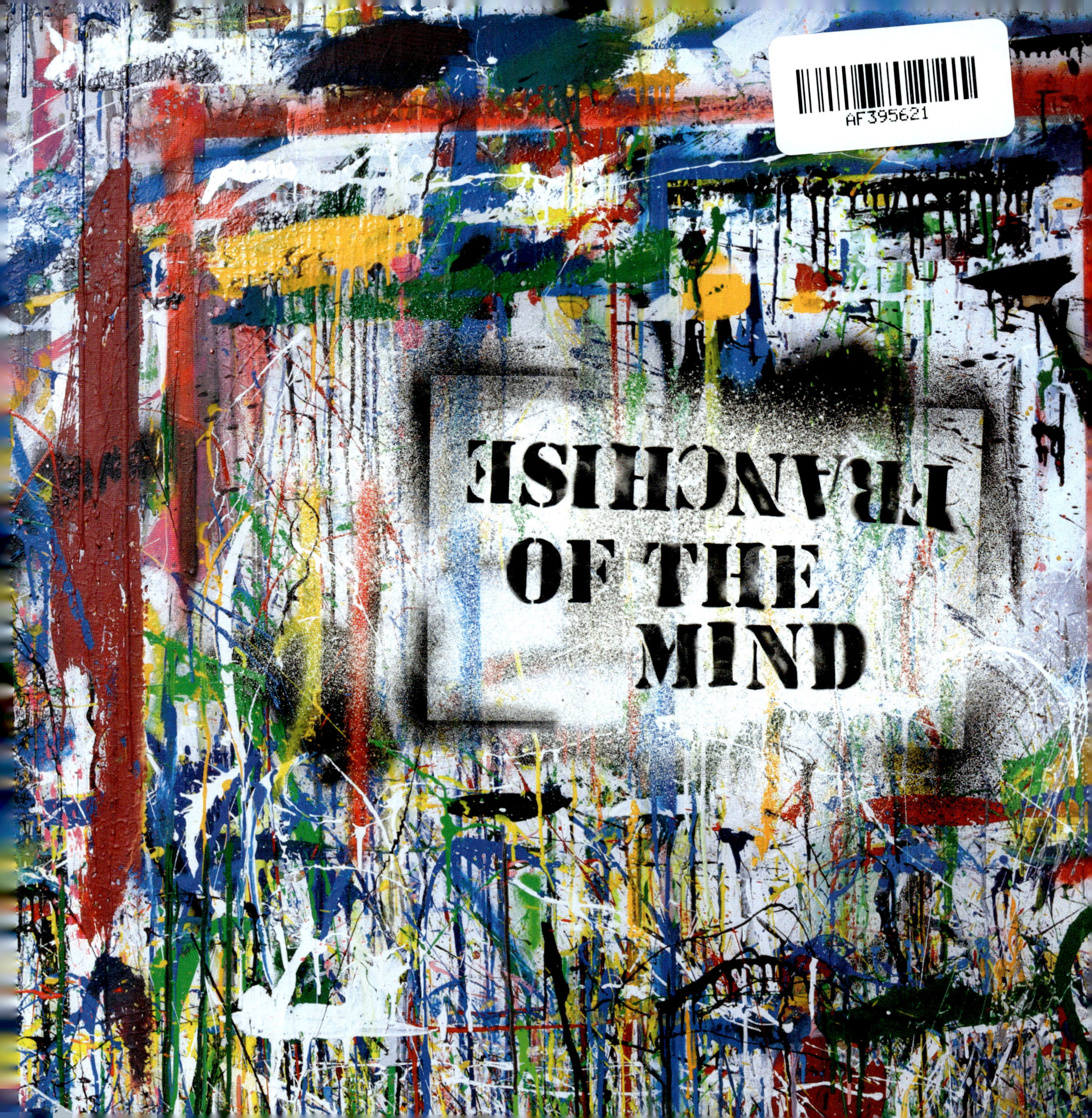
FRANCHISE
OF THE
MIND
AF395621

Text and photography copyright © 2018-2024 DTR Modern Galleries

Mr. Brainwash copyright ©2018-2024: MR BRAINWASH and all related artwork, photography, and editorial provided by the Artist © & ™ Amusement Art, LLC

This edition © B. T. Batsford Ltd., 2024

First published in hardback in 2018

This revised paperback edition published in 2024 by Scala Arts Publishers, Inc.
c/o CohnReznick LLP
1301 Avenue of the Americas
10th floor
New York, NY 10019
www.scalapublishers.com
Scala – New York – London
An imprint of B. T. Batsford Holdings Ltd.

In association with DTR Modern Galleries
458 West Broadway Street
New York, NY 10012
www.dtrmodern.com
Boston – Palm Beach – New York – Washington, DC

ISBN: 978-1-78551-585-9

Library of Congress Cataloguing-in-Publication Data: a catalog record for this book is available from the publisher.

10 9 8 7 6 5 4 3 2 1

mrbrainwash.com
dtrmodern.com

BOOK CURATOR & EDITOR
Ghia Truesdale

DESIGN
Jason Fairchild
Gregory Ronquillo, It's a Wonderful World, Inc.

Printed and bound in China

PHOTOGRAPHY
Elvert Barnes, page 108

Stéphane Bisseuil, page 105

Gavin Bond, page 104

Matt Chung, page 124

Chad Griffith, page 122 and back endpapers

Naj Jamaï, page 6

Olivier Mastey, pages 5, 7, 12, 18, 26, 45, 50, 94, 96, 97, 105, 112, 113, 114, 115, 125 and front endpapers

Kim Ringstad, pages 36, 37

Alicia Vasquez, pages 18, 19, 98, 123

Chris Vidal, pages 98, 120

All other photographs are courtesy of Mr. Brainwash and It's a Wonderful World, Inc.

front cover
Franchise of the Mind
© 2024 Amusement Art, LLC

back cover
Keep Creating
© 2024 Amusement Art, LLC

pages 110–111
Never Never Never Give Up
26" x 50"
Stencil and mixed media on canvas

pages 118–119
Stills from *Exit Through the Gift Shop* used with permission

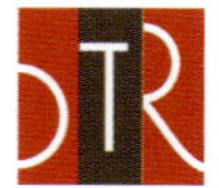

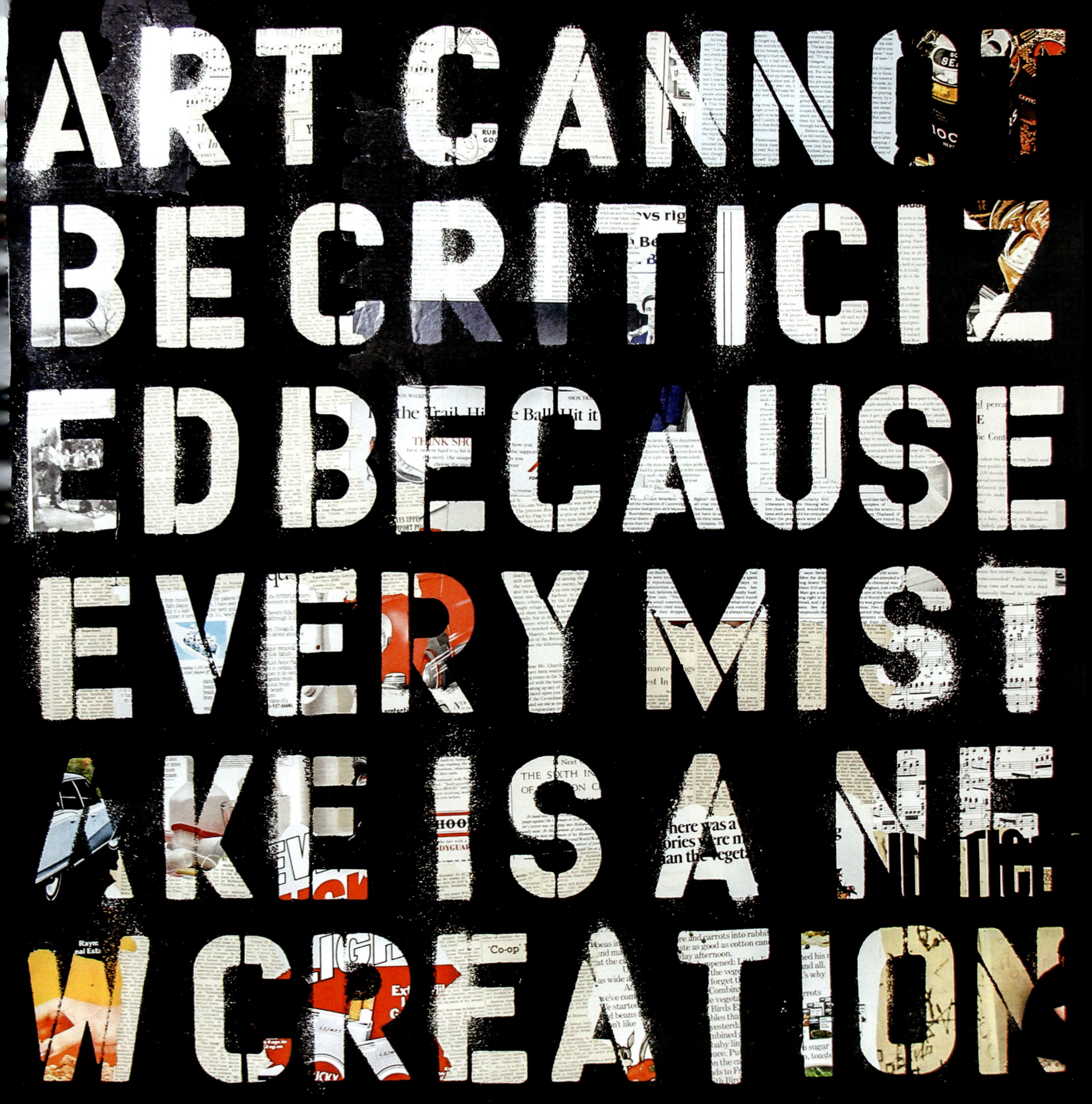

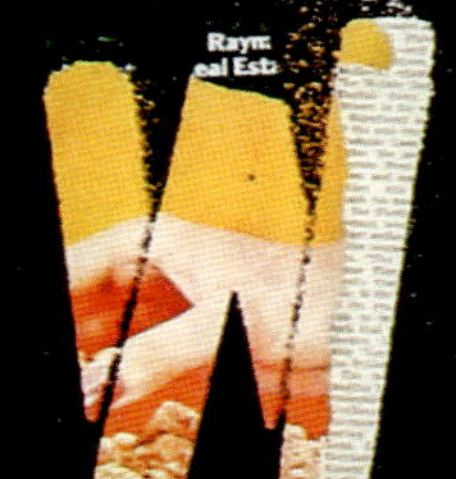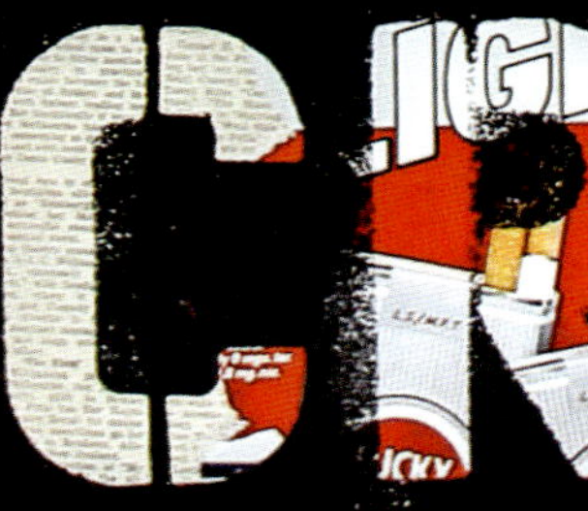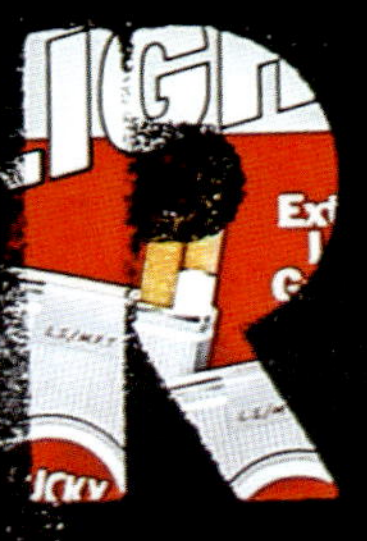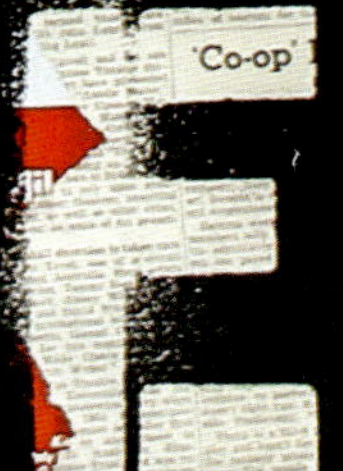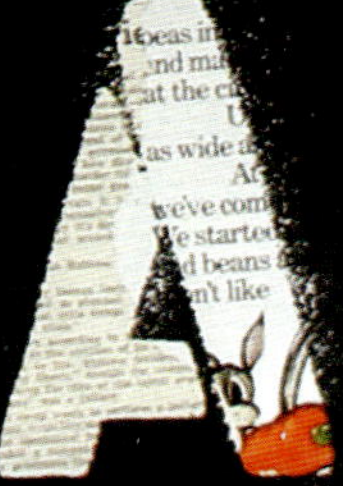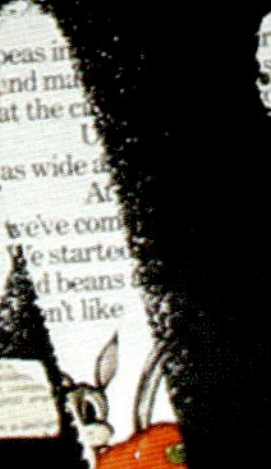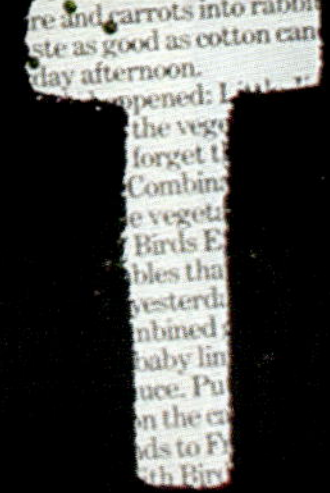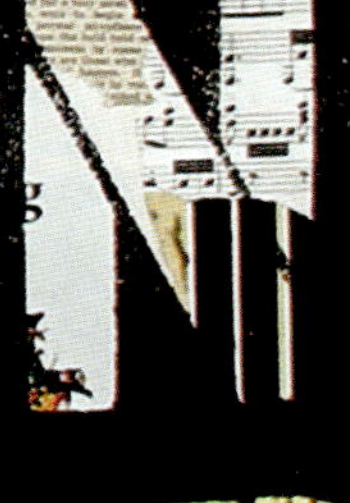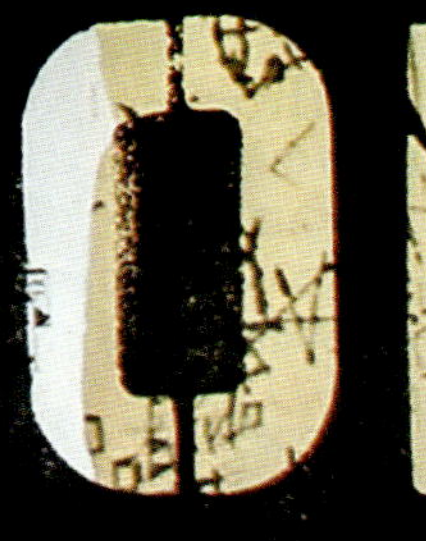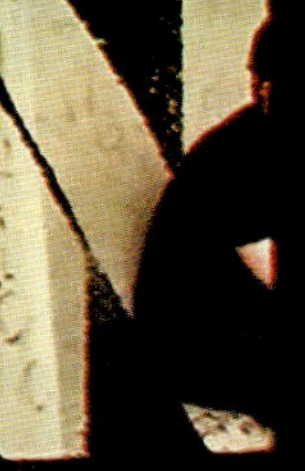

ART CANNOT BE CRITICIZED BECAUSE EVERY MISTAKE IS A NEW CREATION

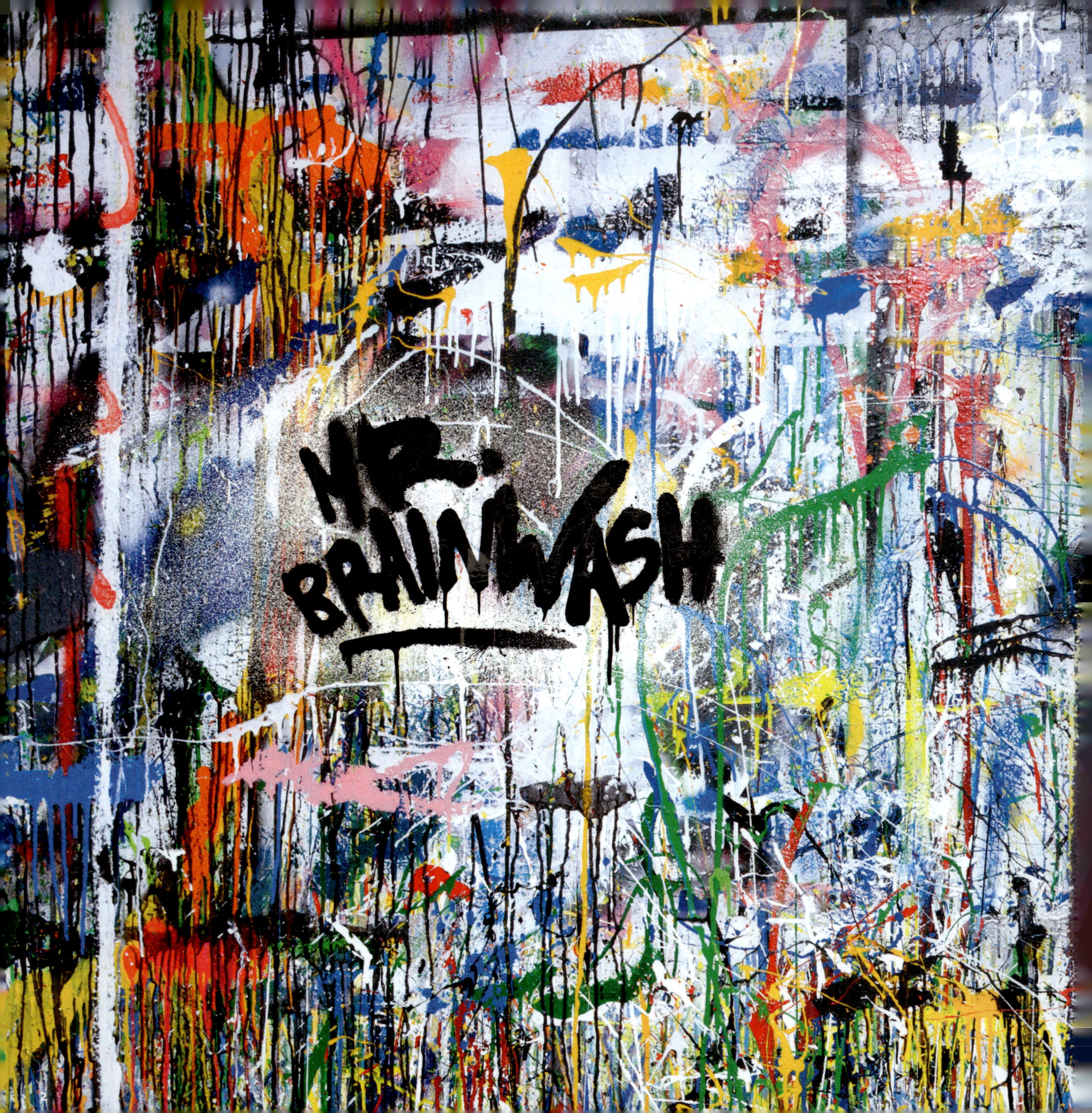

MR.
BRAINWASH

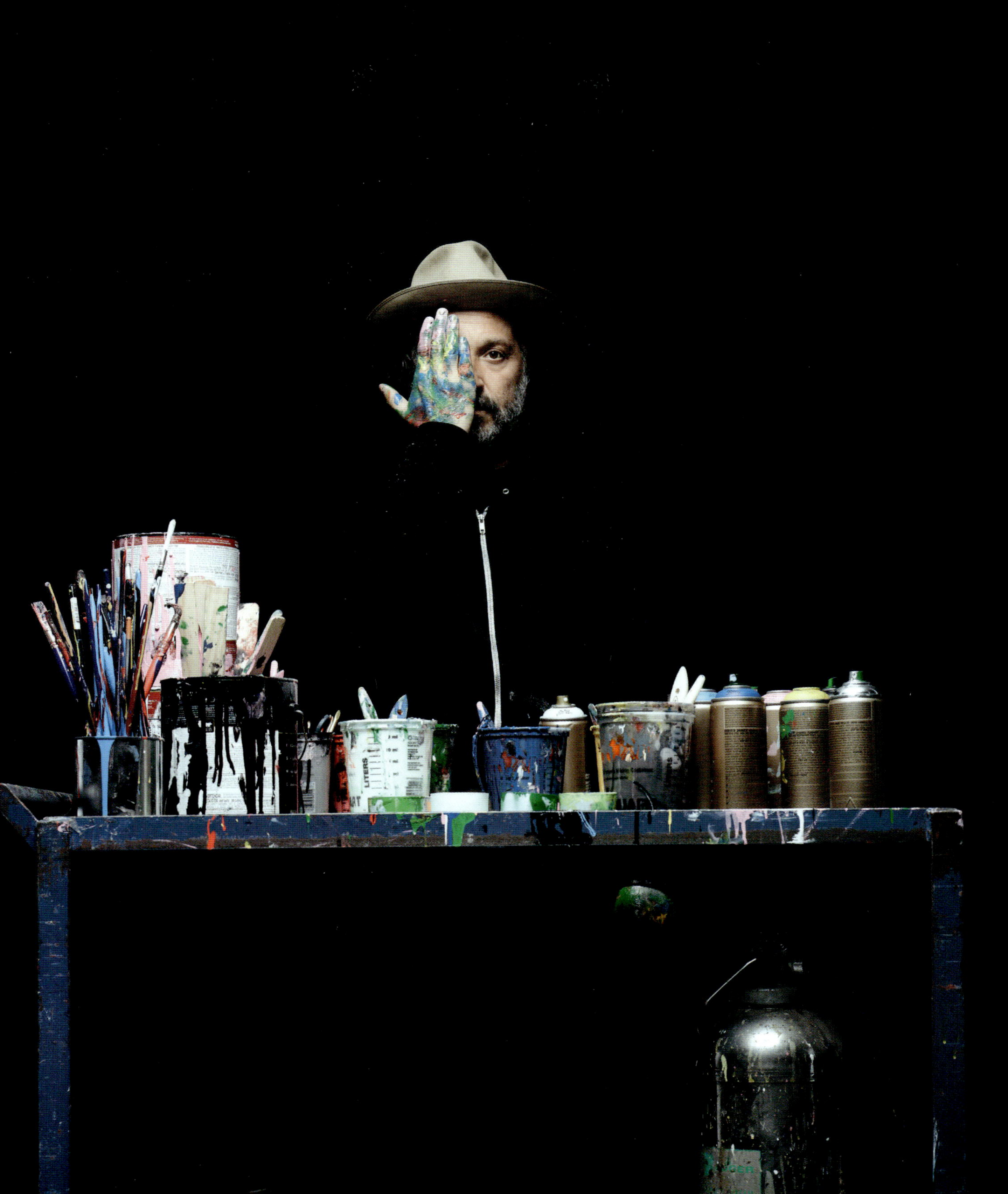

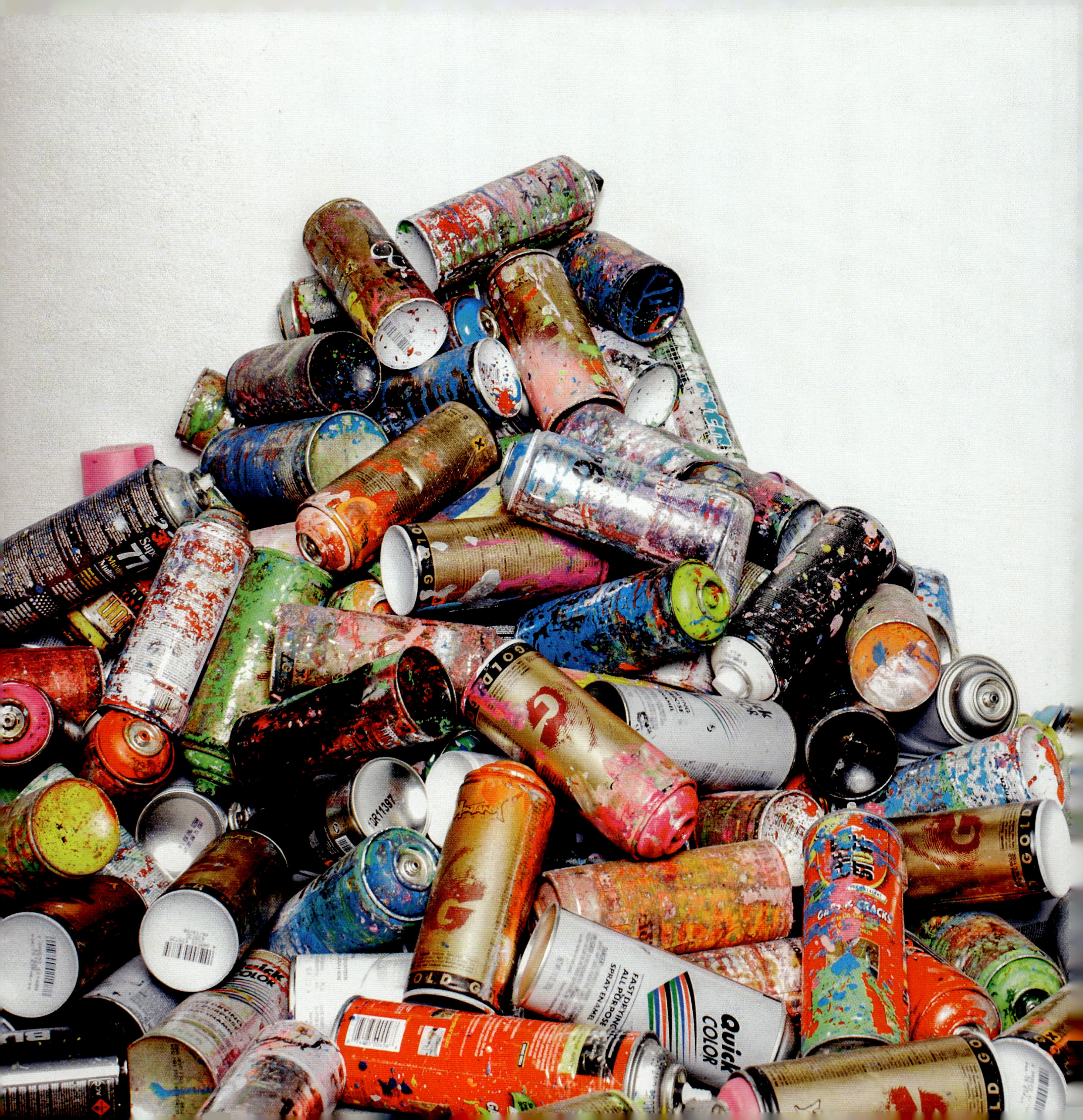

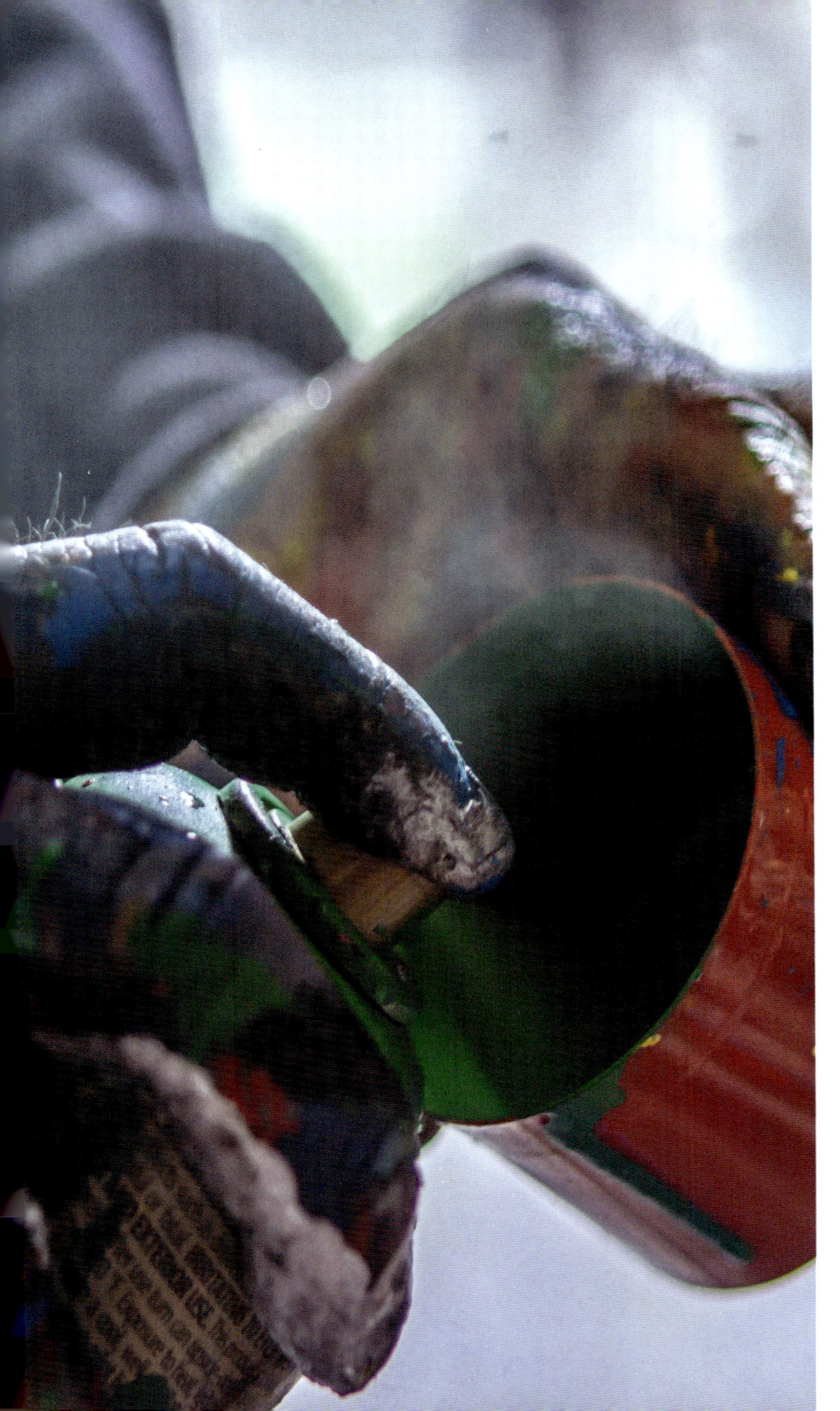

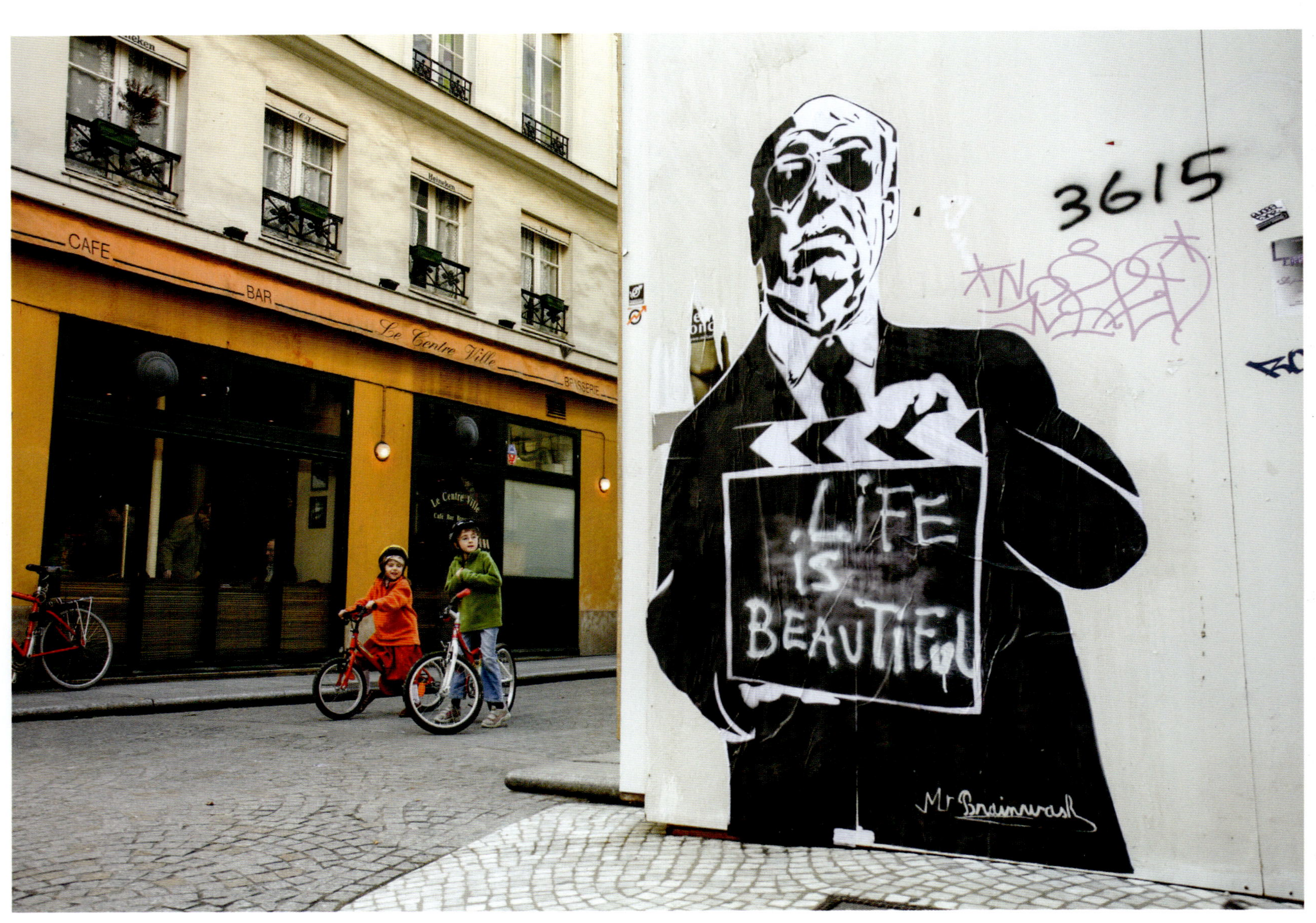
CAFE
BAR
Le Centre Ville
BRASSERIE
Le Centre Ville
Café Bar
3615
LIFE IS BEAUTIFUL
Mr Brainwash

TED VASSILEV

GALLERIST'S STATEMENT

Every surface in the world is a cloak-and-dagger canvas for the Mr. Brainwash franchise of the mind. Captured for the first time in a full-scale trade monograph, Mr. Brainwash (IRL Thierry Guetta, expat francophone) here presents fresh-out-of-the-box pieces together with a retrospective of his earlier works. Heretofore showcased primarily by dead of night, the graffiti artist's positive messages—*Life is Beautiful*; *Love is the Answer*; *Follow Your Dreams!*—are chronicled in this co-publication between Scala Arts Publishers, Inc. and DTR Modern Galleries. Chaotic and playful, the contemporary artist's ardent voice has pushed the envelope of pop culture from the street to the big screen to art galleries worldwide.

My own gut reaction to Mr. Brainwash was to contextualize him among the likes of Jackson Pollock, Willem de Kooning, or Andy Warhol. Similarly, in a personal email to me, art historian Donald Kuspit framed Mr. Brainwash thus:

> To me it's ironical, mocking pop, using a powerful painterliness to undermine the 'stars' he's featuring, all now part of the entertainment industry, and as such without authenticity. Mr. Brainwash's own authenticity is in his vigorous—zealously energetic—gesturalism. Art historically, he is synthesizing hand-painted abstract expressionism, subjective and personal in import (an expression of the unconscious, as has been said), and machine-produced pop art, socially objective and impersonal (or pseudo personal) and mass produced 'illustration' with a kind of ingenious bravado. Formally, he's a master of color—bold, in your face.

Alongside Banksy, Shepard Fairey, and other brinksmen of street art with "roots in rebellion,"[1] Mr. Brainwash was the central figure in the 2010 cult documentary film *Exit Through the Gift Shop* directed by fellow street artist Banksy. In 2006 Mr. Brainwash set aside his video camera to attack the streets with wheat paste, spray cans, brushes, and paint buckets, stenciling images and pegging posters of beloved icons. With a surface area from Los Angeles to New York City and across the globe, Mr. Brainwash quickly franchised the burgeoning street art scene with his proactive missives. Nevertheless, while growing in popularity for the past decade, urban art "still in its infancy on the market" experiences a "complicated relationship" with "the polished platforms of the art world," wherein most "major auction houses and dealers no longer sell pieces" scavenged from public walls, though they are still traded privately.[2]

Mischievous and fun, each colorful work is a journey through Guetta's pop culture wonderland. His works have sold at auction, been collected on all continents, and his massive solo art shows have attracted hundreds of thousands of visitors. He has created cover artwork, album campaigns, music videos, and installations for a variety of the most iconic figures and brands including Madonna, Michael Jackson, Coca-Cola, Levi's, Mercedes, and many others. For Mr. Brainwash and his *franchise of the mind*, I forecast a supernova trajectory like that of Jean-Michel Basquiat, who "came to the art world's attention through his graffiti collective SAMO© at the end of the 1970s," and whose "Untitled" (1982) sold at auction in May 2017 for a staggering sum, followed, as noted by Banksy in a social media bulletin, by a "major new show…at the Barbican [in London]—a place that is normally very keen to clean any graffiti from its walls."[3]

Mr. Brainwash and his *franchise of the mind* emanate dynamism and originality, parallel to American sculptor, Alexander Calder, who trail-blazed the mobile art movement; so too Thierry Guetta "leads where others will follow" in the opulent and discordant world of appropriated and transformational graffiti art.[4]

Thierry Guetta, himself a dedicated philanthropist, deploys Mr. Brainwash installations and sculptures, abstracts and pop art to support nonprofit organizations that otherwise would not have access to the benefits of transformational and appropriation art. Hence our collaboration was a natural segue for DTR Modern Galleries, given my own endeavors in the nonprofit sector and in public arts education through the creation of scholarly books about contemporary artists.[5]

As a gallerist and art lover, I am especially proud to note that *Mr. Brainwash: Franchise of the Mind* has resulted in hatching a plan for an eponymous 2018 exhibit series at DTR Modern Galleries. For this remarkable opportunity, I thank Patrick Guetta, who made possible this collaboration with his brother Thierry Guetta. My heartfelt thanks extend to Thierry Guetta and his *It's a Wonderful World* team, including Alexandra Severine, Chirel Aiche, David Healy, Gregory Ronquillo, Clara Chowaiki, Michaelangelo Loggia, and Olivier Mastey. *Mr. Brainwash: Franchise of the Mind* has been further enriched by the scholarly essays of Eleanor Heartney and Donald Kuspit. And, I must underscore that this book could not have come to fruition on its lightning bolt schedule without our collaborators Jennifer Norman and her Scala Arts Publishers, Inc. team, Hannah Bowen, Tim Clarke, and Claudia Varosio, together with publishing curators Ghia Truesdale, Gail Spilsbury, and book designers Gregory Ronquilo and Jason Fairchild. I am especially indebted to Julia Morris, Gallery Director of DTR, West Broadway in New York City. As ever, I am grateful to my committed staff at DTR Modern Galleries: Lauren Nasella, Bryan Walsh, Suzanne King, Jennie Buehler, Josh Findlay, Helen Schorsch, and Ben Moody.

—TED VASSILEV, DTR MODERN GALLERIES

[1-3] Melanie Gerlis, "Off the Wall: Urban Art Scrubs Up," *Financial Times*, September 23-24, 2017, weekend edition, Collecting, Art & Design section, p. 2. The Basquiat exhibition ran at the Barbican Art Gallery from September 21, 2017 to January 28, 2018.

[4] Virginia Blackburn, "Mobile Art," *Financial Times*, September 23, 2017, "How to Spend It, Smart Arts" weekend magazine feature, p. 39. Includes an interview with gallery owner Ted Vassilev; image is of DTR Modern Galleries' *Landscape Mobile* by Roy Lichtenstein.

[5] *Robert Mars: Futurelics, Past is Present* (New York: Scala Arts Publishers, Inc. and DTR Modern Galleries, 2017) and *Stephen Wilson: Luscious Threads* (New York: Scala Arts Publishers, Inc. and DTR Modern Galleries, 2018).

Ted Vassilev is the owner of DTR Modern Galleries, with locations in Boston, New York, Palm Beach, and Washington, DC.

All you need is passion. All you need is respect. All you need is kindness. All you need is glee. All you need is affection. All you need is dedication. All you need is excitement. All you need is joy. All you need is bliss. All you need is charm. All you need is delight. All you need is humor. All you need is wonder. All you need is dignity. All you need is creativity. All you need is fun. All you need is happiness. All you need is enjoyment. All you need is euphoria. All you need is peace. All you need is laughter. All you need is optimism. All you need is pleasure. All you need is cheer. All you need is enchantment. All you need is hope. All you need is merriment. All you need is positivity. All you need is beauty. All you need is adventures. All you need is friends. All you need is encouragement. All you need is energy.

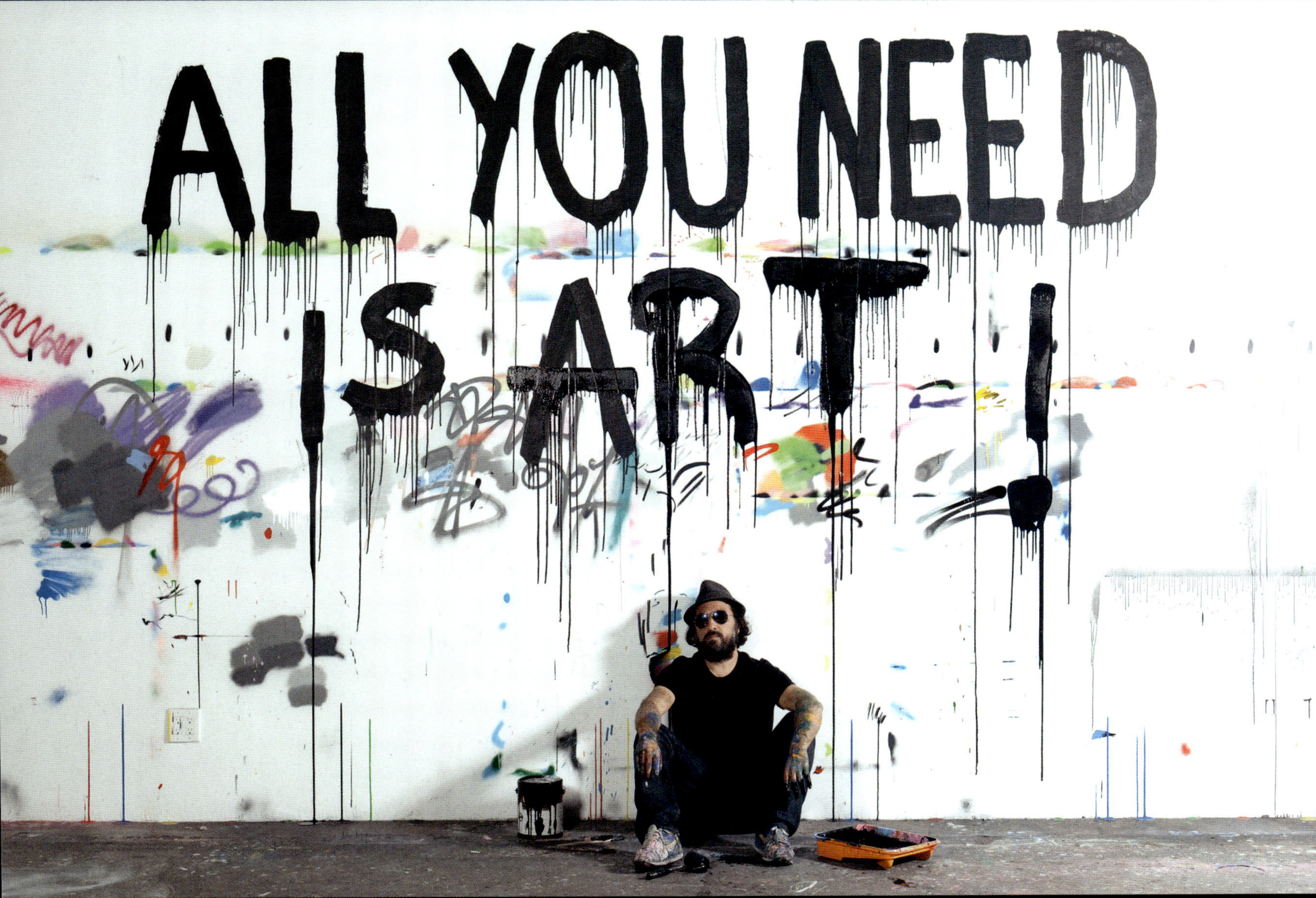

All you need is family. All you need is fortune. All you need is luck. All you need is grace. All you need is harmony. All you need is hugs. All you need is kisses. All you need is knowledge. All you need is loveliness. All you need is nature. All you need is safety. All you need is music. All you need is soul. All you need is vision. All you need is unity. All you need is style. All you need is support. All you need is sincerity. All you need is resolution. All you need is meaning. All you need is intelligence. All you need is honesty. All you need is goodness. All you need is freedom. All you need is faith. All you need is courage. All you need is care. All you need is blessings. All you need is trust. All you need is love. All you need is life. You need it all!

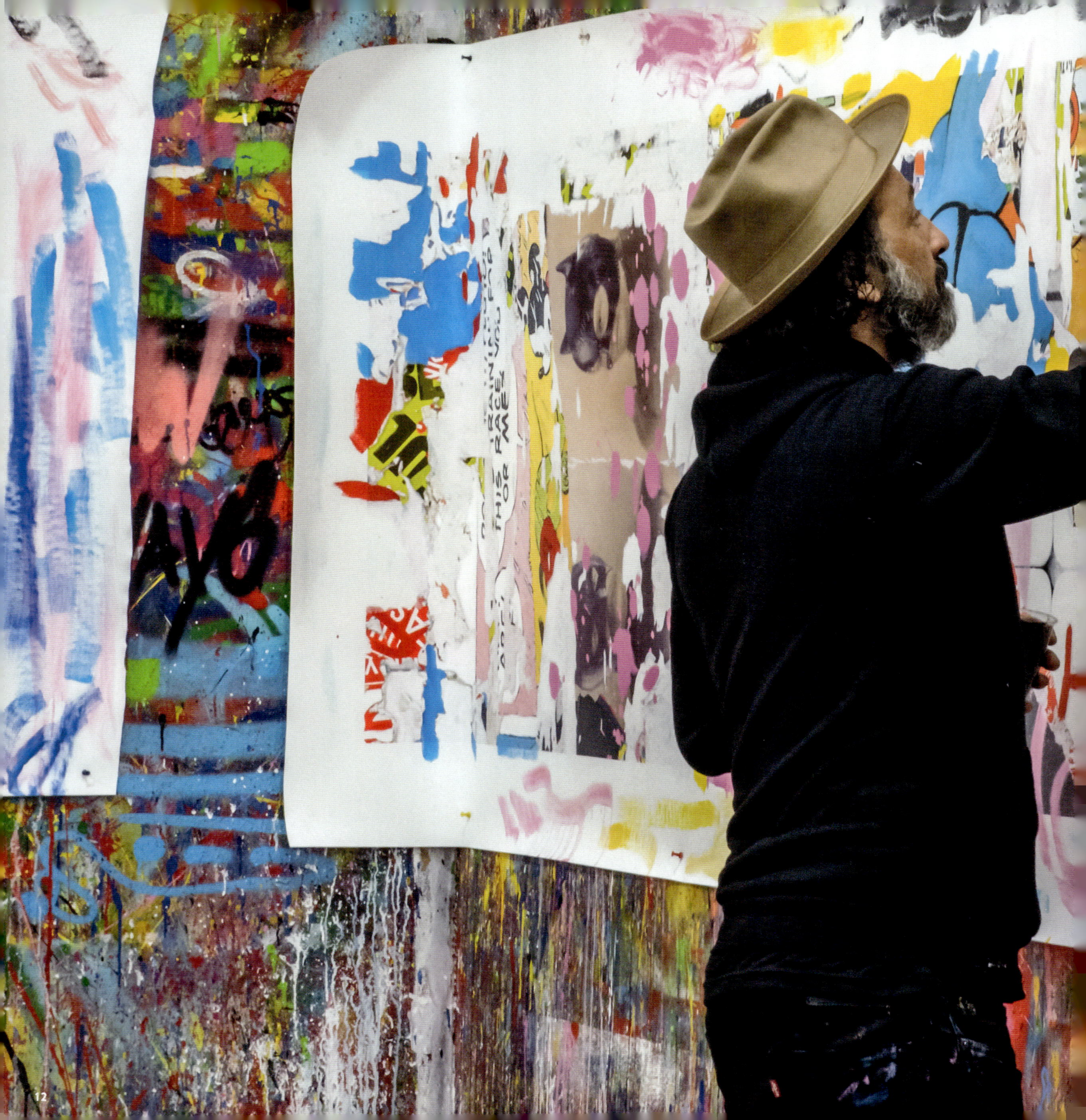
RACE YOU
THIS
OR ME

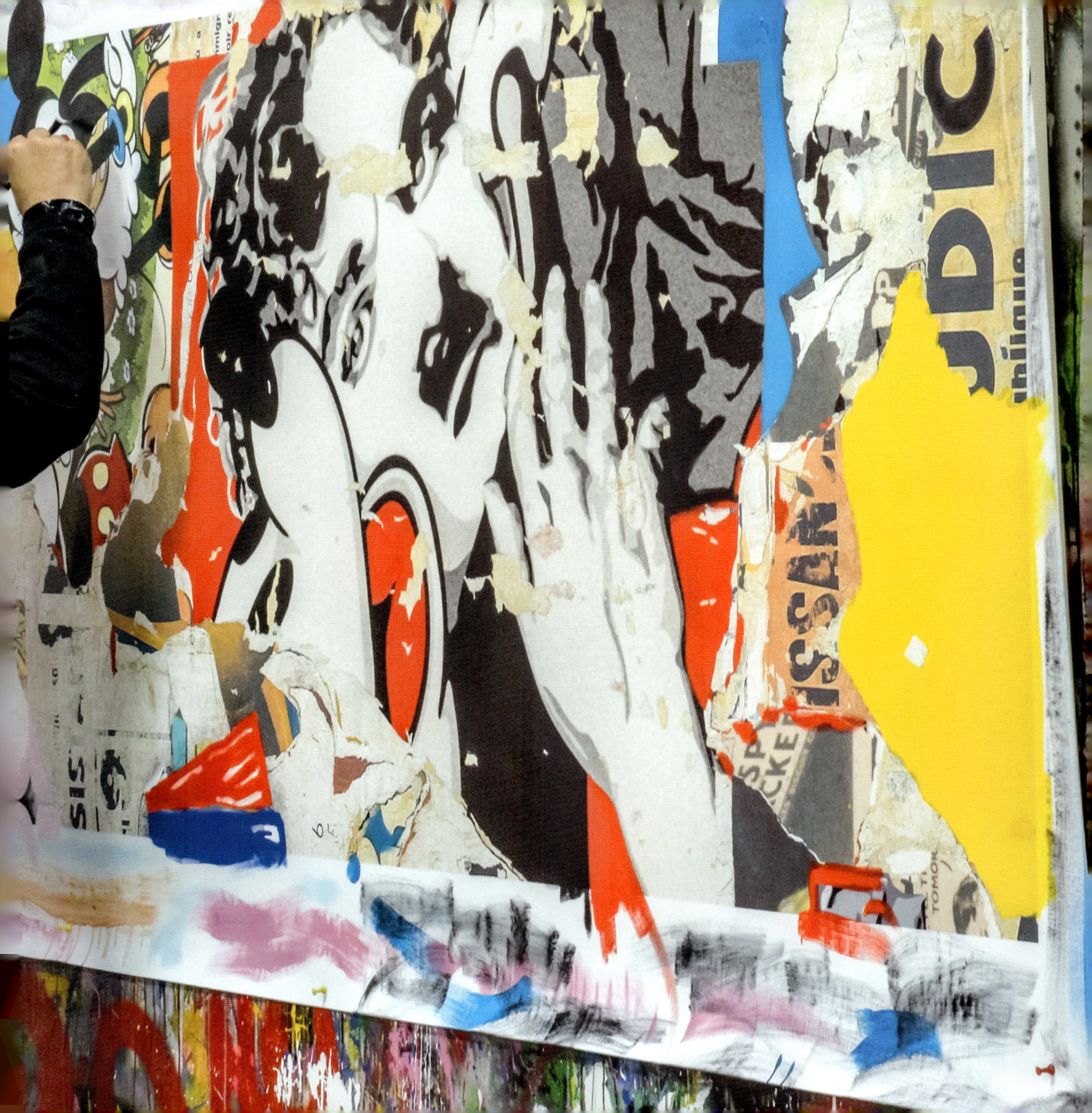

ELEANOR HEARTNEY

MR. BRAINWASH

Andy Warhol knew that celebrity changes everything. Media attention turned him from an awkward commercial shoe illustrator into a worldwide brand, as well as one of the most influential artists of the twentieth century. In the decades since Warhol's death in 1987, the mechanisms by which celebrity is attained and maintained have become even more sophisticated and persuasive. At the same time, celebrity is ever more detached from recognizable accomplishments or verifiable facts. Instead, our cultural consciousness is increasingly crowded with icons who are famous simply for being famous.

Into this brave new world comes Mr. Brainwash. A perplexing and paradoxical figure, he is a vintage clothing entrepreneur turned videographer turned artist whose very existence is open to debate. This, despite the tangible evidence of his art career—numerous solo shows, a body of very real paintings, sculptures, and public murals—and the certifiable reality of a French-born, Los Angeles-based street artist named Thierry Guetta who takes credit both for the *nom de plume* and the extensive output of Mr. Brainwash.

So why the confusion? The mystery surrounding Mr. Brainwash emanates from the vehicle that introduced him to a broad public. This is a 2010 documentary film titled *Exit Through the Gift Shop* directed by Banksy, the famous but also extremely secretive graffiti artist. Banksy has become a celebrated art world figure while protecting his "real" identity from society at large. As a result, his documentary film set off a furor of speculation that (a) Mr. Brainwash was a fabrication, designed to lampoon the art world's gullibility, (b) Mr. Brainwash was Banksy himself playing an elaborate hoax, or (c) Mr. Brainwash was in fact Thierry Guetta, artist and art world phenomenon, as the documentary indicates.

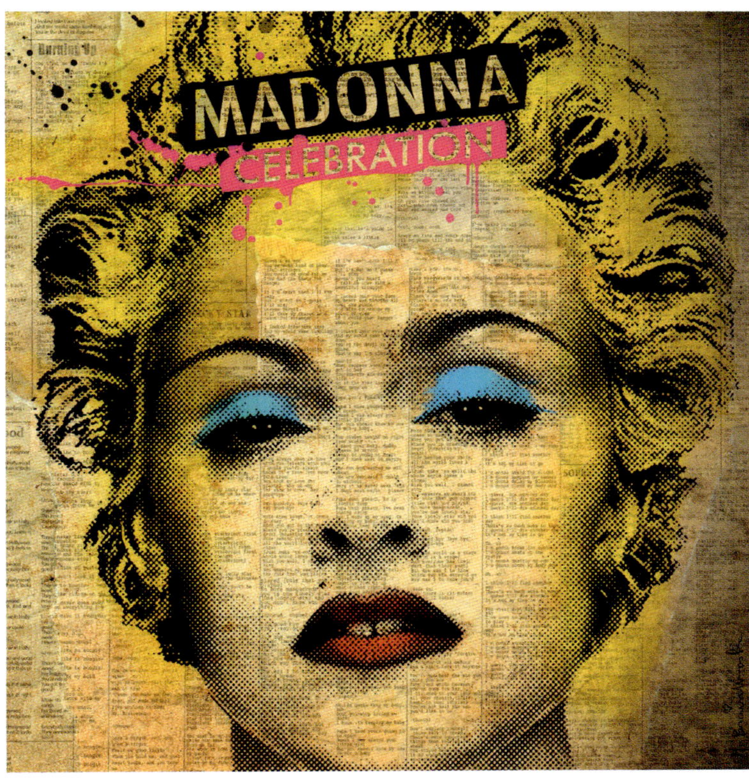

The "facts" are slippery. As narrated in this immensely entertaining film, Thierry Guetta was a would-be filmmaker who spent his early, non-celebrity days with his eye glued to a video camera recording everything within his viewfinder. Upon hooking up with his cousin, a graffiti artist named Invader, he developed a plan to create a documentary about Los Angeles' raffish cohort of street artists. These self-described guerrilla artists spend their days (and nights) affronting the establishment by emblazoning graffiti "tags," stenciled images, and mosaics over public and private buildings. In the process they defy building codes and break laws about private property, always courting arrest. After following them for several years, Guetta managed to amass an unwieldy quantity of footage, during which time he finally met the reclusive Banksy. Eventually Banksy challenged him to stop filming and produce the film. The result demonstrated conclusively that Guetta was not a filmmaker. According to the documentary, Banksy then persuaded him to trade in his camera for a brush, which Thierry proceeded to do under the moniker Mr. Brainwash.

Exit Through the Gift Shop chronicles Mr. Brainwash's unlikely success. To emulate his hero Banksy, he mortgages his house and business to rent a huge warehouse in Los Angeles. He employs an army of assistants to create works for an enormous exhibition composed of paintings, sculptures, and installations that offer mash-ups of high art, historical figures, pop culture imagery, and graffitiesque texts. He exhibits considerable media savvy, trumpeting the show with posters, interviews, and announcements in the local press even while his assistants are scrambling to finish the works. In the end, the show, with the uplifting title *Life Is Beautiful*, is a giant triumph, reportedly racking up over a million dollars in sales. Having been thus auspiciously launched on his artistic career, Mr. Brainwash today continues to enjoy commercial and media success. Among his high-profile commissions are the album covers for Madonna's greatest hits collection, *Celebration* and Michael Jackson's posthumous *Xscape*.

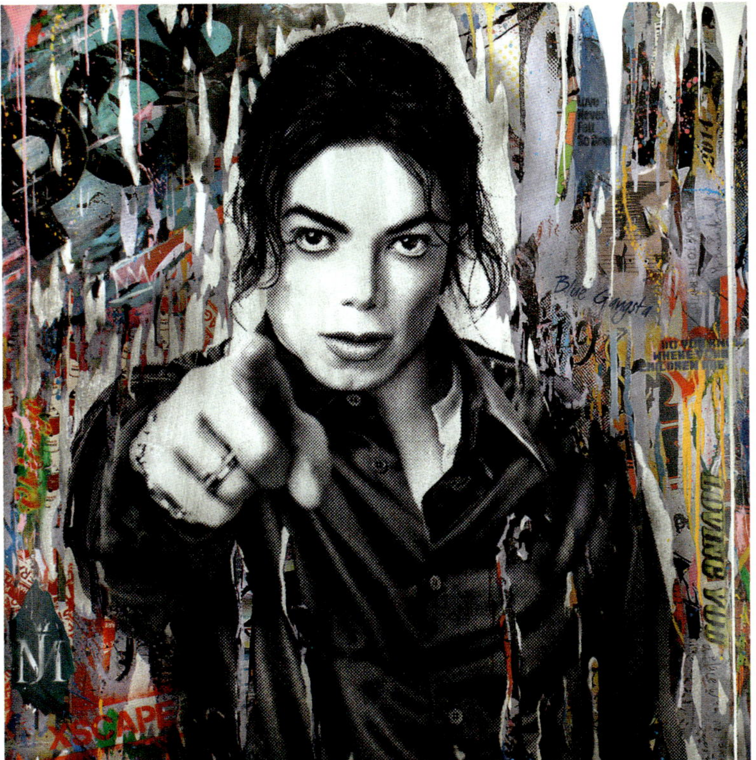

top
**Madonna, Celebration
album cover**
Silkscreen and
mixed media on canvas

bottom
**Michael Jackson,
Xscape album cover**
Silkscreen and
mixed media on canvas

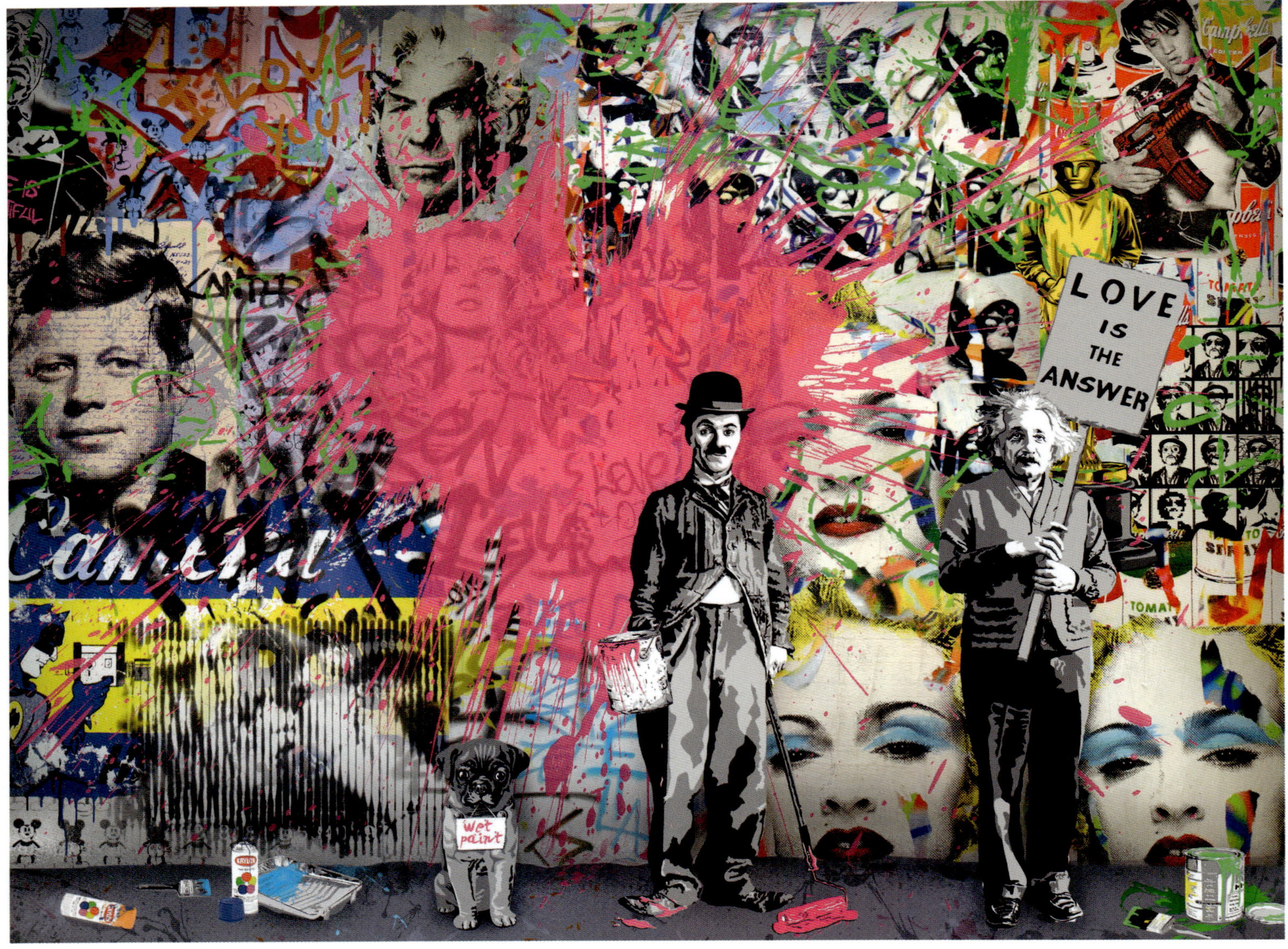

Juxtapose
38" x 50"
Silkscreen edition print

The saga of Mr. Brainwash as told by Banksy is fascinating on many levels. Whether strictly factual or not, it tells us a great deal about the current intermingling of the worlds of art, entertainment, advertising, and commerce. This is exactly the nexus of concerns that preoccupied Andy Warhol. Mr. Brainwash's subjects, who include famous actors, rock stars, politicians, and artists, as well as his own rise to fame are testament to the power of celebrity in a media-driven world. Meanwhile, by circling around the world of graffiti and street art, Mr. Brainwash's career underscores the paradoxical nature of a system in which an art of subversion can become the toast of the establishment. The deliberate irony of his name attests to his consciousness of the peculiarities that surround his career and the ambiguities of his persona.

What is undeniable is the existence of the artworks created by Mr. Brainwash. Employing scans, stencils, and screen prints, his paintings operate within the sphere opened up by Warhol and expanded by graffiti artists like Keith Haring, Jean-Michel Basquiat, Shepard Fairey, and Banksy. And in fact, these artists, and others, are often referenced in his works. Warhol's soup cans are repurposed in Mr. Brainwash's paintings as the aerosol spray cans that are the street artist's primary tool. Haring's flying figure makes an occasional appearance, as does Banksy himself. One occasionally spies the face of Basquiat amid scribbles and drips that resemble those found in his own work. The paintings also include figures from outside the art world, among them Albert Einstein, Charlie Chaplin, and Jimi Hendrix, as well as fictional characters such as Batman, Mickey Mouse, Popeye, and Snoopy. Marilyn Monroe's distinctive coiffure as immortalized by Warhol clings to the unlikely heads of figures like Leonard Nimoy, Barack Obama, and Michael Jackson. Texts weave in and out, some scrawled on like the tags of graffiti artists, others drawn from street signs that urge *Caution*, or warn *Construction Ahead*, or *Road Closed*. The stenciled, scanned, or otherwise appropriated images are overlaid with splashes and drips of paint that suggest both the street artist's stealth inscriptions and the gestural brushstrokes and marks associated with abstract expressionism.

This amalgam of images and sources places Mr. Brainwash squarely within the pop tradition. The collapse of the boundary between high and low culture is so pervasive now that we take for granted the juxtaposition of Mickey Mouse and Einstein or Superman and John F. Kennedy. The leveling begun by Warhol is accelerated within the digital world as the whole of human history becomes available for appropriation and reinterpretation. In such a world, it seems perhaps that a figure like Mr. Brainwash was inevitable. One can trace the seeds of his artistic career back to his early obsession with making video recordings of everything around him. Just as his camera once indiscriminately devoured everything in its path, so today his canvases are receptacles for the never-ending flow of celebrity news, superhero fantasies, historical memes, and nostalgic memories that swirl about us every day. Meanwhile, Mr. Brainwash's own identity is as beguiling and capricious as the images that wash over our screens and flash momentarily on our Facebook feeds. Is he his own invention or ours? When we look at his works, do we see him or ourselves?

When Warhol said, "In the future, everyone will be famous for fifteen minutes," he was both overstating and understating the case. In cyberspace everything constantly changes while never actually disappearing. Fame is as fleeting as it is unerasable. Mr. Brainwash captures the paradoxes of our culture by embodying paradox himself.

—ELEANOR HEARTNEY

Eleanor Heartney is an art critic based in New York City. She is the author of numerous books, articles, and monographs, including *Postmodernism*, *Postmodern Heretics*, and *Art & Today.* She is a Contributing Editor to *Art in America* and *Artpress* and has written extensively on contemporary art issues for publications such as *ARTnews*, *Art and Auction*, *The New Art Examiner*, *The Washington Post*, and *The New York Times.*

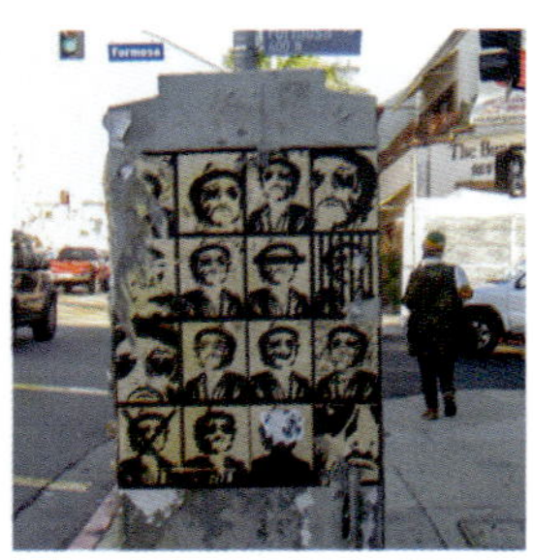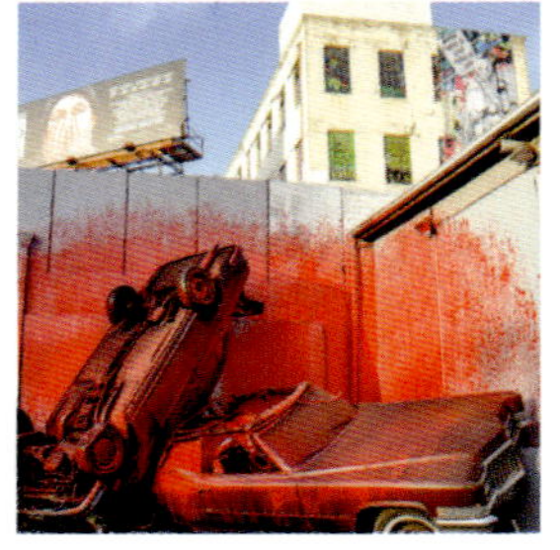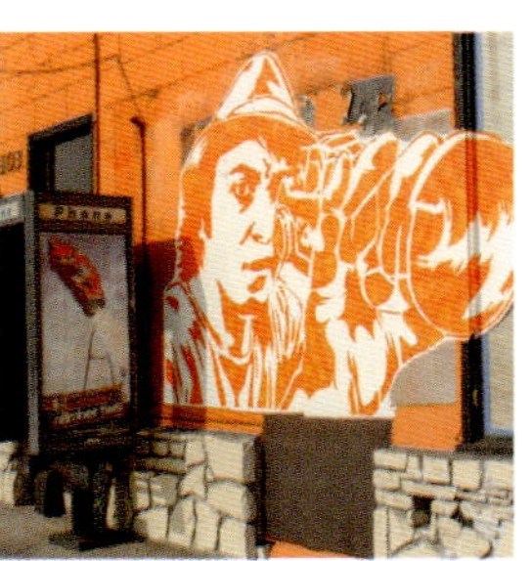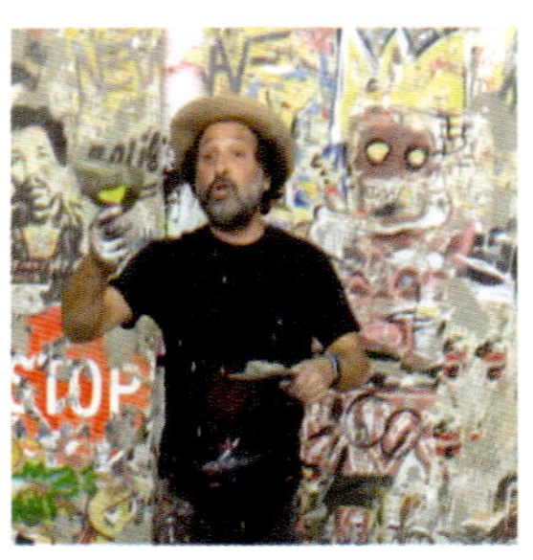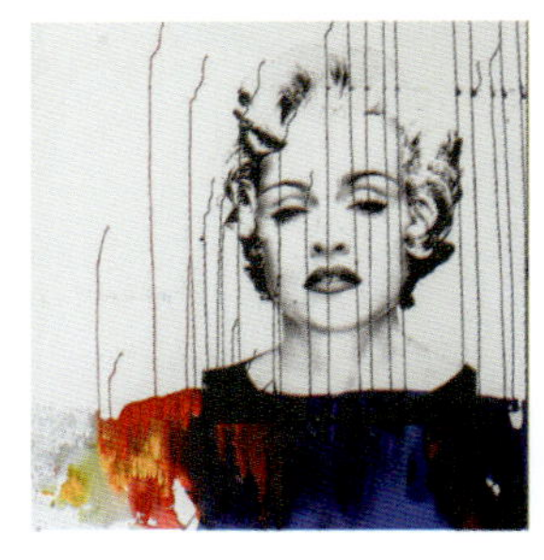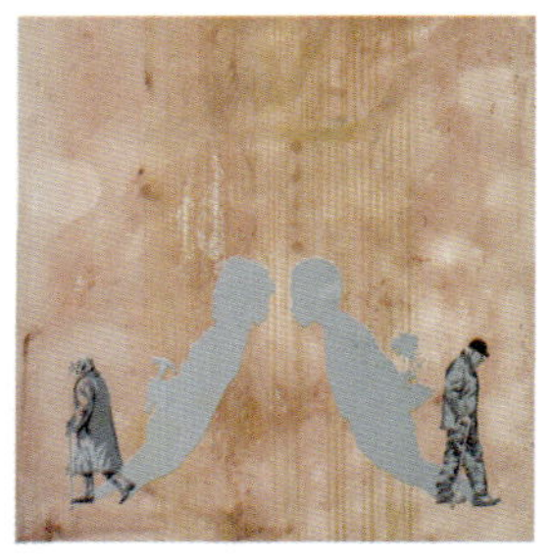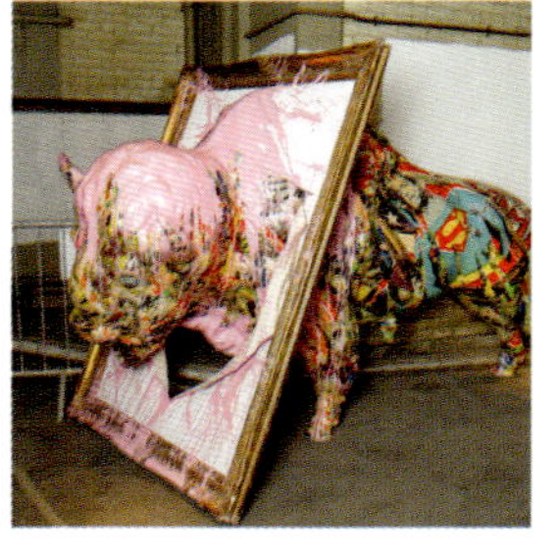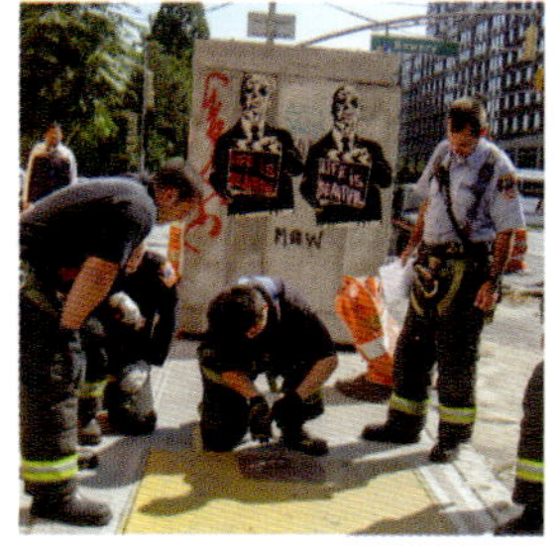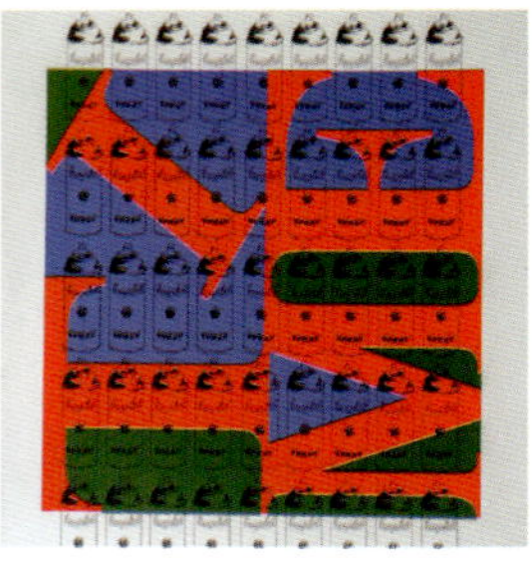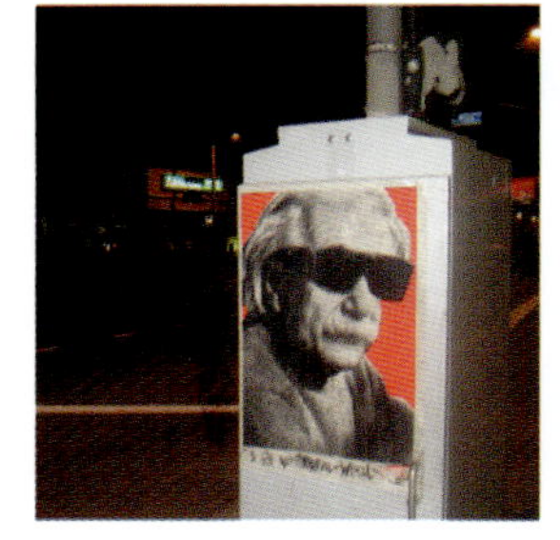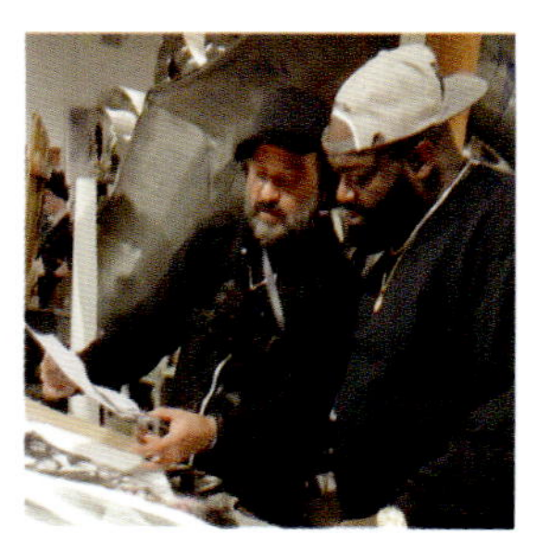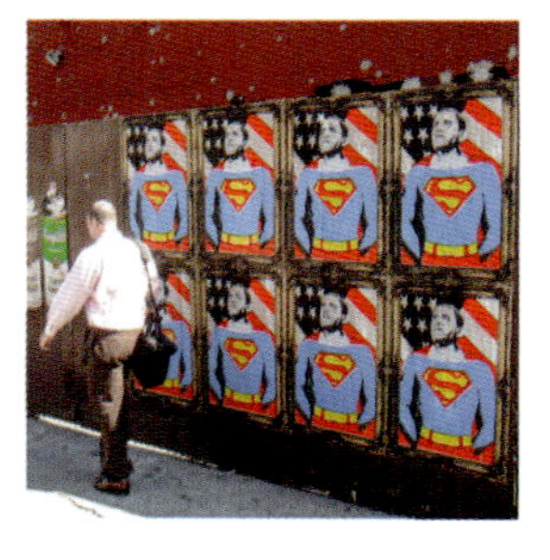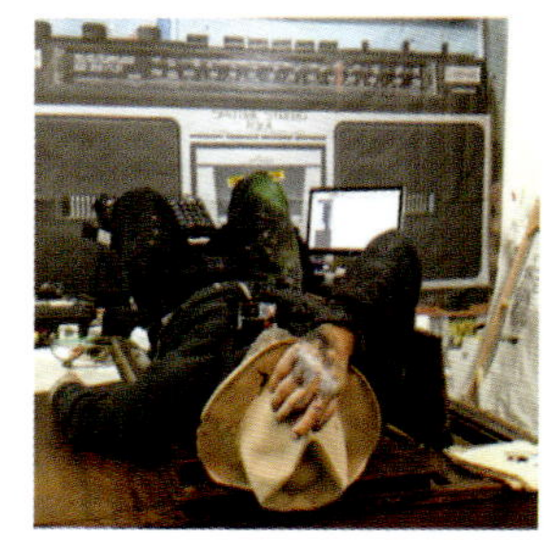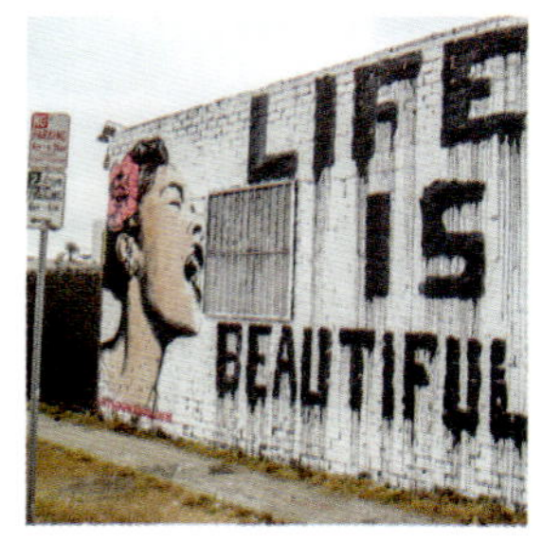

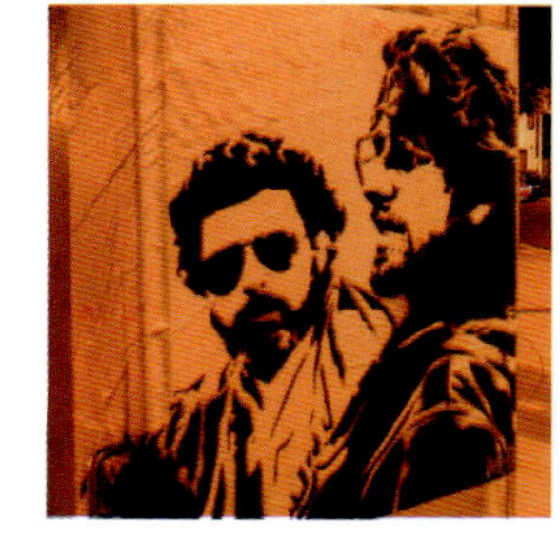
LIFE
IS
BEAUTIFUL

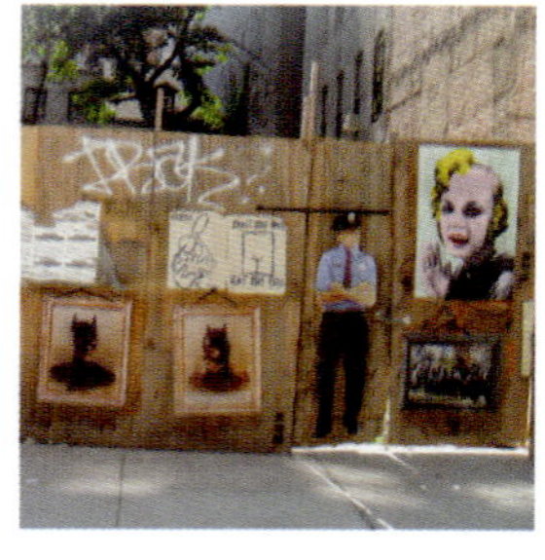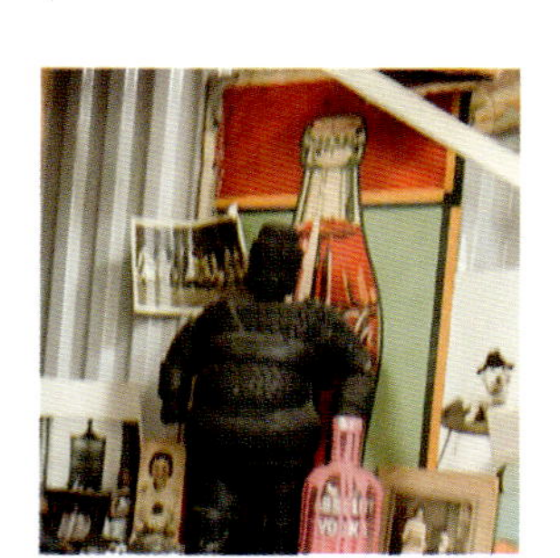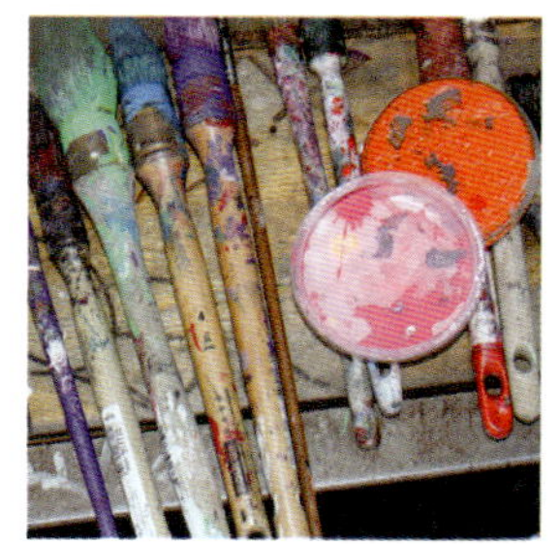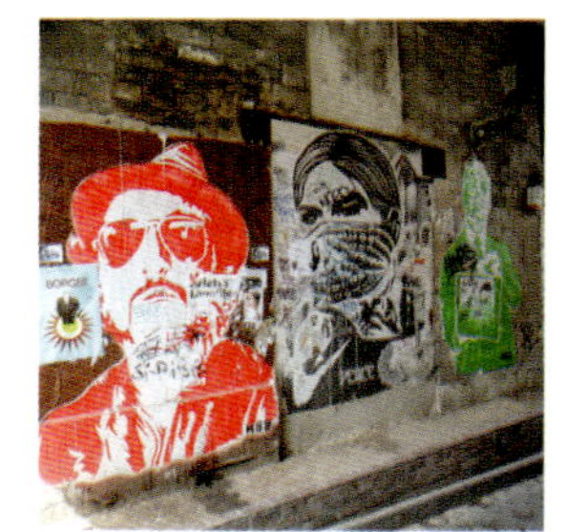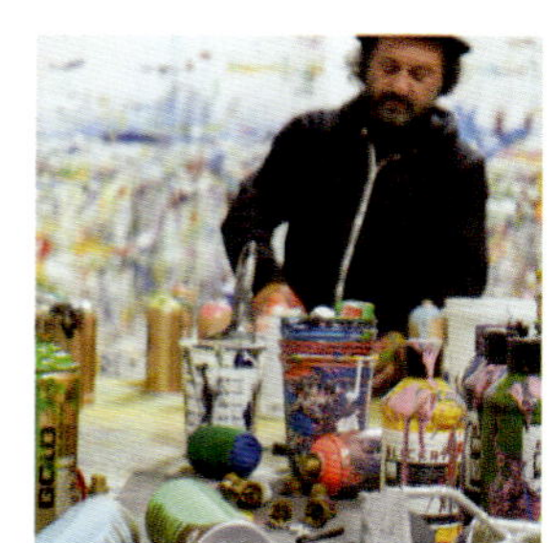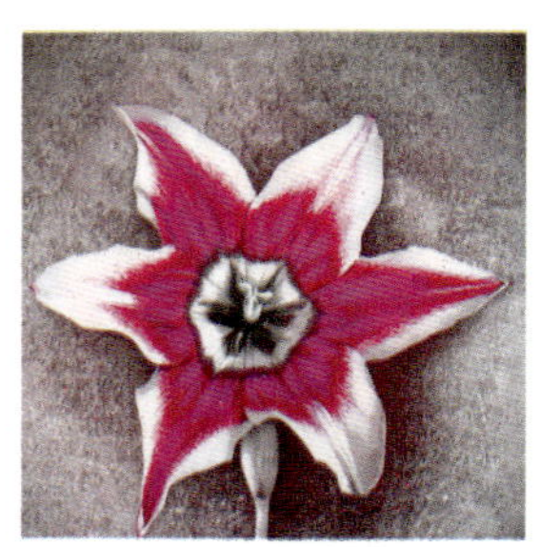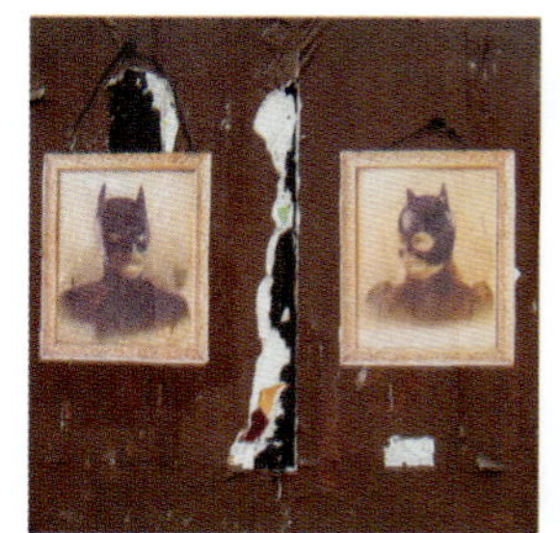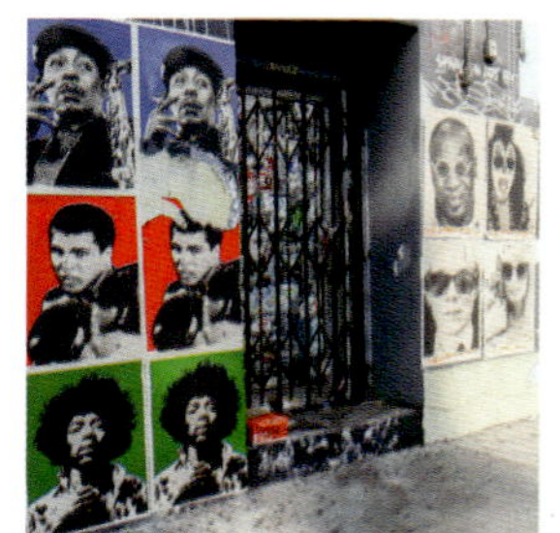

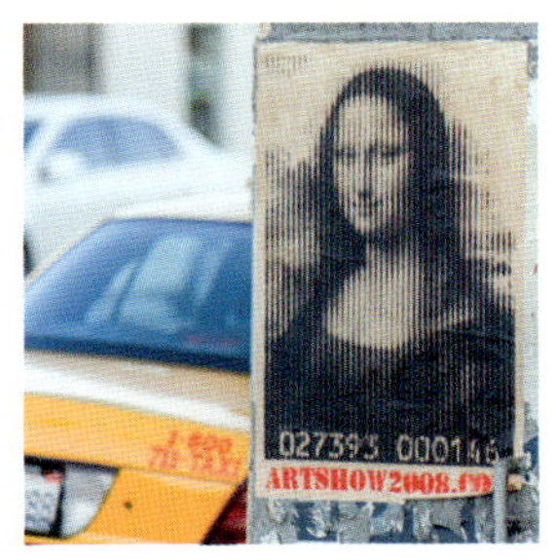
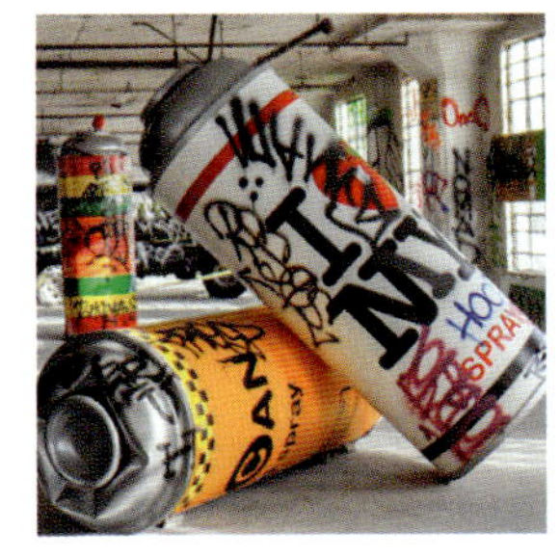
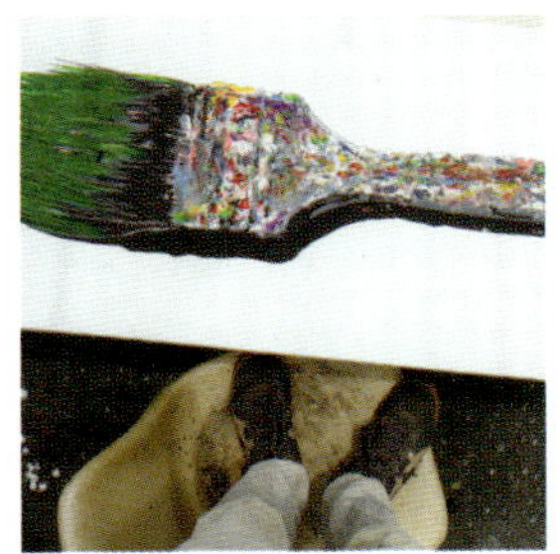
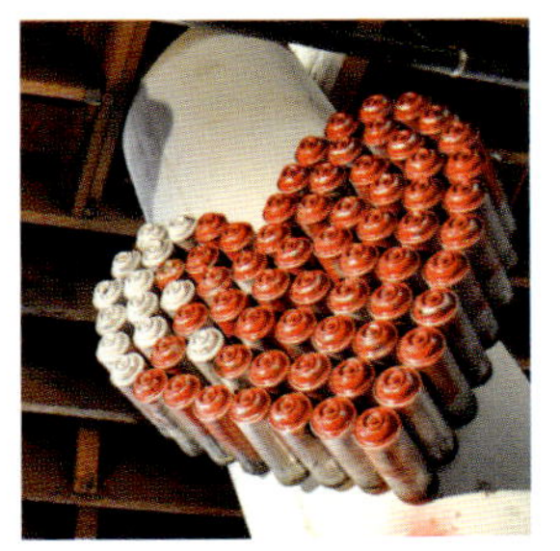
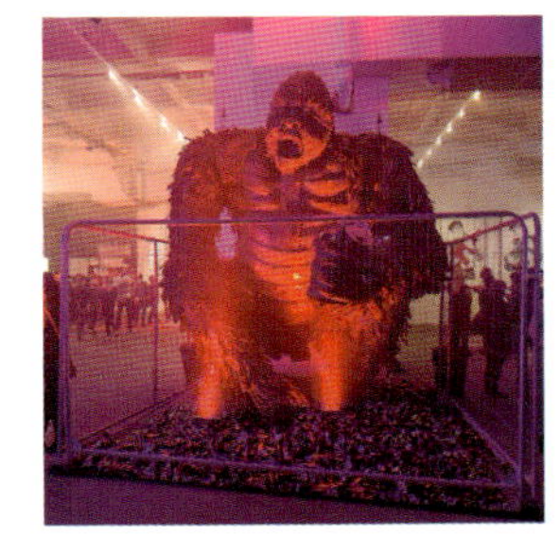
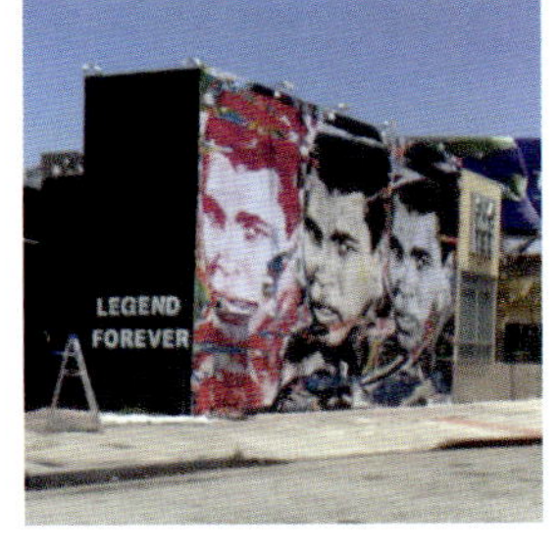
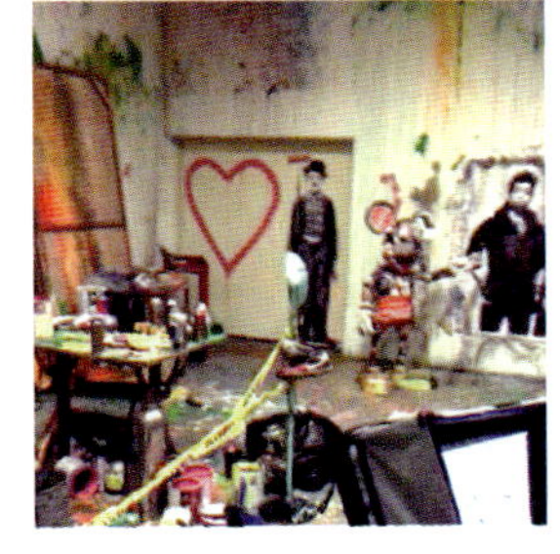
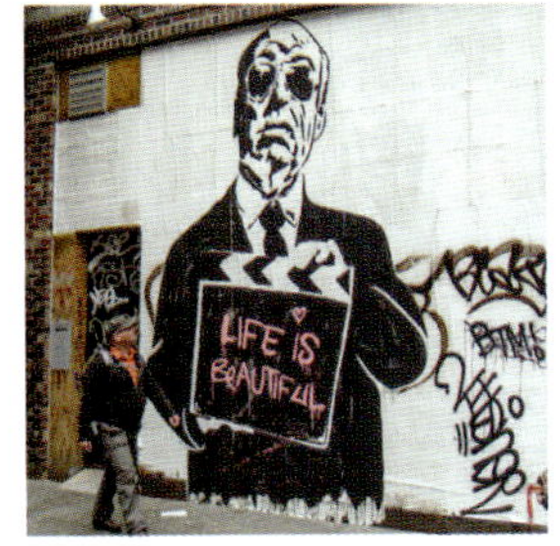
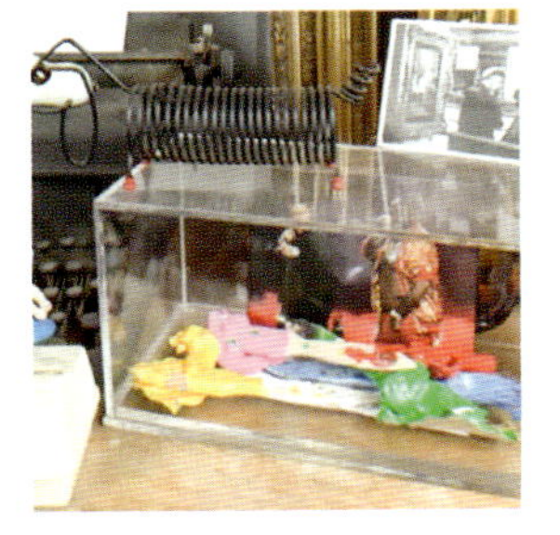
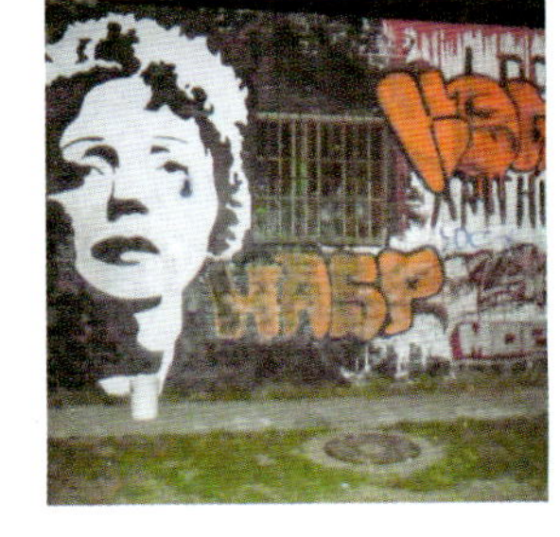
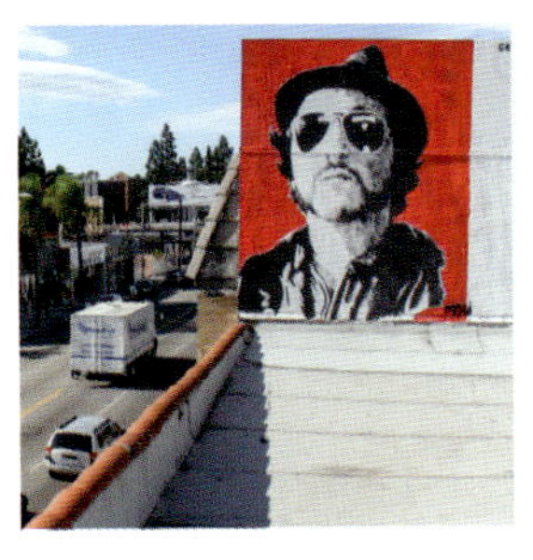
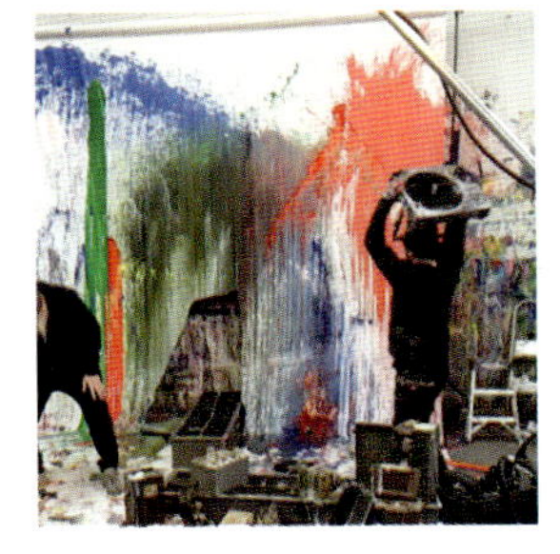
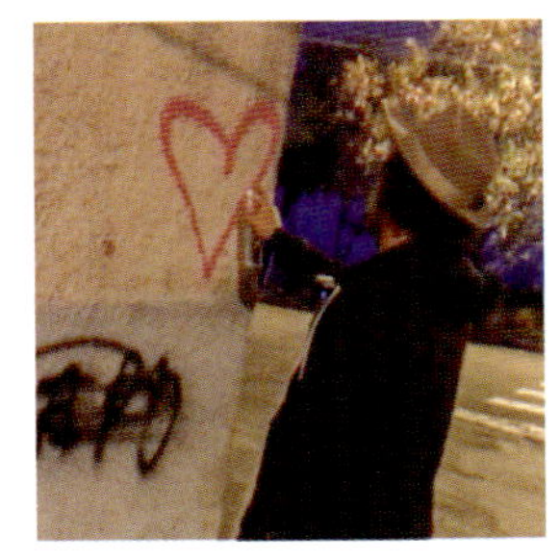
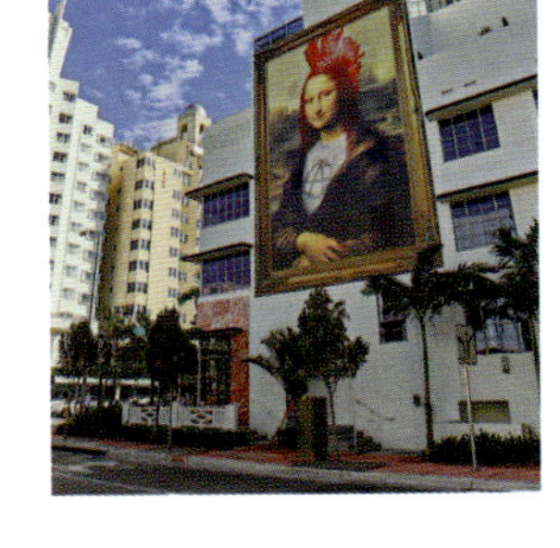
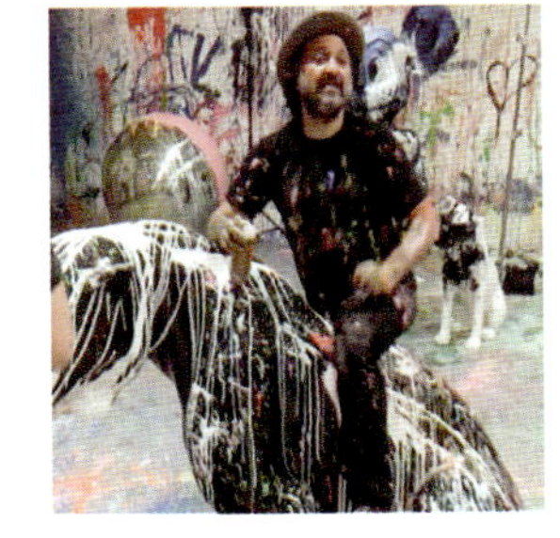
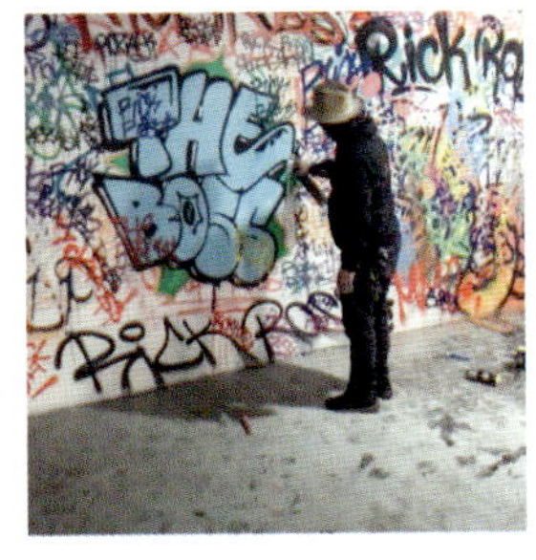
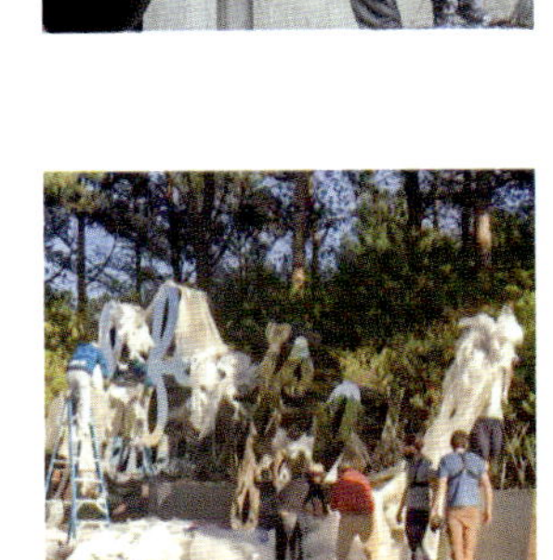
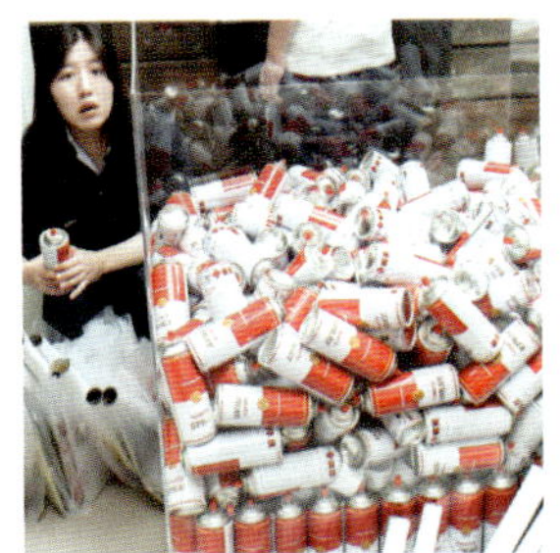
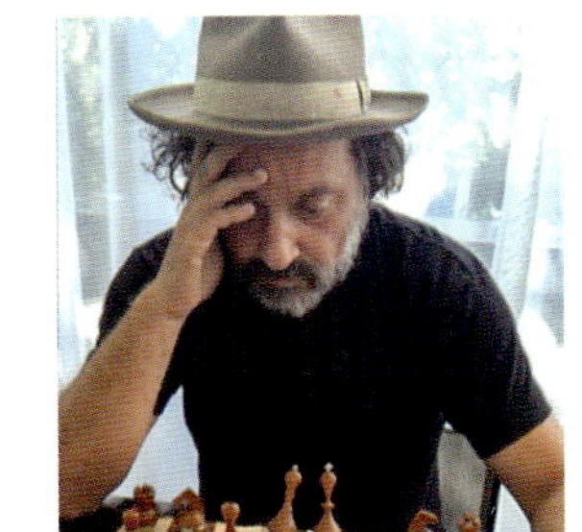
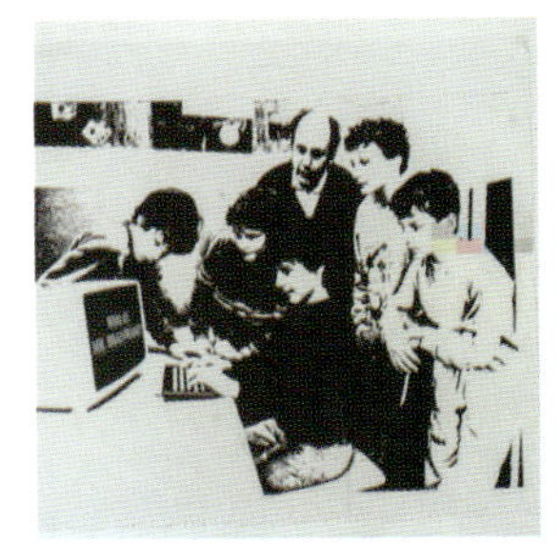
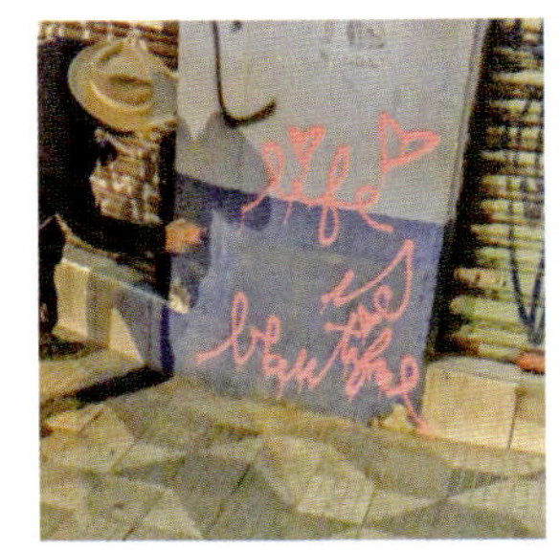
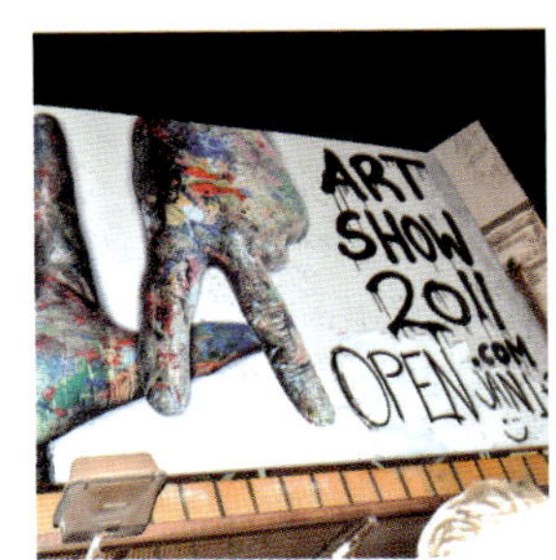
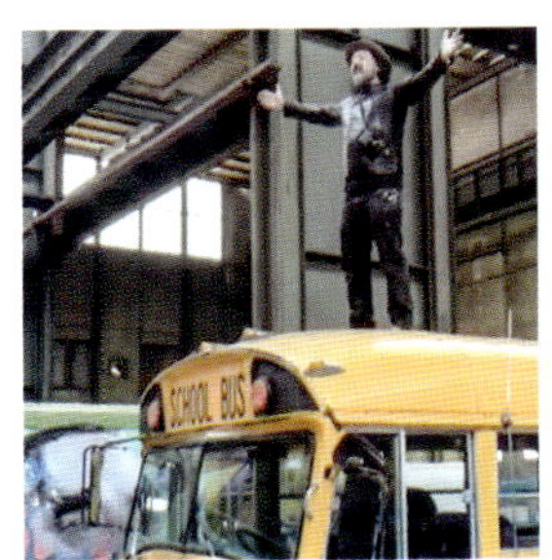
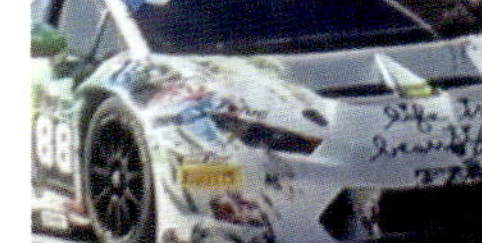

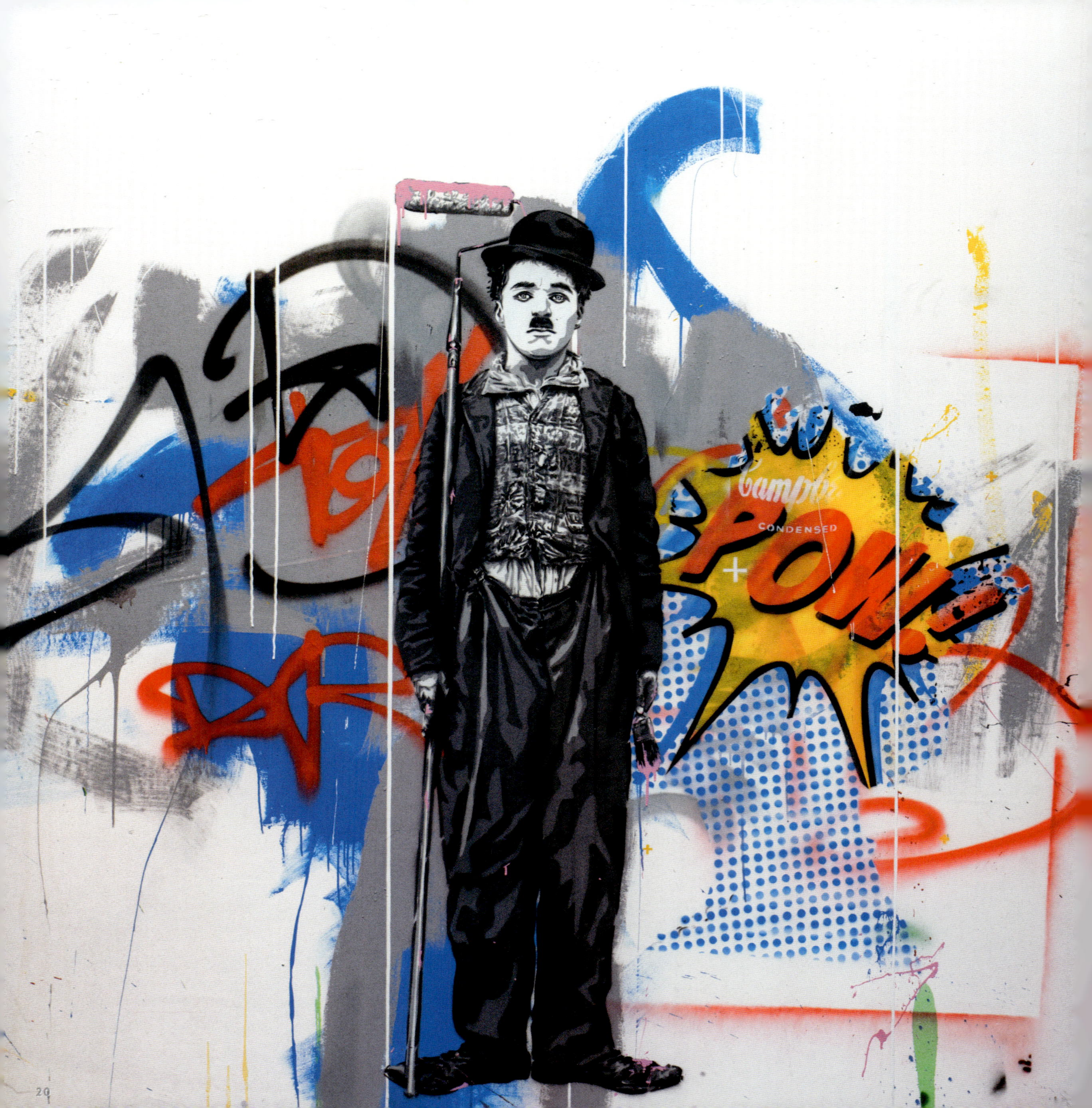
Campbell
CONDENSED
POW!

DONALD KUSPIT

MR. BRAINWASH: THE PAINTER OF POSTMODERN LIFE IN ART HISTORICAL PERSPECTIVE

Mr. Brainwash's paintings are dazzling, intense, delirious: overrun by painterly gestures, applied with seemingly reckless abandon—under the spell of gravity, colorful paint cascades down the surface, a veritable waterfall in *Banksy Thrower*, *Batman vs. Superman*, *Chaplin*, and *Everyday Life*, or explodes on the canvas, as in *Brigitte Bardot*, *Einstein*, and *Einstein 2*.

The vivid paint bombards the illustrious personages, all colorless ghosts, as the black, white, and gray of which they are ingeniously composed suggests. Their flatness and fixed expressions contrast with the haptic energy of the expressive paint, just as their photographic verisimilitude contrasts with the overall abstractness of the works. At once abstract and representational—modernist in their assertion of the material medium and socially realistic in their imagery—they seamlessly fuse aesthetic opposites. Graffiti abounds—"Love" and "Punks" are scrawled on the wall of *Einstein*, the Keith Haring winged sacred child between them reminding us that Haring began his career scrawling graffiti on the walls of subways—and absurd juxtapositions abound, among them the small figure of Einstein and the billboard-large face of Warhol. Einstein holds a sign declaring that "Love is the Answer" in both works devoted to him, and a "sign" of Warhol, in the form of his Campbell's soup cans, appears in *Einstein 2*. Also appearing in both Einstein works is a black and white poster of man holding a clapboard, with the words "Life is Beautiful" scrawled on it in *Einstein*, even though his contorted mien suggests that it is not.

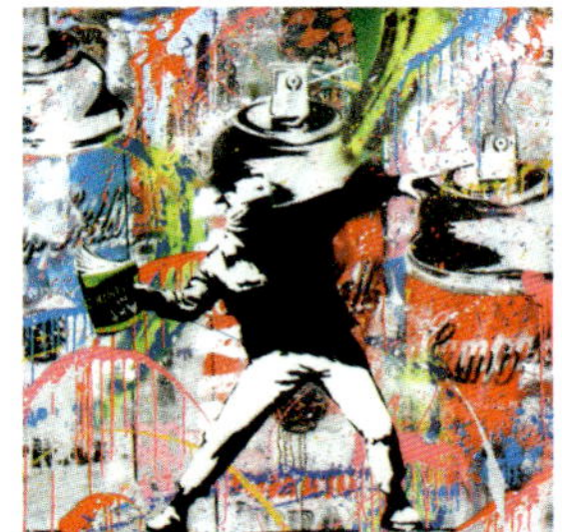

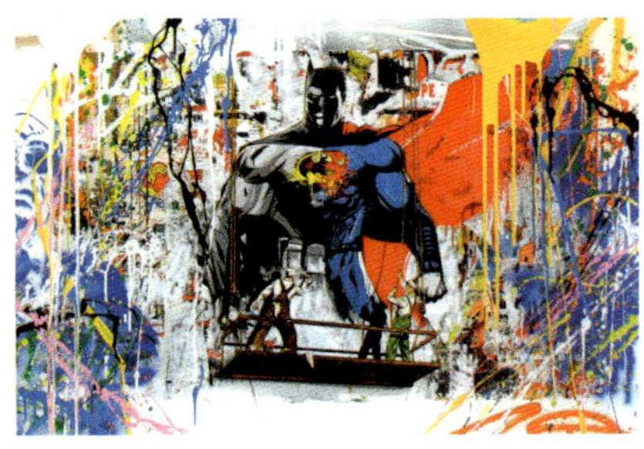

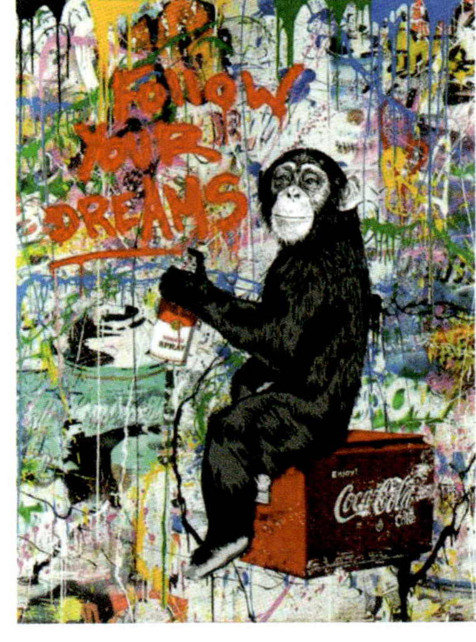

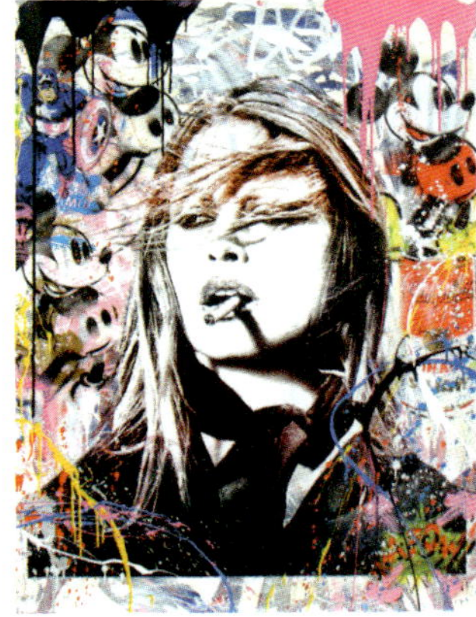

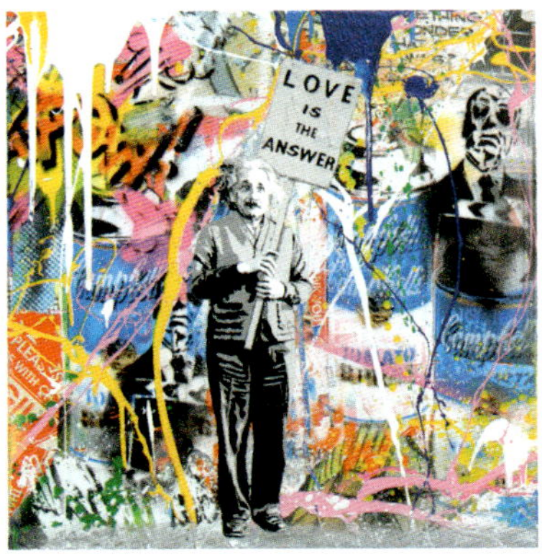

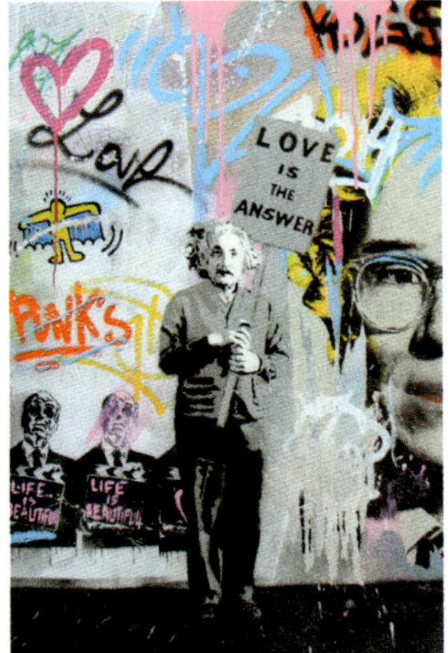

left to right, top to bottom

Banksy Thrower
36" x 36"
Stencil and mixed media on paper

Batman vs. Superman
25" x 38"
Silkscreen and mixed media on paper

Everyday Life
64" x 48"
Stencil and mixed media on paper

Brigitte Bardot
50" x 38"
Silkscreen and mixed media on paper

Einstein 2
20" x 20"
Silkscreen and mixed media on canvas

Einstein
36" x 24"
Silkscreen and mixed media on canvas

opposite
Chaplin
89" x 94"
Stencil and acrylic
paint on canvas

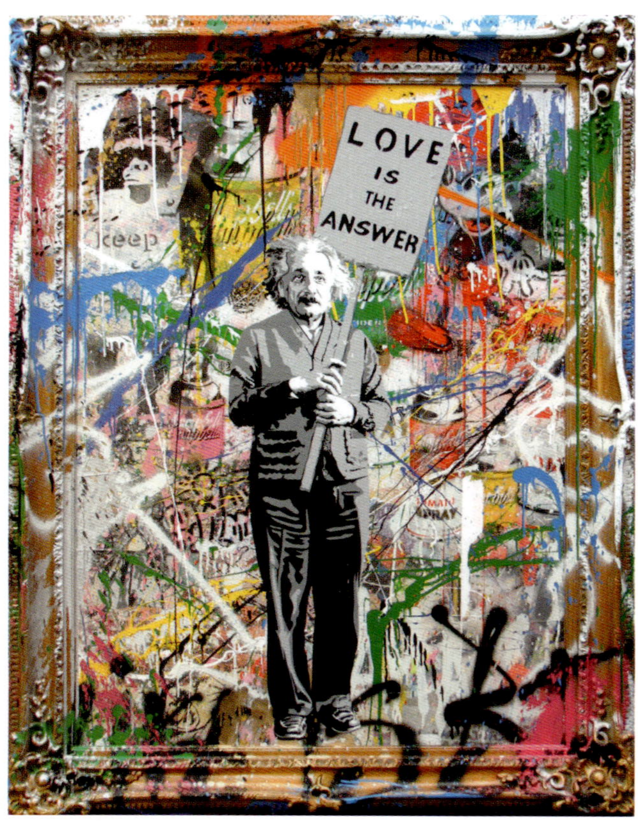

Einstein
57" x 45"
Silkscreen and mixed media on canvas

All the figures in the paintings are, in principle, comic book figures—a point made explicitly clear by the appearance of Mickey Mouse in *Brigitte Bardot* and *Chaplin*. That is, they're all stars in the popular culture, not to say waxworks in a theater of the absurd, their faces and figures photographically embalmed and idealized—facilely immortalized—in what is better called the "common culture." In a famous essay of the same name, Baudelaire described "The Painter of Modern Life" as a "man of the crowd," and the crowd is a social space where the commonplace rules—a democratic space in which everyone and everything are equal yet uneasily together, sometimes at odds, sometimes making common cause. The crowd is a paradox: a space of difference and sameness—heterogeneous yet homogeneous—at once. Mr. Brainwash is a man of the crowd, a painter of *commonplaces*: famous figures that have become visual clichés, and familiar thoughts that have become conceptual clichés. Every cliché is instantly recognizable and comprehensible—matter of fact to the point of banality. But the crowd of commonplace images and ideas that flood Mr. Brainwash's paintings exist in the mind of a brainwashed postmodern public, that is, a manipulated and with that peculiarly mindless public.

Brainwashing is a method of mind control—menticide, it has sometimes been called, on the model of suicide—designed to break down a person's thought patterns, that is, way of thinking, and in the case of Mr. Brainwash's works, their thinking about art. Ever since Clement Greenberg's famous 1939 essay "Avant-Garde and Kitsch" celebrated *avant-garde* art—more particularly, abstract art (then still a novelty, not imported to New York until European avant-garde artists arrived in the city after the Second World War had devastated Europe)—and deplored popular art, conceived as *kitsch* ("mass-produced" art, often "sentimental," "heartfelt," and "garish," that is, facilely "sensational," as well as made for a commercial purpose), avant-garde art has been the preferred and dominant mode of art. A refined art appealing to refined taste, avant-garde art is by definition aesthetically superior to popular art, all the more so because it is handmade—painting that showed the sign of a hand, and with that conveyed an individual sensibility, was the exemplary avant-garde art for Greenberg, as it was for Harold Rosenberg, who regarded it as the "signature" of the artist, and as such an expression of his personality—rather than anonymous, impersonal, machine-made, and "unsigned," like commercial kitsch art. Kitsch was "arty," but it was not exactly "art." Greenberg's 1939 essay followed in the wake of Alfred Barr's notable 1936 diagram tracing the development of avant-garde art, climaxing in what Barr called "non-geometrical abstract art" and "geometrical abstract art," implicitly dismissing popular art, unmentioned, as beside the creative point.

But when European abstract art, in effect an aristocratic art, arrived in democratic America, it met a certain resistance, evident in the social realism that continued to be popular, as the acclaim accorded Edward Hopper and Ben Shahn indicated. Kitsch remained popular, even as avant-garde art was accorded elite status, an ironic way of dismissing it as incomprehensible. And, slowly but surely—and inevitably in a democratic society—artists began to integrate "artless" kitsch and "artful" avant-garde art, according each equal significance and assimilating each into the other, as pop art, particularly Roy Lichtenstein's and Andy Warhol's, made clear. The Museum of Modern Art's 1990 exhibition *High and Low: Popular Culture and Modern Art* broke down the distinction completely, suggesting that each was as aesthetically valid and culturally important as the other, and arguing that each had its own integrity. Mr. Brainwash's paintings are the climactic statement of this "equalization," with a subtle difference: they indicate that it puts us in a mental state of what the deconstructionists call "undecidability" or uncertainty. For if both are equal, both become peculiarly inconsequential, leaving us in a sort of emotional and cognitive limbo. Looking at a Mr. Brainwash painting, the spectator commits mental suicide by being stuck in uncertainty, like Buridan's ass, or, if he embraces the extremes in a kind of *Eureka moment* of insight into the self-contradictory whole, he acknowledges the absurdity of art and of his own mind, and achieves "a free state of creativity" as Mr. Brainwash calls it.

I suggest that the chimpanzee in *Everyday Life* is the emblematic spectator—and emblematic artist. Art makes a monkey of us all. Mr. Brainwash's painting are playful, theatrical, "grandstanding"—he monkeys with art to subversive effect even as he celebrates its contradictions. The monkey is clearly a graffiti artist—a symbolic self-portrait of the ironical Mr. Brainwash—and American, as the carton of Coca-Cola on which he sits suggests. He mocks painting even as he popularizes it: anyone can make a painting—a rather dramatic, impassioned, profoundly expressive painting— all he has to do is buy a can of spray paint, which is what the monkey uses, find a wall to spray, and monkey with art. "Follow Your Dreams," the monkey writes on the luridly graffitied walls, suggesting that he has followed his dream of becoming an artist—a painter.

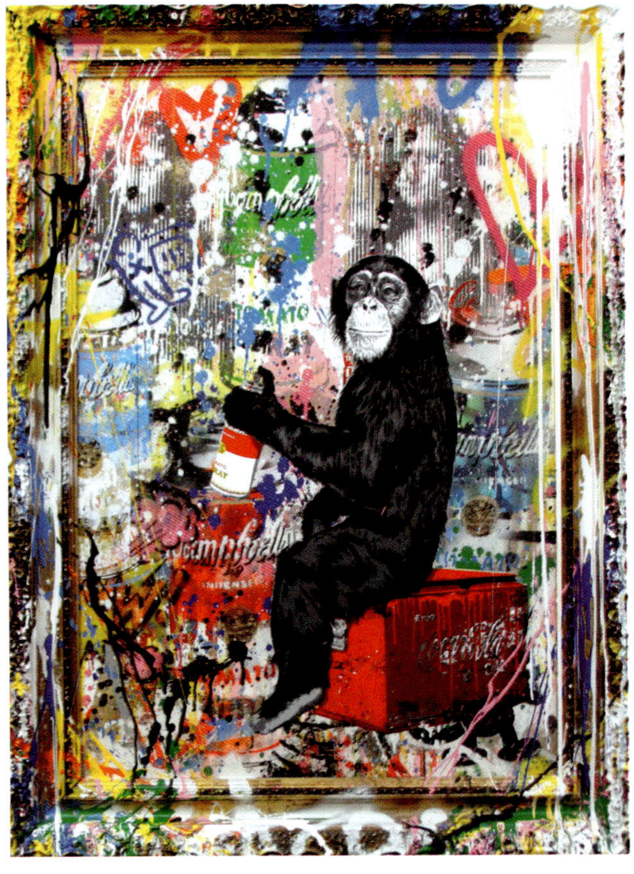

Everyday Life
39" x 29"
Silkscreen and mixed media on canvas

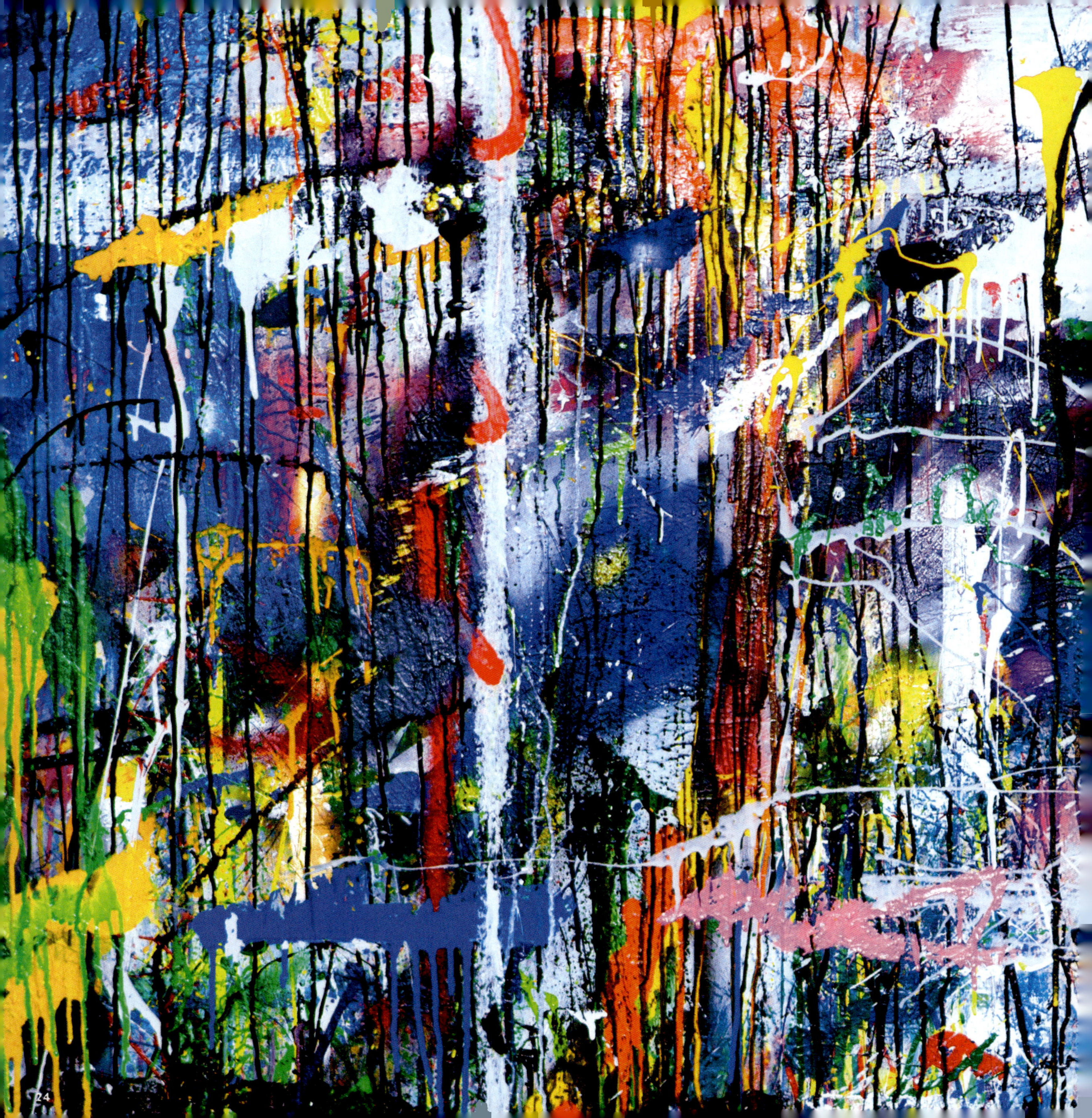

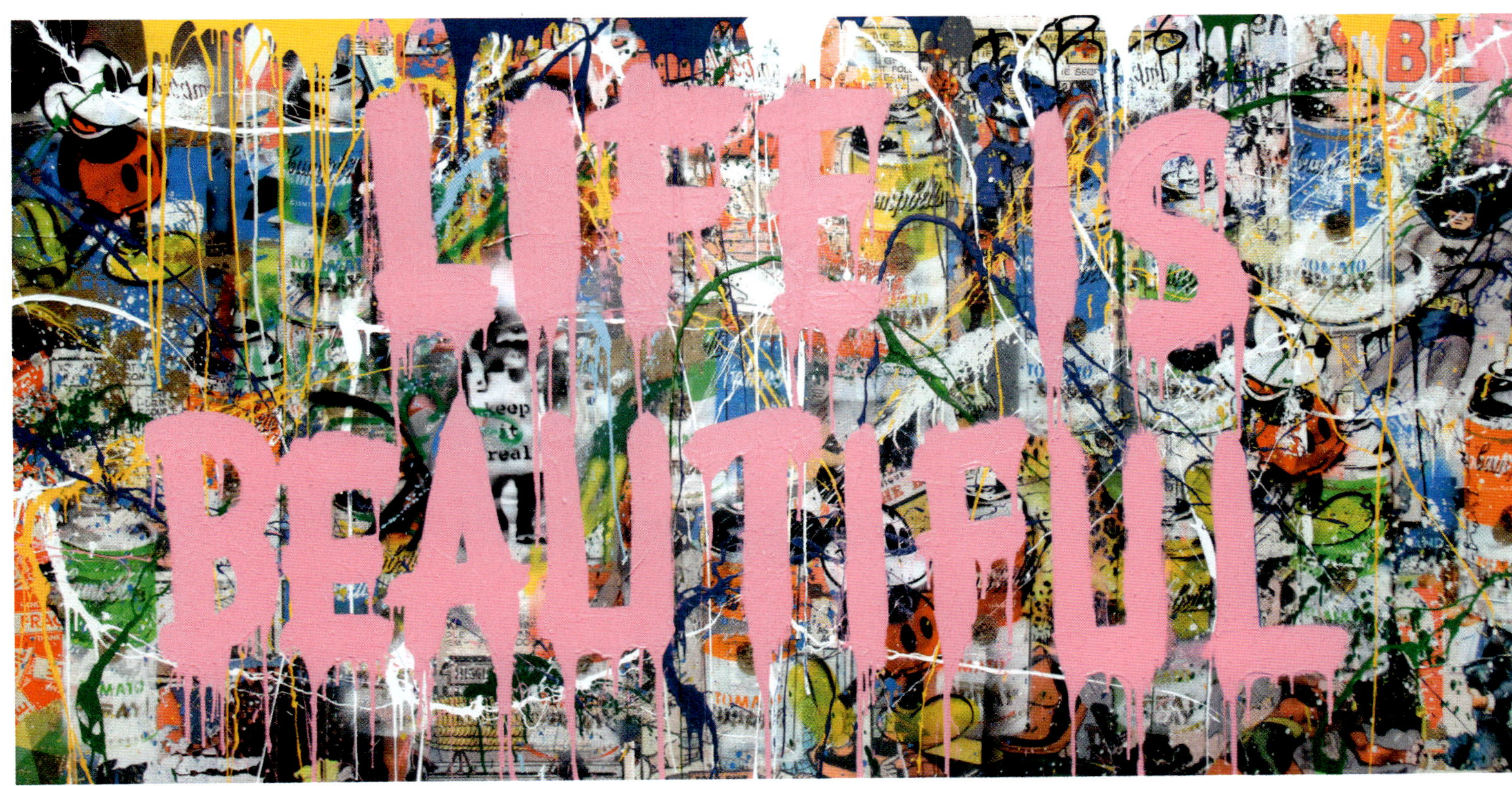

A subtle nihilism informs Mr. Brainwash's paintings, the nihilism of the brainwashing that the sociologist Herbert Marcuse famously called "repressive desublimation," an elaboration of Freud's idea that we can either repress our sexual and aggressive instincts or sublimate them by giving them sociocultural form and expression. According to Marcuse, in postmodern society there is no sublimation of instincts—let it all hang out, whether in life or art—and there is the repression of meaning. Mr. Brainwash's paintings are an ironically desublimated abstract expressionism—they're erotically aggressive, but their eroticized aggression, not to say in-your-face, over-the-top expressivity, is as peculiarly trifling as their signs and figures are. Mr. Brainwash's painting points a finger to remind us that all art has become popular, and with that, lost inner meaning, and has become a way of brainwashing us, claiming a franchise of the mind.

—DONALD KUSPIT

Donald Kuspit is one of America's most important art critics. He is Distinguished Professor Emeritus of Art History and Philosophy at the State University of New York at Stony Brook and former Professor of Art History at the School of Visual Arts. He has received fellowships from the Ford Foundation, Fulbright Commission, National Endowment for the Arts, National Endowment for the Humanities, Guggenheim Foundation, and Asian Cultural Council, among other organizations. He has doctorates in philosophy (University of Frankfurt) and art history (University of Michigan), as well as degrees from Columbia University, Yale University, and Pennsylvania State University. He is a contributing editor at *Artforum* and *Per Contra*, and the author of dozens of books on art, including *A Critical History of 20th-Century Art* (2005), *The End of Art* (2004), and *Psychostrategies of Avant-Garde Art* (2000).

opposite
Close-up of workshop wall

above
Life Is Beautiful
48" x 95"
Mixed media on canvas

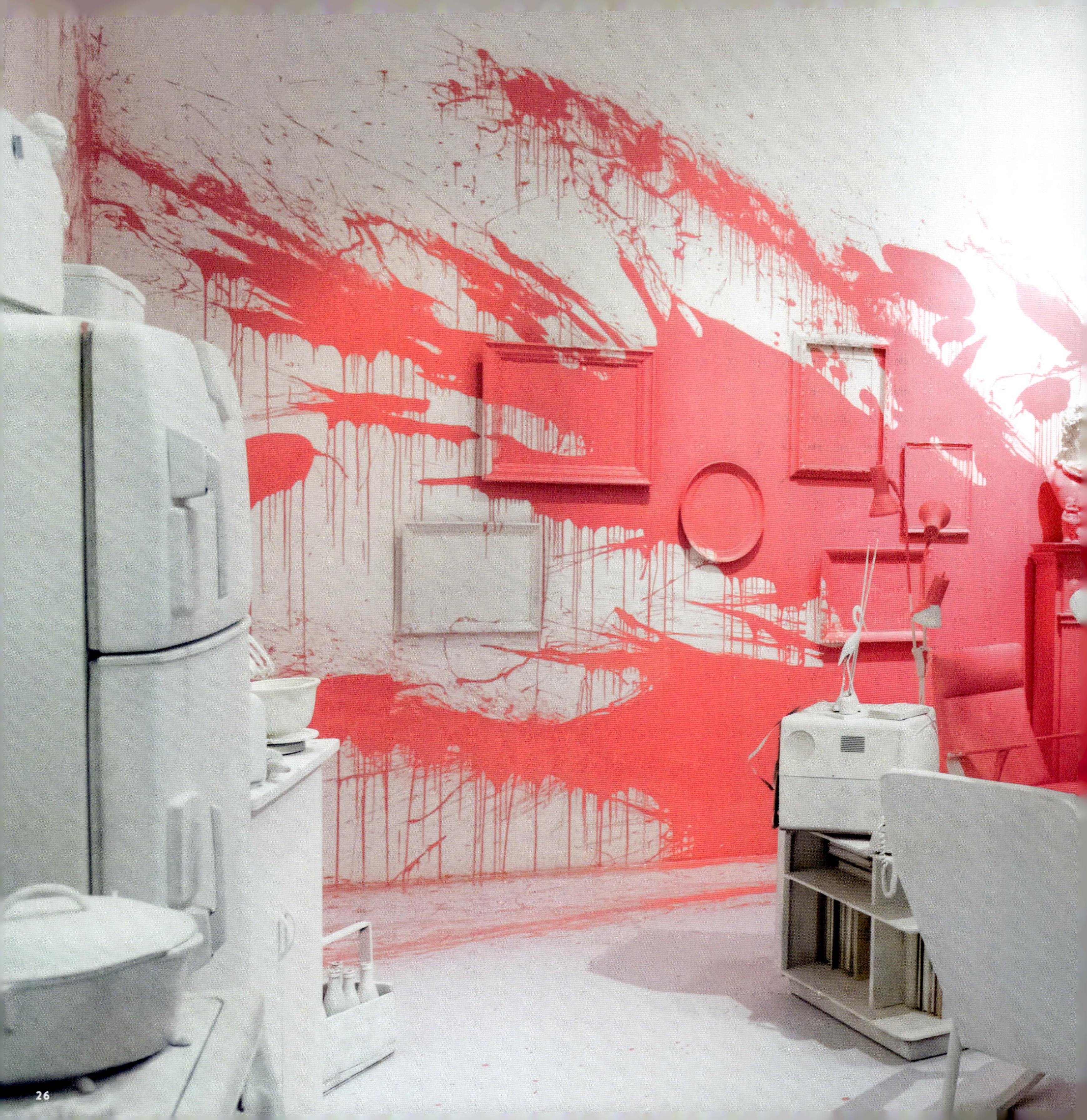

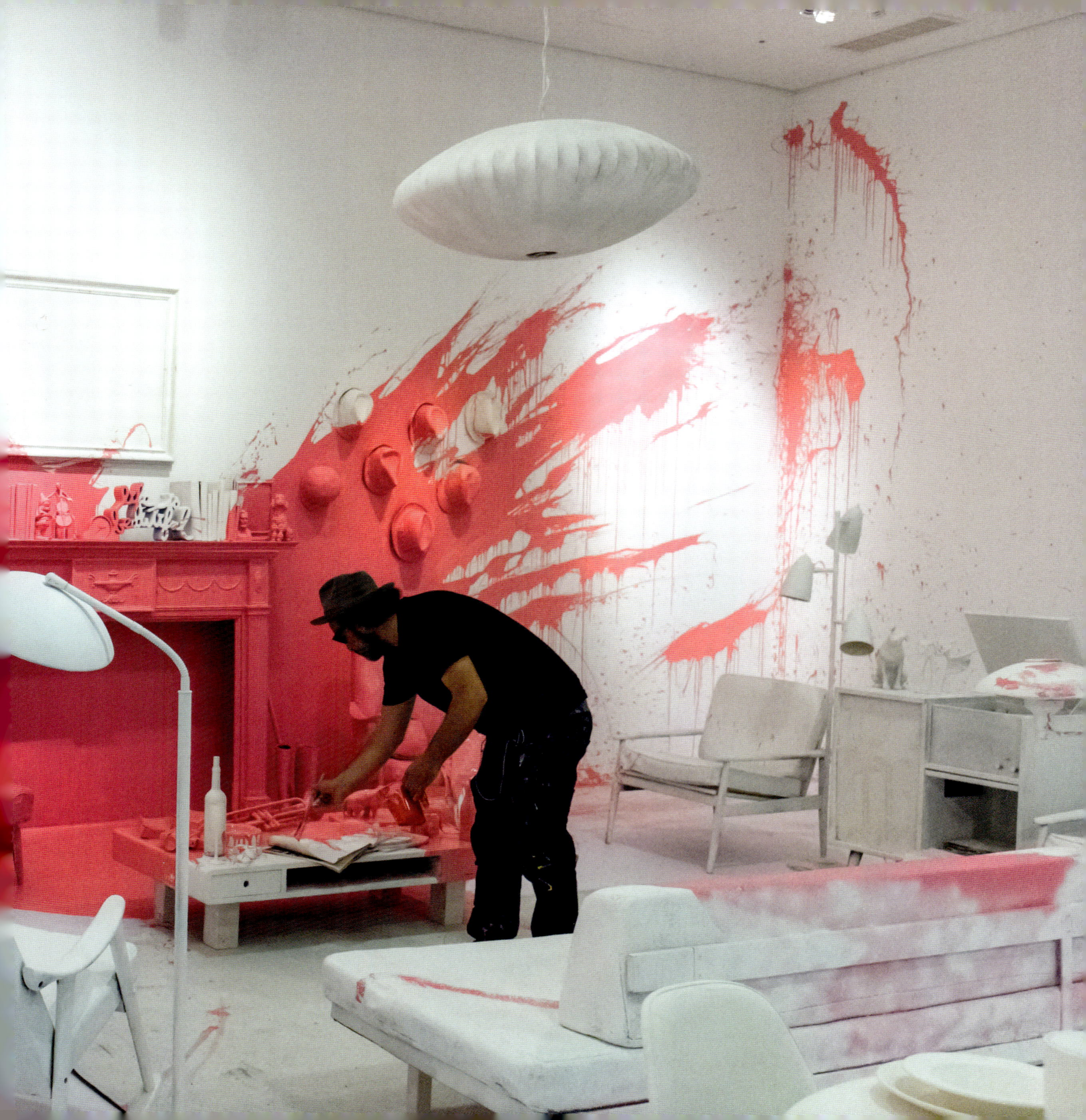

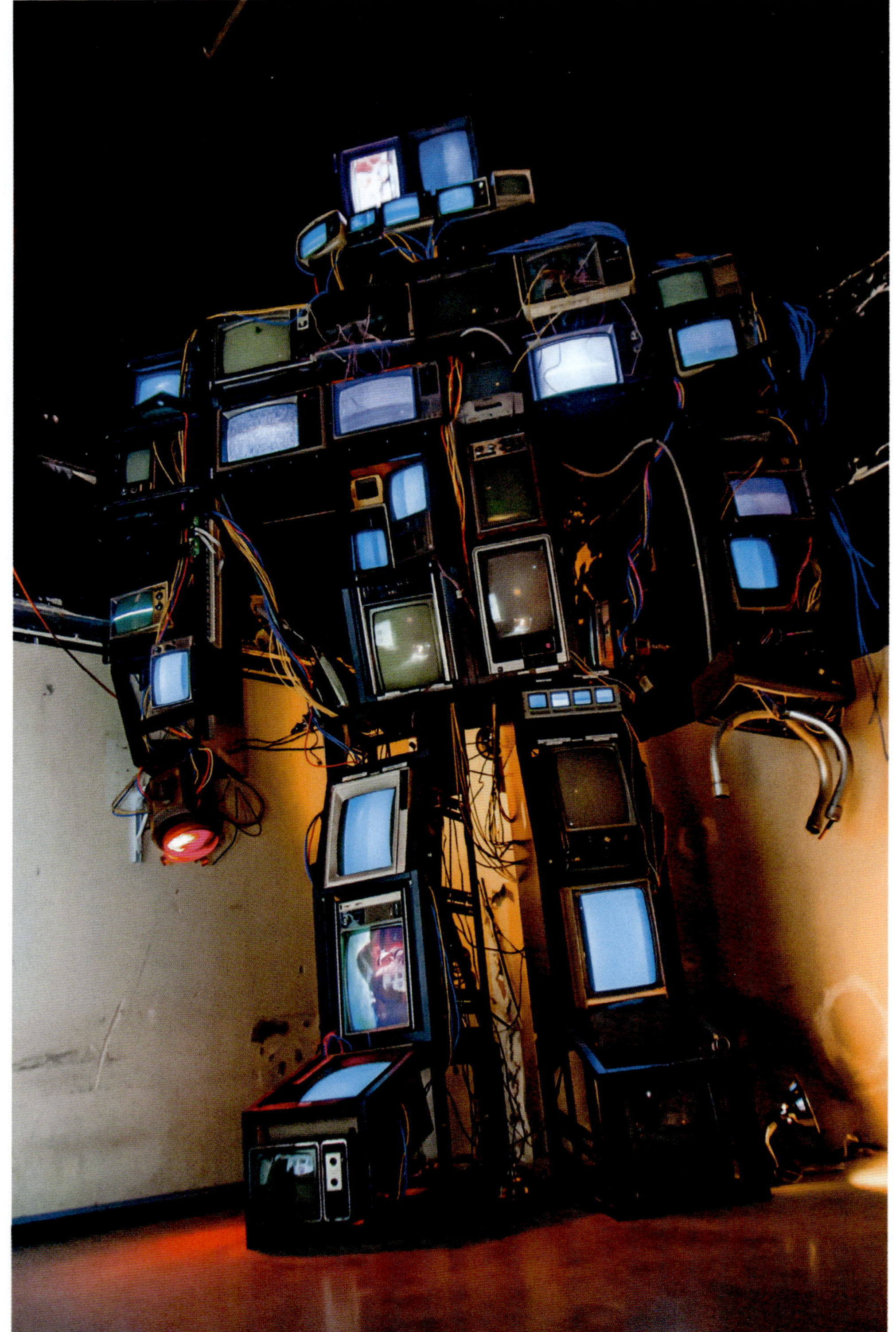

TV Man
20 feet tall
Repurposed televisions
and metal frame

FIRST SOLO SHOW:
LIFE IS BEAUTIFUL

Hollywood 2008

Promising a show like no one had ever seen, Mr. Brainwash appropriately chose the city's first film studio (then called the Nestor Film Company) as the location for his debut into the art world. The former CBS Columbia Square studios in Hollywood opened its doors for the first time on June 18, 2008, the site having been closed since 2007.

Mr. Brainwash transformed this once-pristine news and radio network into a gallery space that held a variety of mediums, from sculptures to installations, paintings to prints, all in his grandiose style. Though he fell off a ladder while preparing for *Life Is Beautiful*, a broken leg wasn't enough to stop Mr. Brainwash from creating the biggest art opening Los Angeles had ever seen.

Crowds lined up for hours around the block, with eager art-seekers even rushing through the gates past security in order to take a peek at Mr. Brainwash's work. Originally booked to run for just five days, *Life Is Beautiful* stayed open for a further two months. And as word about Mr. Brainwash spread, his pieces appeared in galleries and shows around the world.

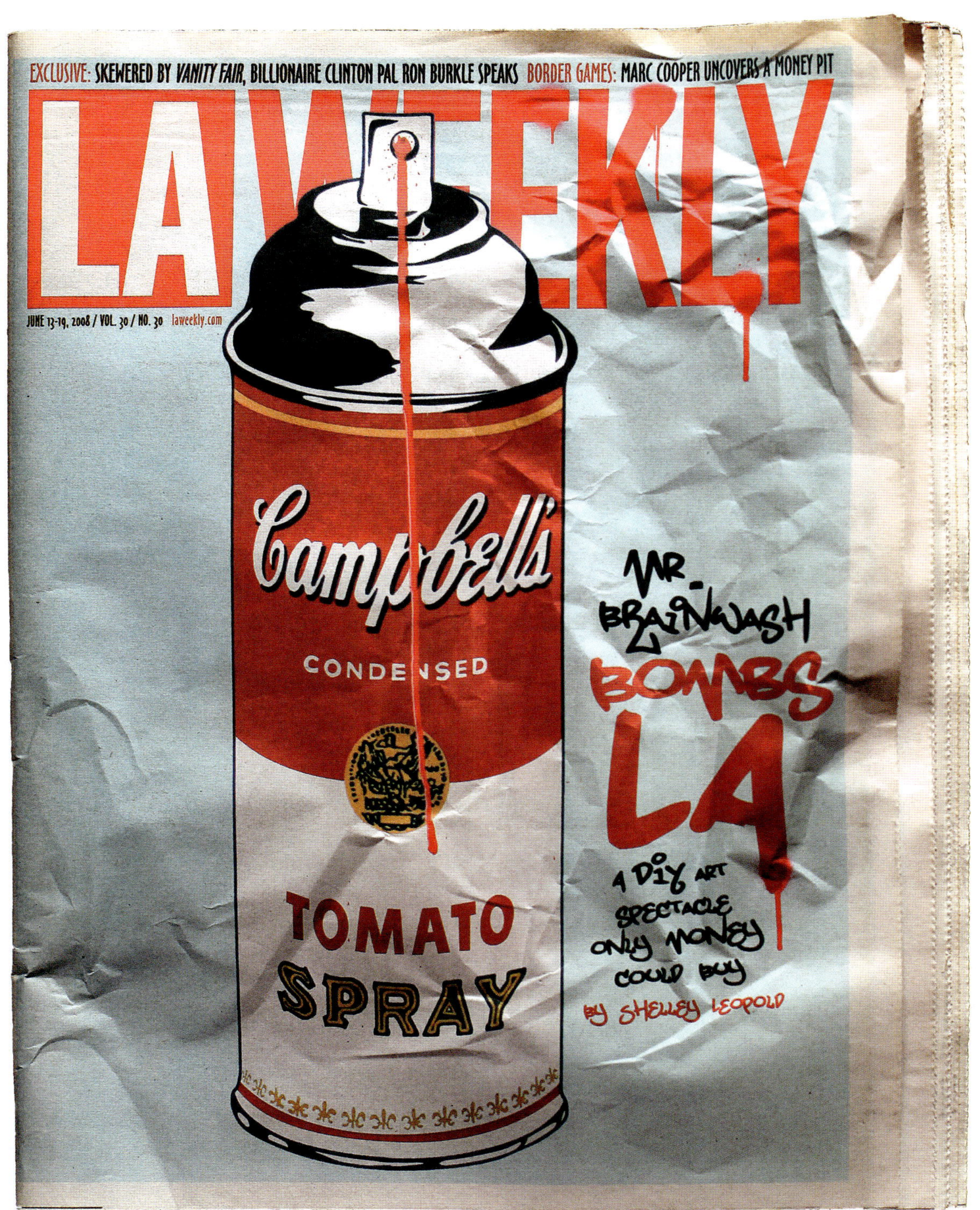

EXCLUSIVE: SKEWERED BY VANITY FAIR, BILLIONAIRE CLINTON PAL RON BURKLE SPEAKS   BORDER GAMES: MARC COOPER UNCOVERS A MONEY PIT
LA WEEKLY
JUNE 13-19, 2008 / VOL. 30 / NO. 30   laweekly.com
Campbell's
CONDENSED
TOMATO
SPRAY
MR. BRAINWASH BOMBS LA
A DIY ART SPECTACLE ONLY MONEY COULD BUY
BY SHELLEY LEOPOLD

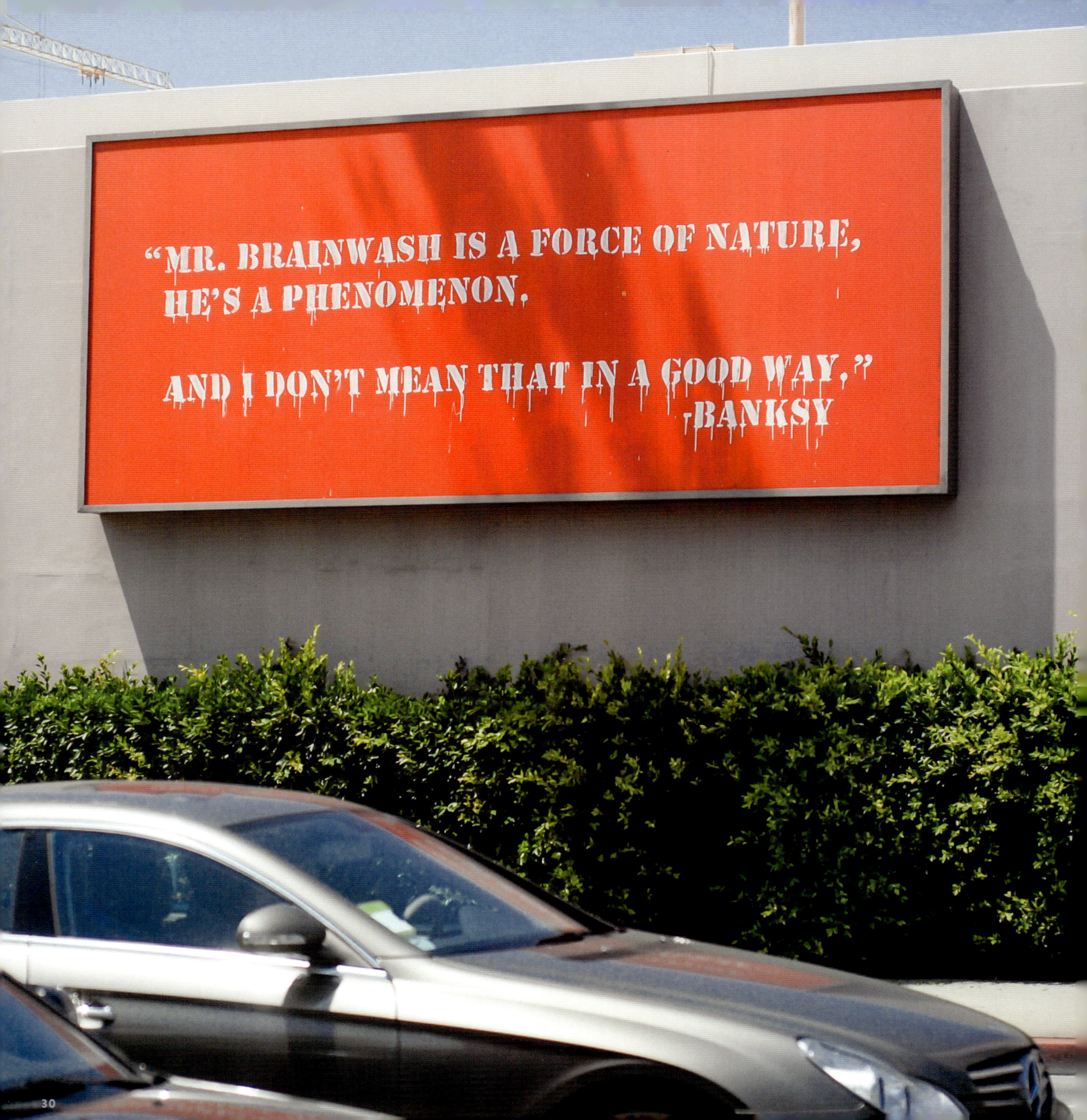

"MR. BRAINWASH IS A FORCE OF NATURE,
HE'S A PHENOMENON,

AND I DON'T MEAN THAT IN A GOOD WAY,"
-BANKSY

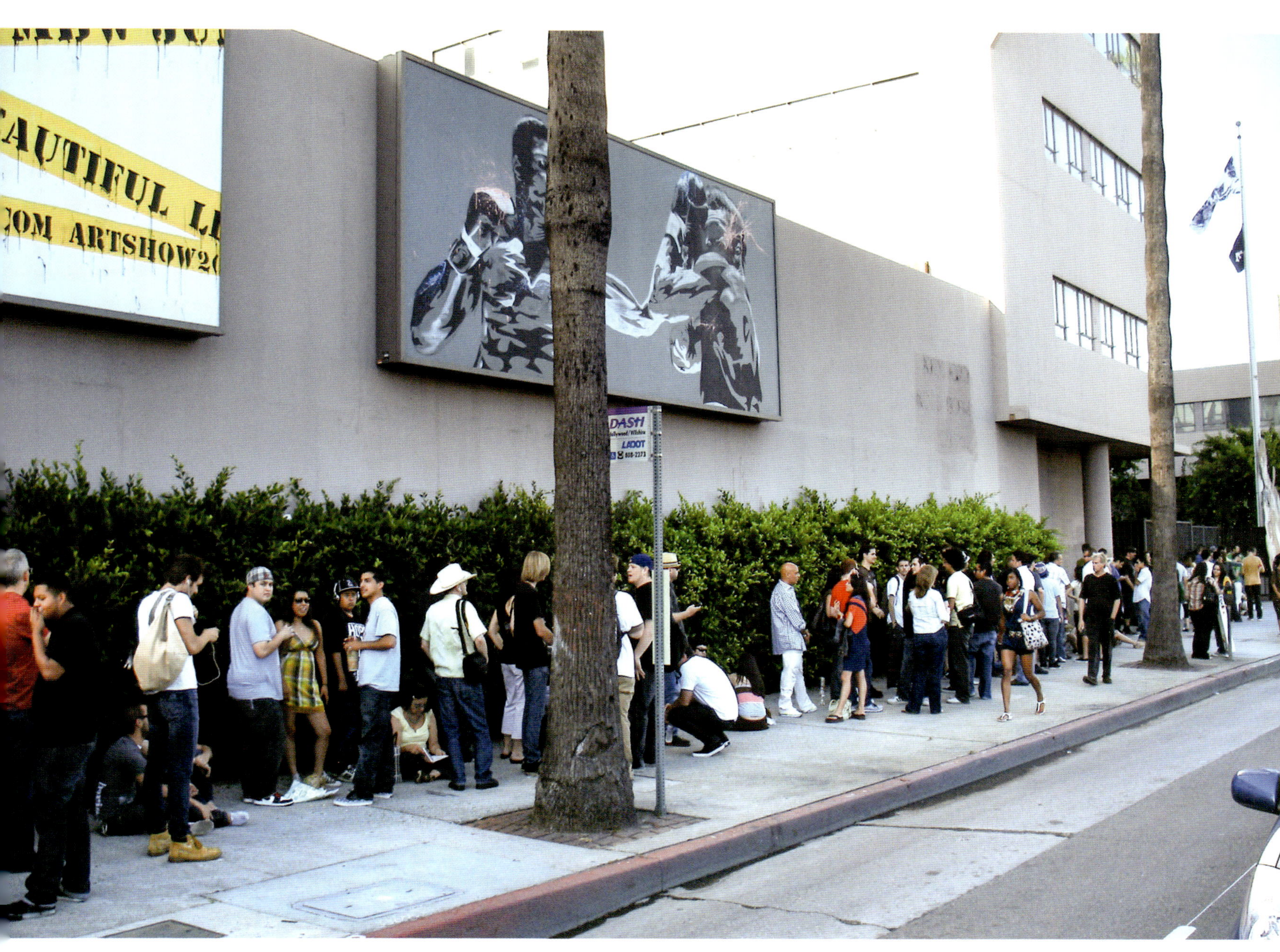
EAUTIFUL L
OM ARTSHOW2
DASH
Hollywood/Wilshire
LADOT
808-2373

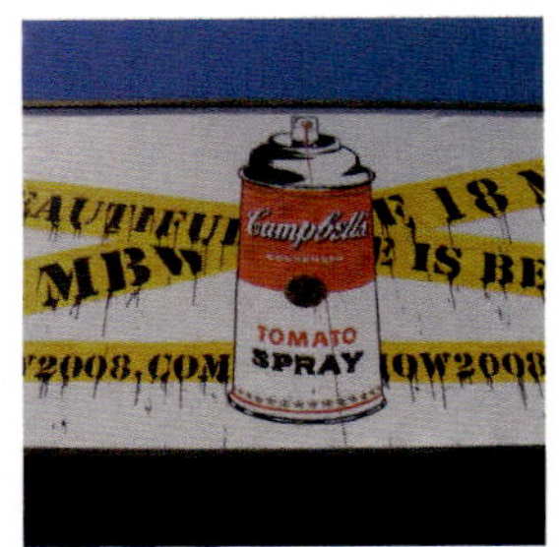
Campbell's
TOMATO
SPRAY
EAUTIFUL
MBW
2008.COM

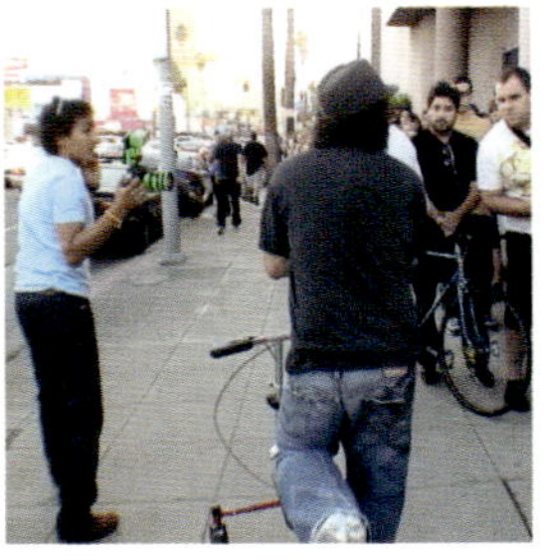
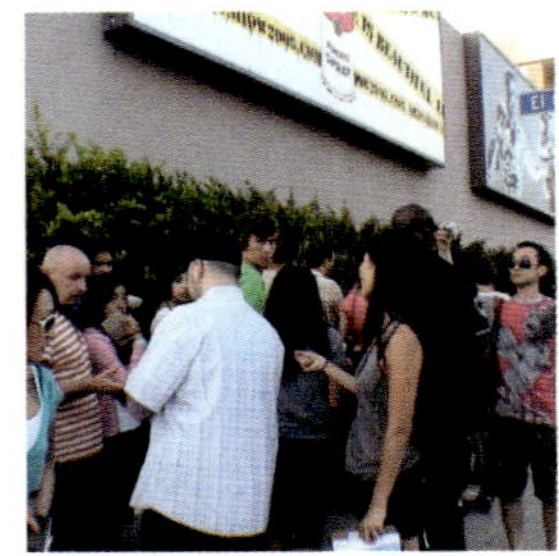
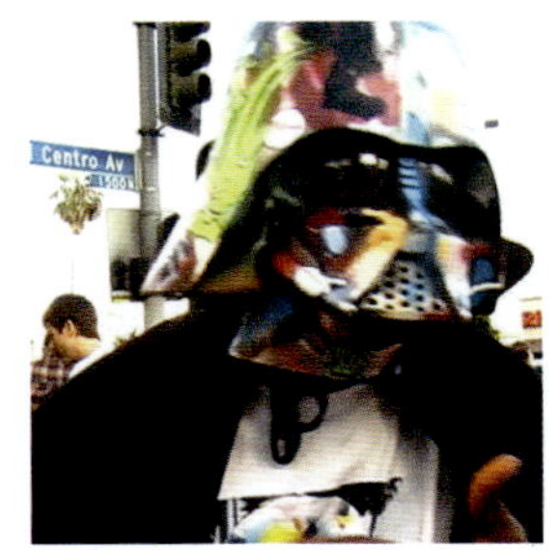
Centro Av

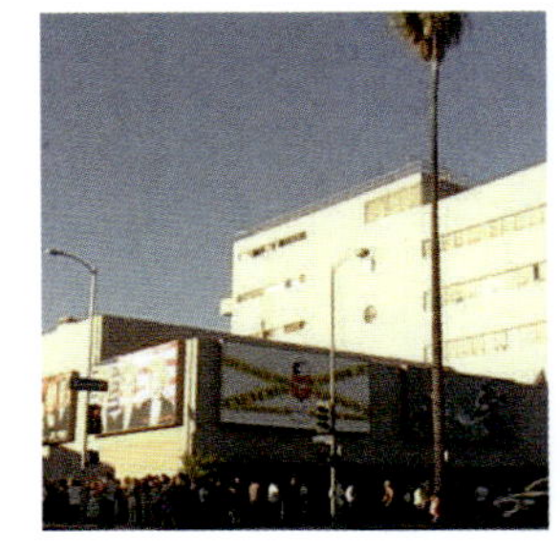

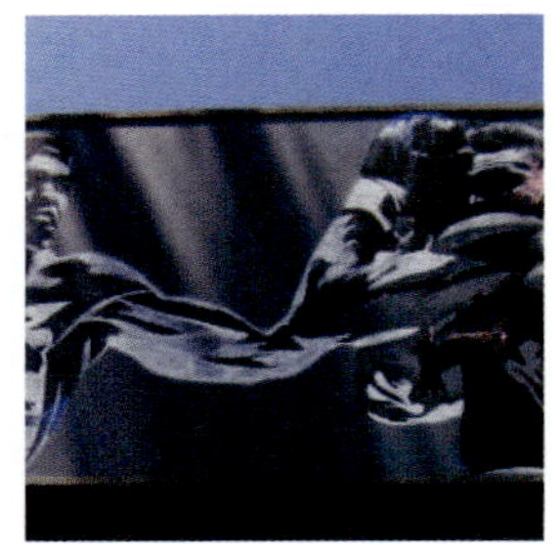

MBW SOLO SHO
OPENS JUNE 18
6121 SUNSET

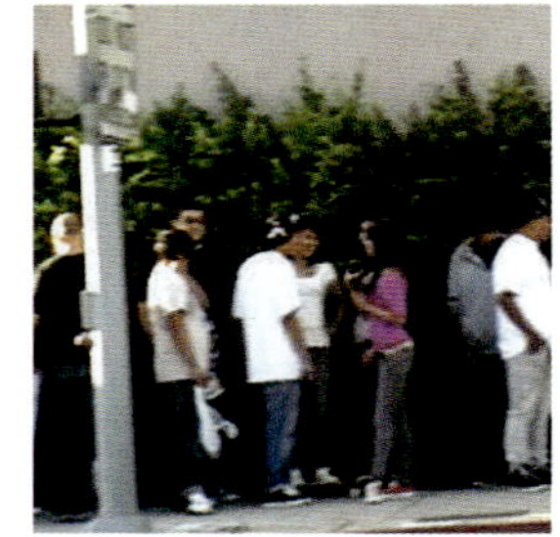
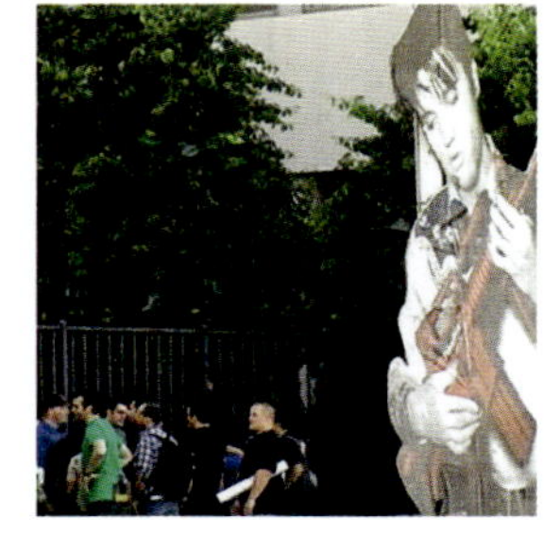
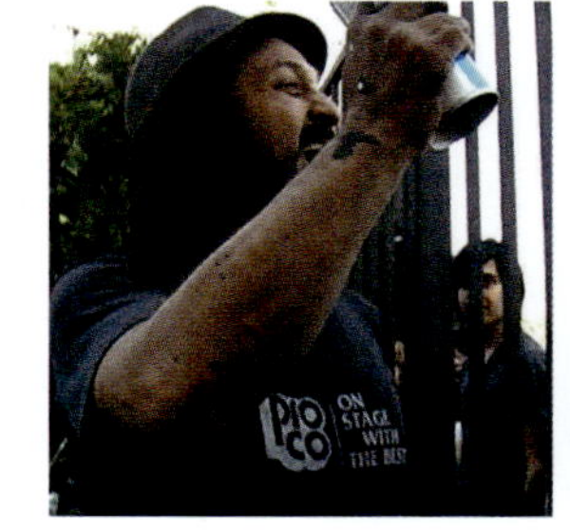

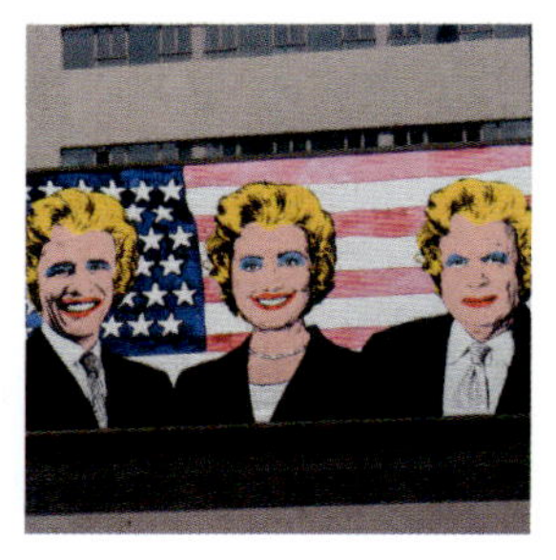
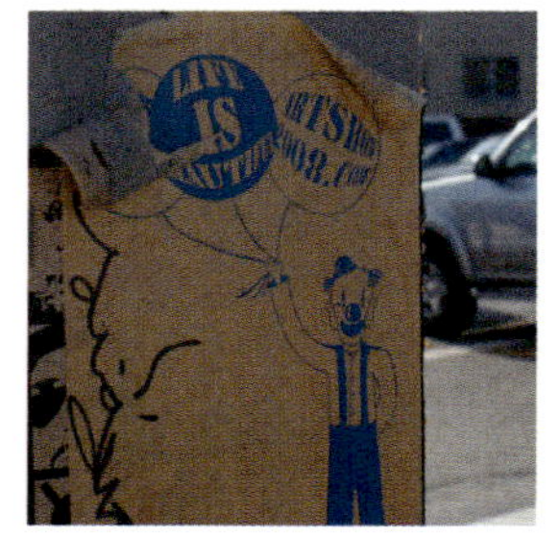
LIFE IS

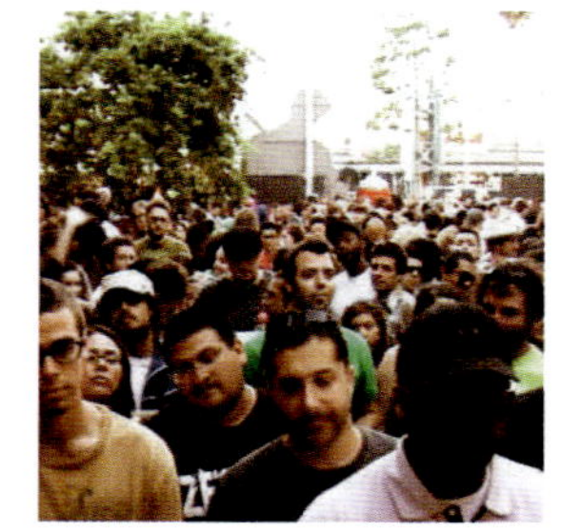
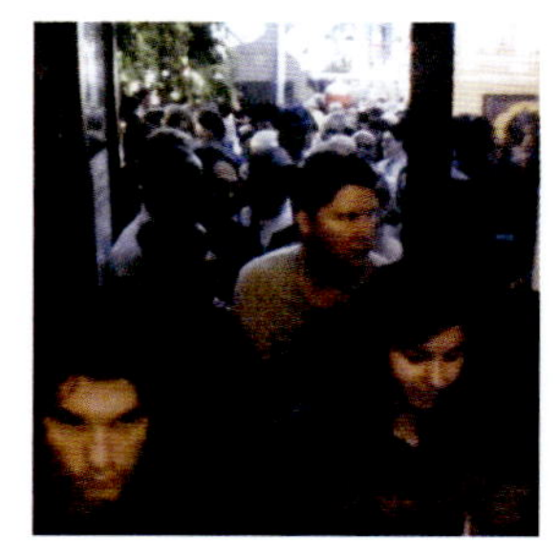
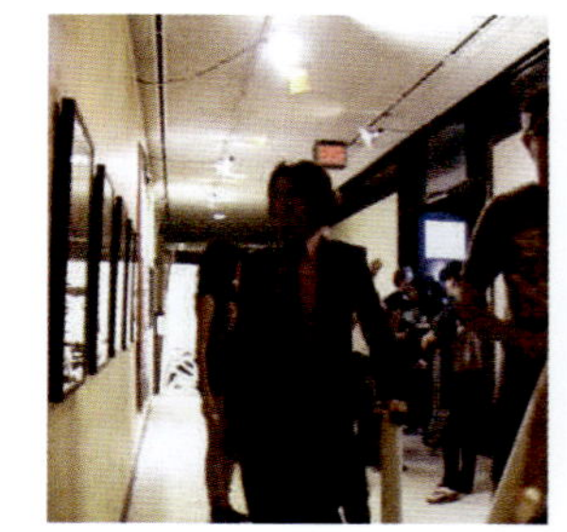

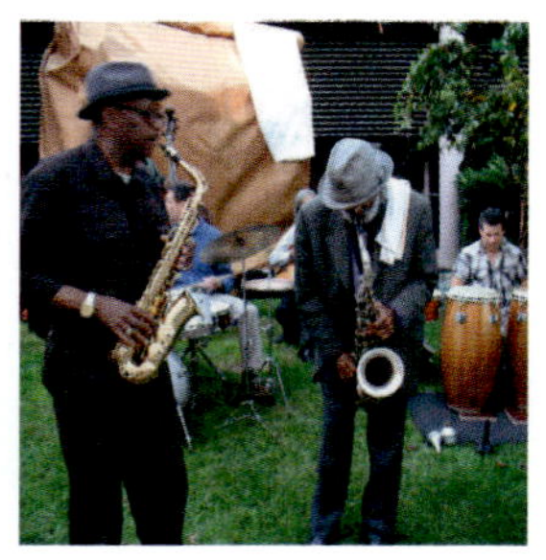
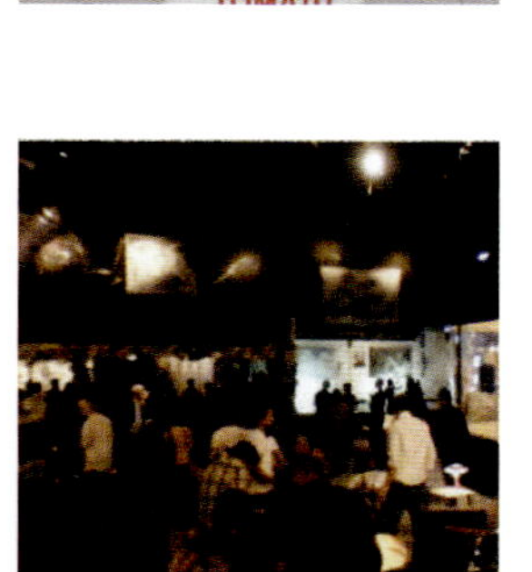
Campbell's
CONDENSED
TOMATO

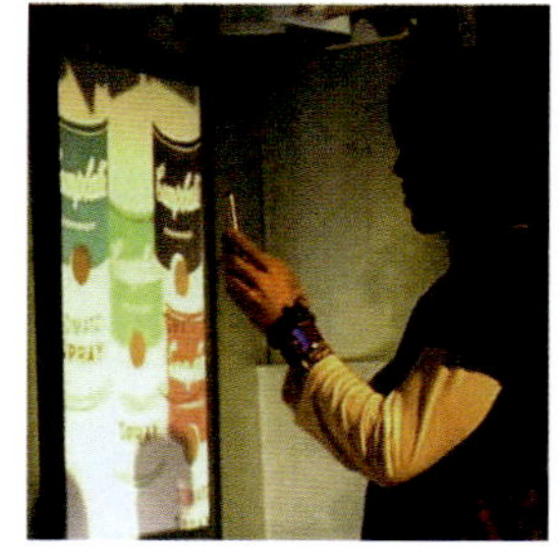
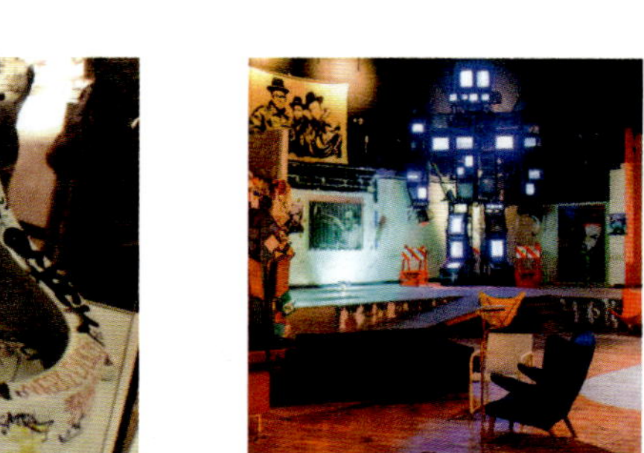
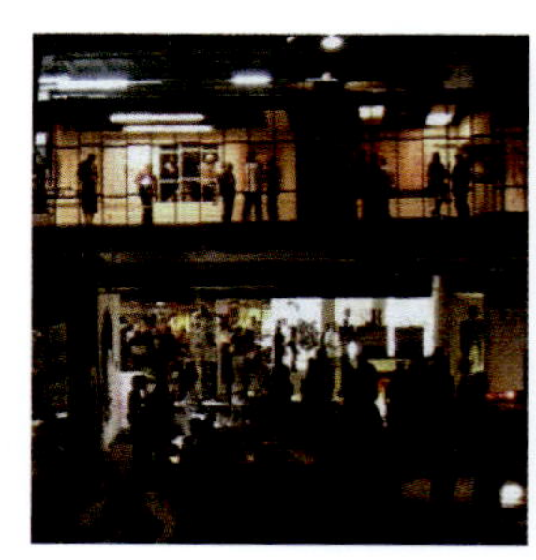

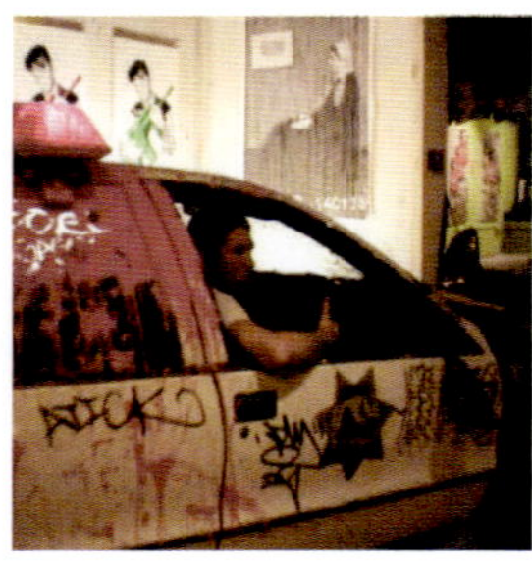
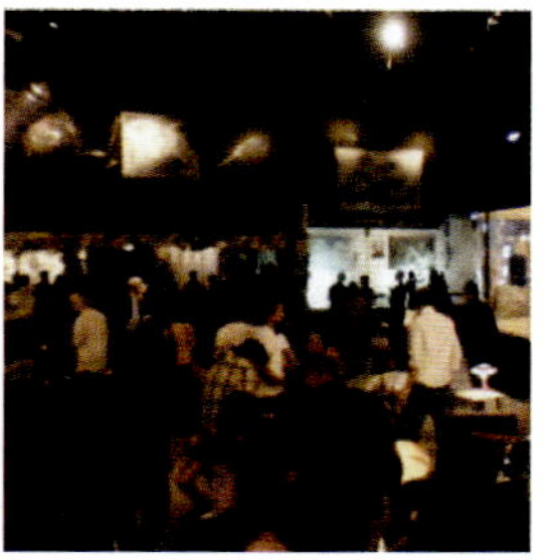
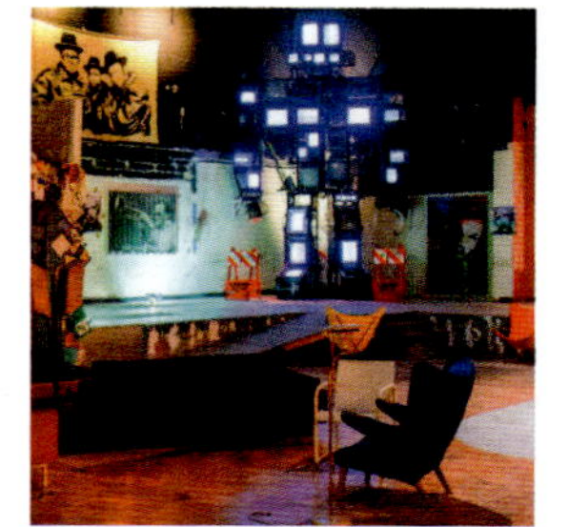
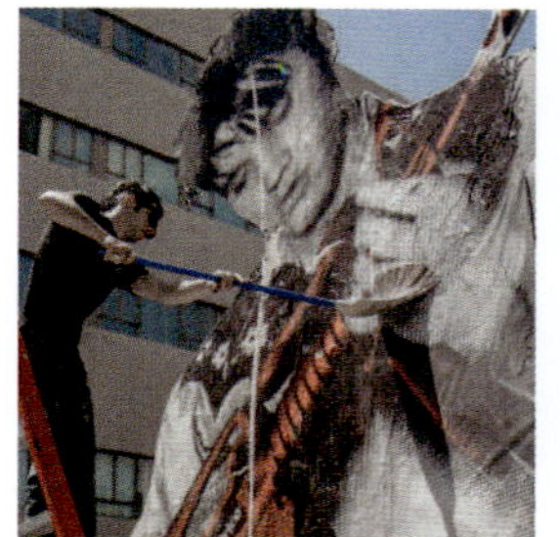

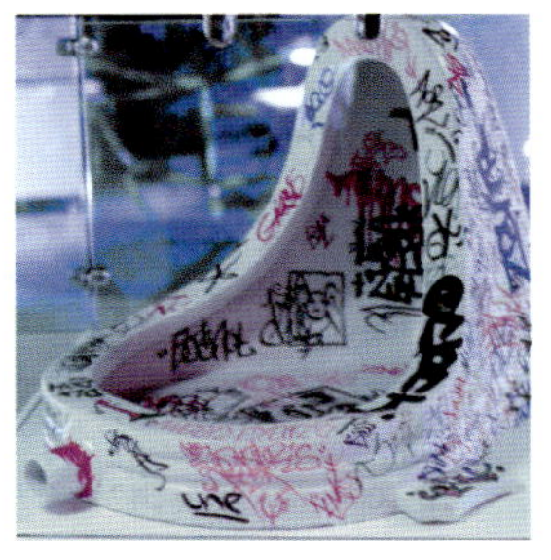 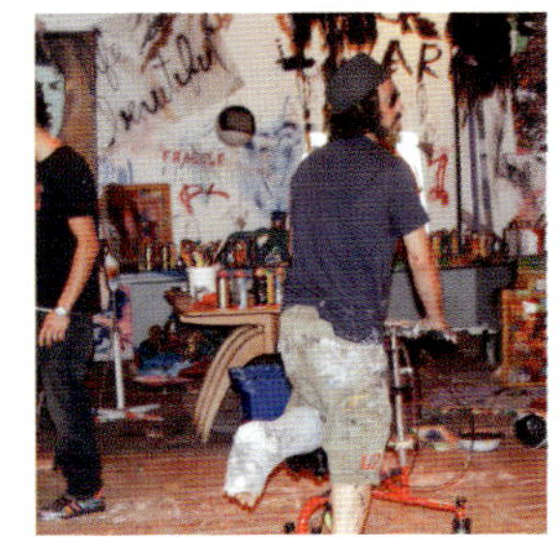  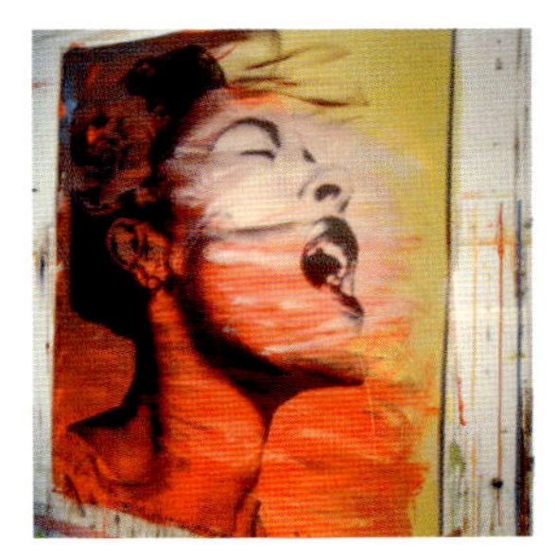 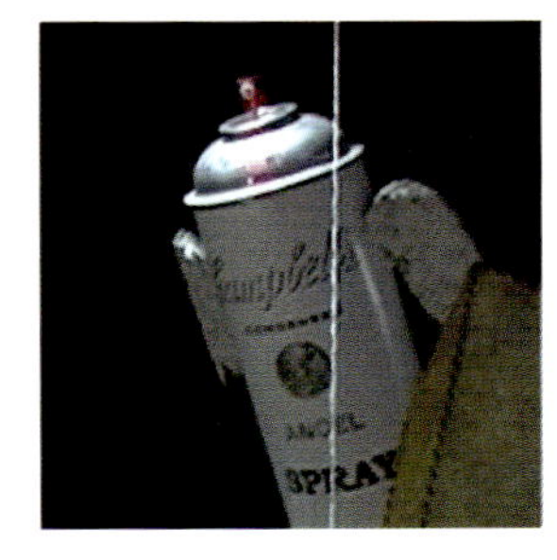
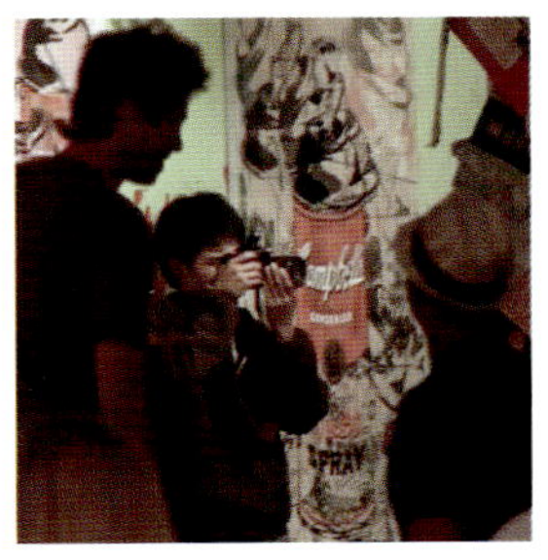 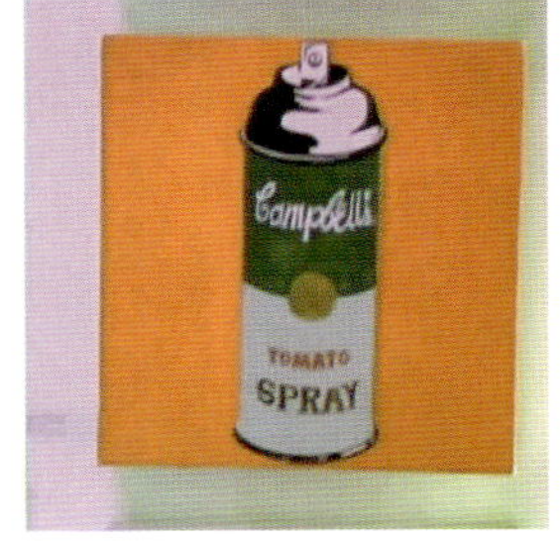 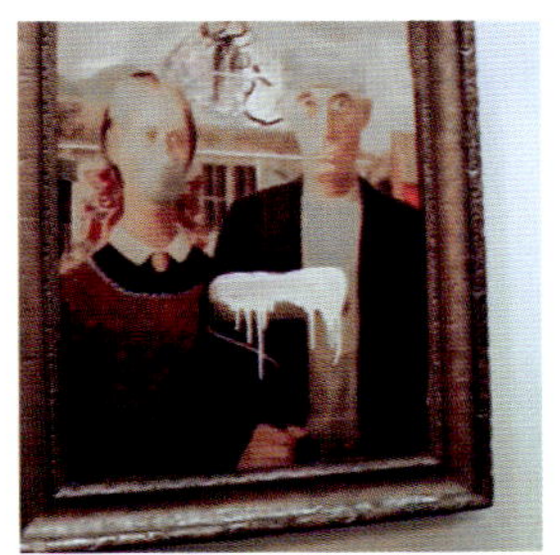 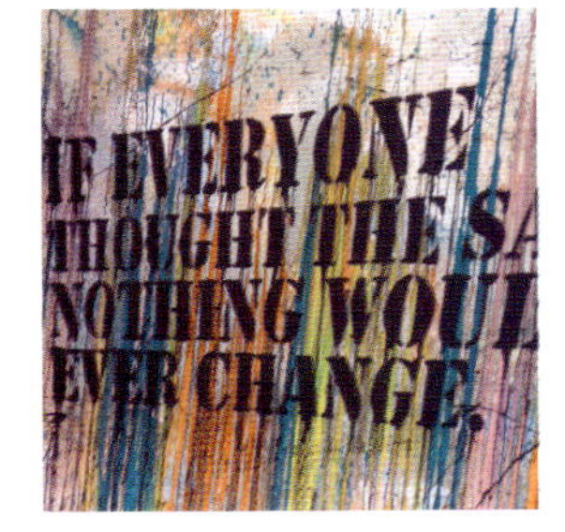 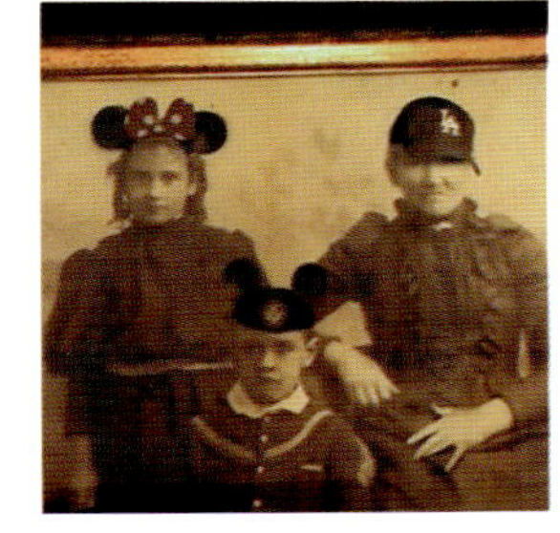
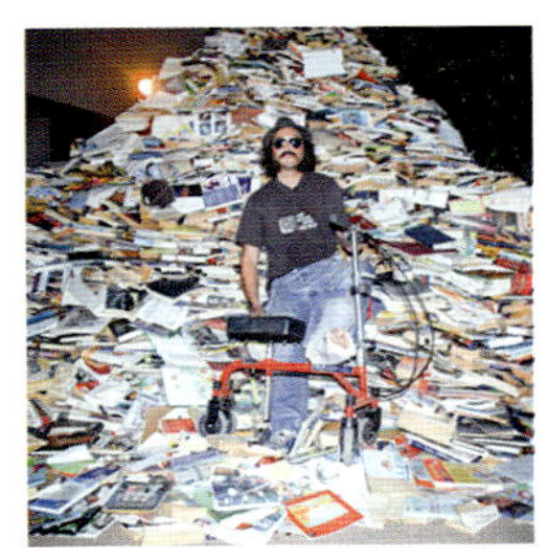 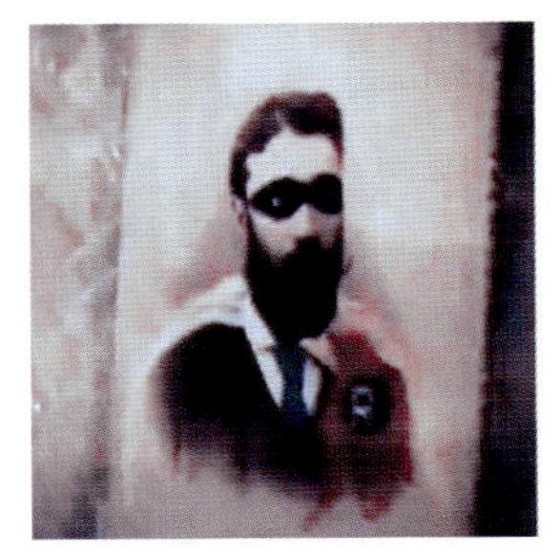 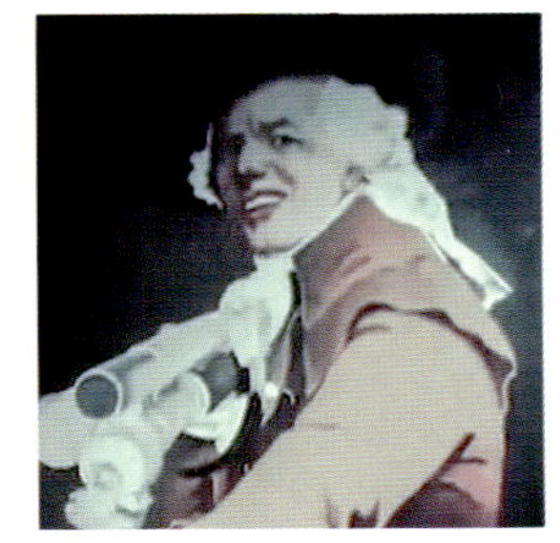 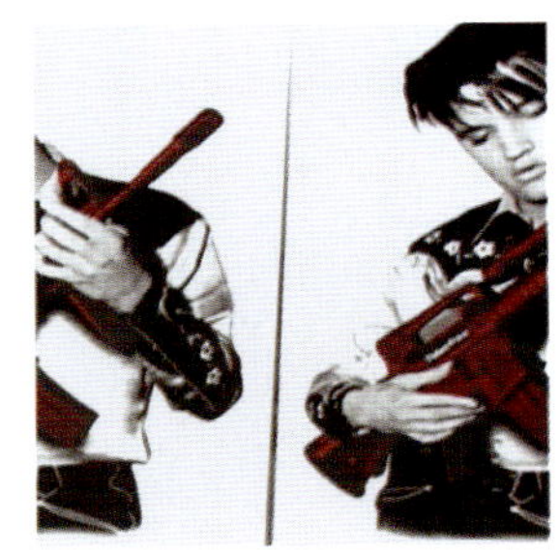 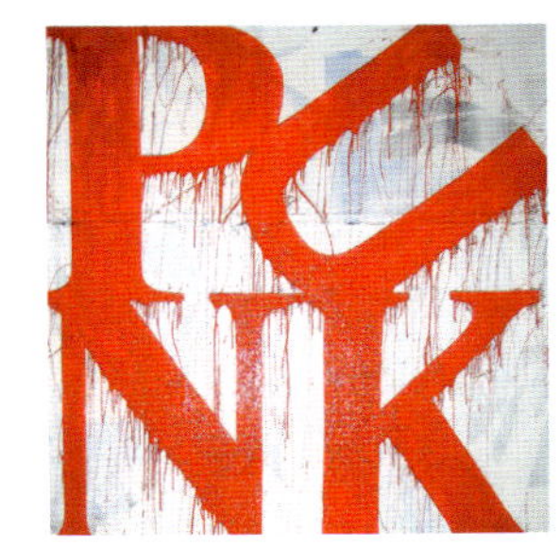
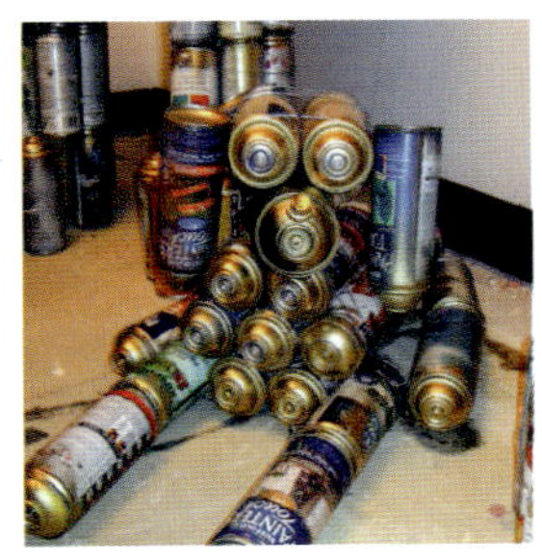 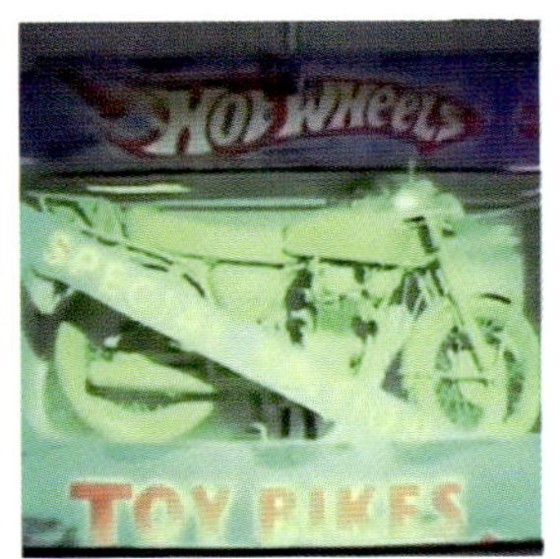 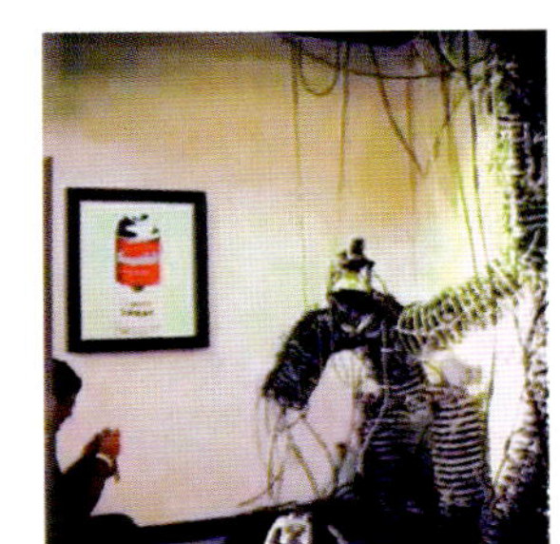 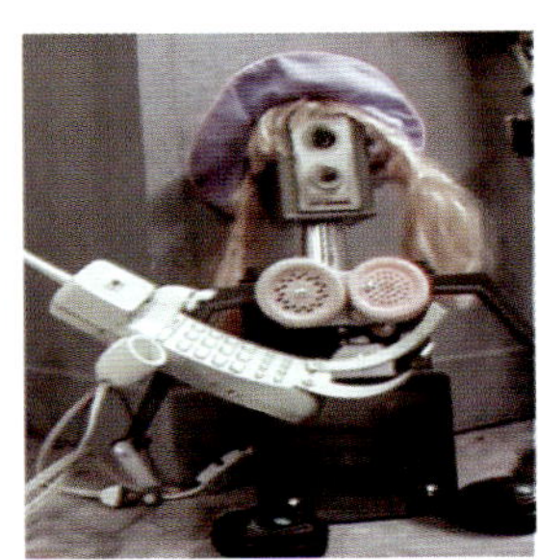
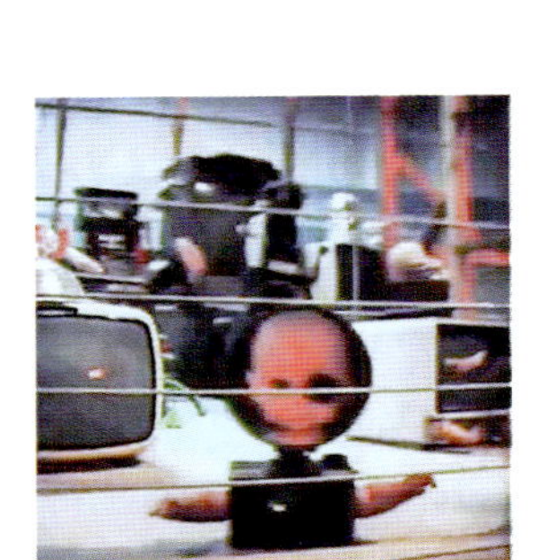 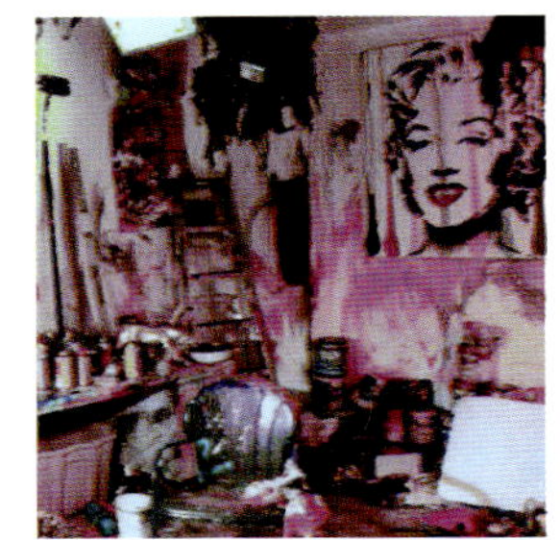 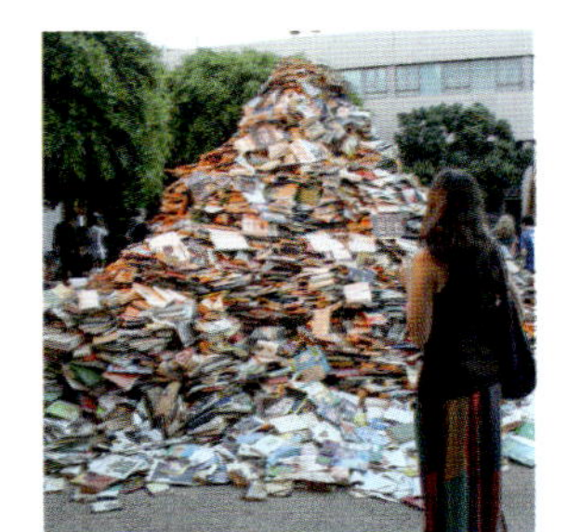 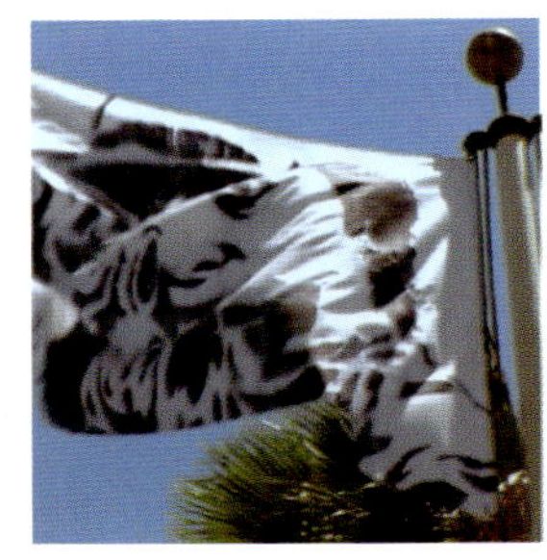 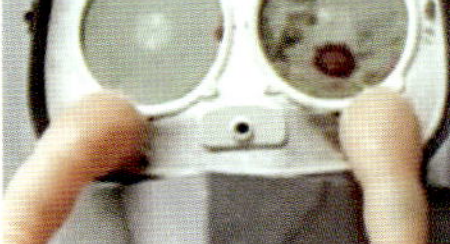

AGAIN. I WILL NEVER WRITE ON THE WALLS AGAIN
I WILL NEVER WRITE ON THE WALLS AGAIN. I WILL NEVER WRITE ON THE W
I WILL NEVER WRITE ON THE WALLS AGAI
AIN. I WILL NEVER WRITE ON THE WALLS AGAIN
AIN. I WILL NEVER WRITE ON THE WALLS AGAIN. I W
AIN. I WILL NEVER WRITE ON THE WALLS AGAIN. I WILL N
I WILL NEVER WRITE ON THE WALLS AGAIN. I WILL NEVE
I WILL NEVER WRITE ON THE WALLS AGAIN. I WILL NEVE
AGAIN. I WILL NEVER WRITE ON THE WALLS AGAIN. I WILL NE
I WILL NEVER WRITE ON THE WALLS AGAIN
LS AGAIN. I WILL NEVER WRITE ON THE WALLS AGAIN. I WILL
WALLS AGAIN. I WILL NEVER WRITE ON THE WALLS AGAIN.
I WILL NEVER WRITE ON THE WALLS AGAIN
I WILL NEVER WRITE ON THE WALLS AGAIN. I WILL

ON THE WALLS AGAIN. I WILL NEVER WRITE ON THE WALLS AGAIN. I W
N THE WALLS AGAIN. I WILL I WILL NEVER WRITE ON THE WALLS AGAIN.
THE WALLS AGAIN. I WILL NEVER WRITE ON THE WALLS AGAIN. I WILL NEVE
I WILL NEVER WRITE ON THE WALLS AGAIN
ON THE WALLS AGAIN. I WILL NEVER WRITE ON THE WALL AG
WRITE ON THE WALLS AGAIN. I WILL NEVER WRITE ON THE
I WILL NEVER WRITE ON THE WALLS AGAIN. I WILL NEVER W

WALLS AGAIN. I WILL NEVER WRITE ON THE WALLS AGAIN.
I WILL NEVER WRITE ON THE WALLS AGAIN. I WILL NEVER WR,T

I WILL NEVER WRITE ON THE FLOOR AGAIN. I WILL NEVER WRI
WILL NEVER WRITE ON THE FLOOR AGAIN
WILL NEVER WRITE ON THE FLOOR AGAIN. I WILL NEV
WILL NEVER WRITE ON THE FLOOR AGA
WILL NEVER WRITE ON THE FLOOR
WILL NEVER WRITE ON THE FLOOR

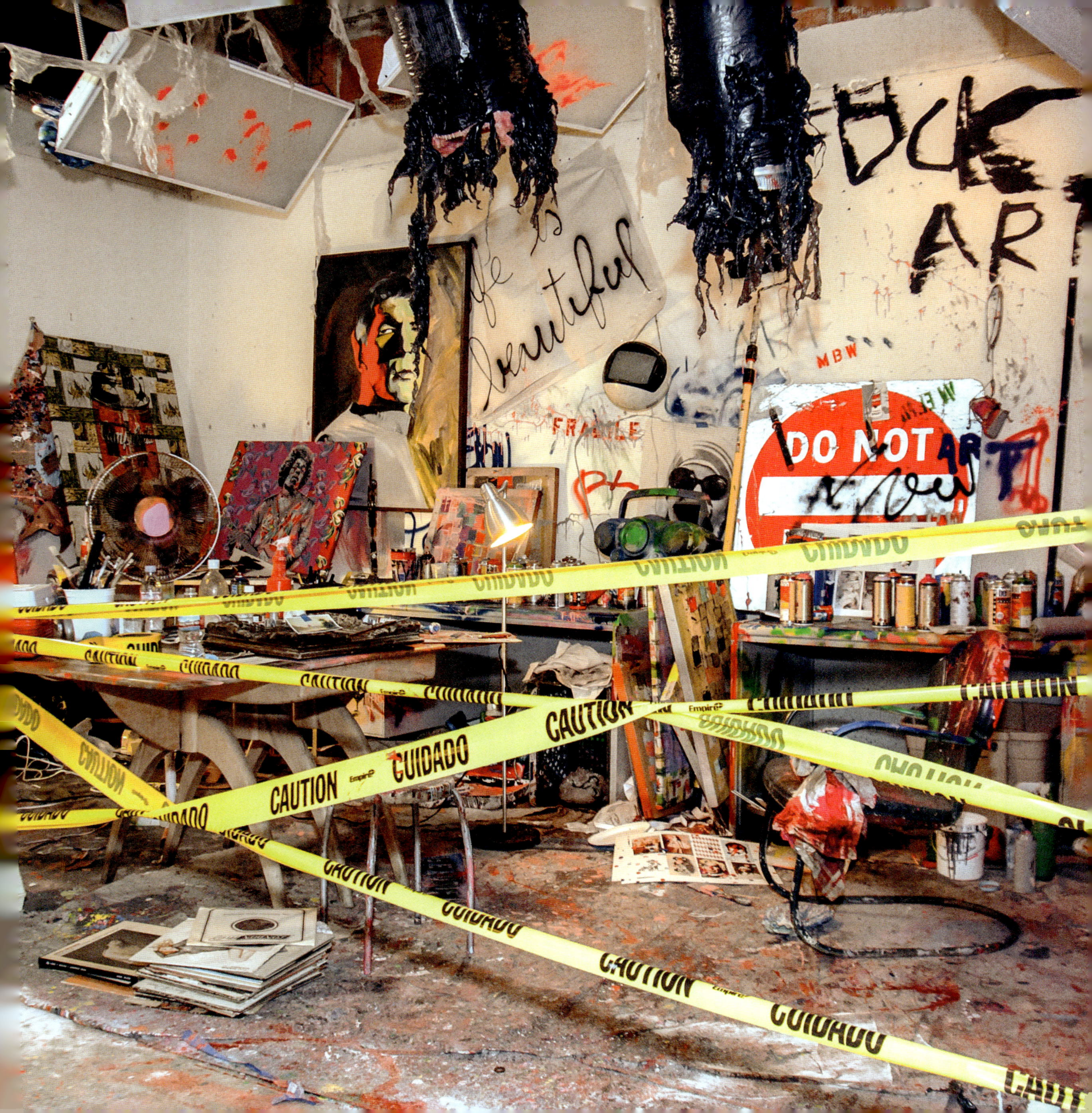

life is
beautiful
FUCK
ART
MBW
FRAGILE
DO NOT
CAUTION
CUIDADO
Empire

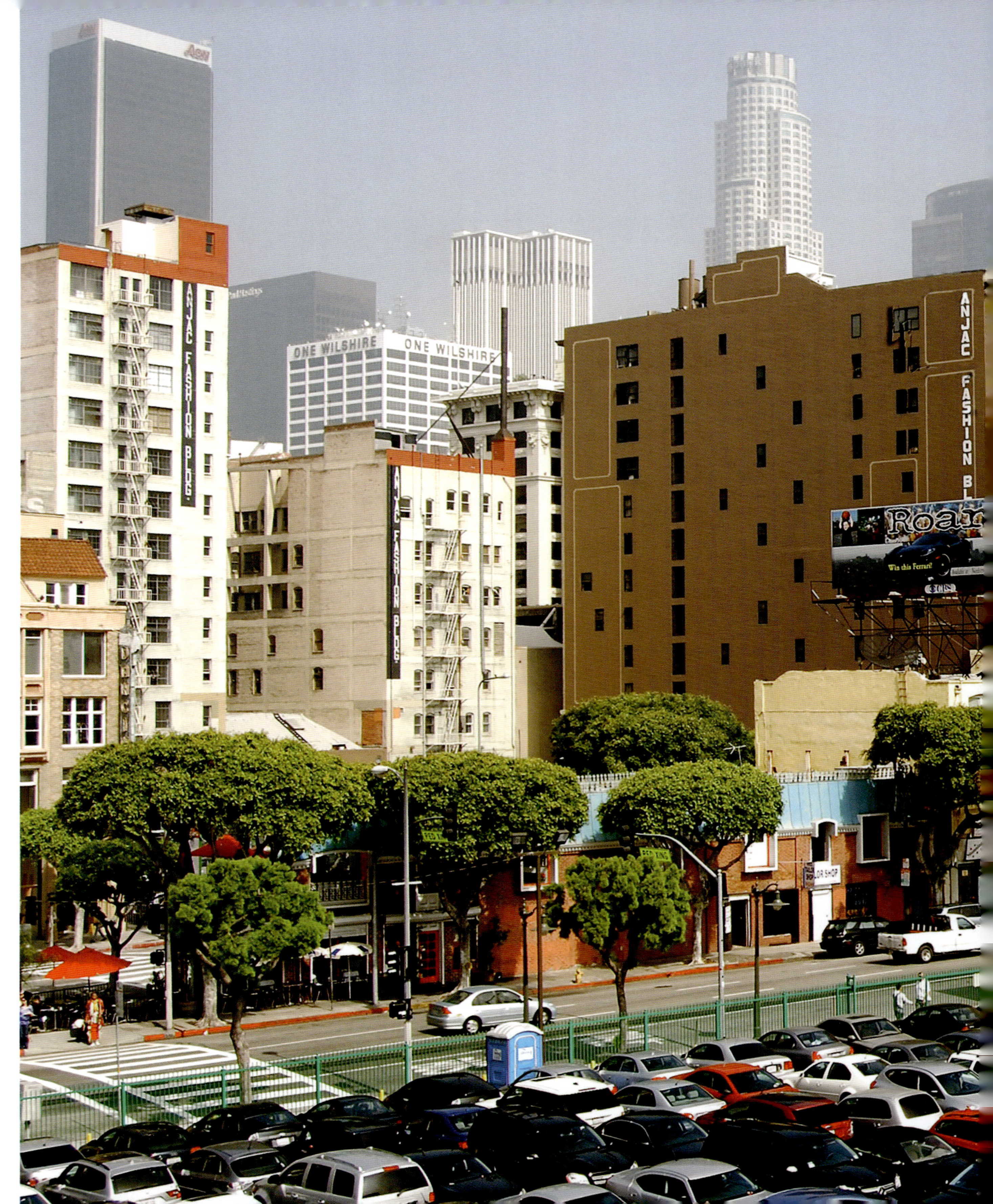

ANJAC FASHION BLDG.
ANJAC FASHION BLDG
ANJAC FASHION BLDG
ONE WILSHIRE
ONE WILSHIRE
AON
Roar
Win this Ferrari!

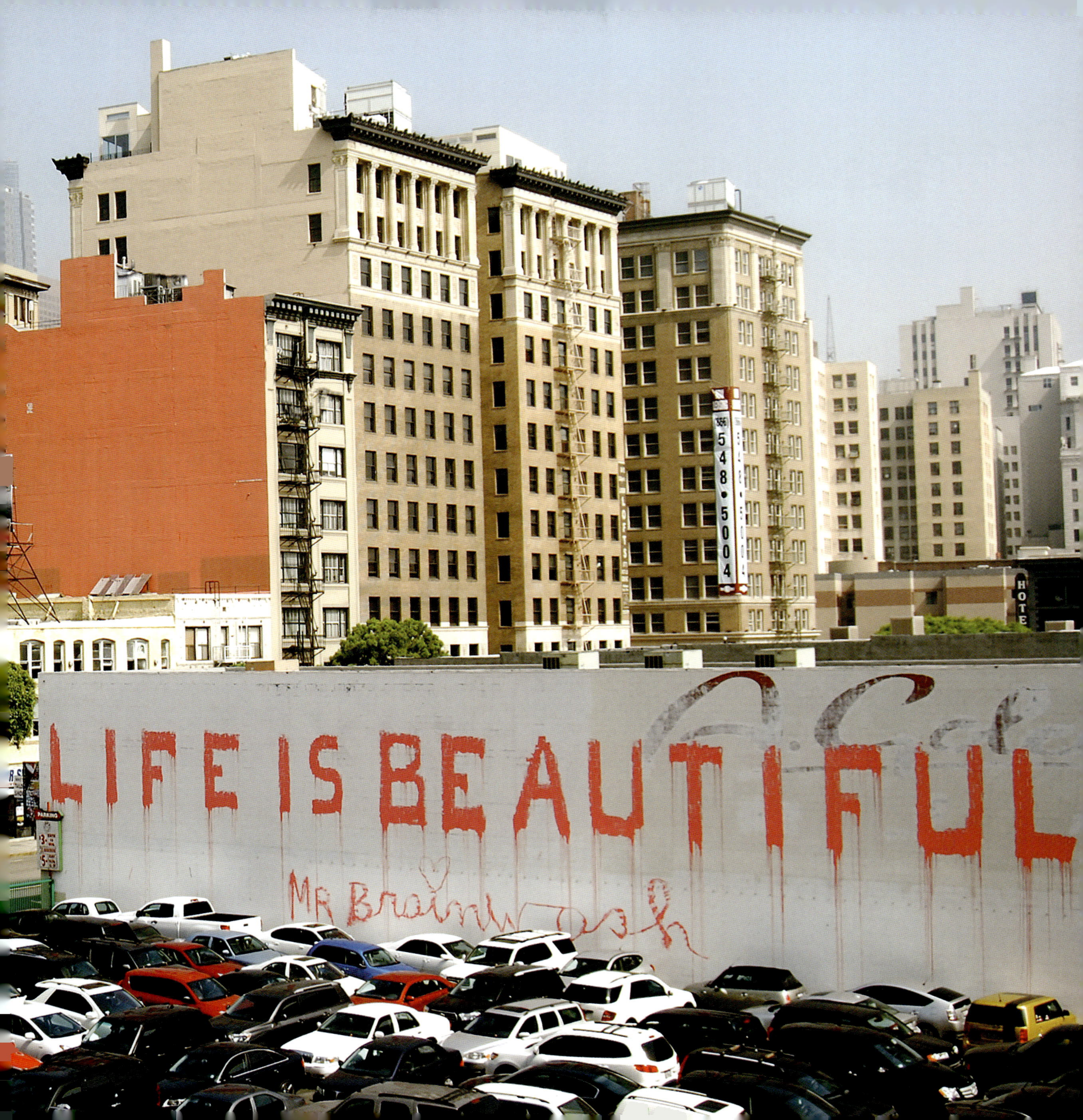

LIFE IS BEAUTIFUL
MR Brainwash

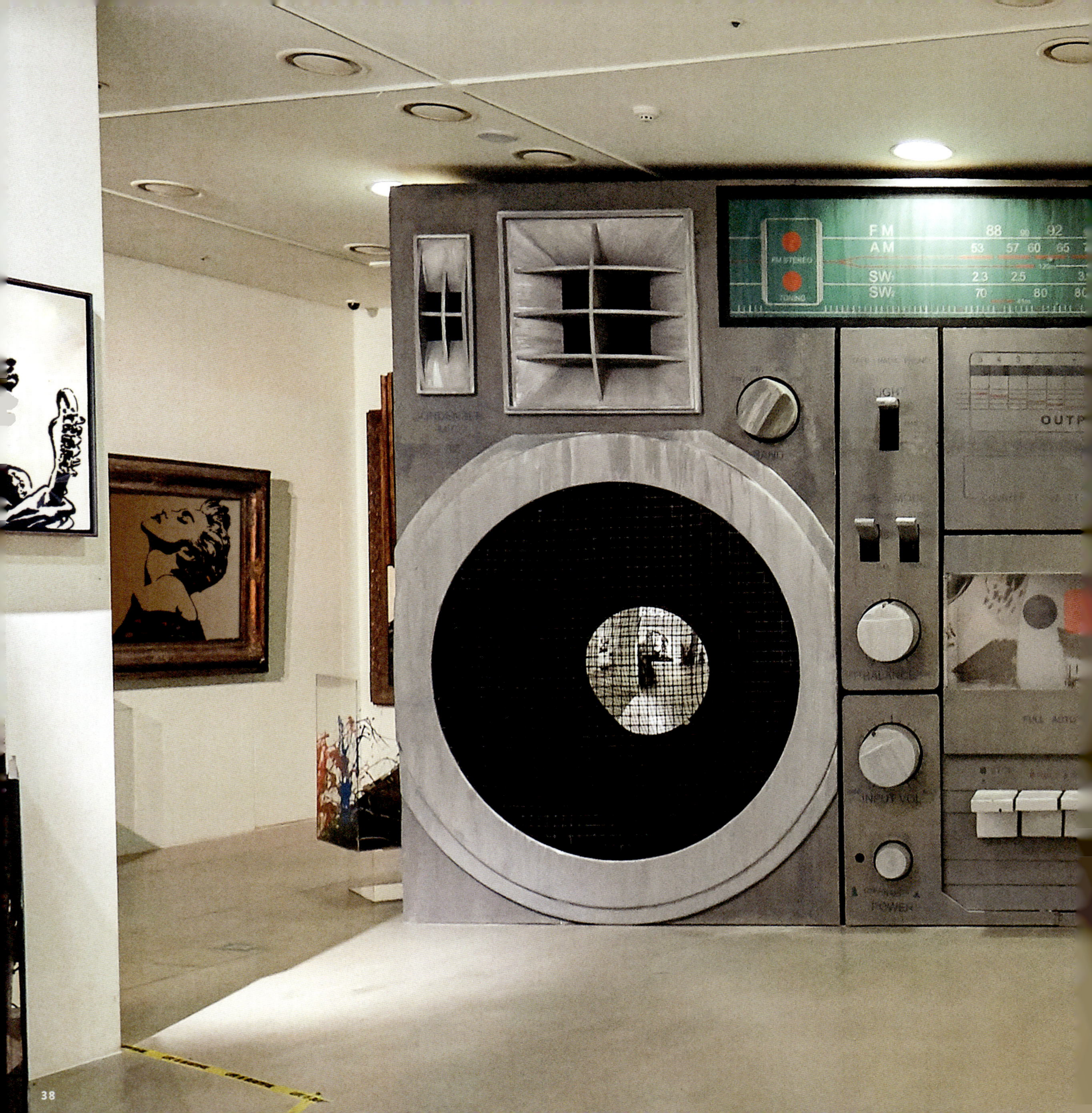

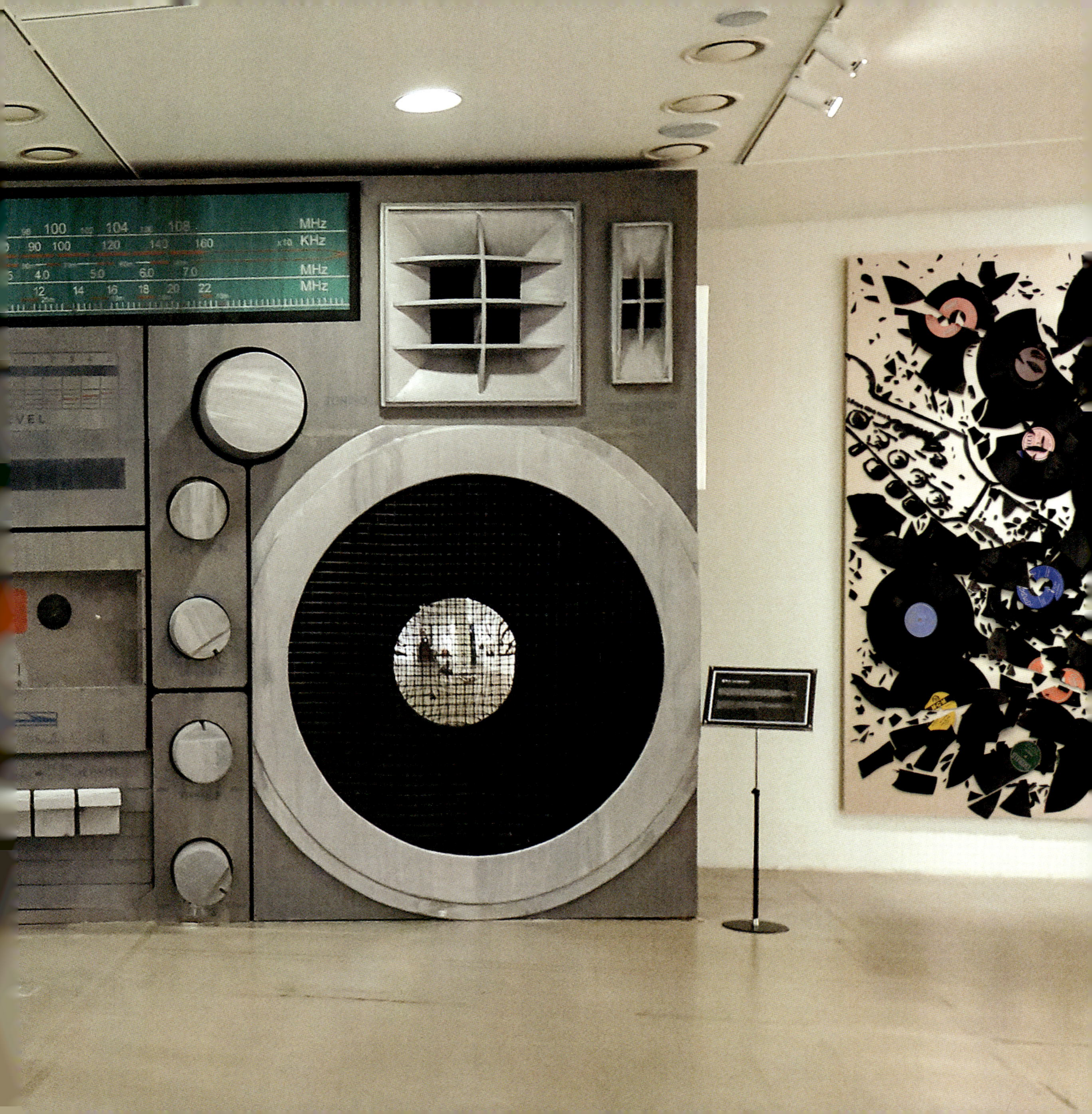

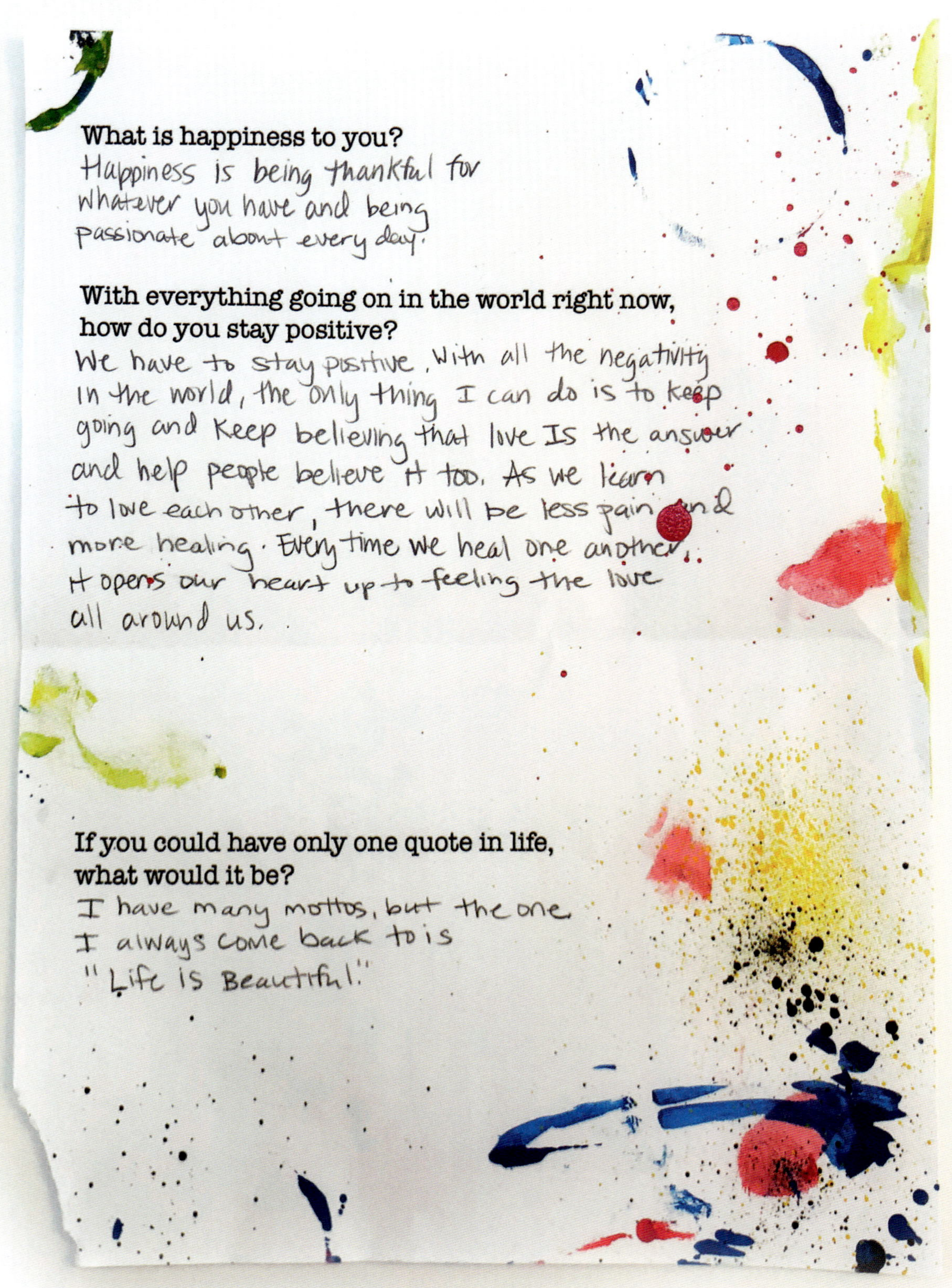

What is happiness to you?
Happiness is being thankful for whatever you have and being passionate about every day.

With everything going on in the world right now, how do you stay positive?
We have to stay positive. With all the negativity in the world, the only thing I can do is to keep going and keep believing that love Is the answer and help people believe it too. As we learn to love each other, there will be less pain and more healing. Every time we heal one another, it opens our heart up to feeling the love all around us.

If you could have only one quote in life, what would it be?
I have many mottos, but the one I always come back to is "Life is Beautiful."

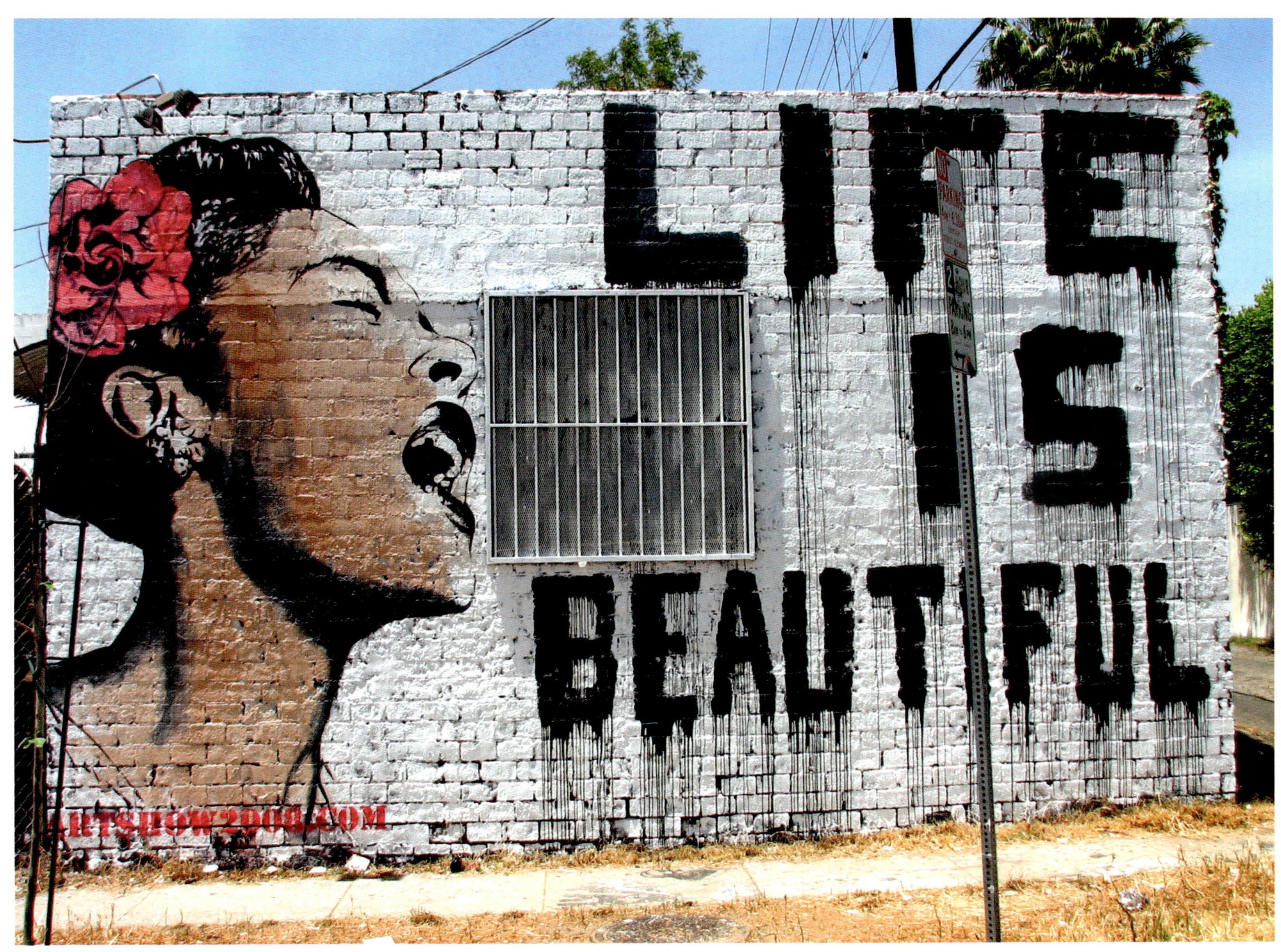

pages 38–39
Giant Boombox
12' x 23'
Metal and wood installation

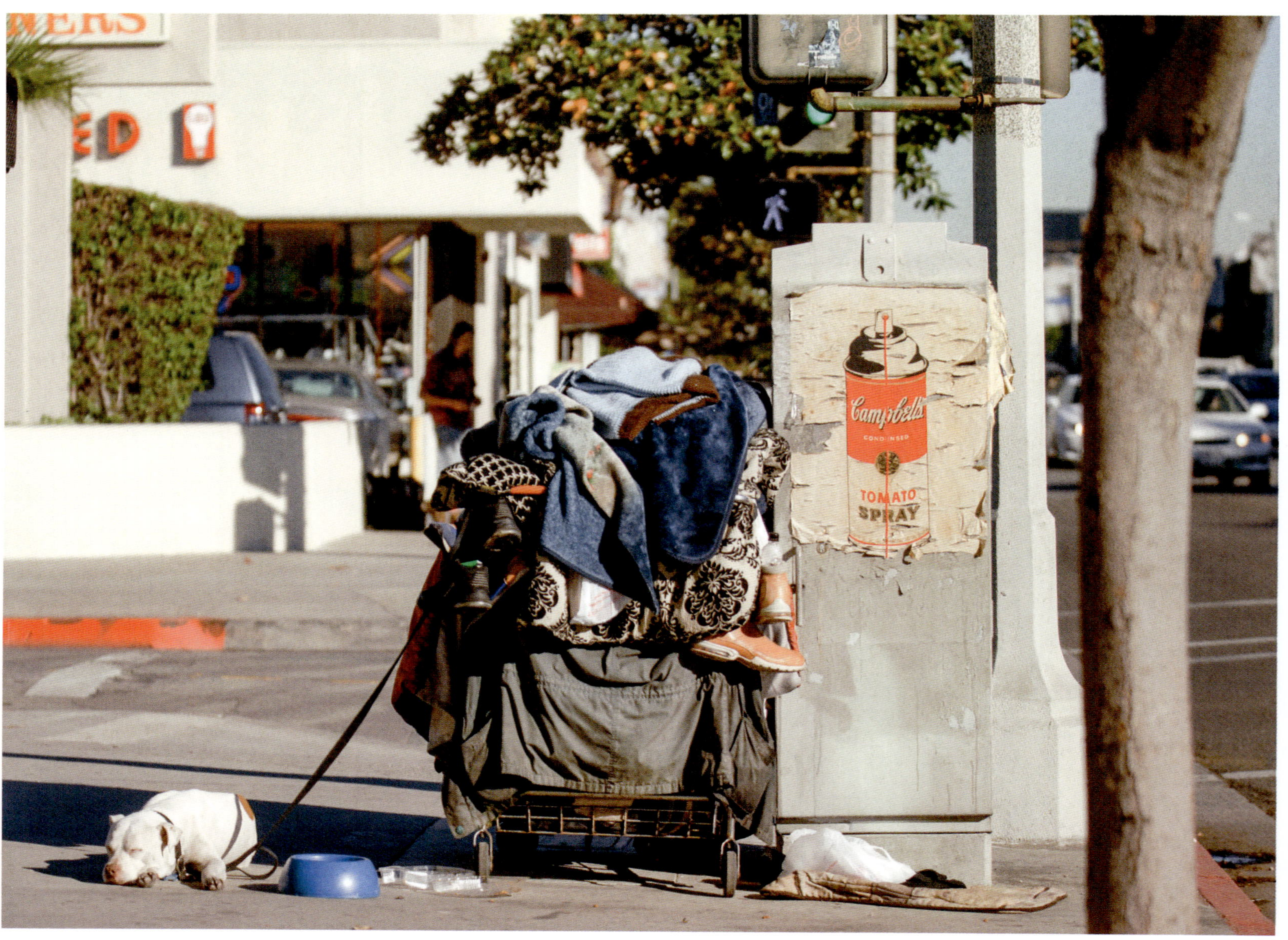
Campbell's
COND-NSED
TOMATO
SPRAY

**What kind of truth have you discovered
when making art?**

It's not important what I'm doing today
tomorrow, or the next day, the only thing that
is important is that I'm living my life as an
art form. I will never stop making art and
living, because I need one to do the other.
My art is a projection of what I feel. It
could be on canvas, on film on a wall, in a
sculpture. But ultimately, all of my art wants
to scream that life is a gift and life is
beautiful. Life isn't fair, but it's the way
you live it that matters. You can take away
beauty from something bad. Although life is
only one simple word, it is everything.

**What do we have to look forward to with your work
in the future? Any big plans?**

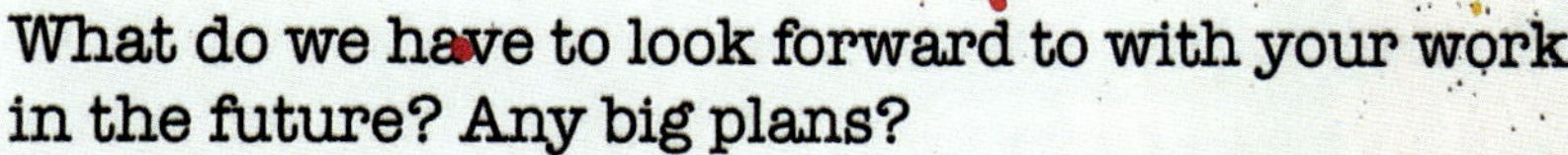

I never stop planning and each plan is usually
bigger than the last. Many people ask me "How
are you doing? What are you working on?" I just
keep working. This is what my life is because work
for me is not work anymore. It's what my life
has become so I will never stop.

What did you want to be growing up?

I don't know because I still haven't
grown up. I'm still a kid growing every day.

**What travels or adventures have had the most
significant impact on you?**

I just love traveling to different countries
and being able to create in new places. When
I did shows in London, Korea, and Mexico I
was able to create a whole new universe in a
different country with new people and new
cultures. Every country I've visited has led me
to learning and growing as an artist and as a
person. My heart is open and absorbs all that
country has to offer.

Are you still filming?

I always film. It's not as crazy as it was
before, where I had a camera attached
to my hand 24/7, but I do attach a Go-Pro
and record a lot of what is around me.
Your life is a crazy journey.
And as someone who filmed for 12 years,
non-stop, I can't just let it go. The movie
I'm making isn't over - it's just started.

**If you could be another artist from the past or present
for one day, who would it be, and what would you make?**

If I were DaVinci, I would make ten Mona Lisas.
I'd have fun with any artist I would become.
Even so, I try not to be someone that I'm not. I try to be me,
myself and be a better person every day, loving and
accepting what lies in front of me. I'm very thankful for
all these artists because they added color and light
to the world we live in today, from Marcel Duchamp, to
Magritte, to Picasso and Basquiat, and on and on and on.
The only thing they have in common is passion. I believe
that it's all about what you love and respecting it.
And never, never, never giving up.

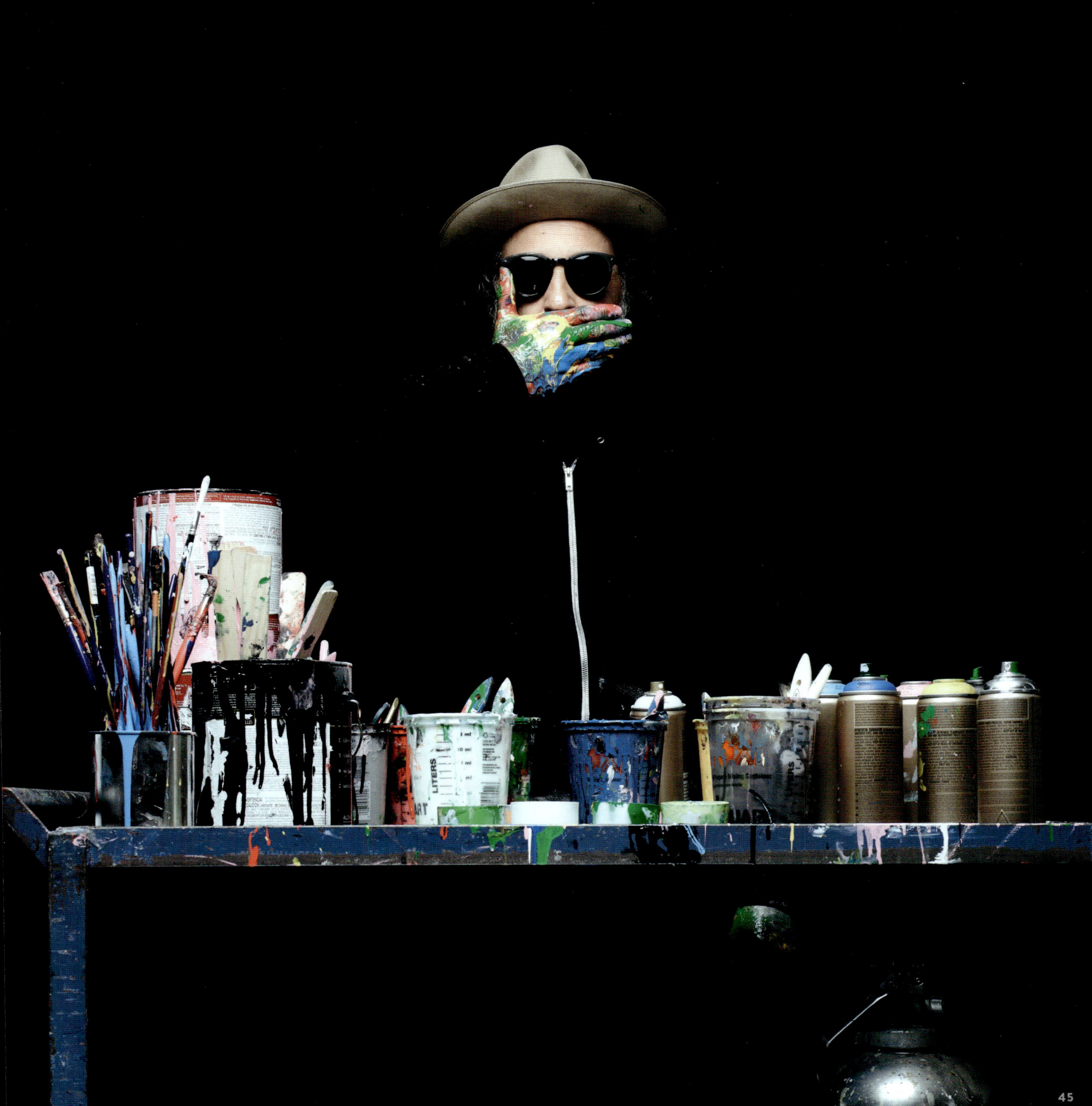

How do you feel about art in art museums?

Art is art. There is no street art, or pop art.
So all art belongs in museums. It doesn't matter
who you are or what you make. What matters
is that you make something and believe it.

What does spray paint mean to you?

Spray paint is just another way to express color.
It doesn't matter if you use crayons or acrylics
or spray paint - they are all colors communicated
in a different way. Tomorrow, they may invent
a new way to create color and I would accept
it. Immediately. But to the person who created
the spray can, I say "Thank you. It's beautiful, quick
fun and I can take it anywhere."

What is street art to you?

Street art represents freedom. Freedom
of expression and freedom of location.
You can't close the street, it's always open,
and there's always an opportunity for people
to experience your work. The wonderful
thing about street art is that it isn't
permanent. It represents a beautiful moment
in time that can't ever be recreated. I
love that there is street art happening
everywhere. It's all beautiful.

What are your hobbies?

My hobby is just to wake up in the morning and to see where life takes me until I go to sleep. I enjoy exploring the adventures of life, whatever they might be. Life is this powerful force that I approach everyday with passion because if you don't have passion, life does not glow as brightly. The beautiful thing is that each day is a brand new opportunity to make something happen, to live from your heart.

Of course in life, there are ups and downs, but without the low points the high points wouldn't be as beautiful. I've found that it isn't about where you are, but how you are going to get there. There is no secret. When you want to do something, you just have to believe it and work for it.

How long have u been making art?

I have been making art my whole life because art is a part of you. It's who you are. I had dreams when I was younger, but I never imagined it would take me this far. It goes to show that reality can go even deeper than the dreams I've created and the life I imagined. I hope that my art, which I make for everyone, will continue to grow with them.

What's your favorite color?

I love them all. From the colors that come straight from the spray can or paint tube to the ones that are created when you mix two colors together. I love every aspect of color. For me, color is life so it's the same question, there isn't one I love more than the other.

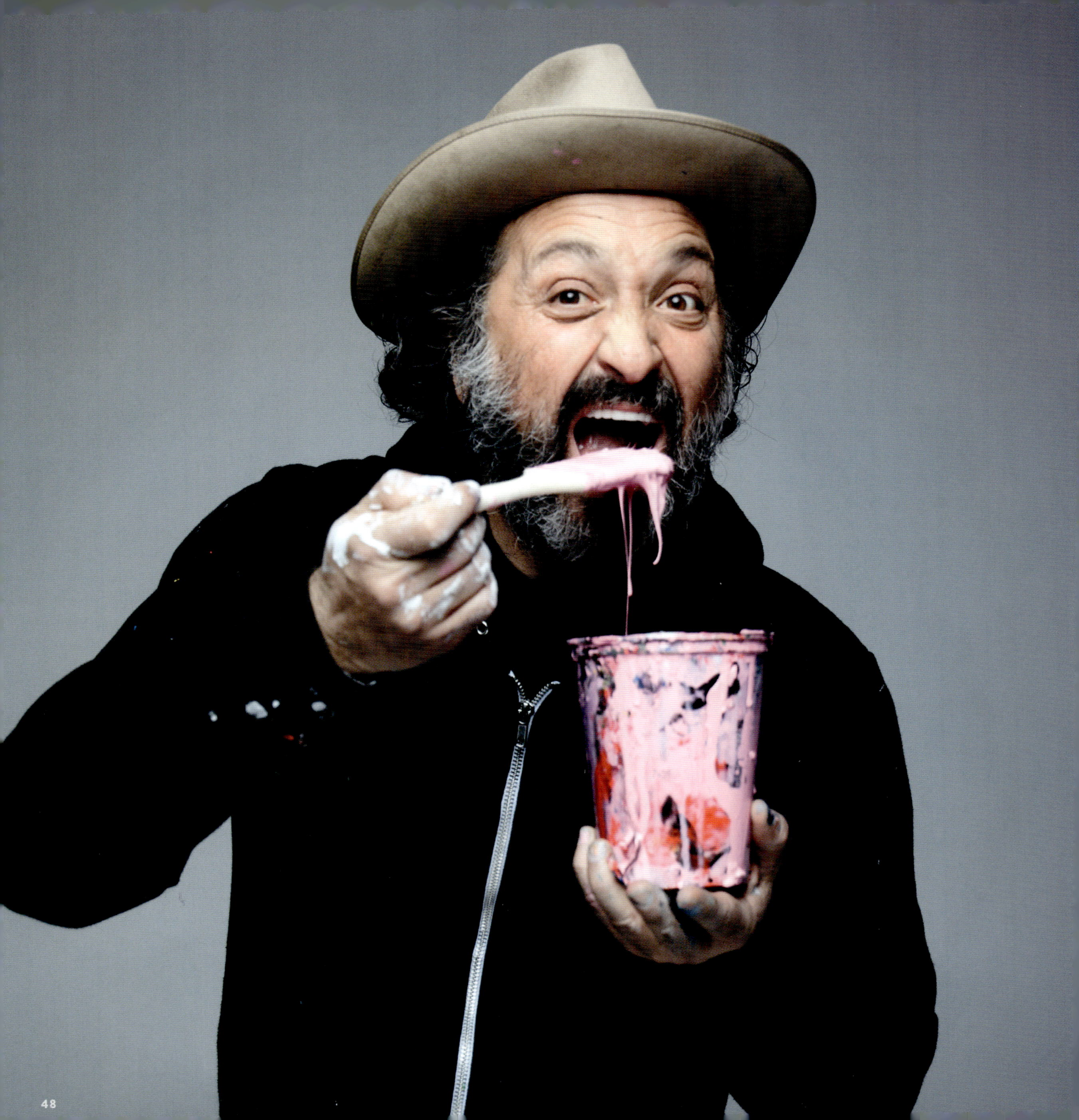

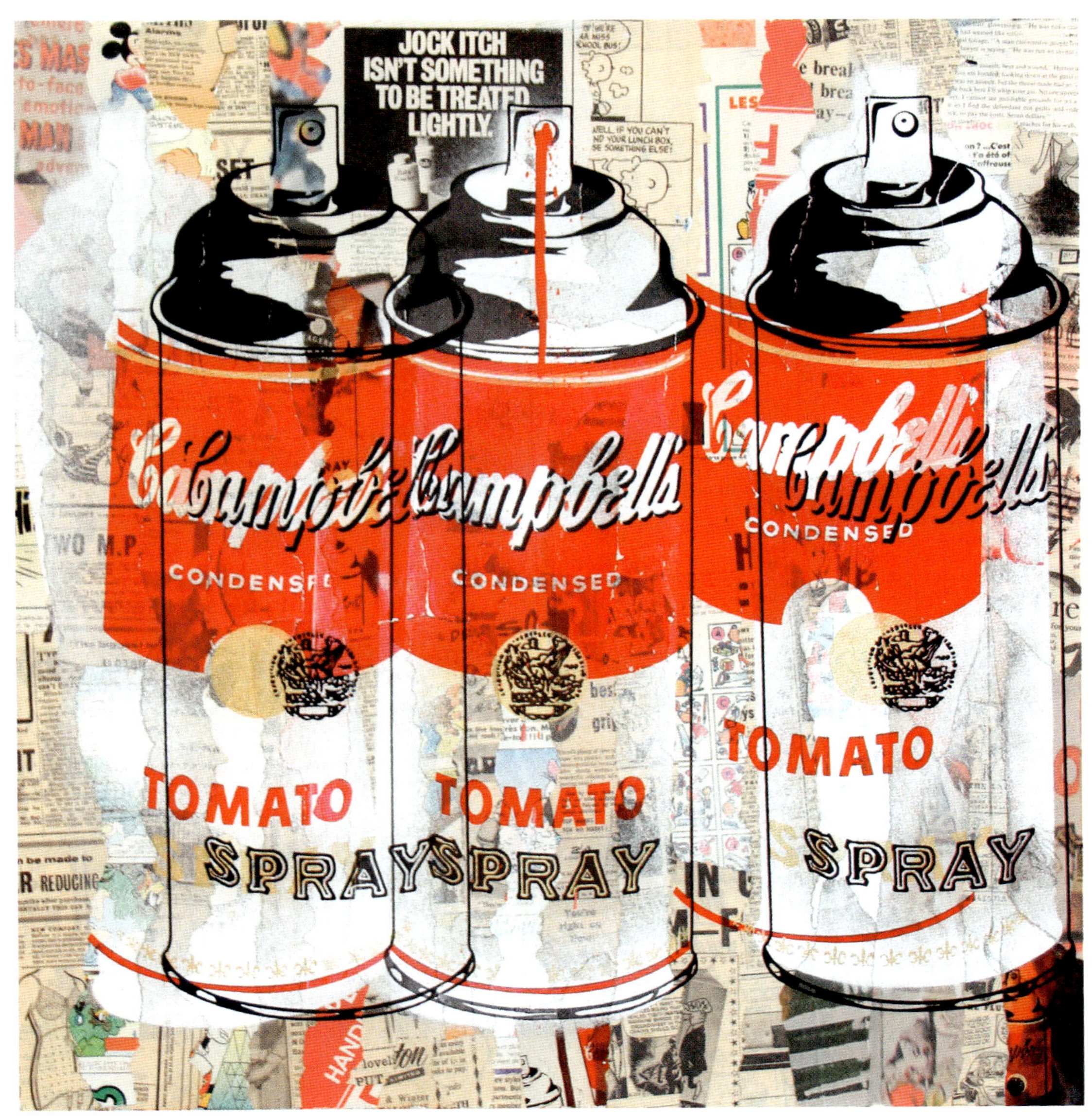

Tomato Spray
22" x 22"
Silkscreen and
mixed media on canvas

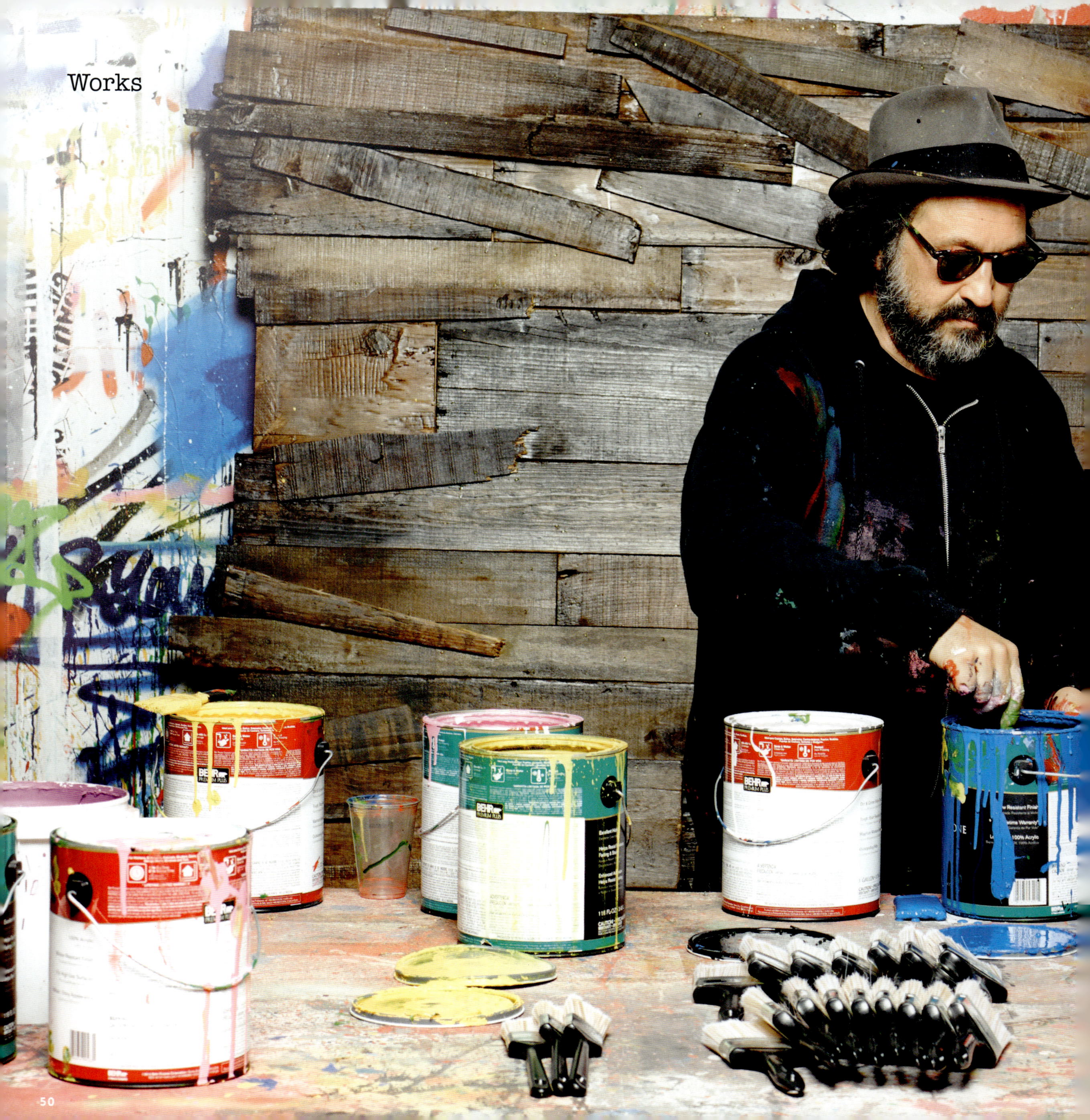

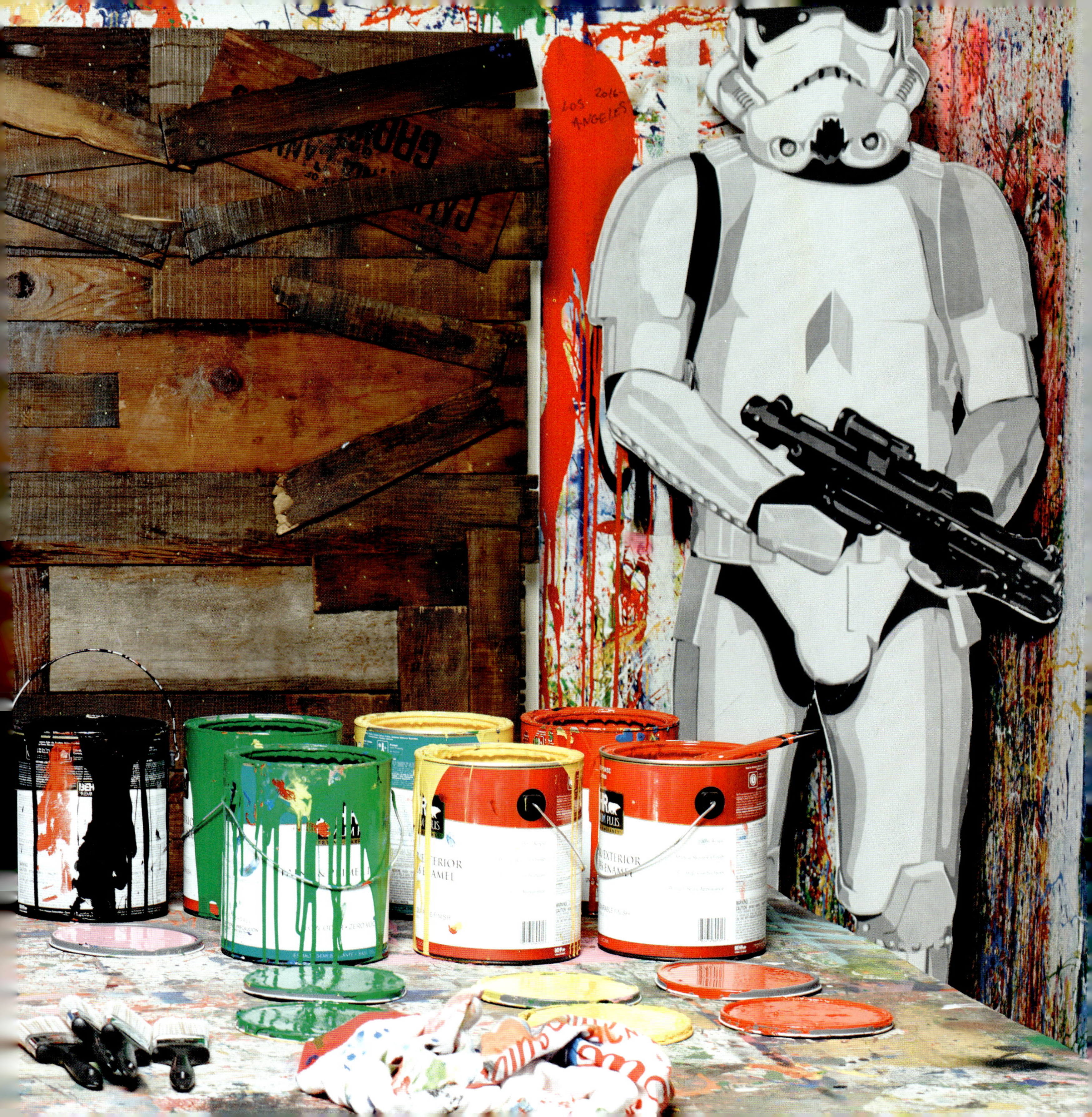
LOS 2016
ANGELES

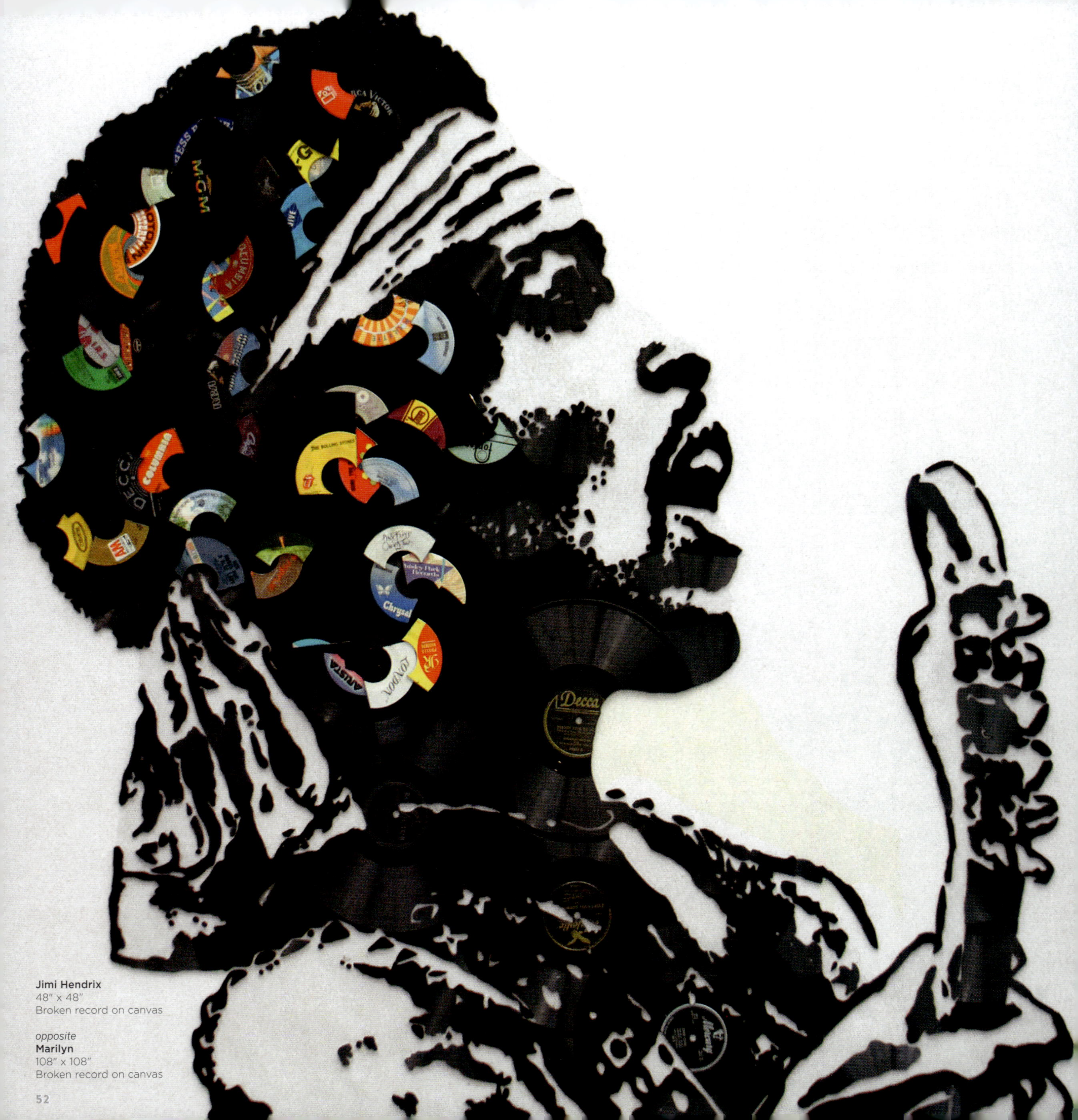

Jimi Hendrix
48" x 48"
Broken record on canvas

opposite
Marilyn
108" x 108"
Broken record on canvas

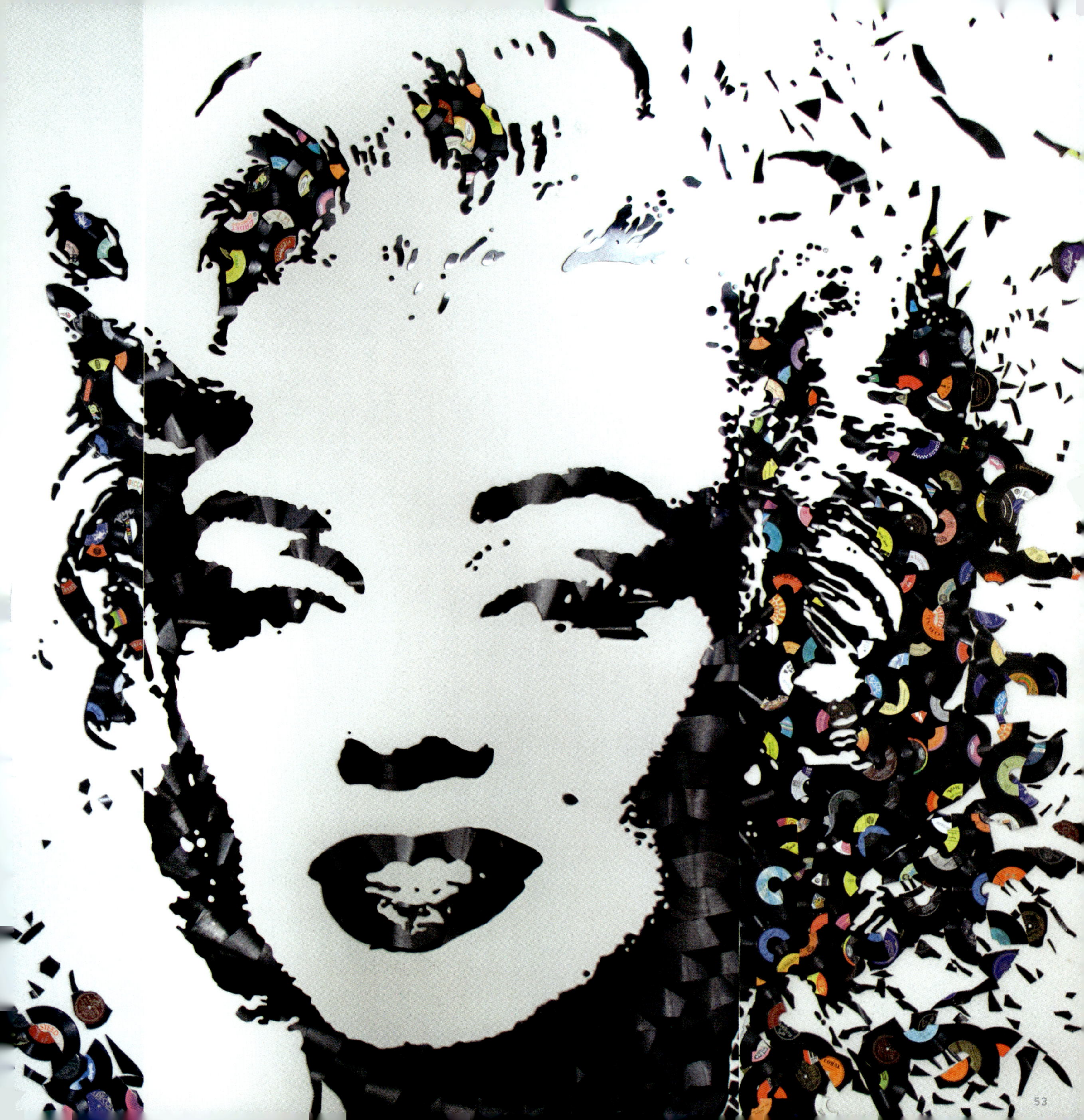

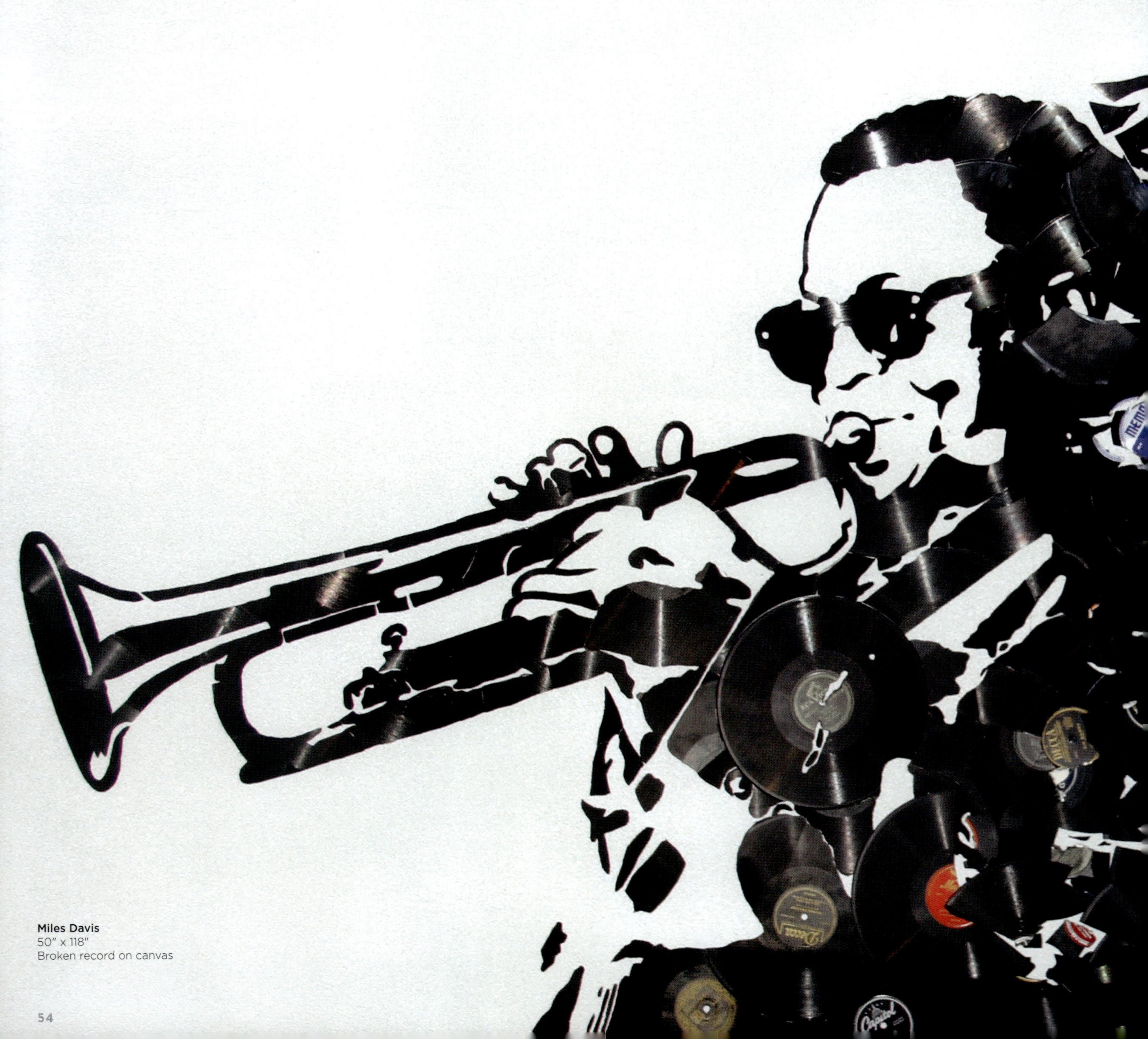

Miles Davis
50" x 118"
Broken record on canvas

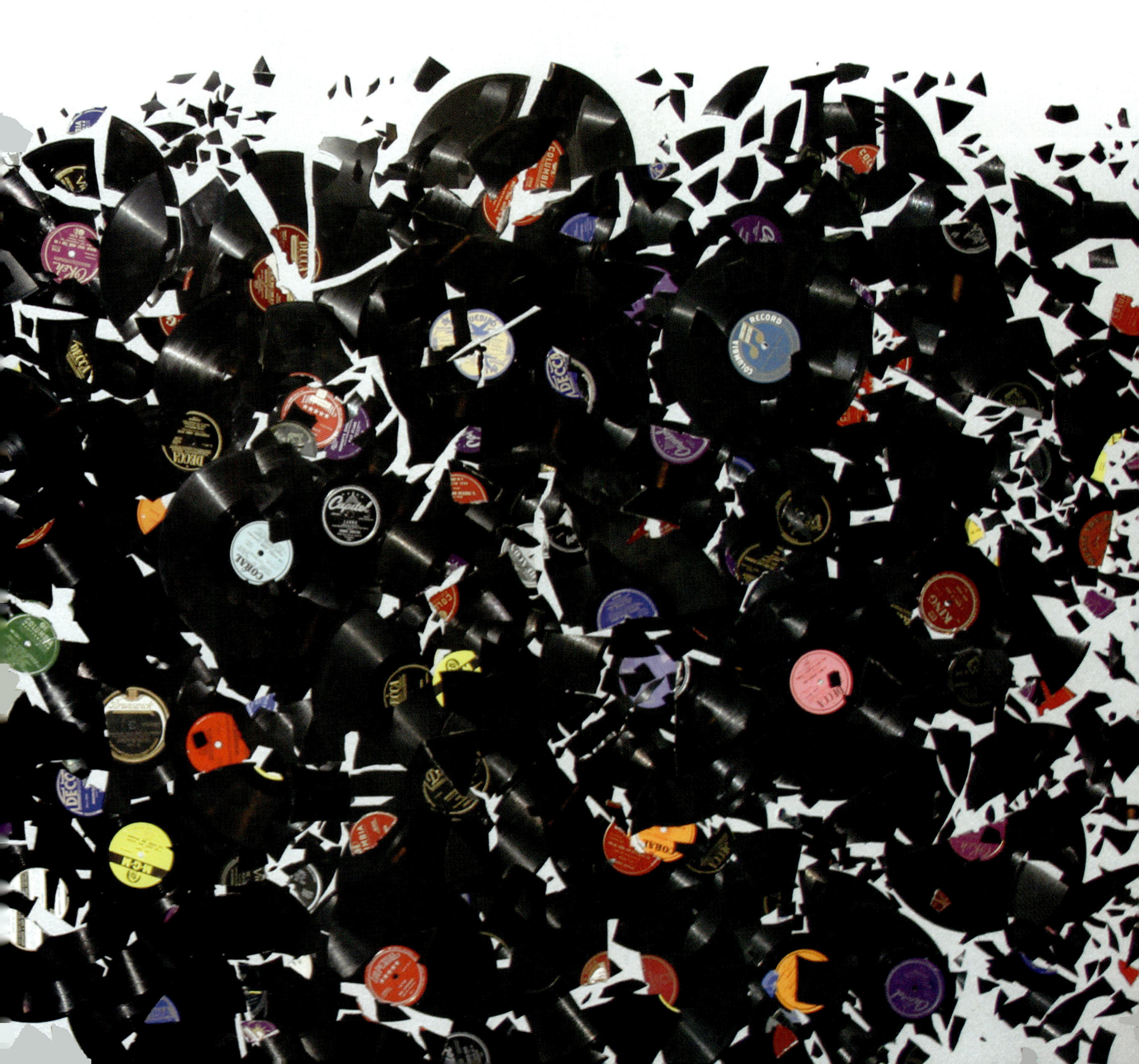

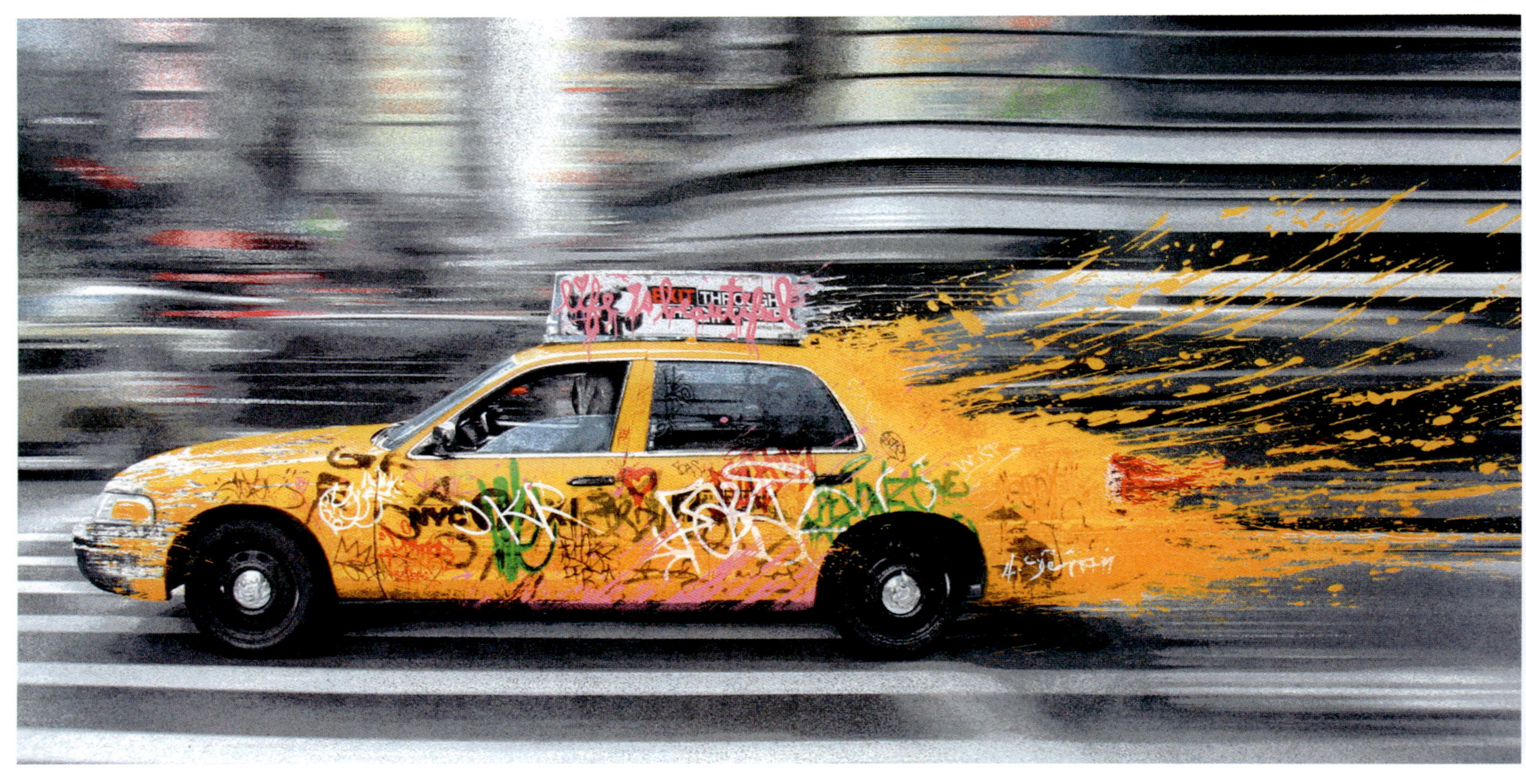

Going to NY
21" x 40"
Silkscreen edition print

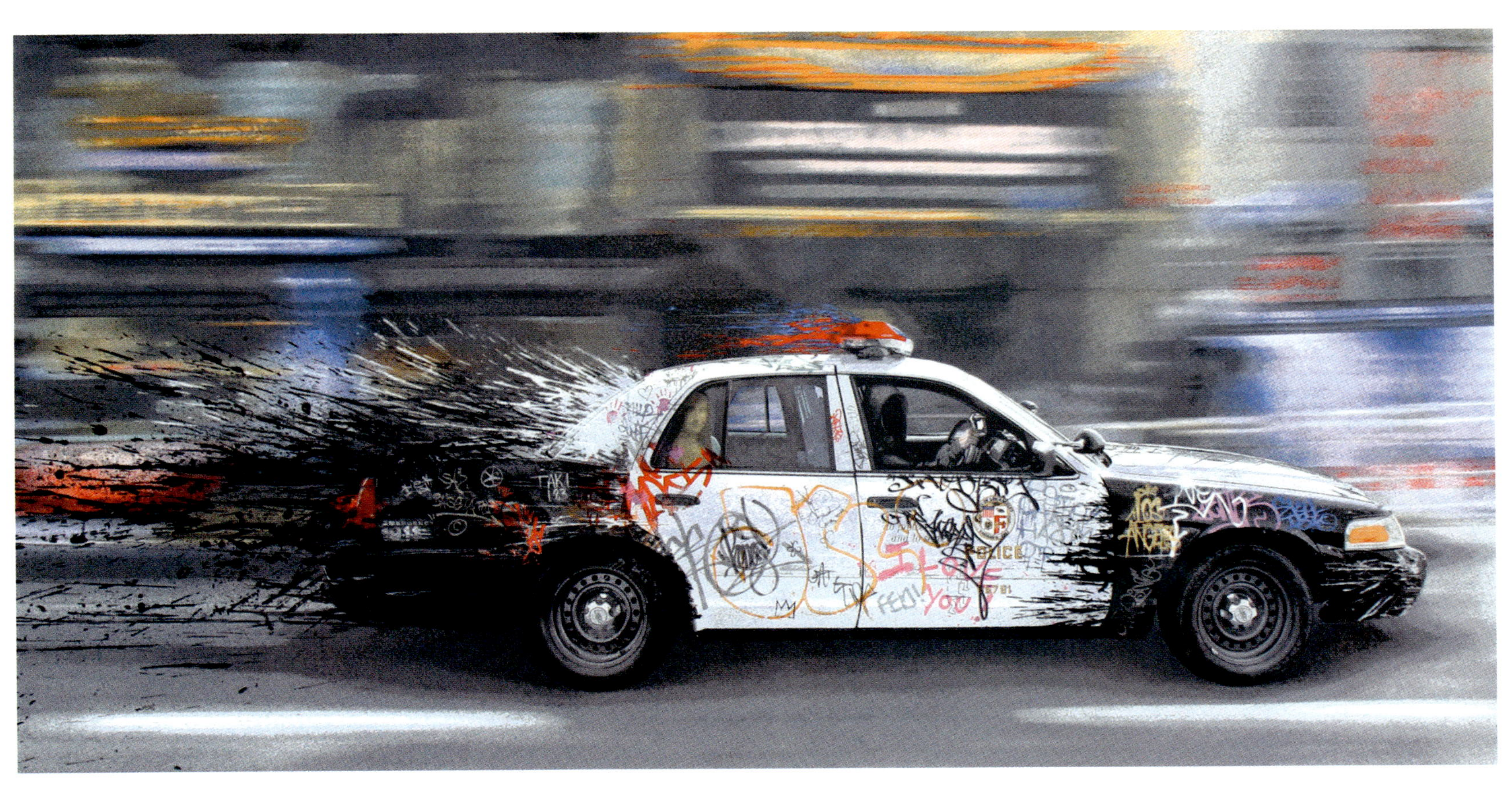

MetroPolisa
21" x 40"
Silkscreen edition print

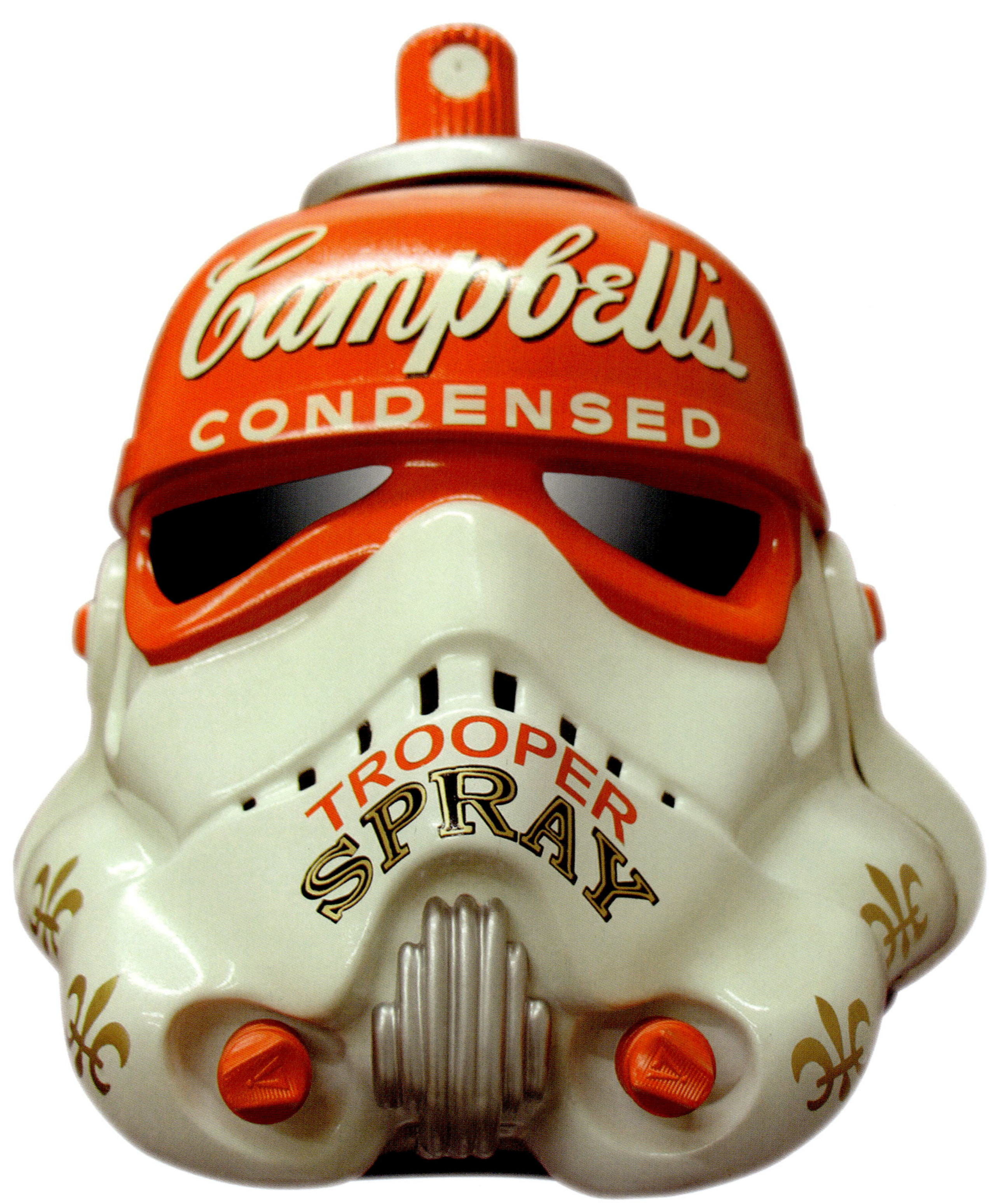

Campbell's Stormtrooper
15" x 12" x 12"
Fiberglass and acrylic paint

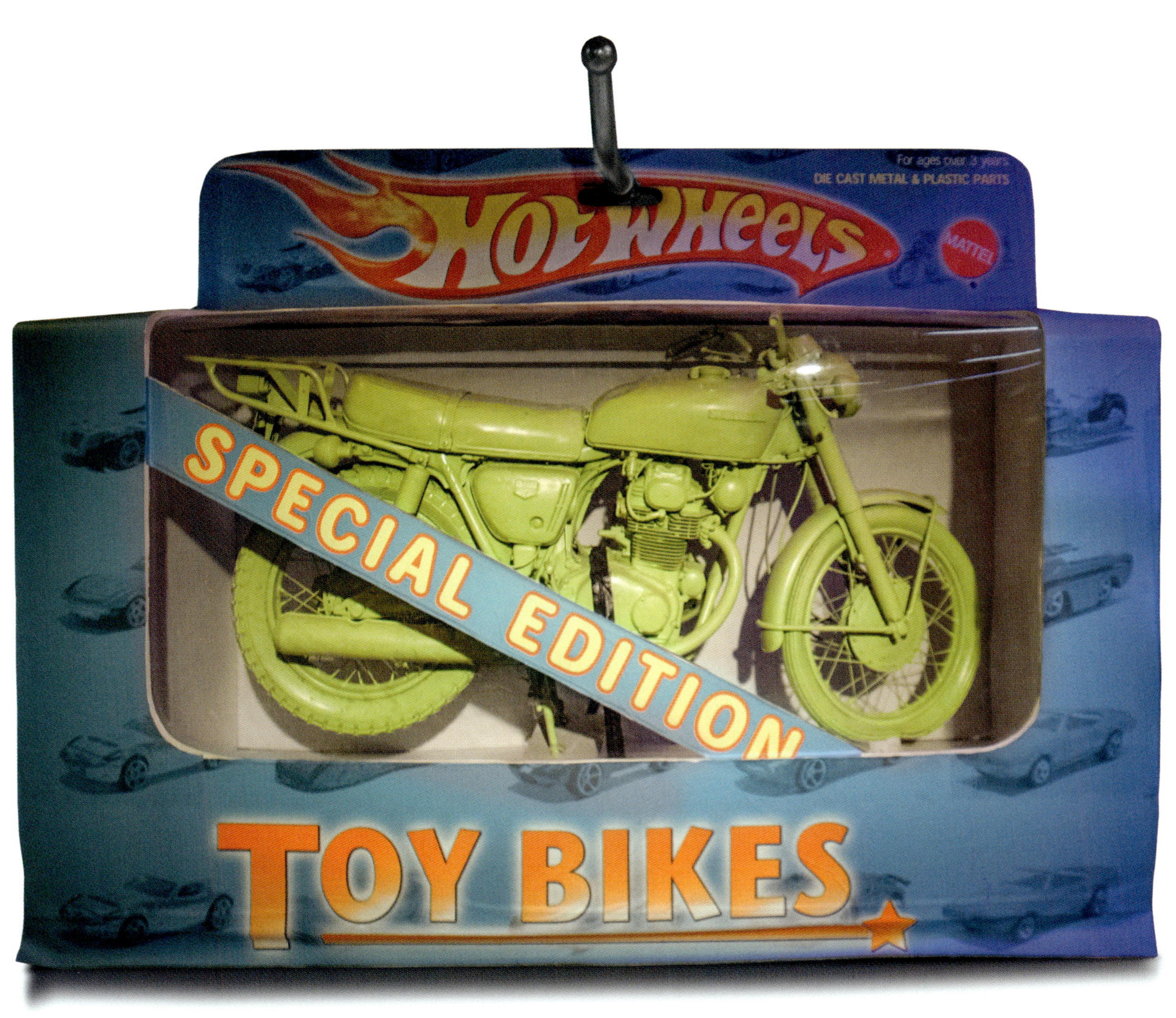

Giant Motorcycle Toy
9' x 13'
Real motorcycle, metal and cardboard packaging

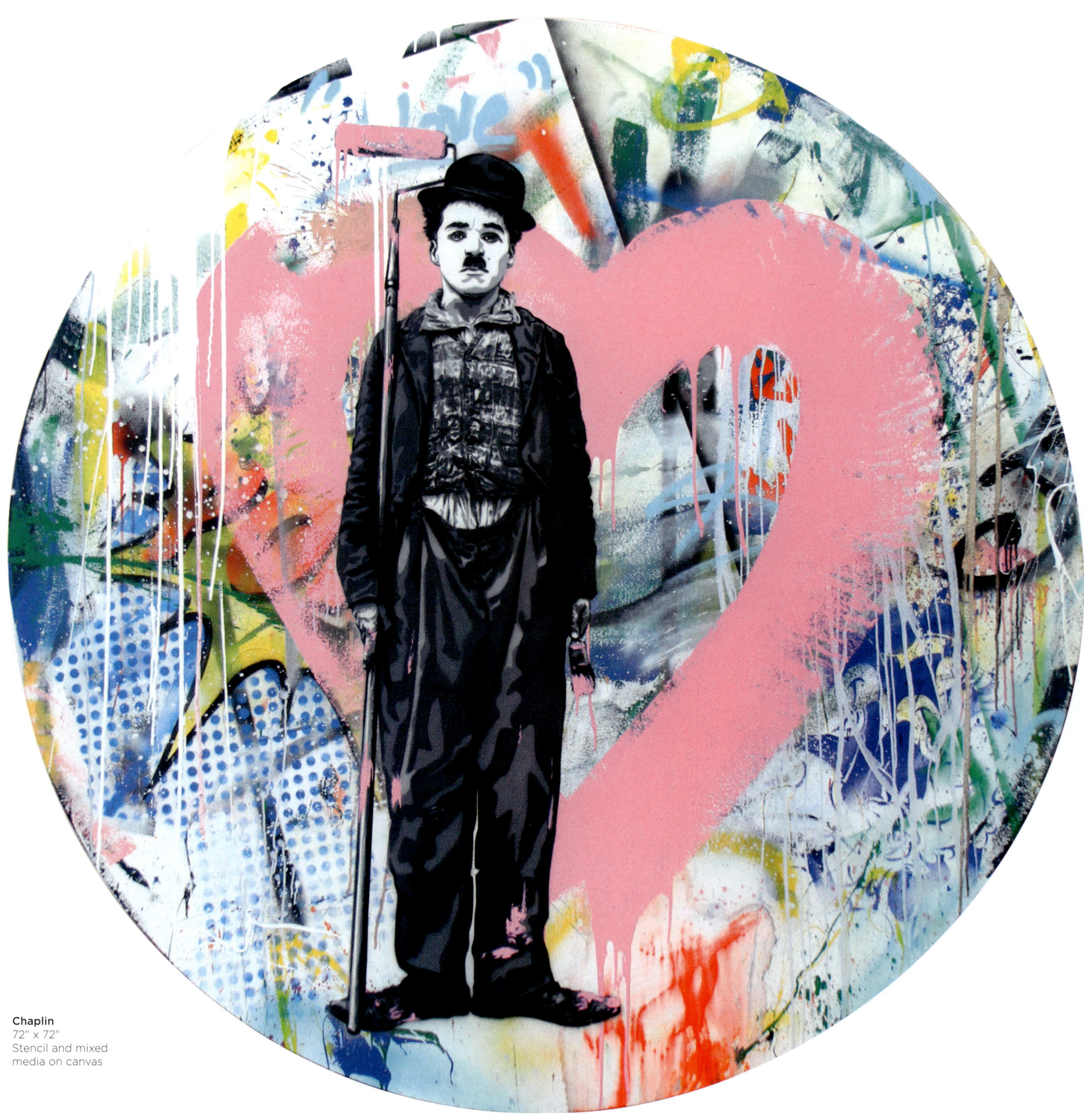

Chaplin
72" x 72"
Stencil and mixed
media on canvas

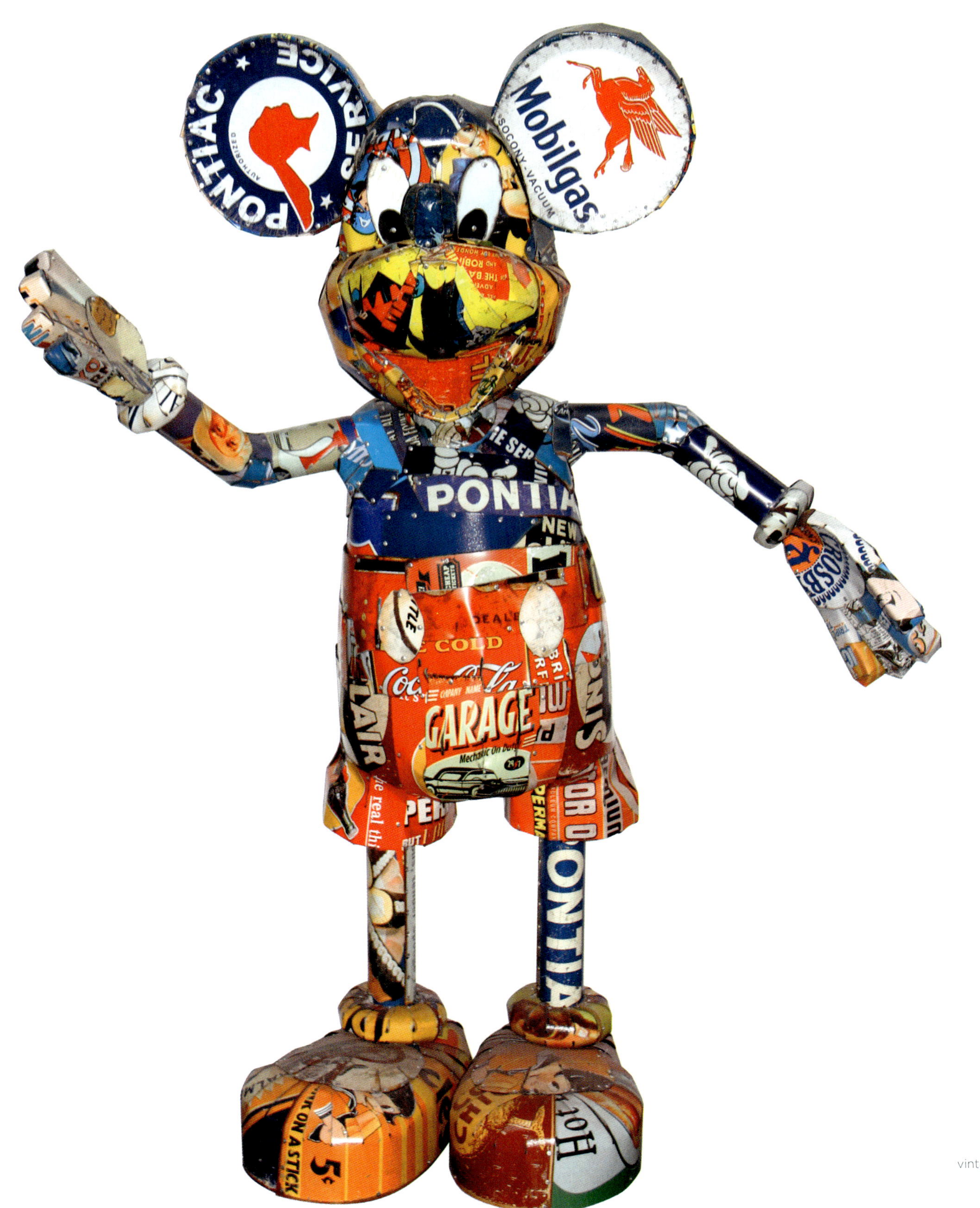

Mickey Mouse
5 feet tall
Repurposed
vintage metal signs

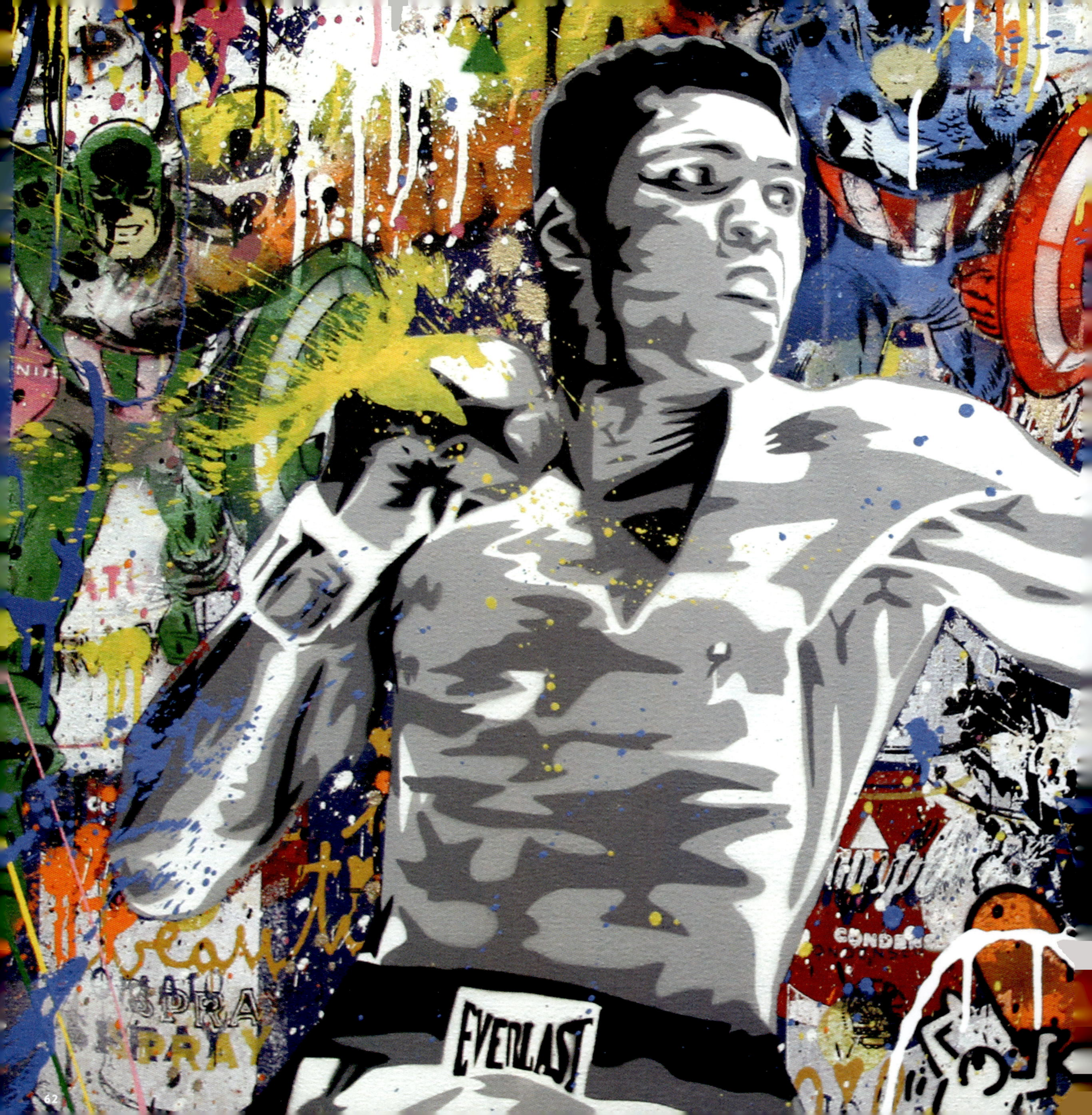

EVERLAST

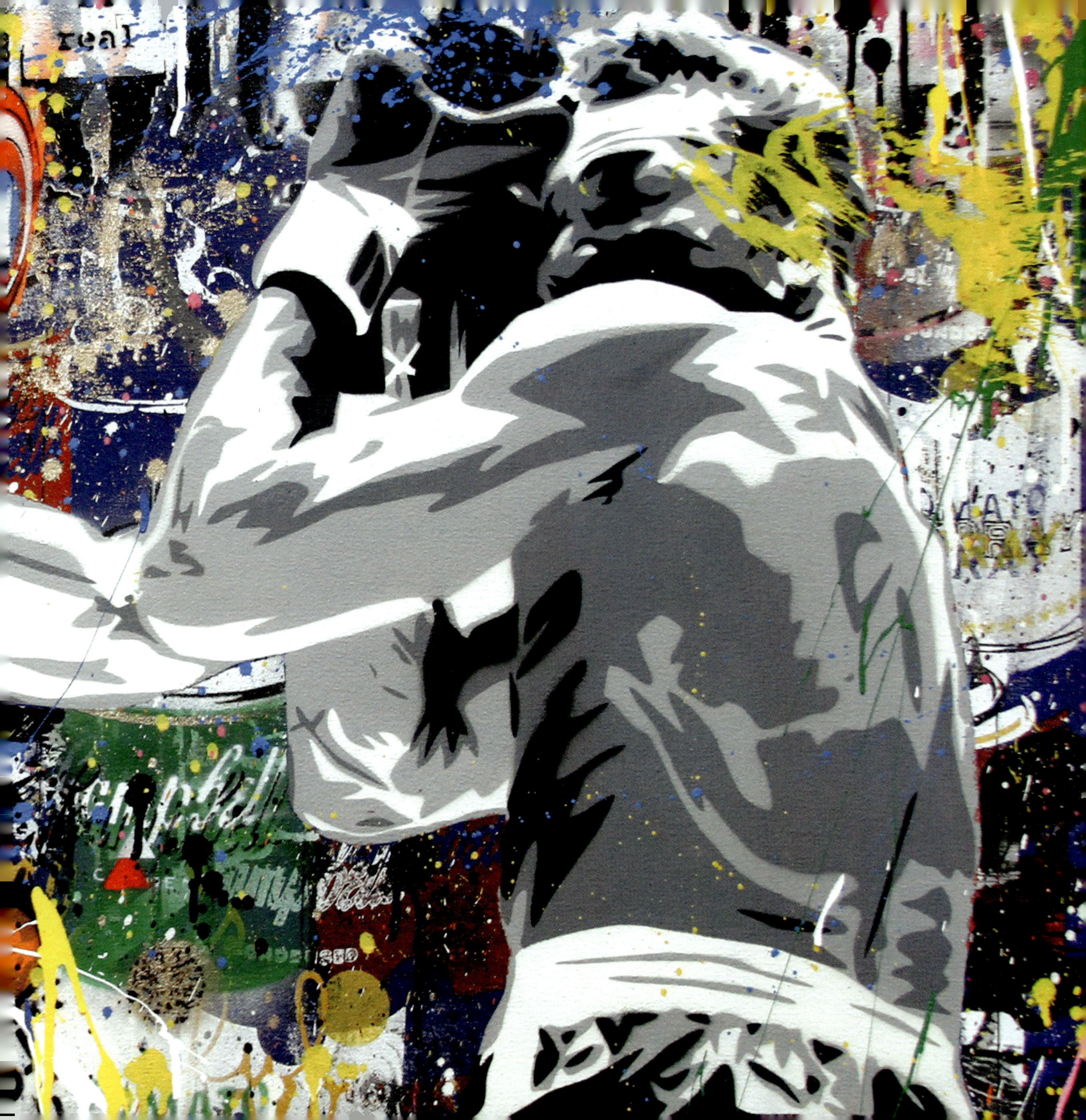
real

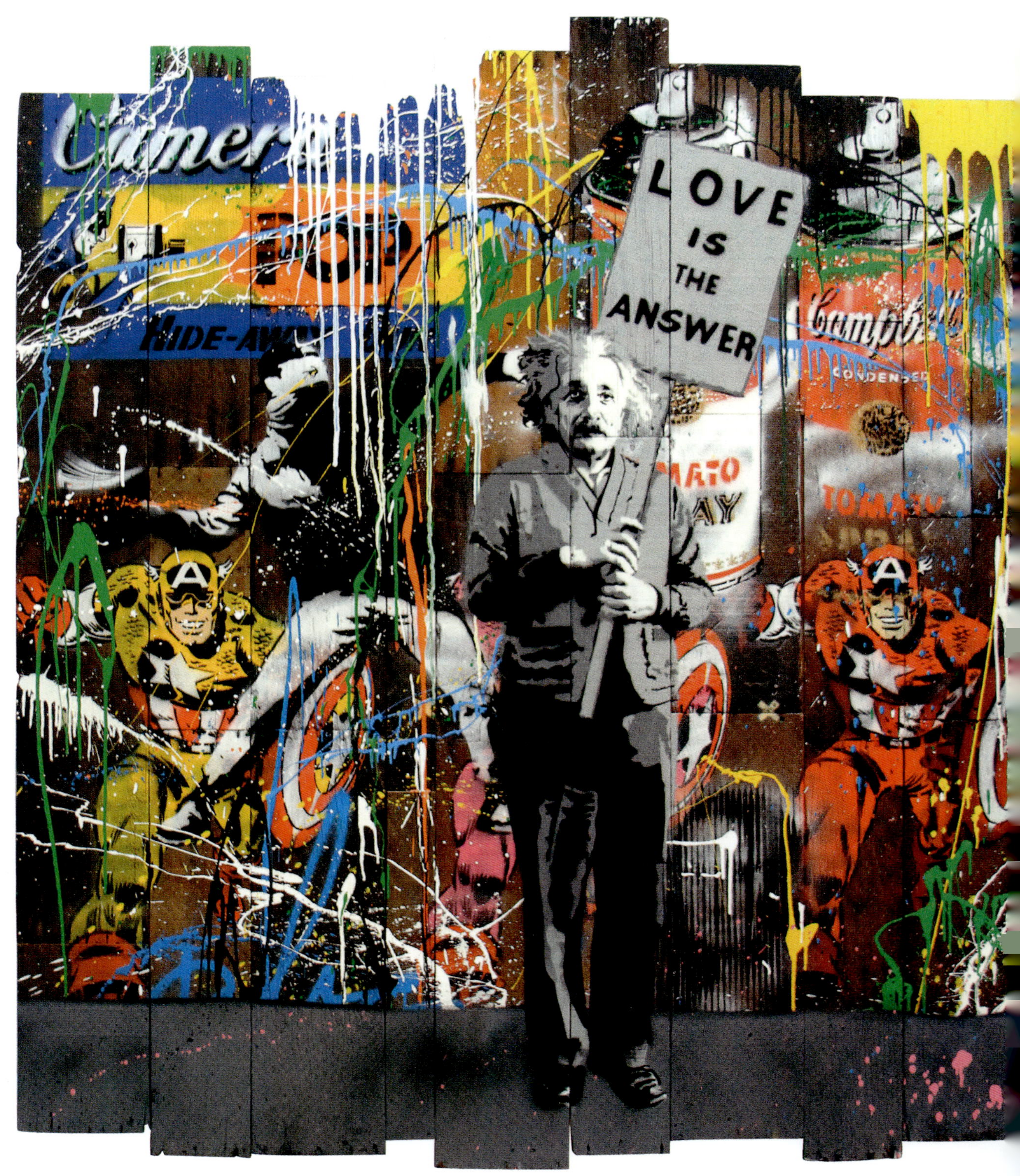

pages 62–63
Legend
34" x 51"
Mixed media on
archival paper

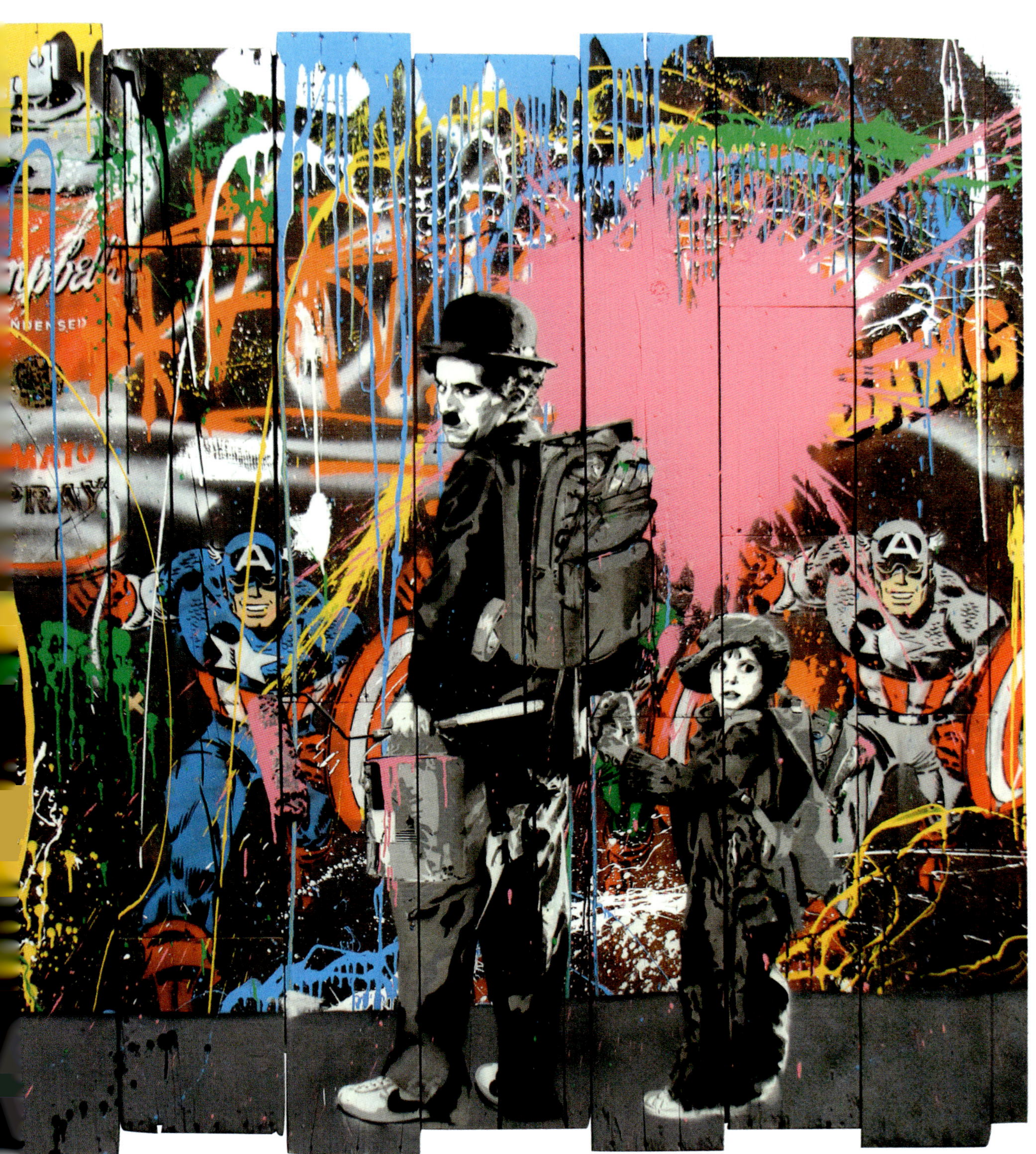

Einstein
65" x 118"
Stencil and acrylic paint
on wood

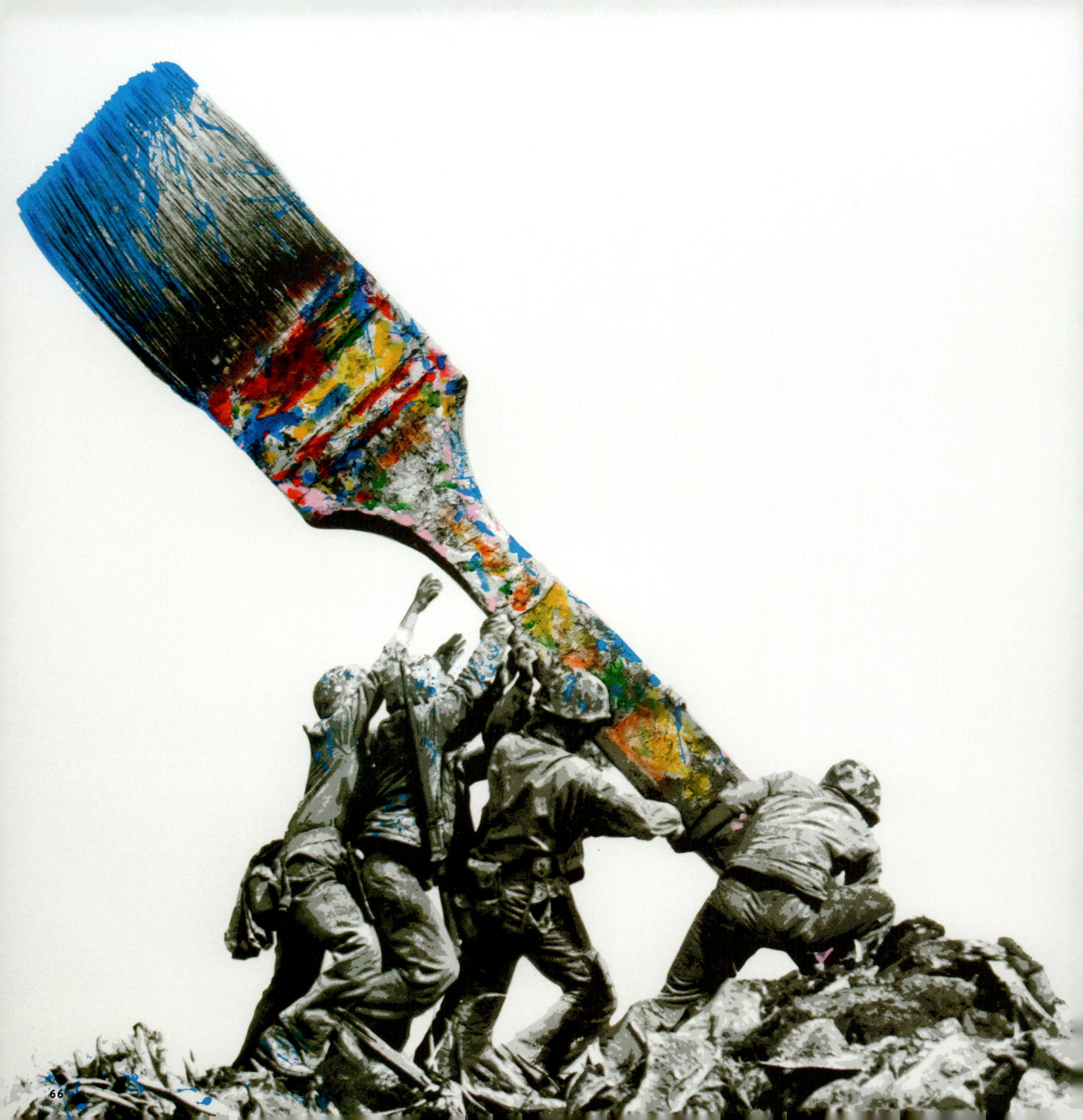

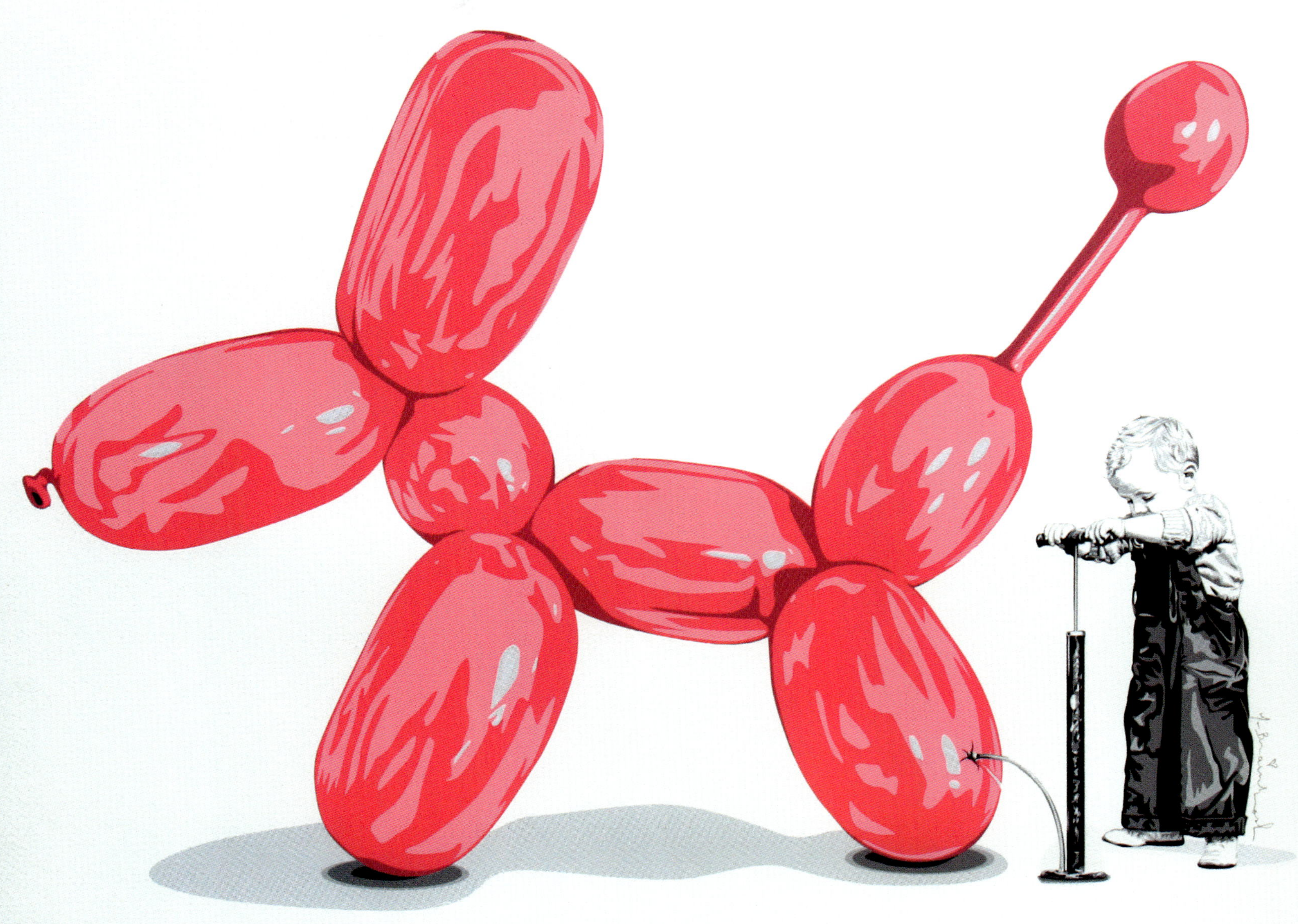

opposite
Brush
50" x 32"
Silkscreen edition print

Poppy Pink
22" x 30"
Silkscreen edition print

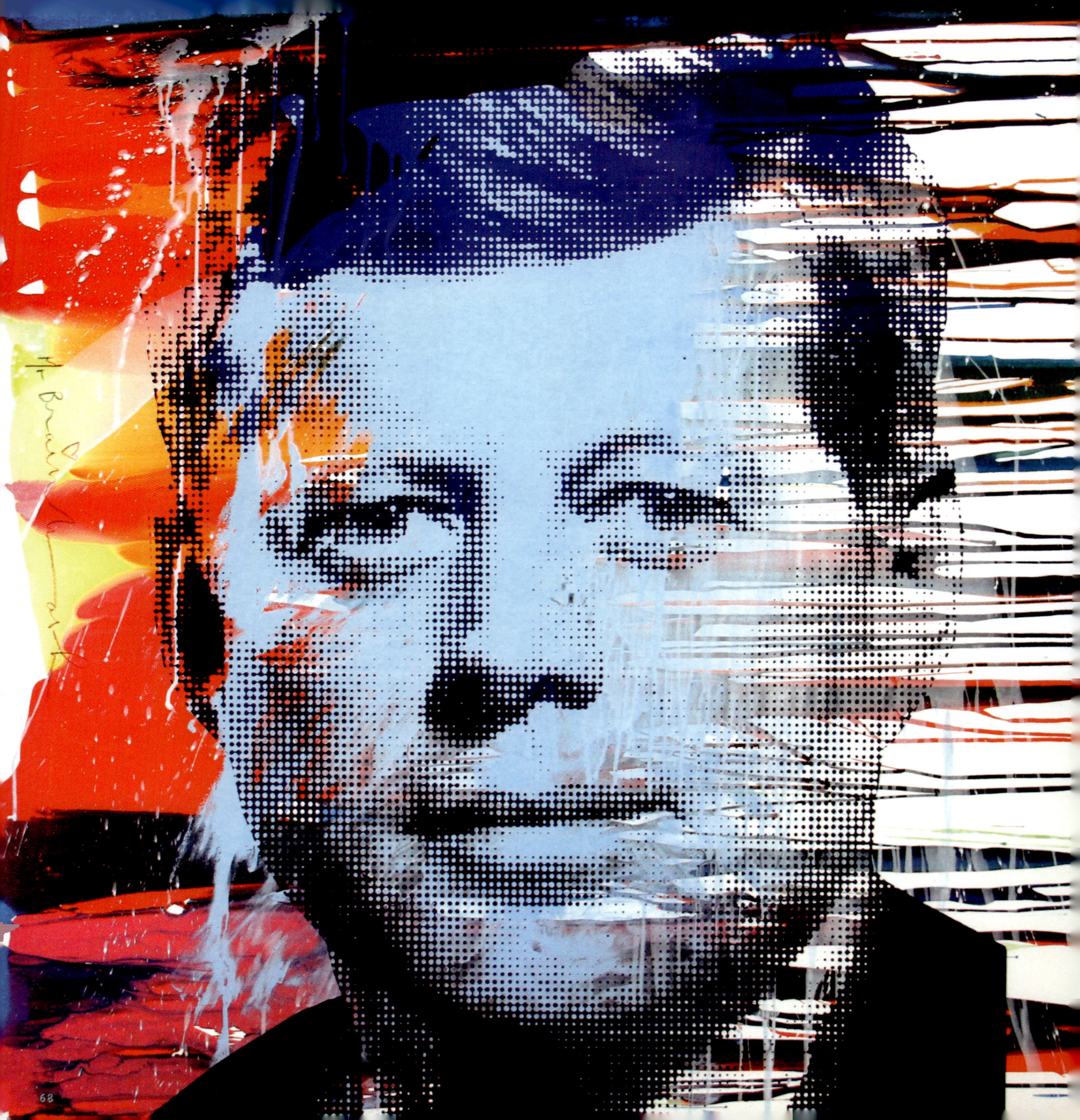

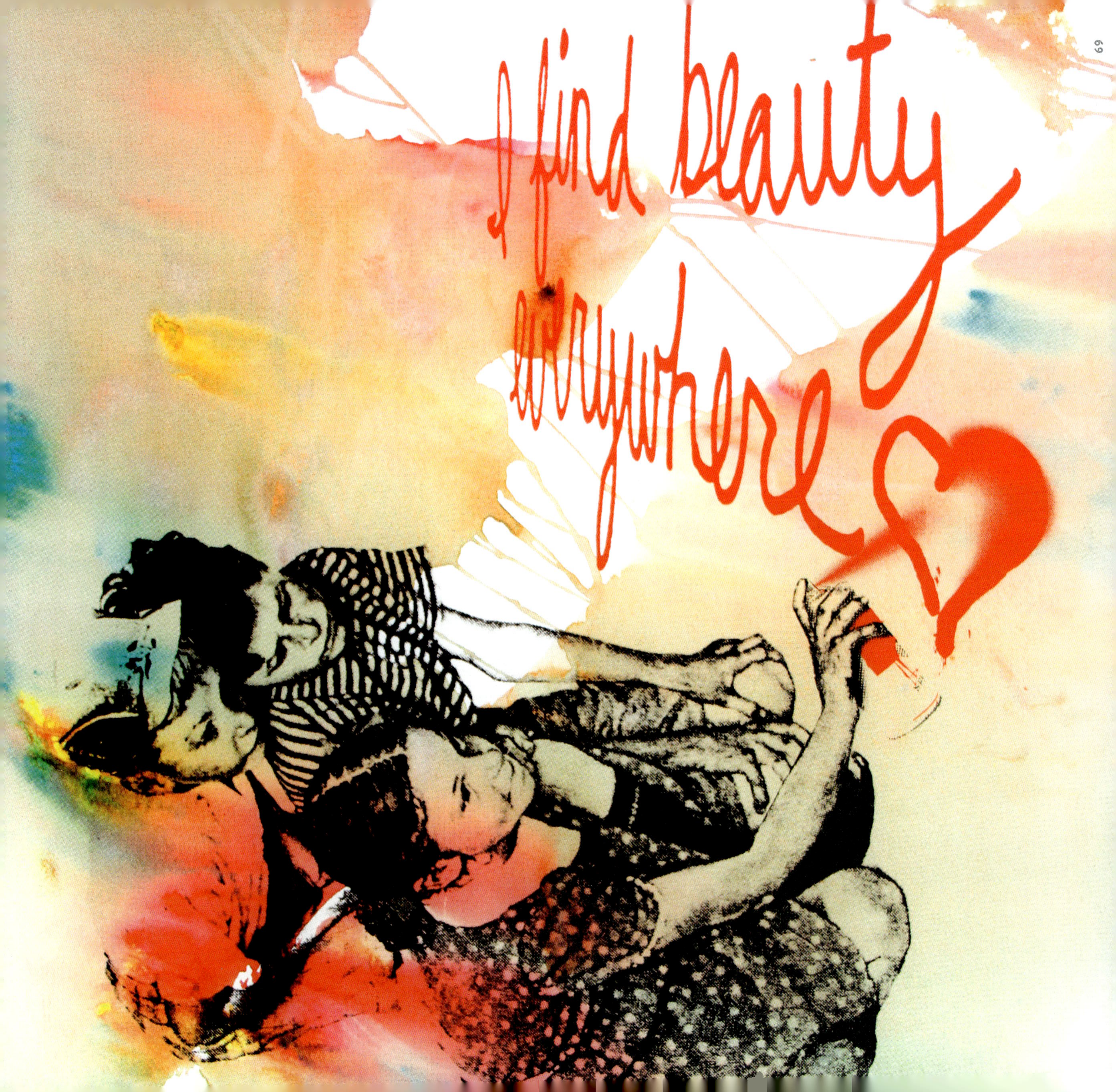
I find beauty everywhere

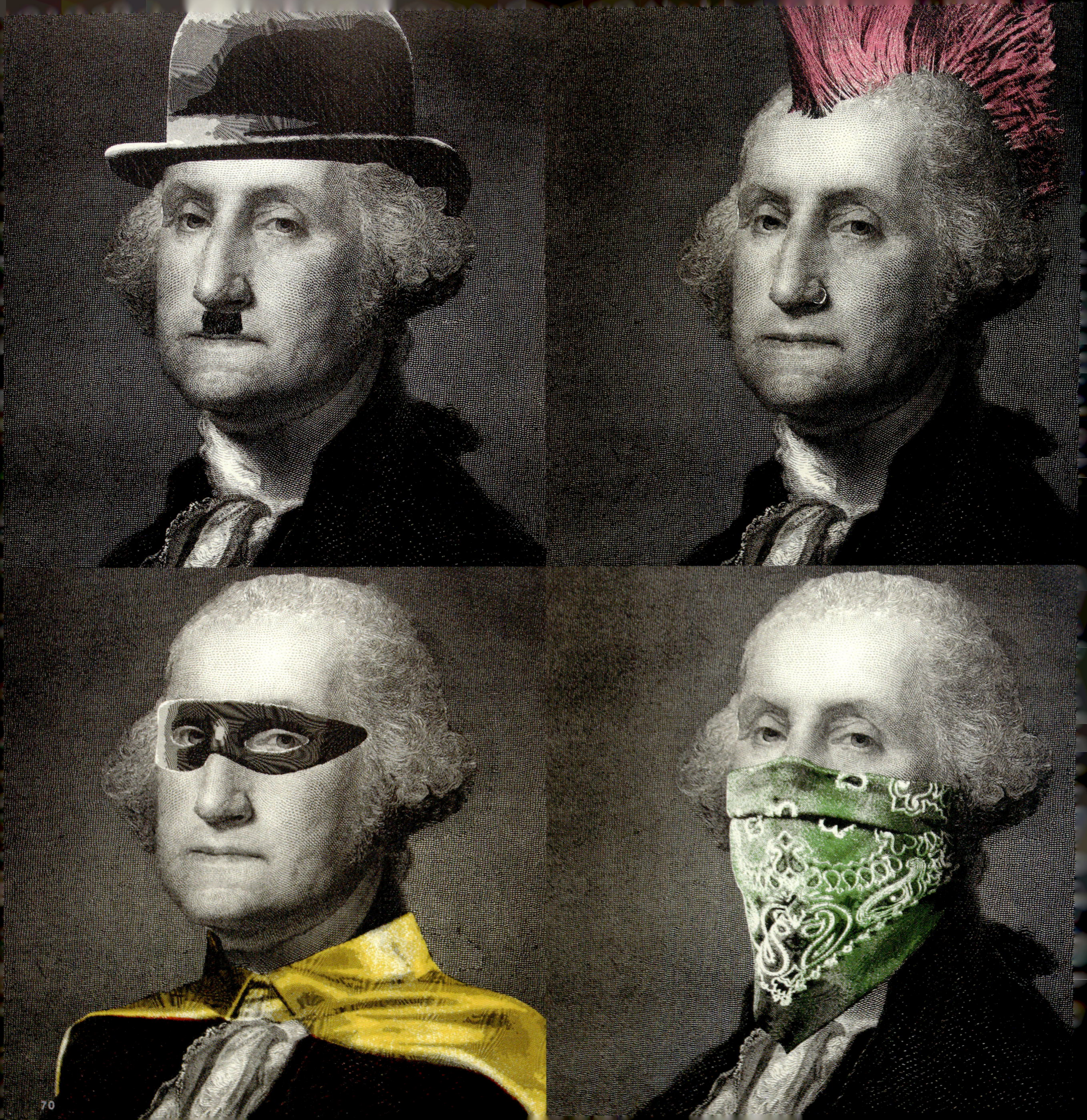

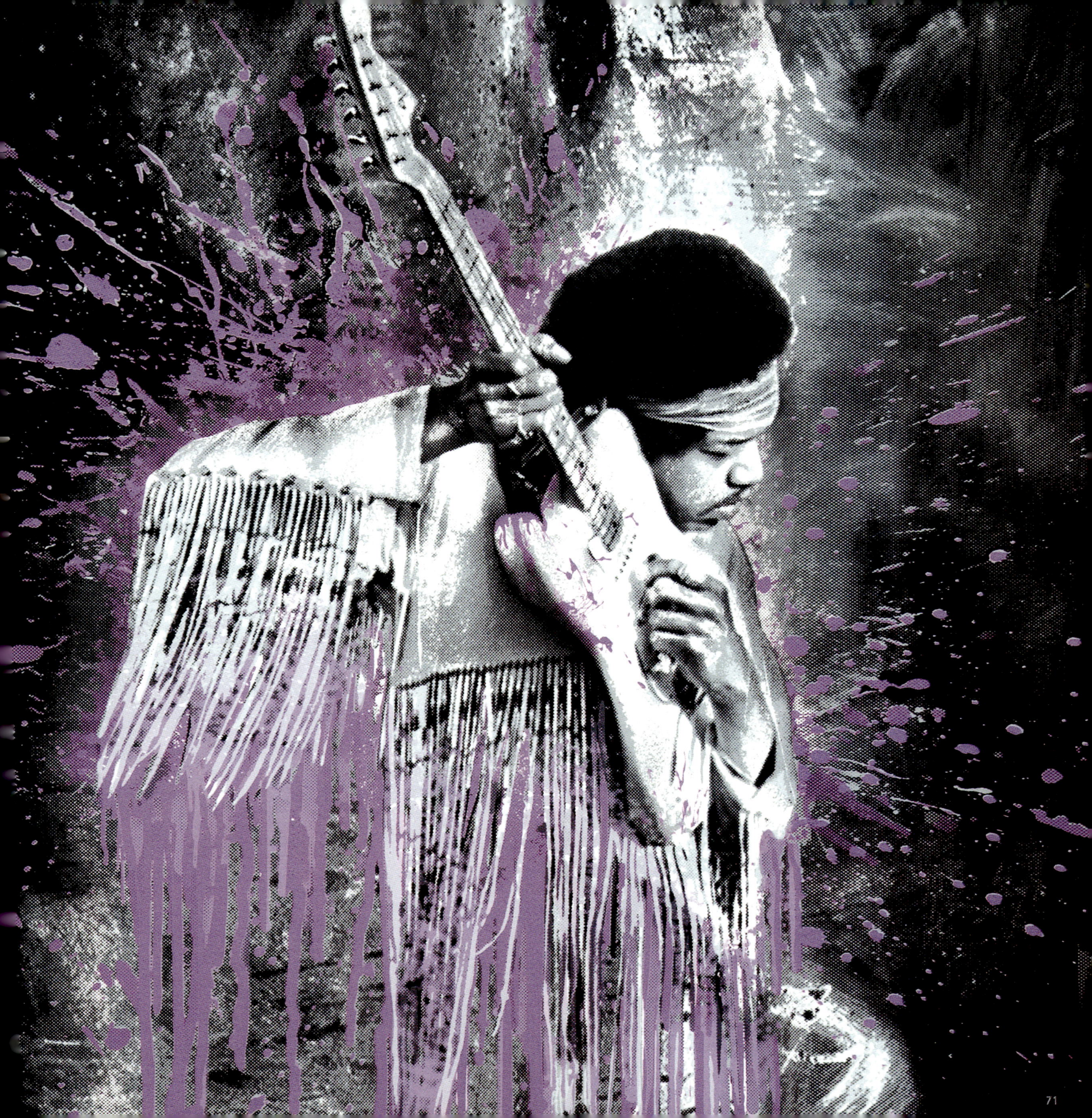

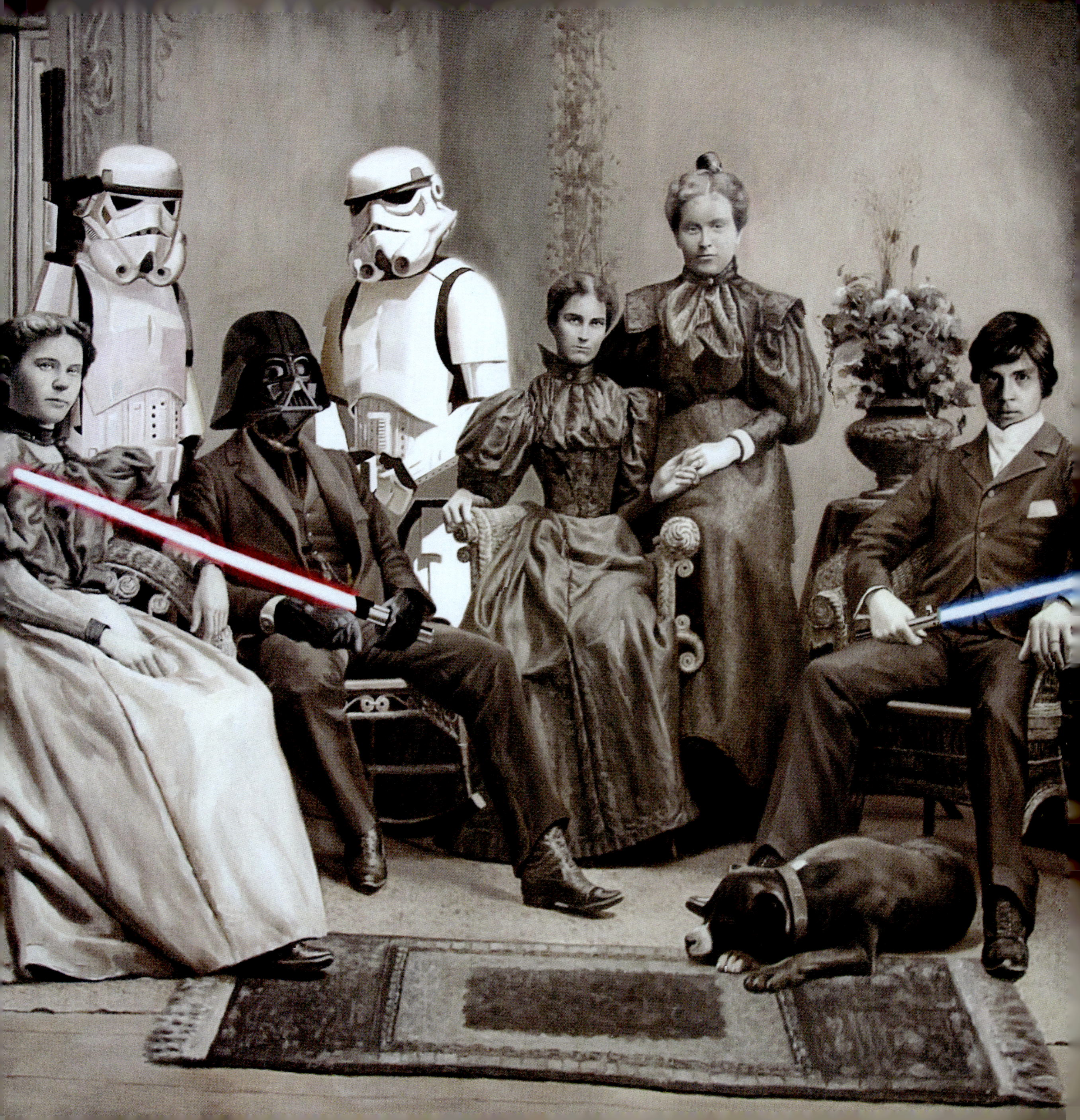

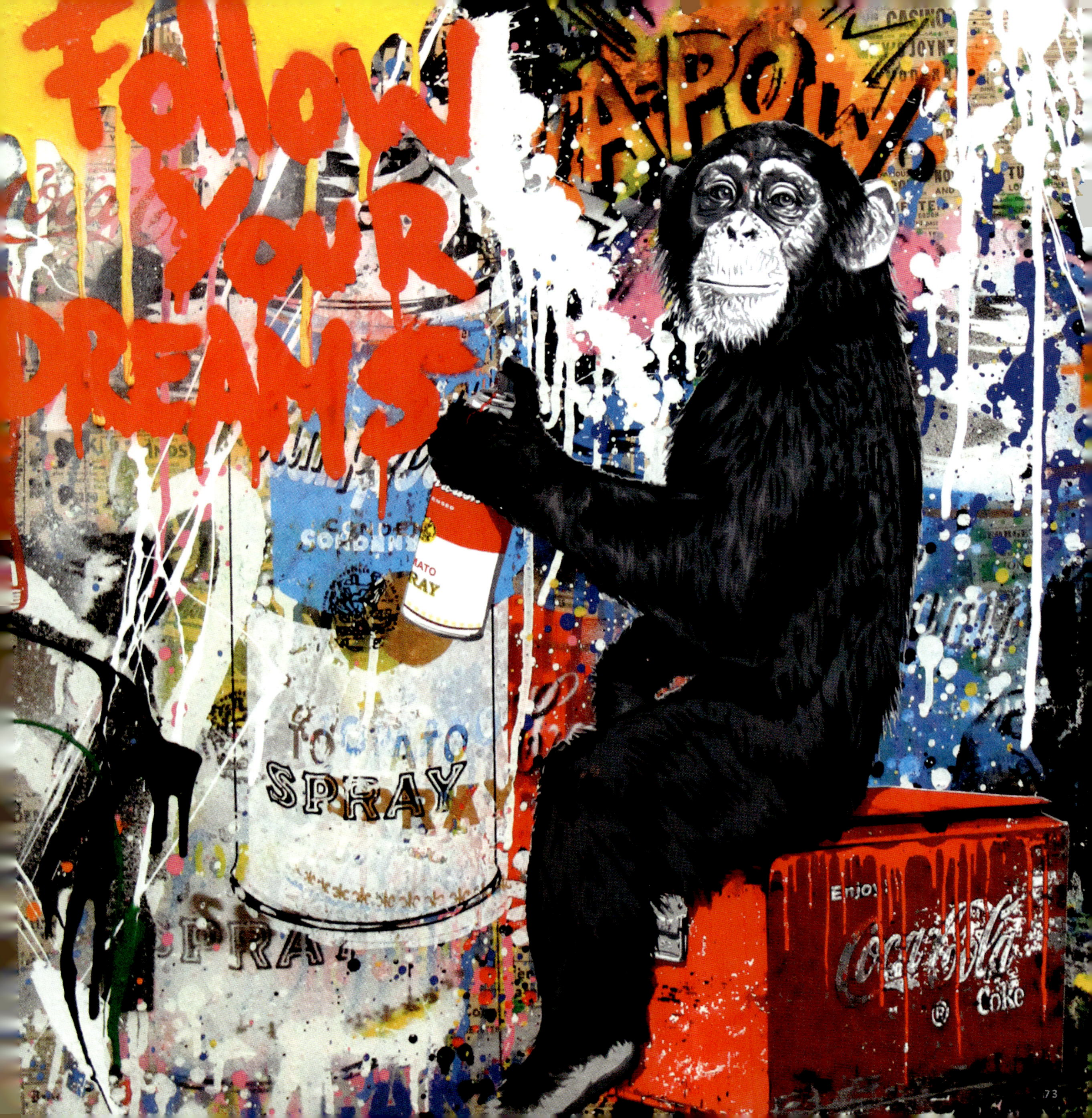

Follow your DREAMS
KA-POW
TOMATO SPRAY
TOMATO SPRAY
SPRAY
Enjoy Coca-Cola Coke

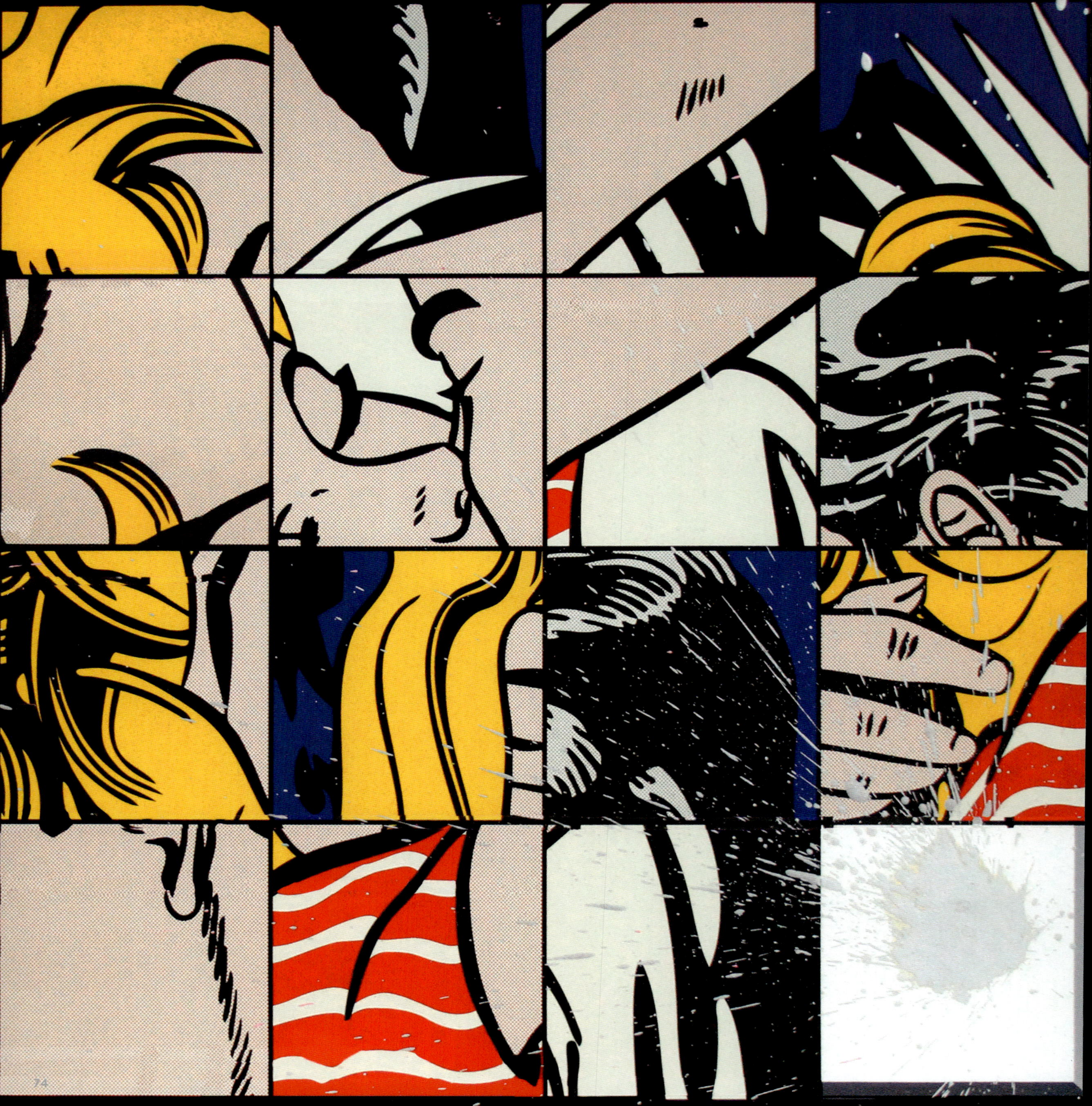

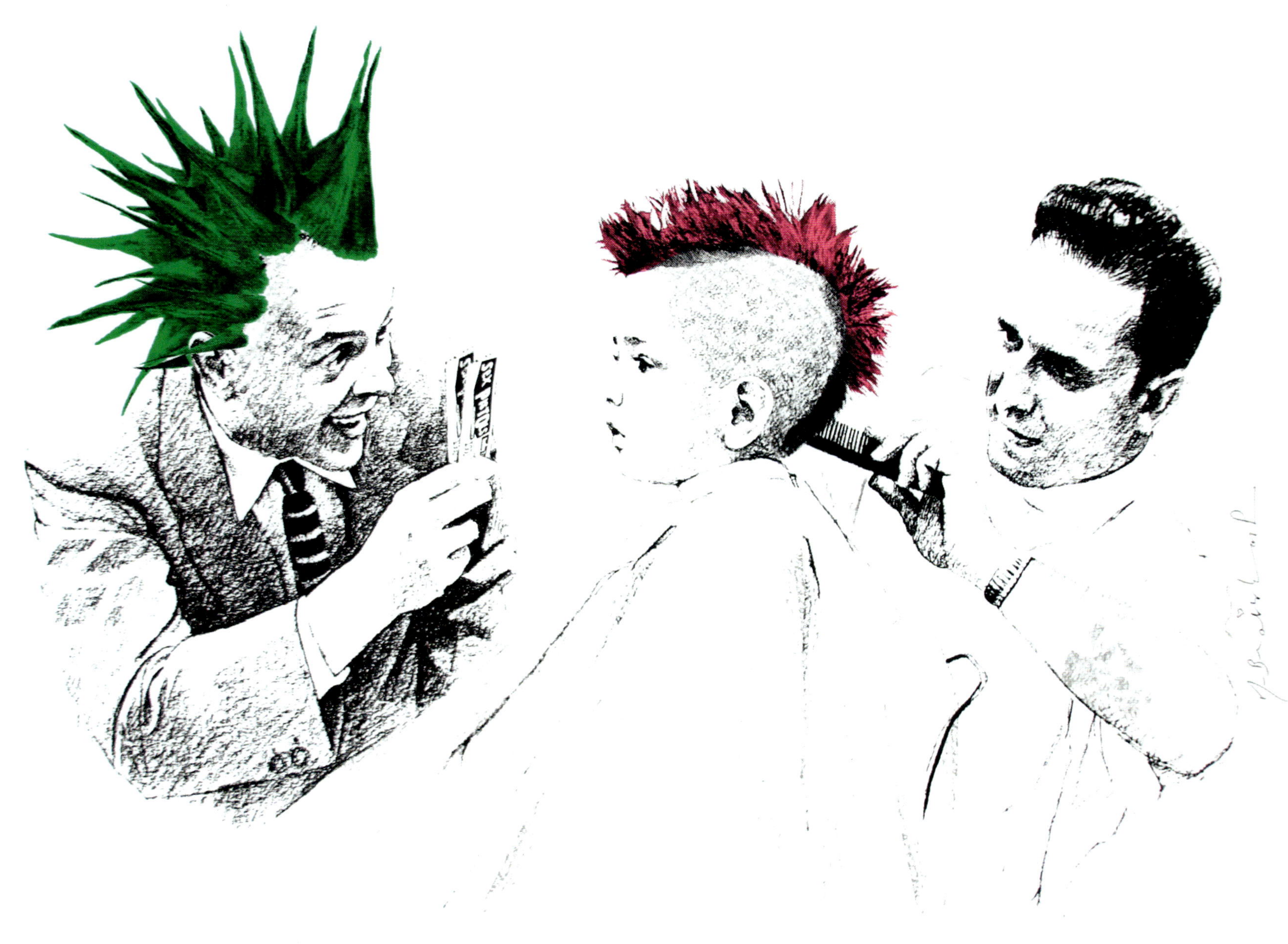

My First Concert
21" x 25"
Silkscreen edition print

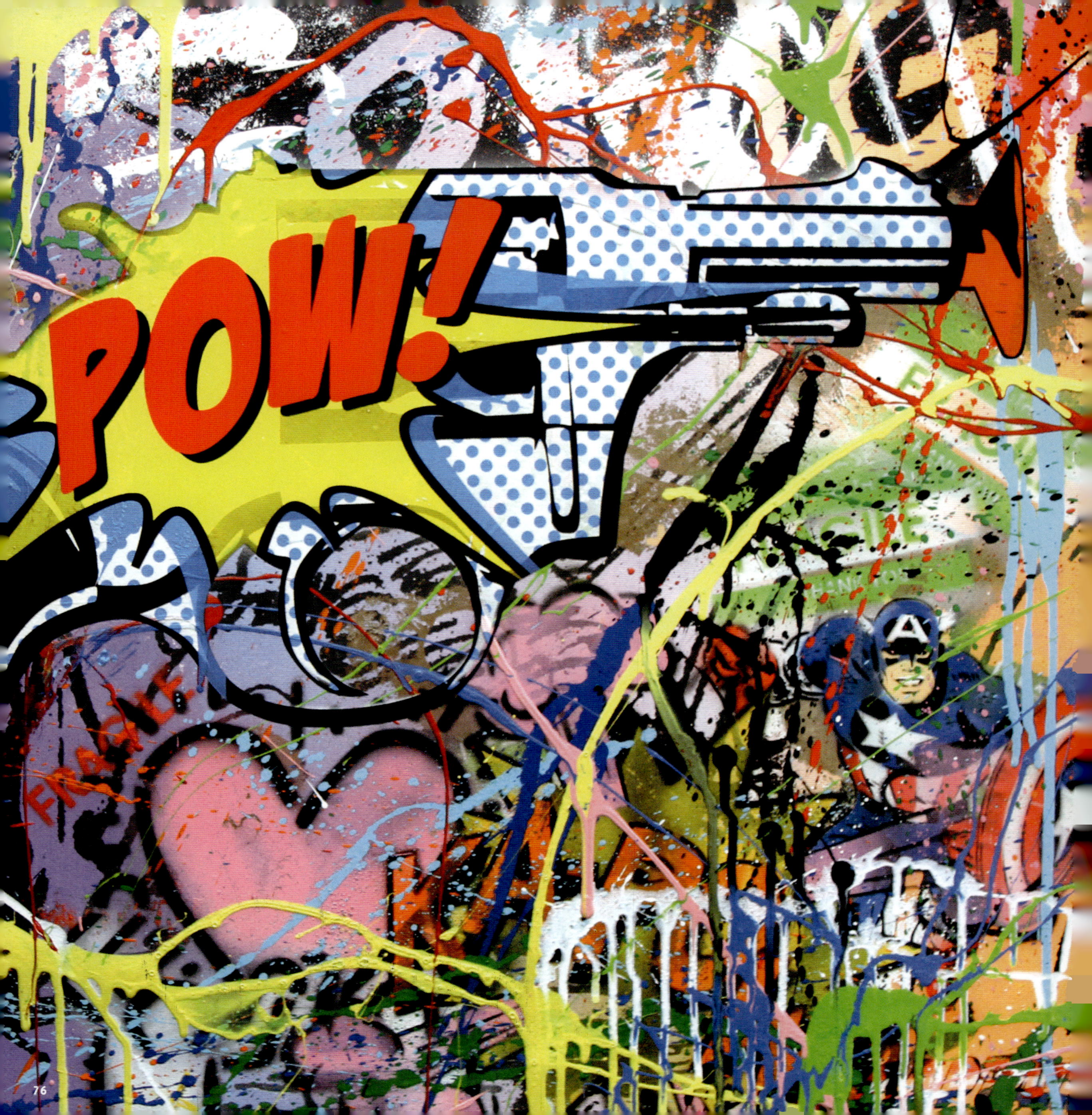

POW!

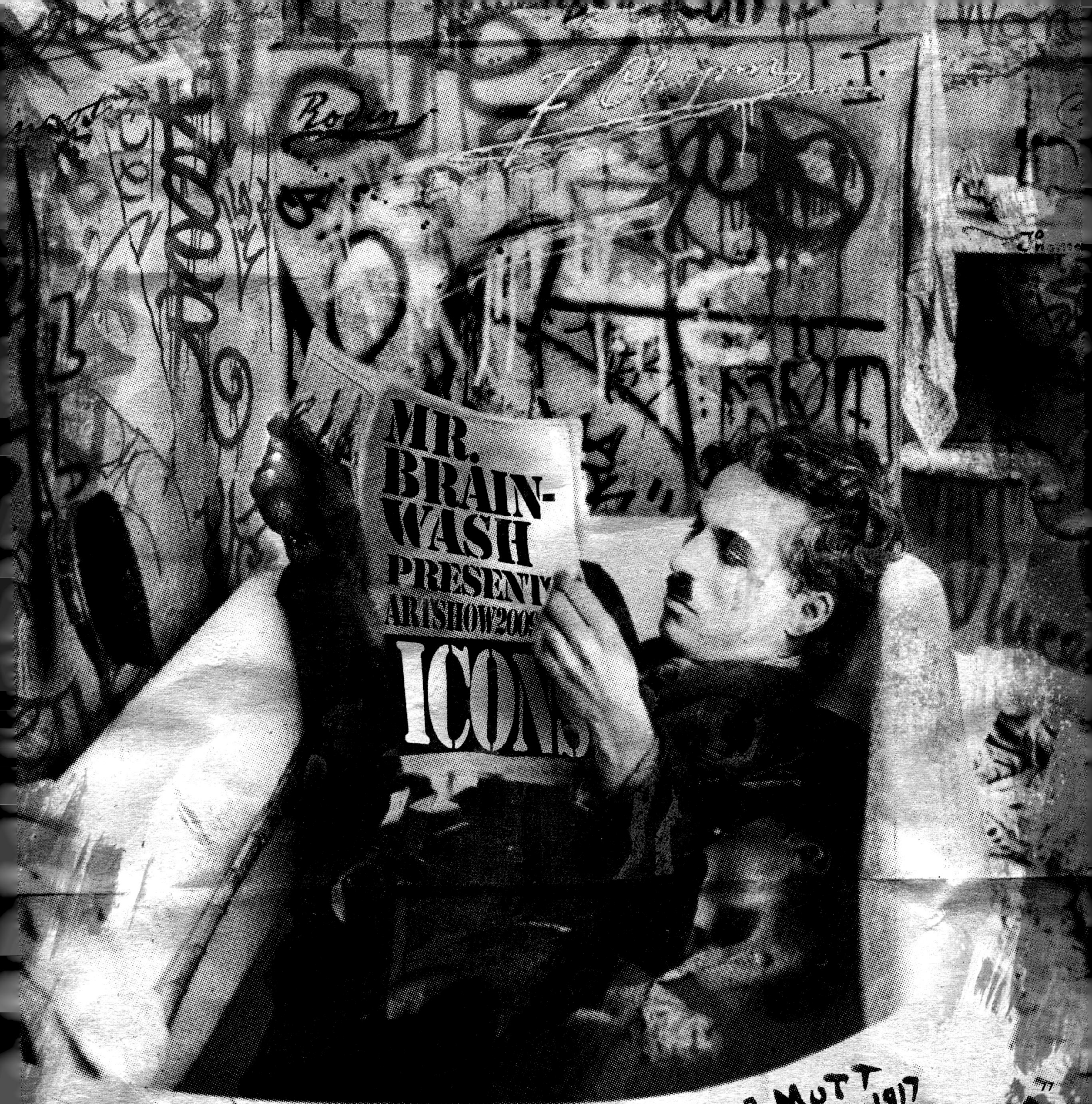
MR.
BRAIN-
WASH
PRESENT
ARTSHOW2009
ICON.
MUTT
1917

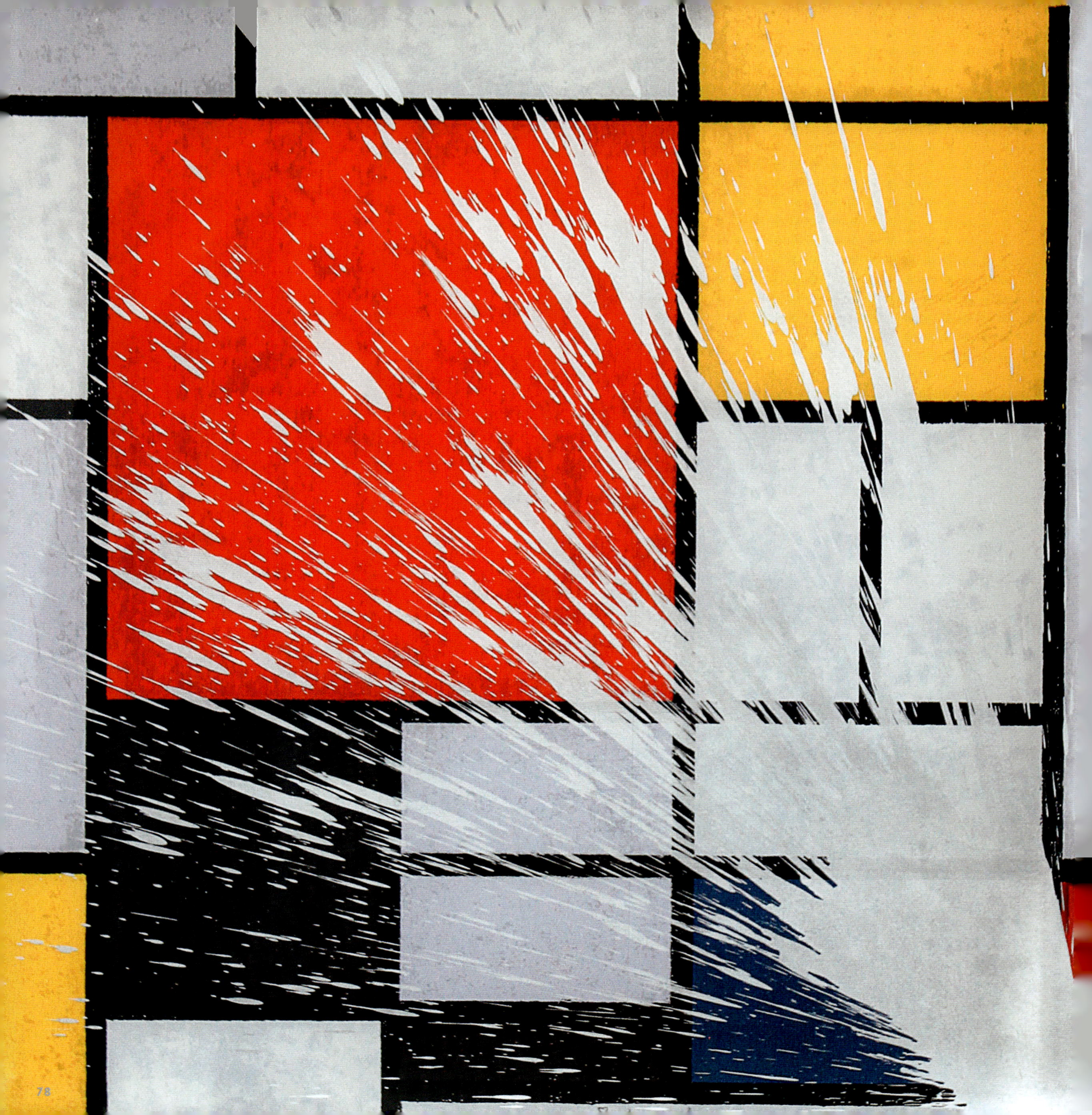

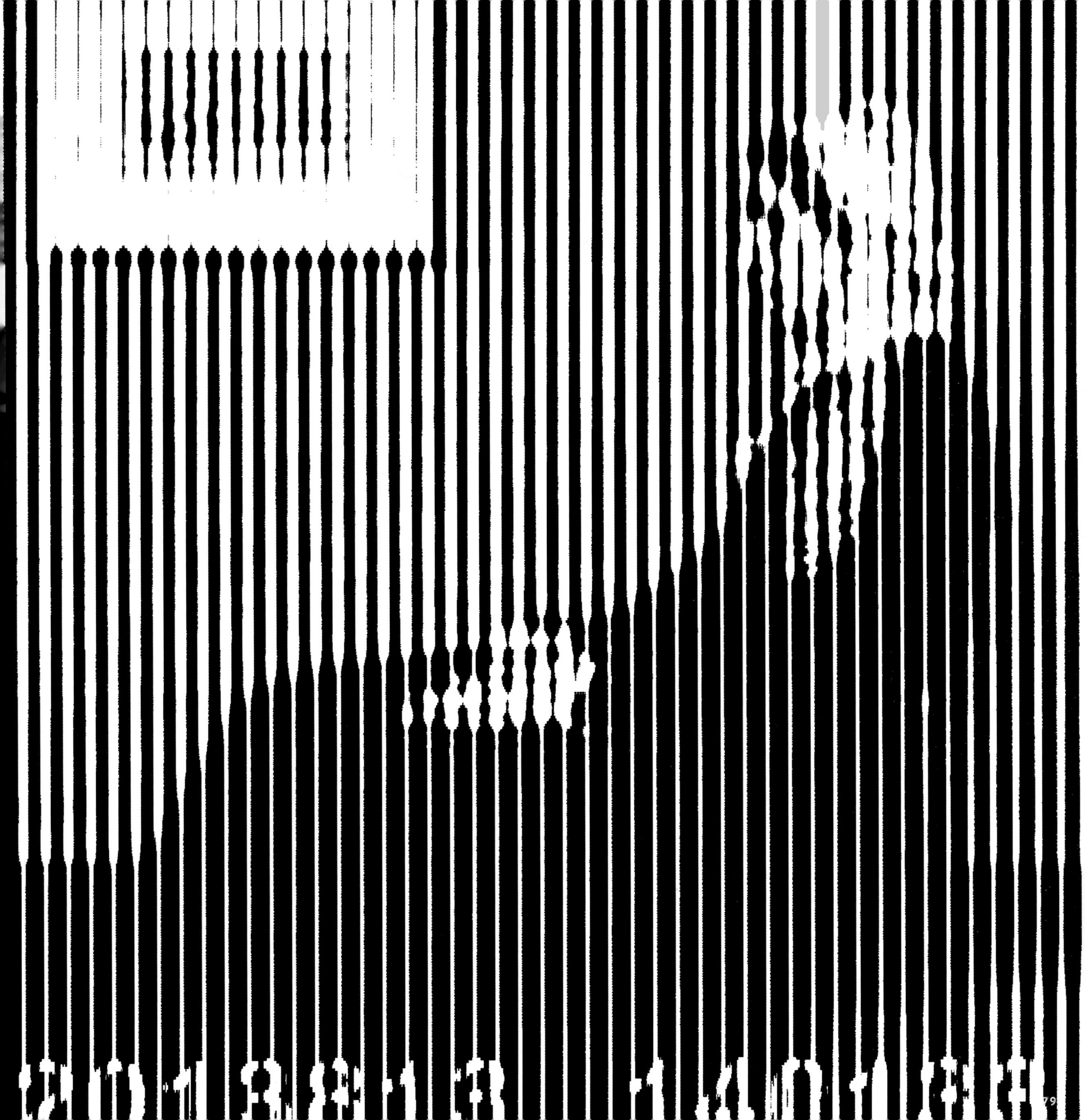

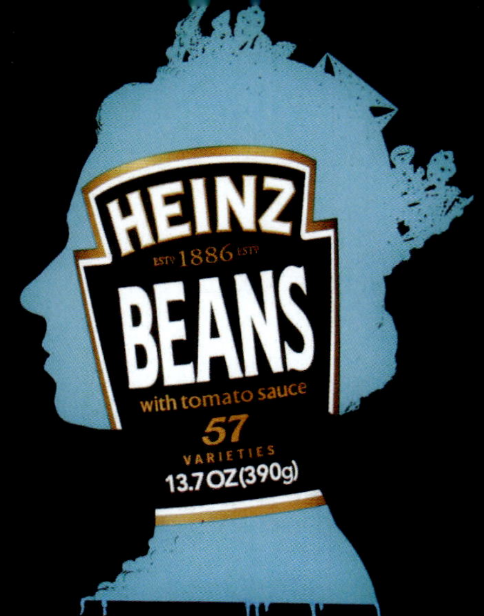
HEINZ
ESTD 1886 ESTD
BEANS
with tomato sauce
57
VARIETIES
13.7 OZ (390g)

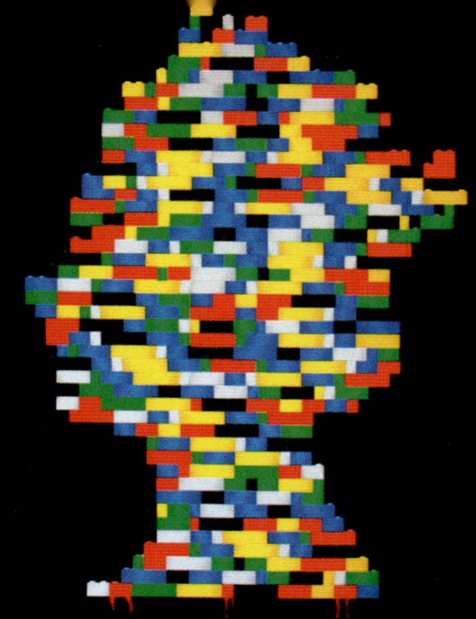

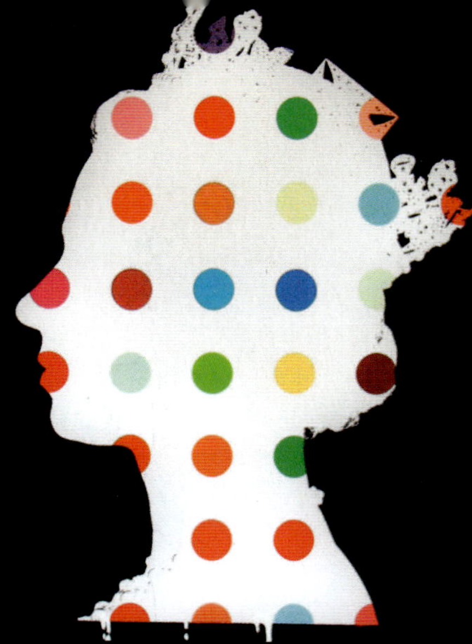

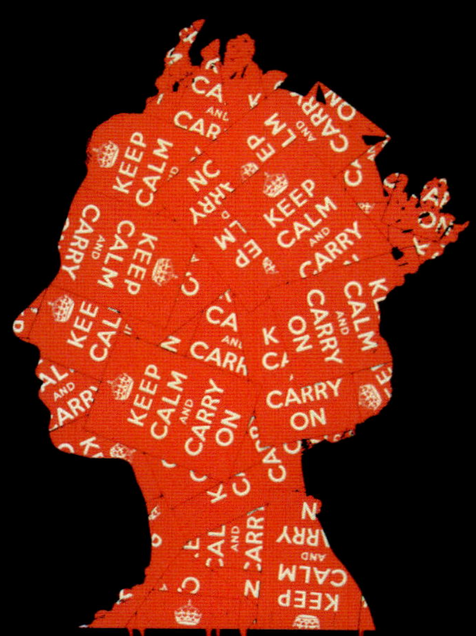
KEEP CALM AND CARRY ON

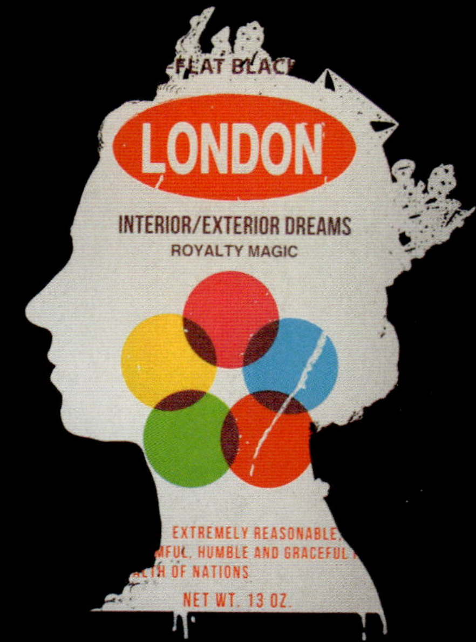
FLAT BLACK
LONDON
INTERIOR/EXTERIOR DREAMS
ROYALTY MAGIC
EXTREMELY REASONABLE
FUL, HUMBLE AND GRACEFUL
LTH OF NATIONS
NET WT. 13 OZ.

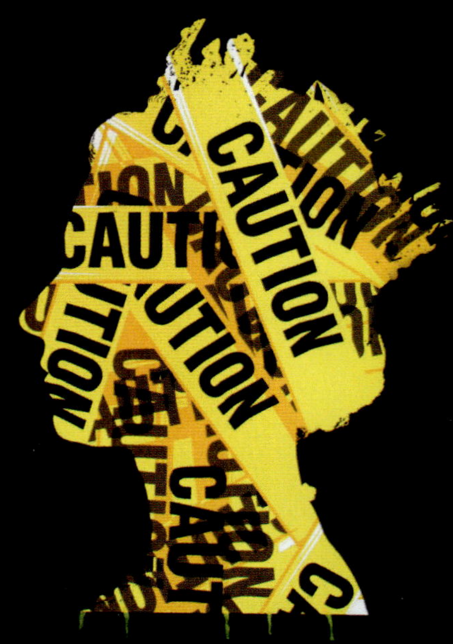
CAUTION

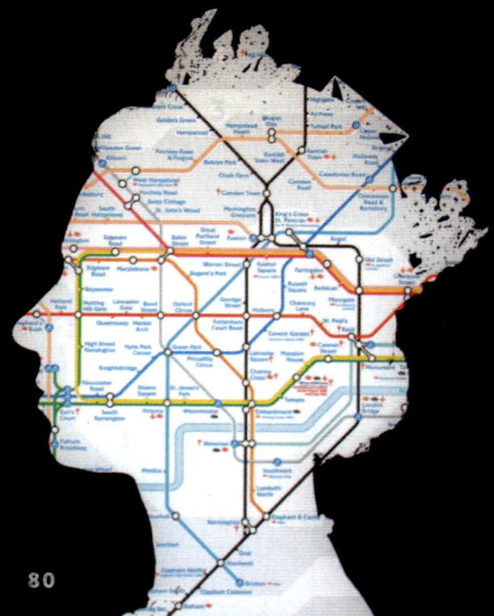

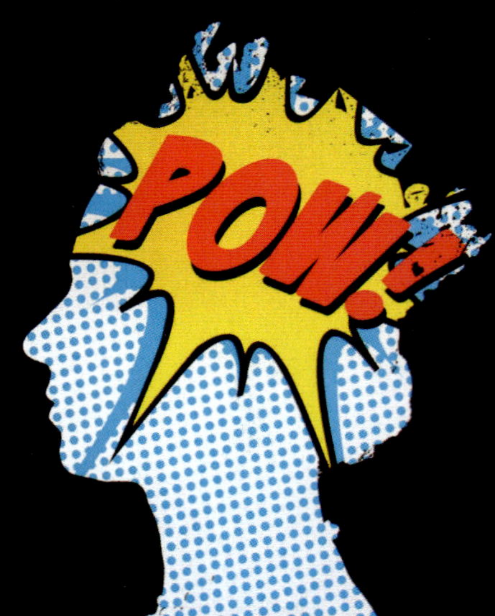
POW!

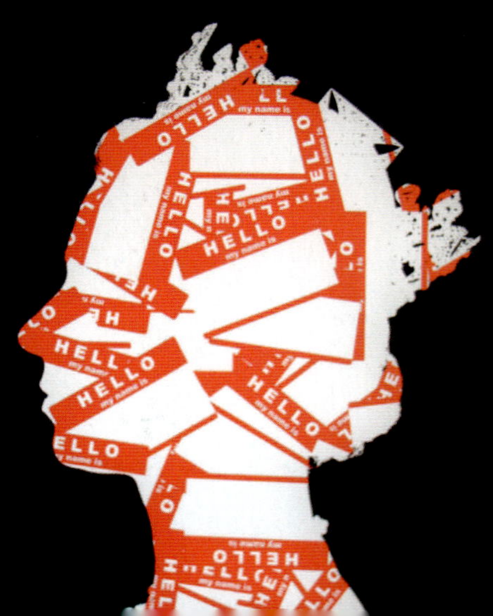
HELLO my name is

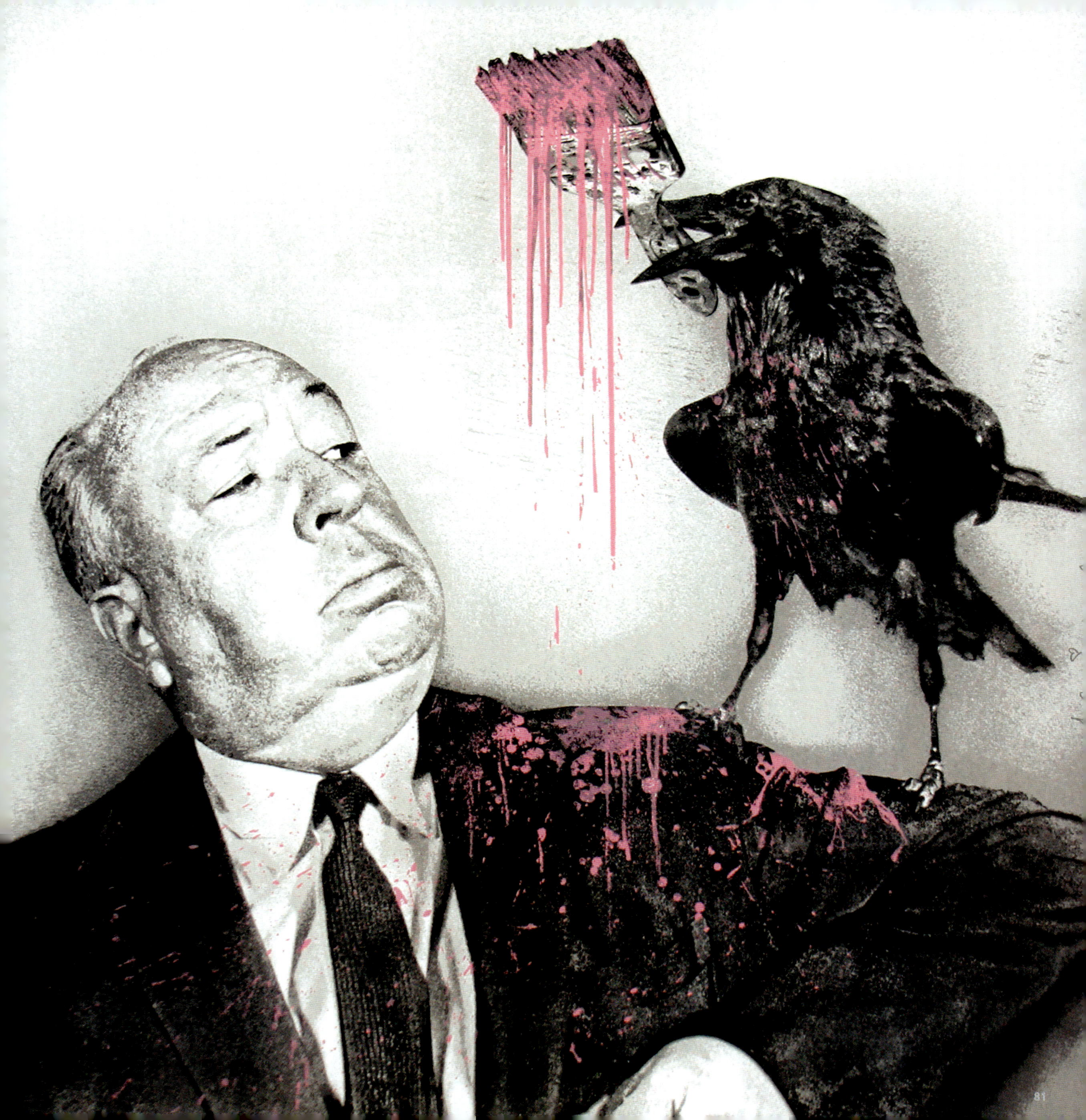

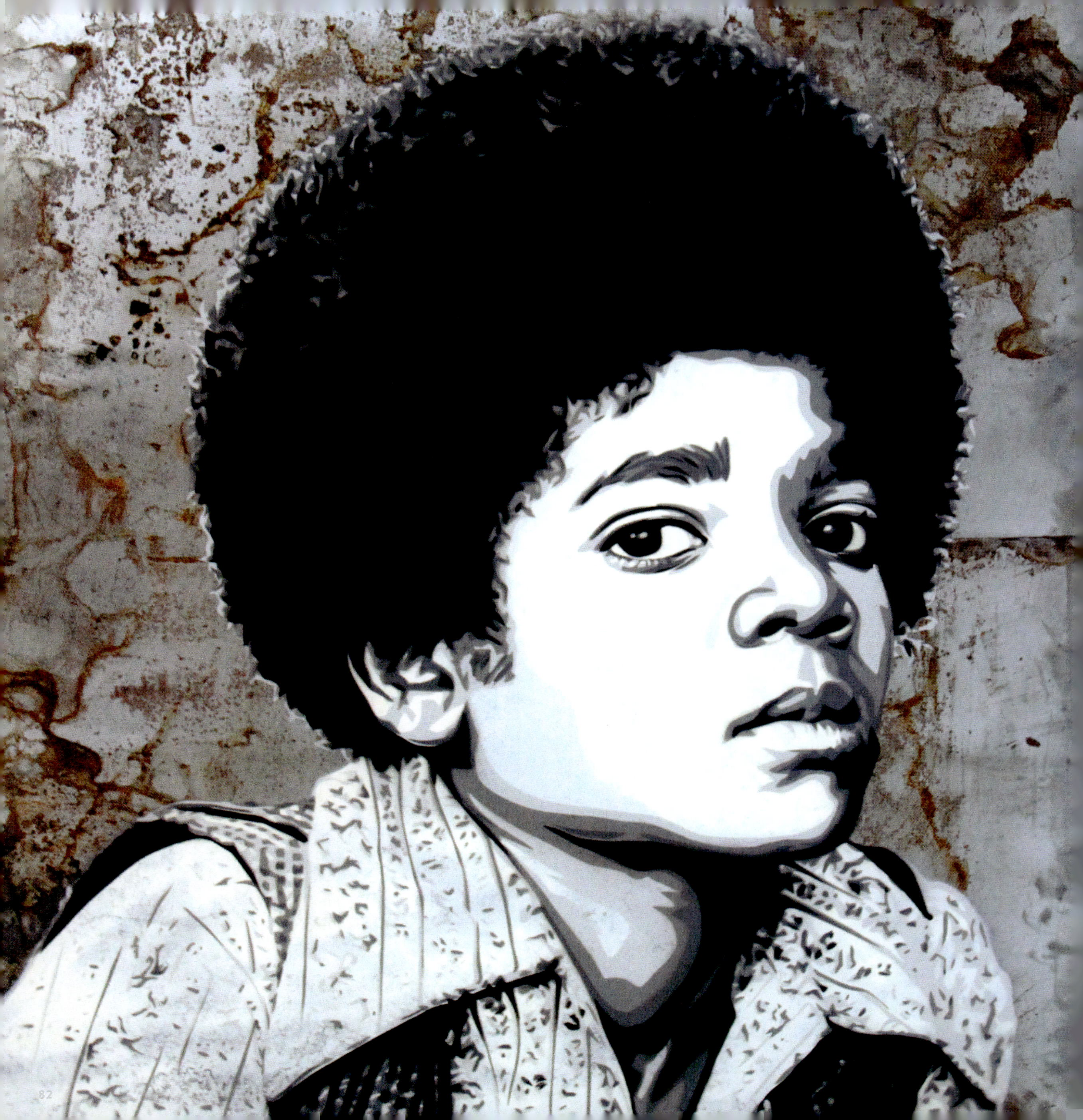

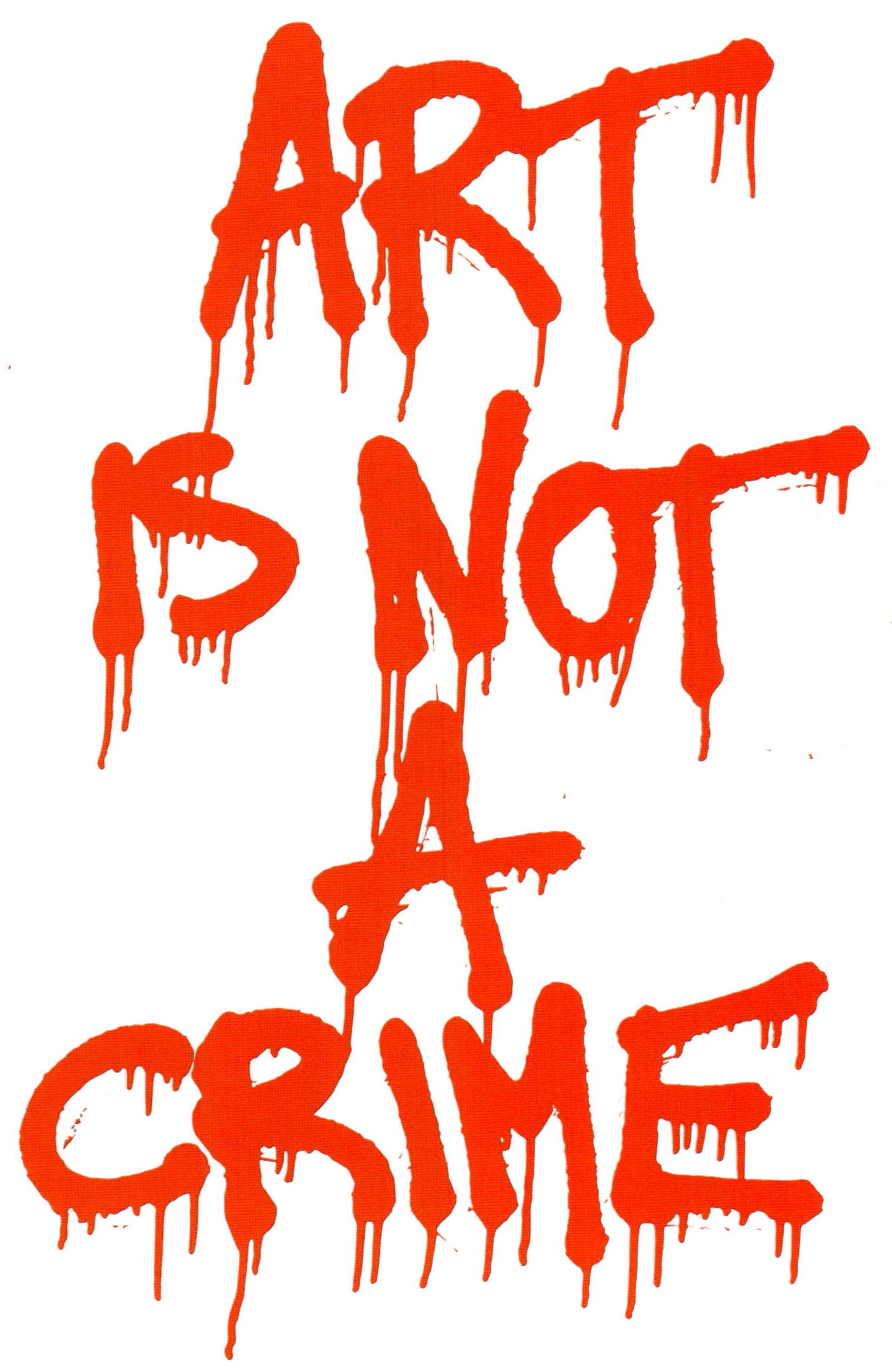

Art Is Not a Crime
30" x 22"
Silkscreen edition print

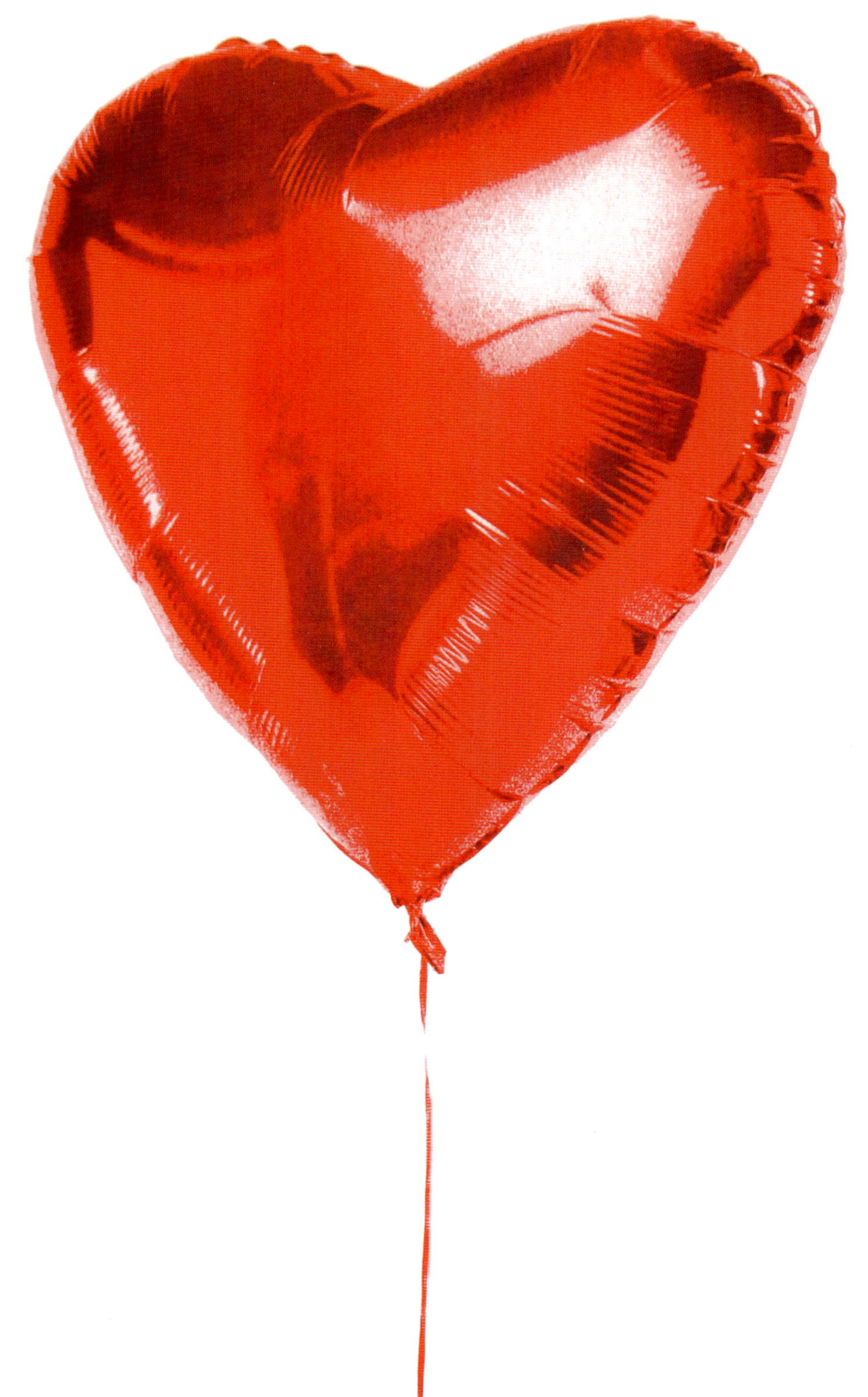

**Hold on to My
He(ART)**
30" x 22"
Silkscreen edition print

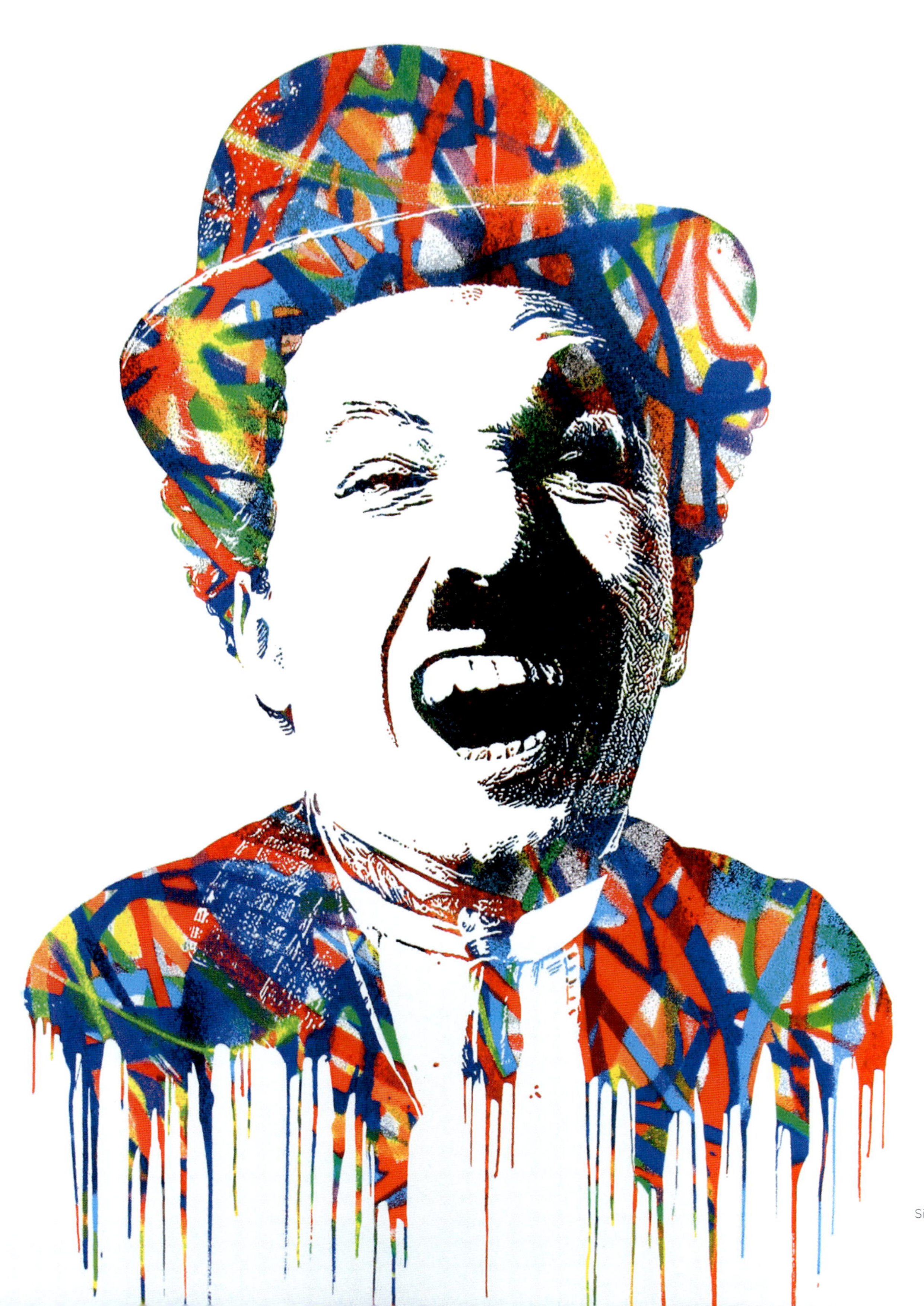

Charlie
30" x 22"
Silkscreen edition print

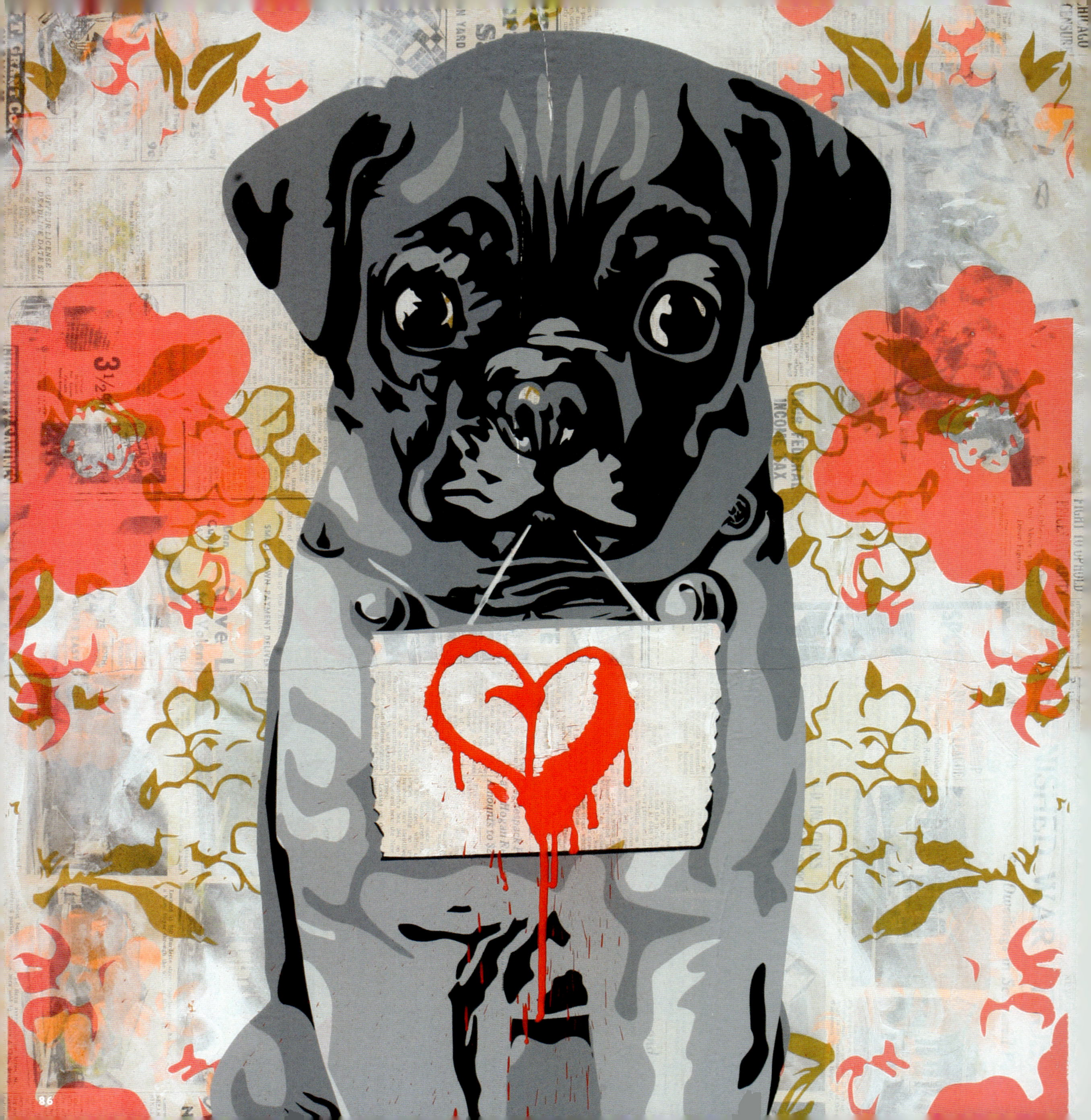

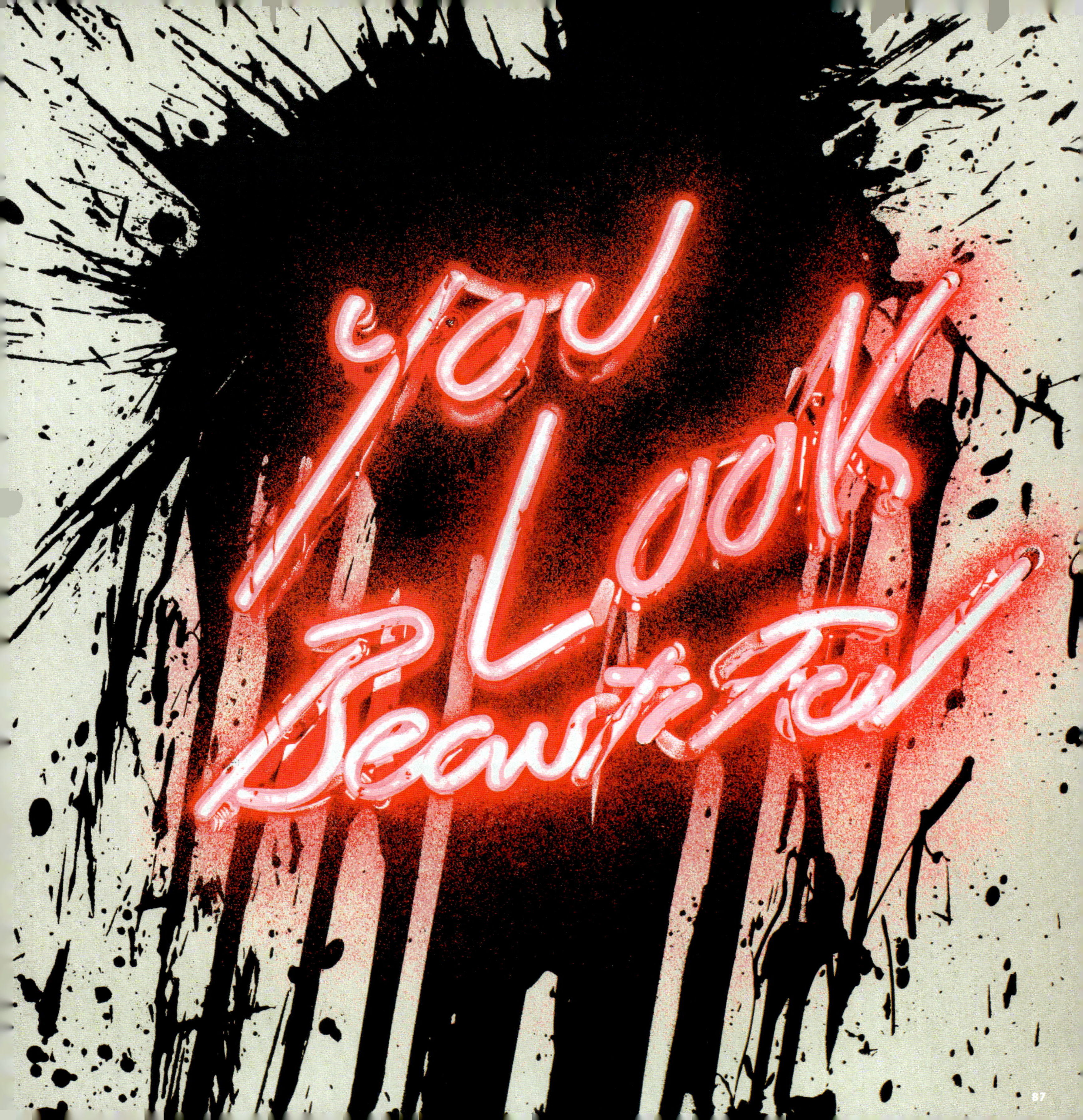

you
Look
Beautiful

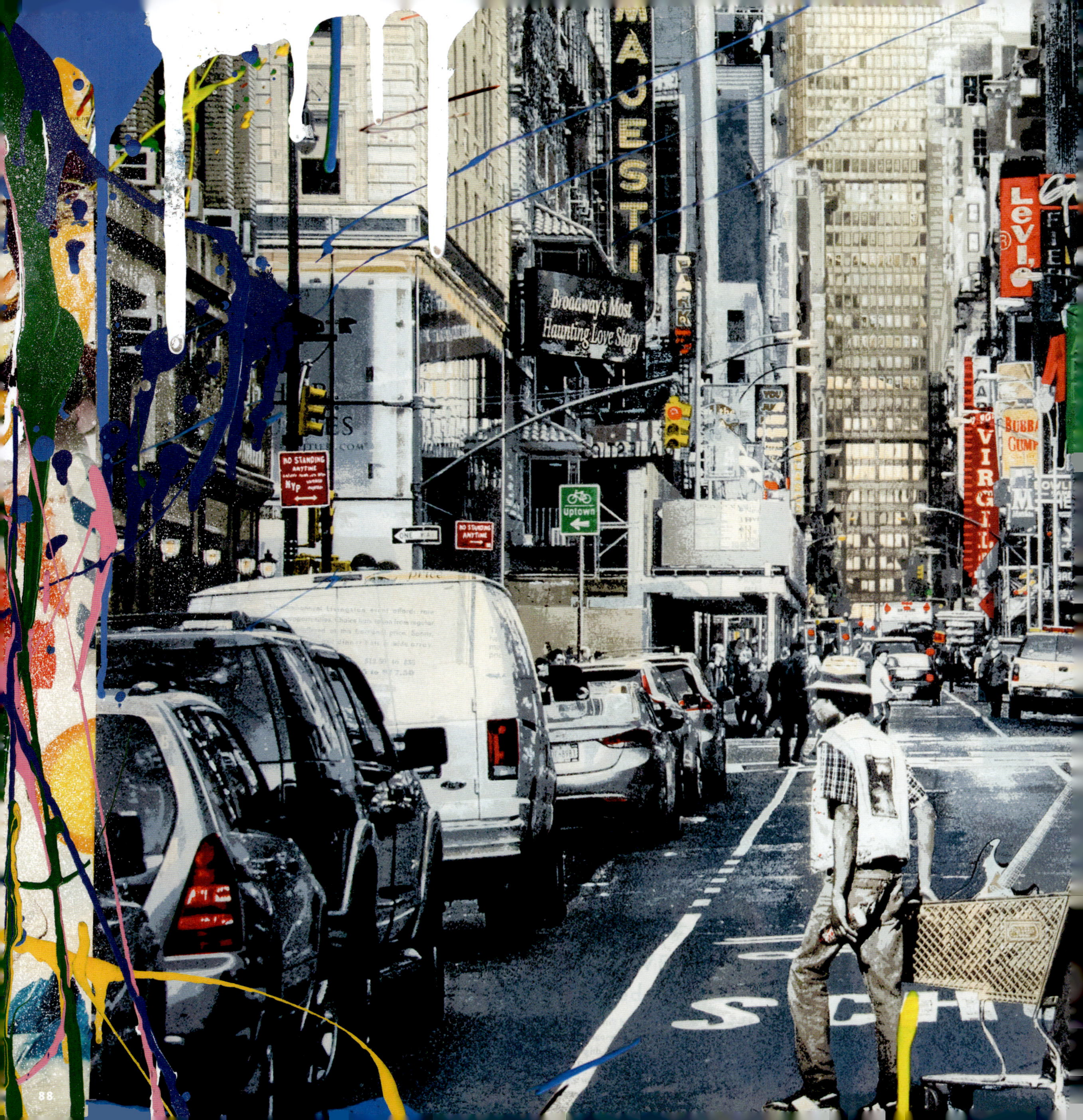

MAJESTI
Broadway's Most
Haunting Love Story
PARK
Levi's
VIRGI
BUBBA
GUMP
NO STANDING
ANYTIME
NYP
ONE WAY
NO STANDING
ANYTIME
Uptown
S CH
88

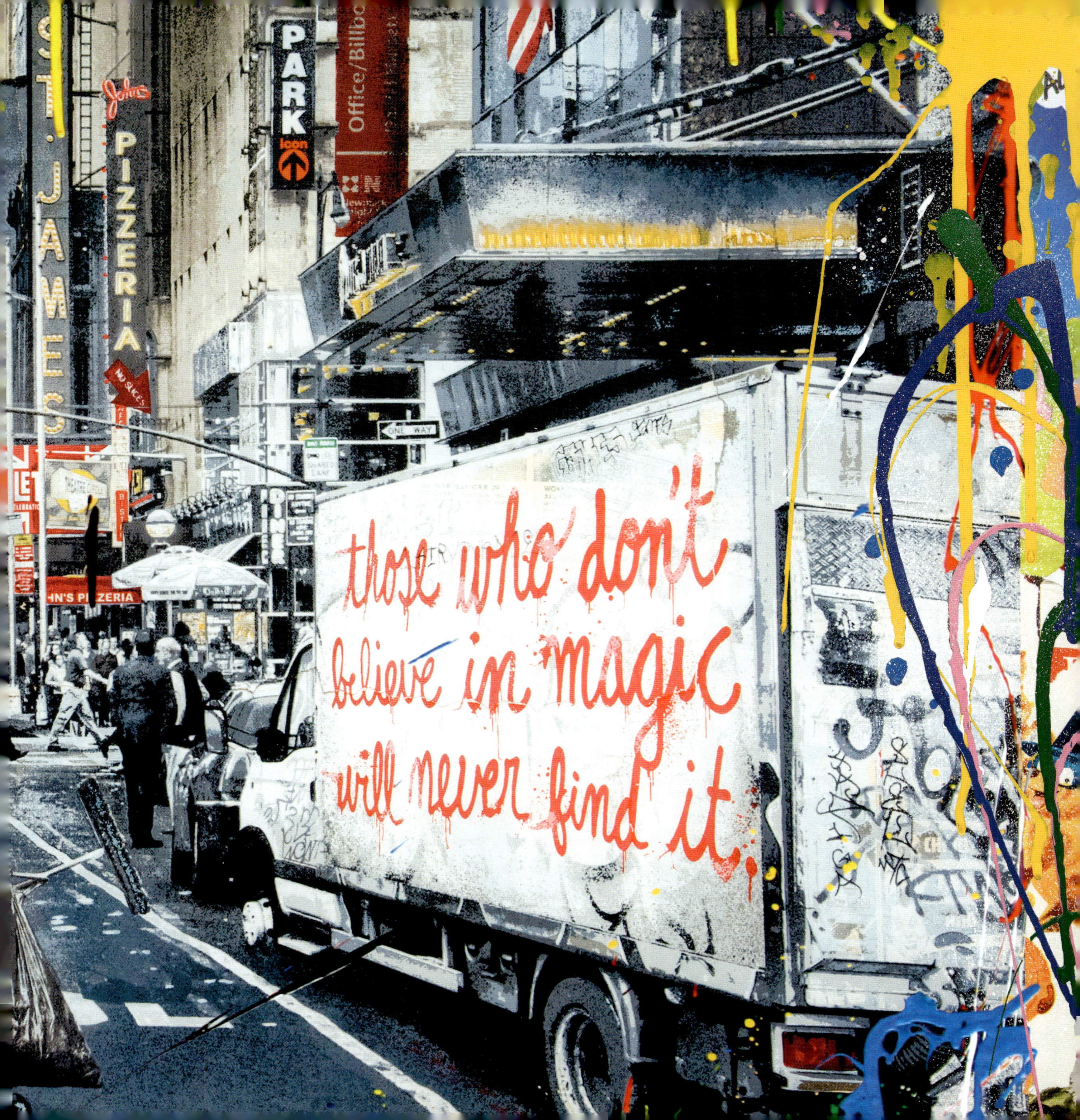

ST. JAMES
John's PIZZERIA
NO SLICES
PARK
icon
Office/Billbo
ONE WAY
those who don't believe in magic will never find it.

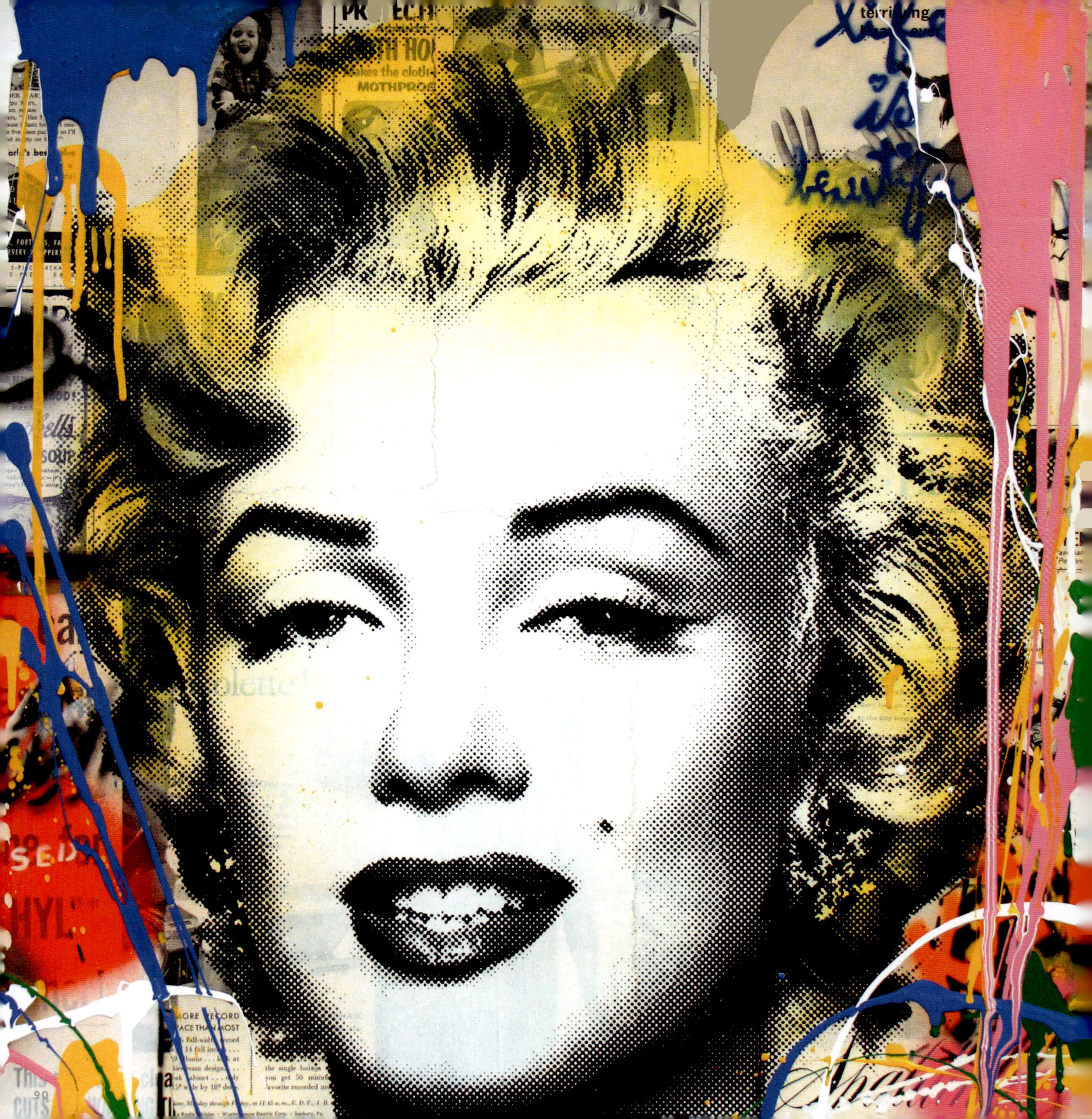

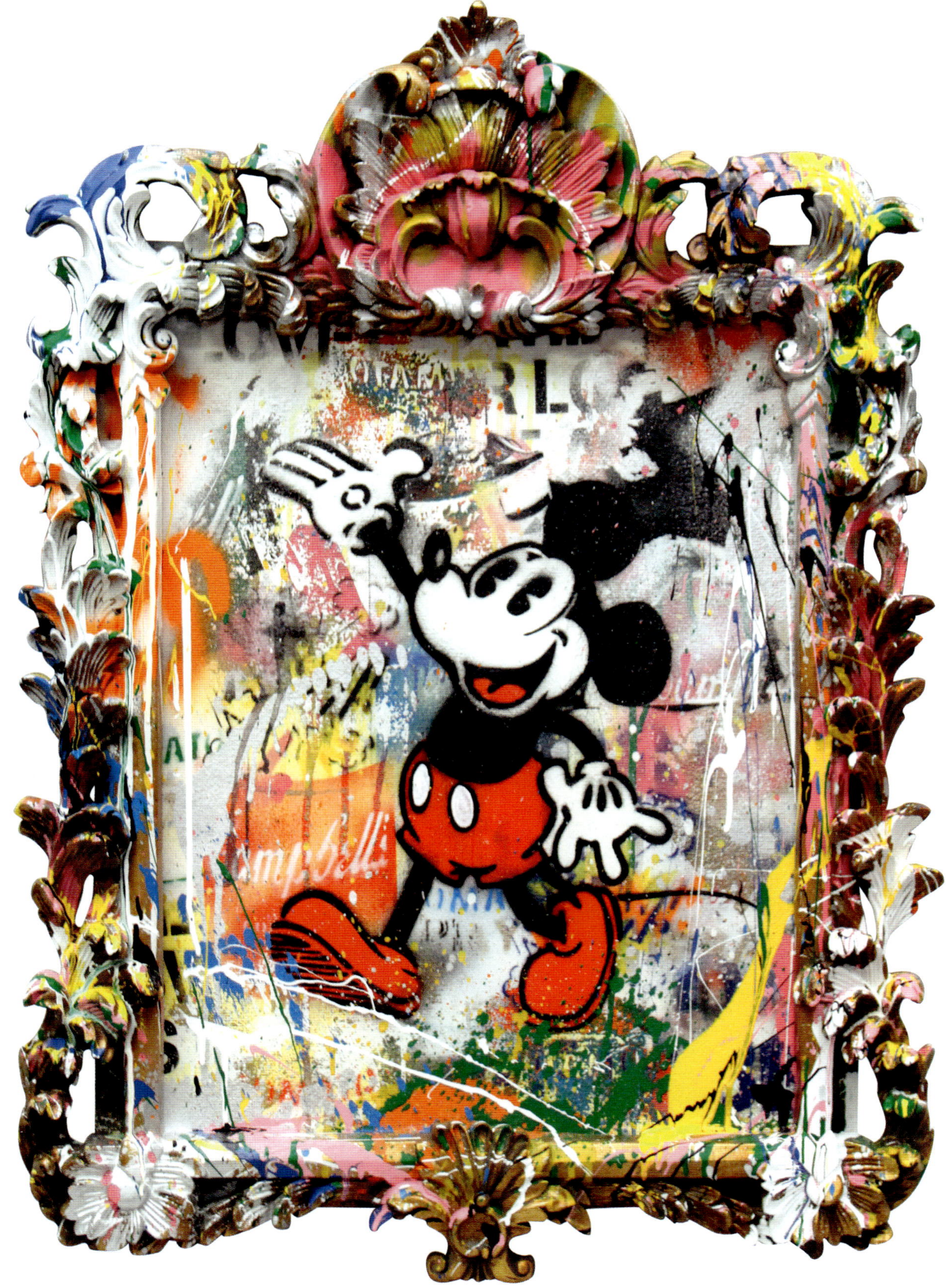

page 86
Heart Dog
30" x 22"
Silkscreen
and mixed
media on
paper

page 87
**You Look
Beautiful**
32" x 32"
Silkscreen
edition print

pages 88–89
Broadway
28" x 40"
Silkscreen
and mixed
media on
paper

opposite
Marilyn
22" x 22"
Silkscreen and
mixed media
on paper

Mickey
22" x 35"
Stencil and mixed
media on canvas

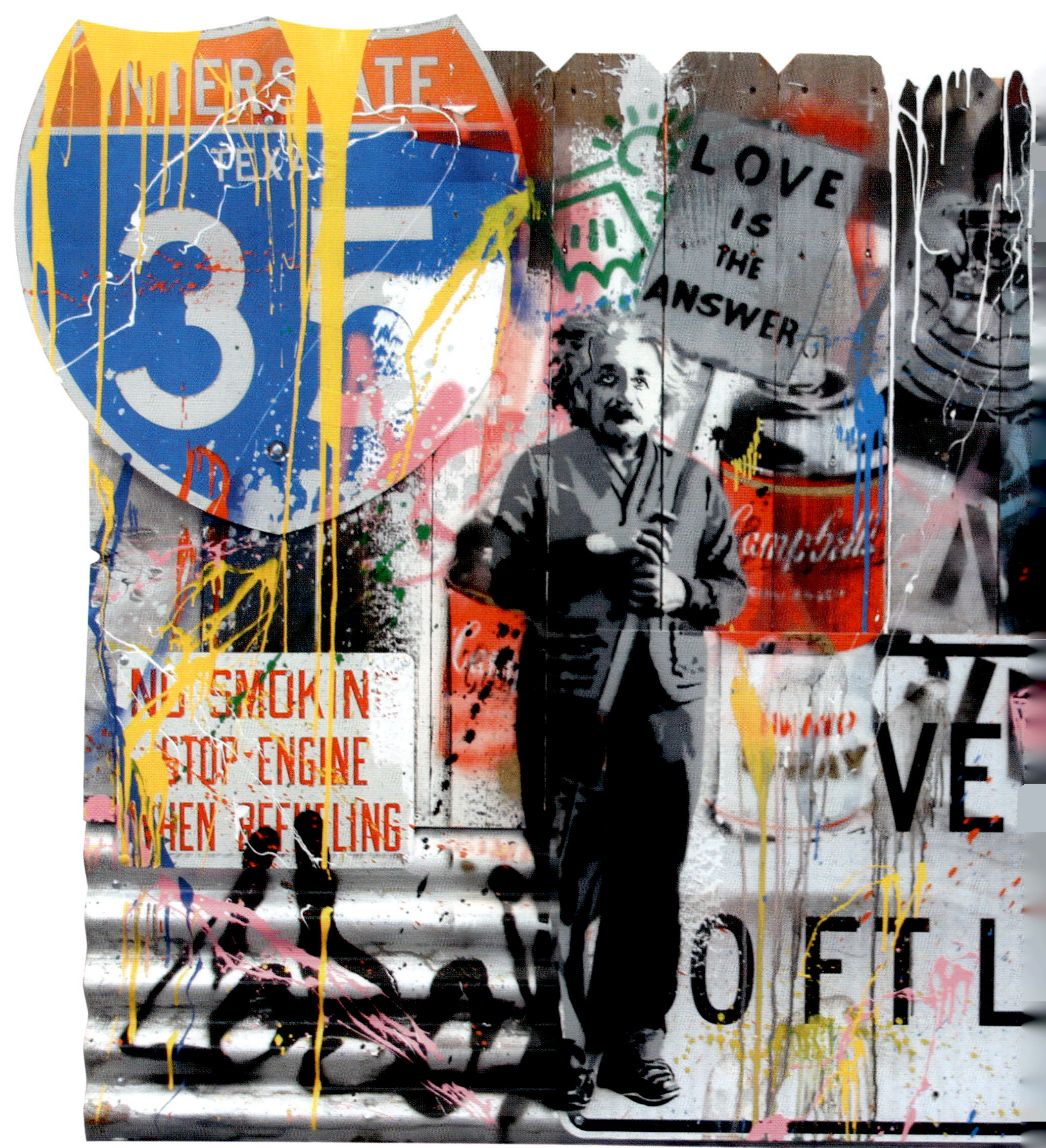
INTERSTATE
TEXAS
35
LOVE
IS
THE
ANSWER
NO SMOKIN
STOP ENGINE
WHEN REFUELING
Campbell's
VE
OFL

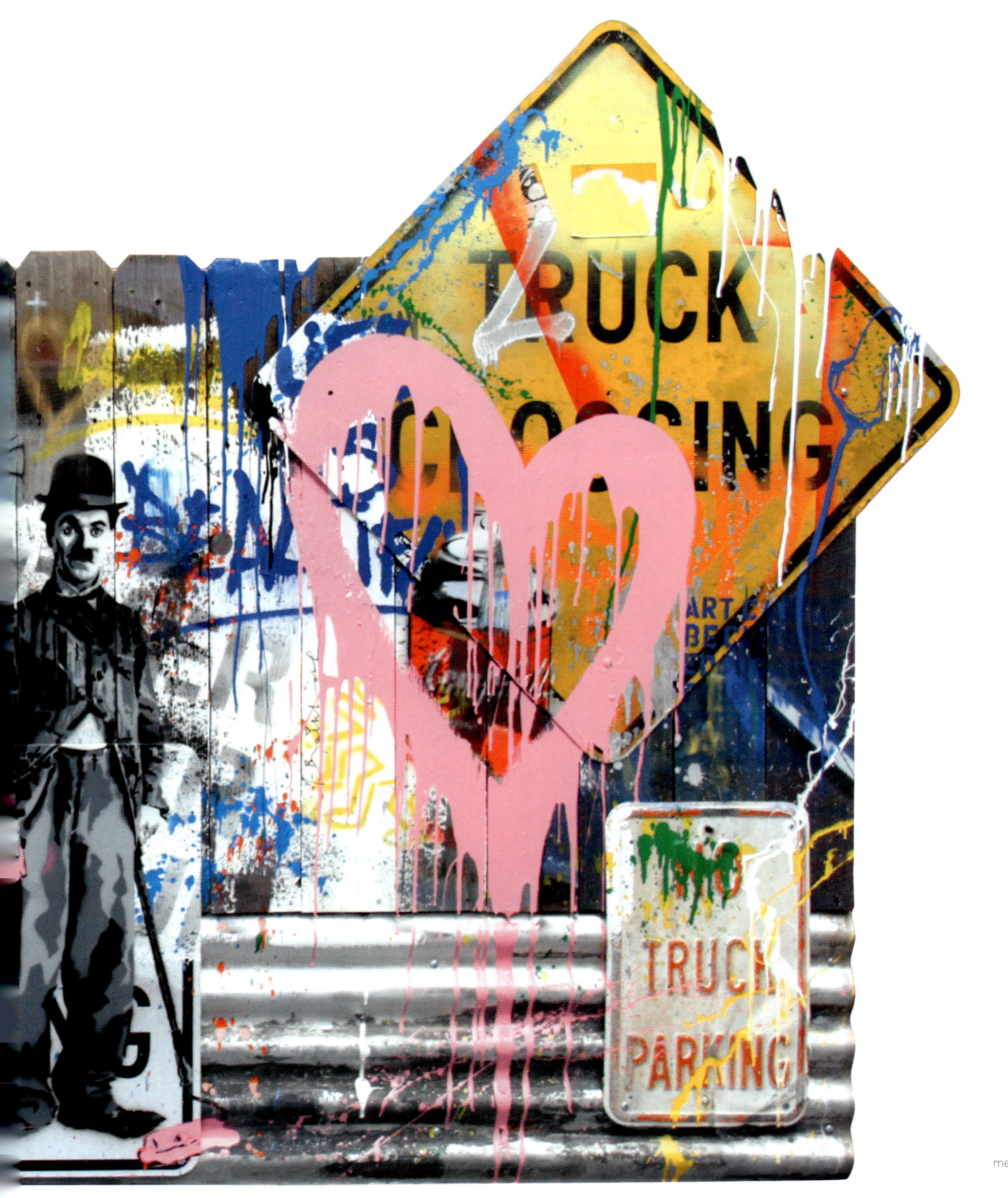

Juxtapose
64" x 106"
Stencil and mixed
media on metal and wood

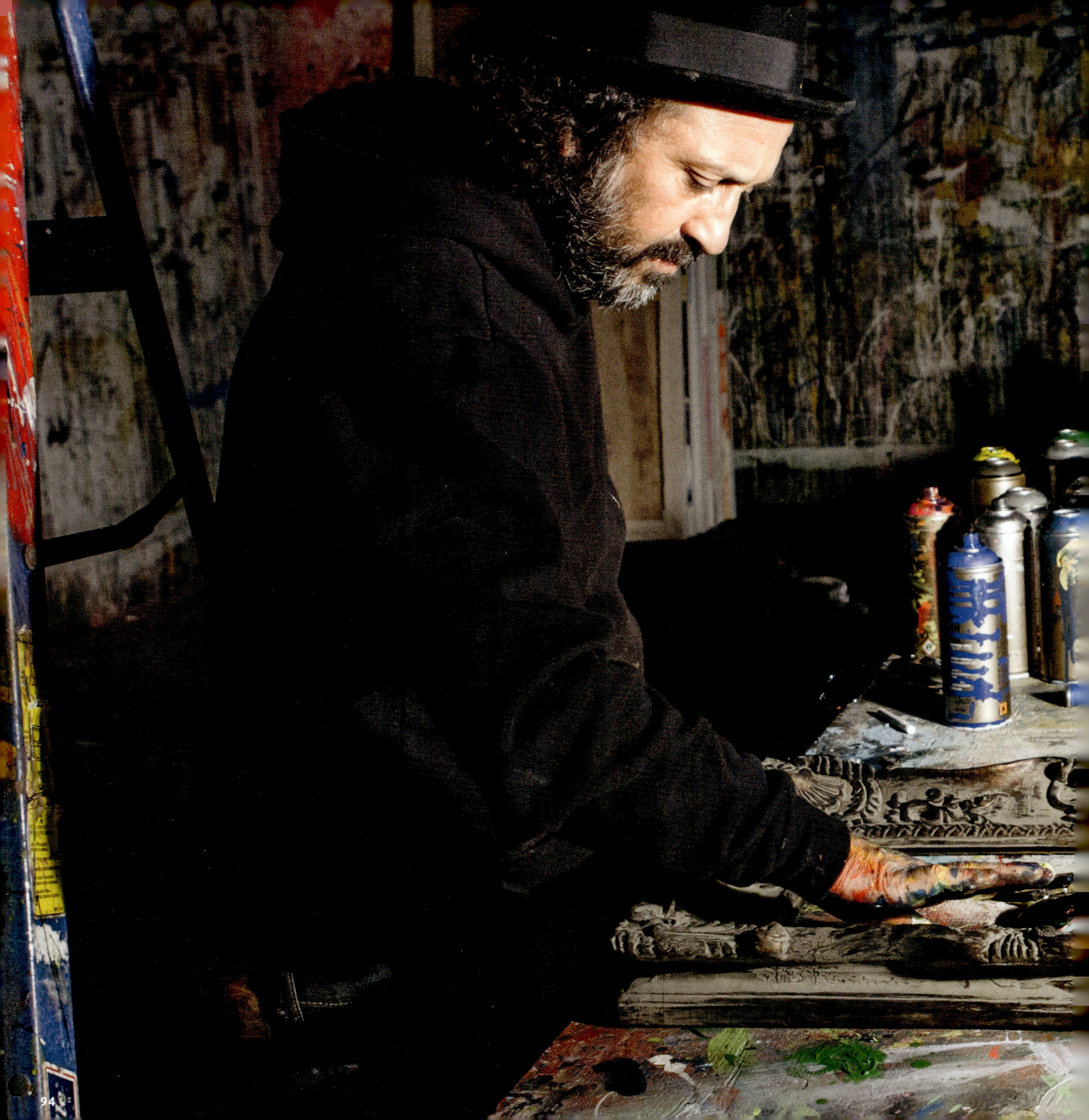

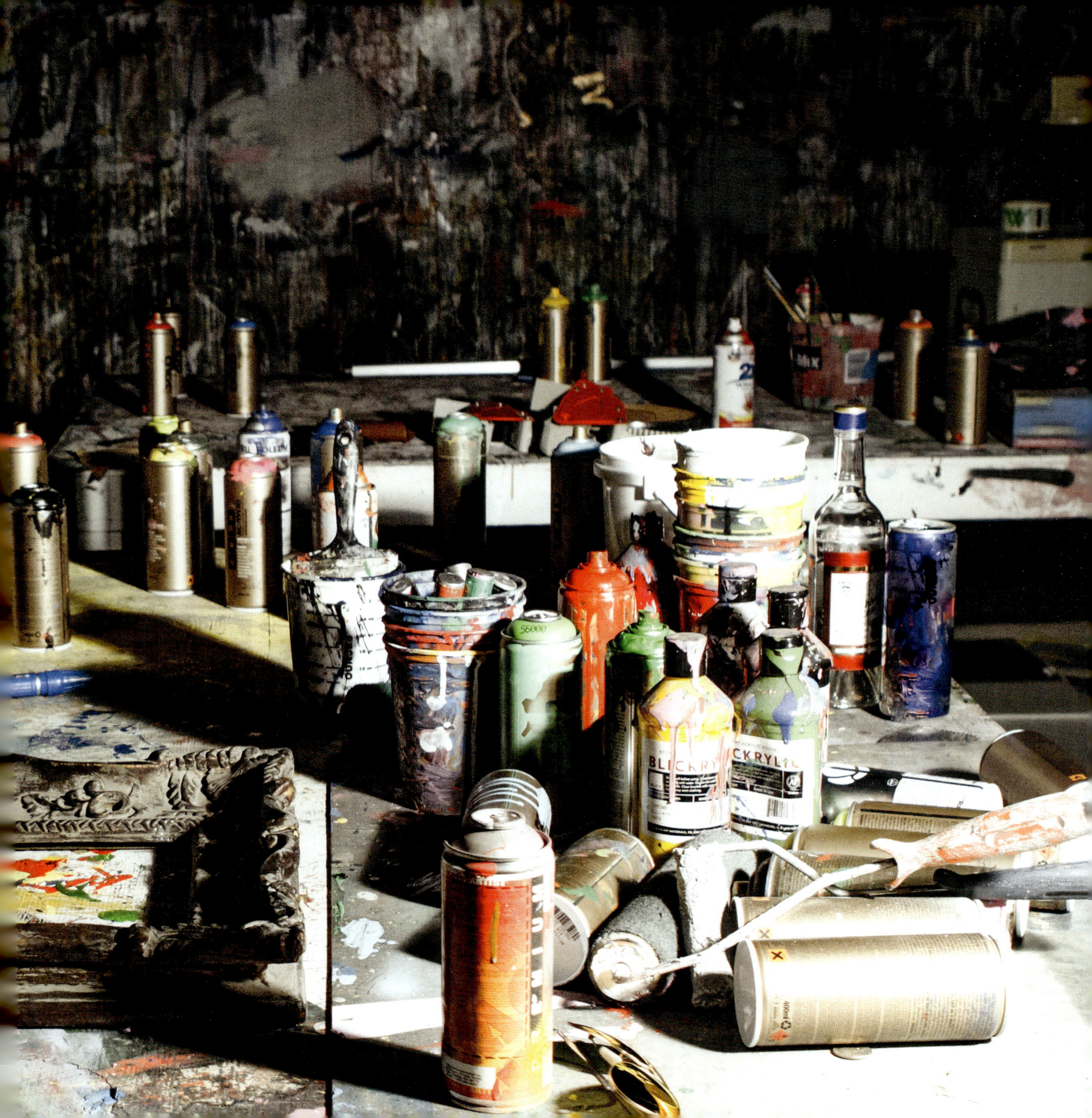

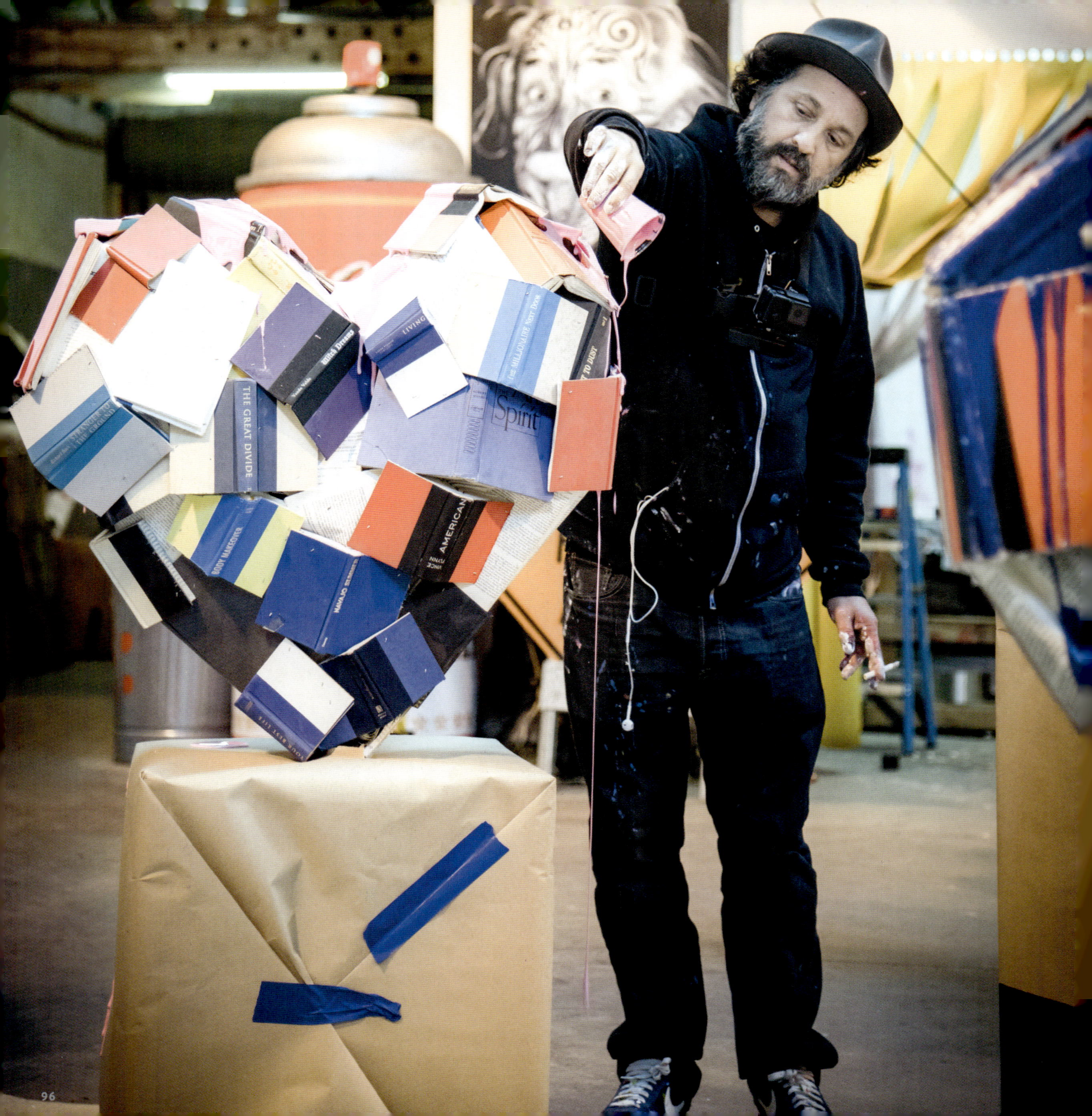

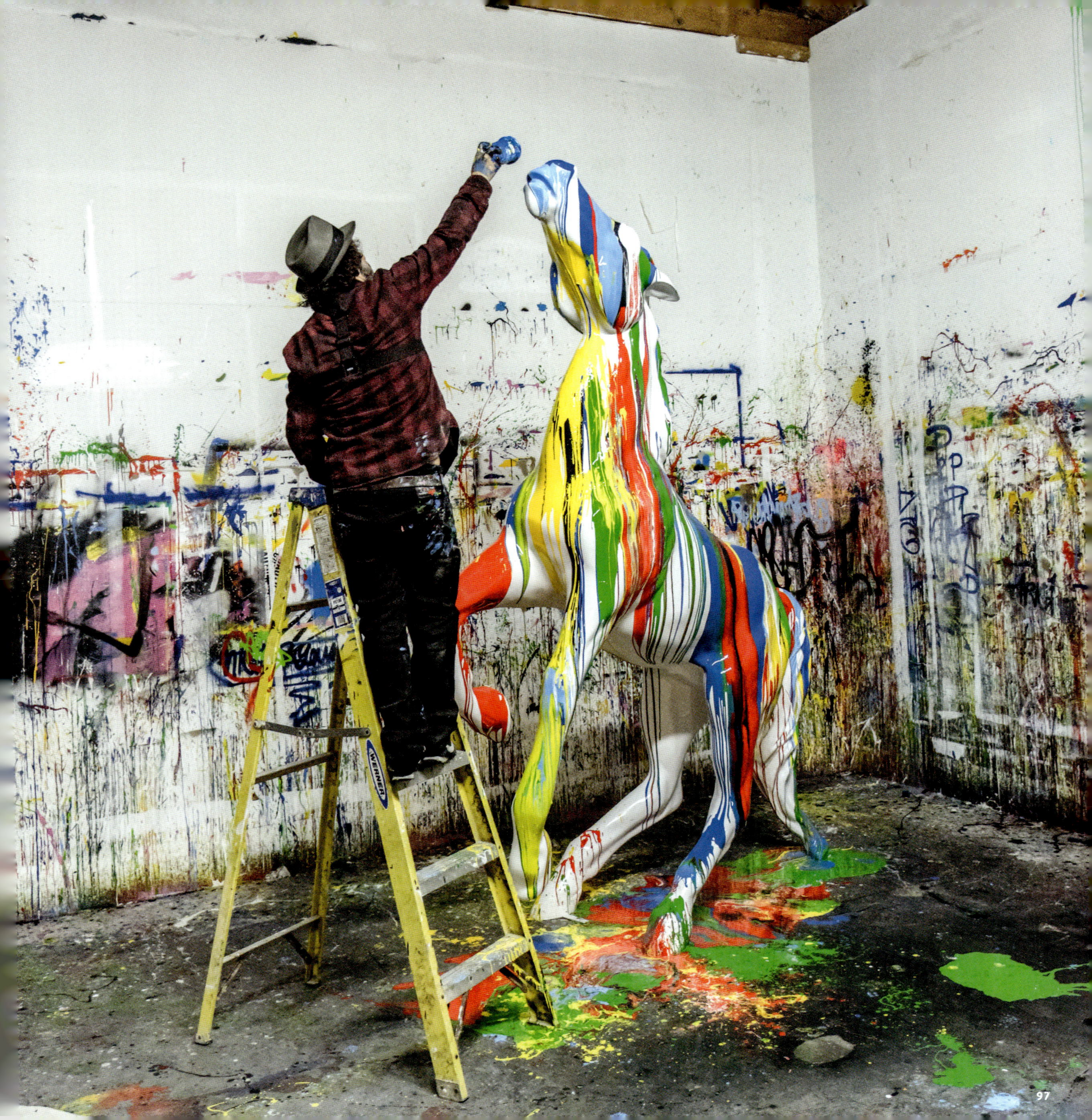

Tire sculptures

Mr. Brainwash's desire to use tires in art came when he learned they cannot be recycled easily. He wanted to reclaim this waste in a way that would positively affect the world. Works of art created with tires, such as those shown here, are not only timeless, but literally last forever.

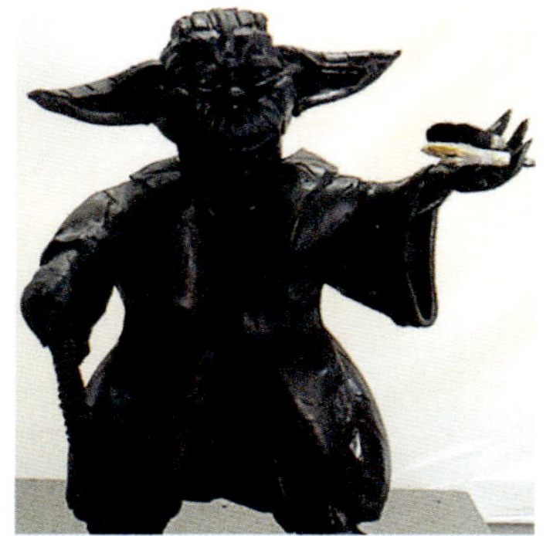
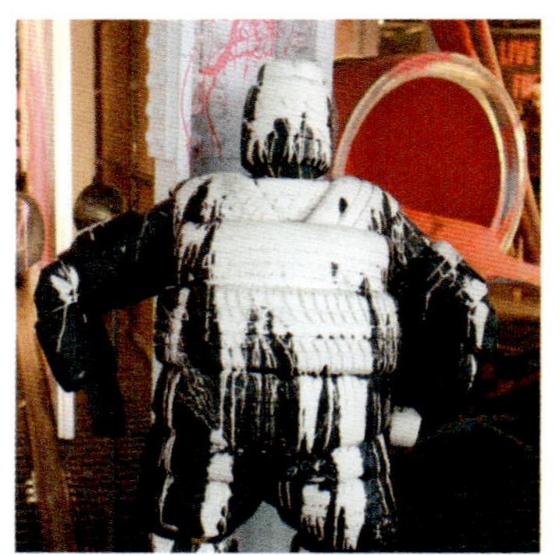
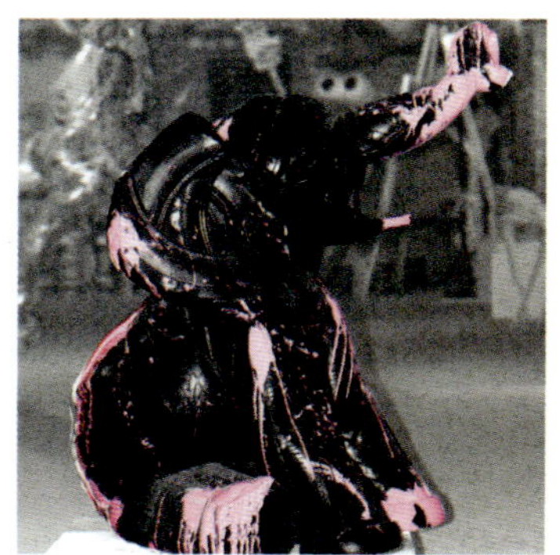
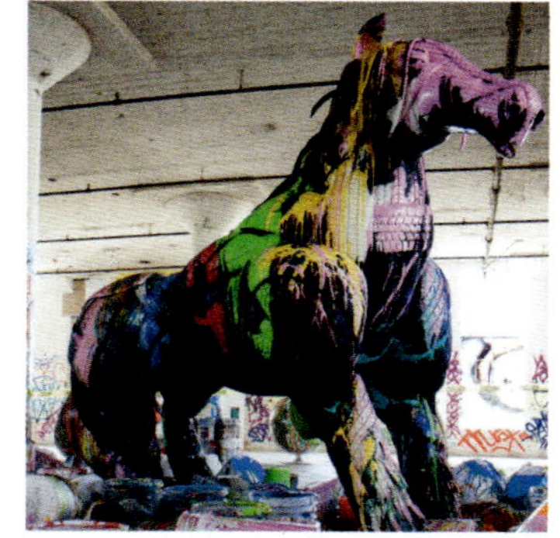
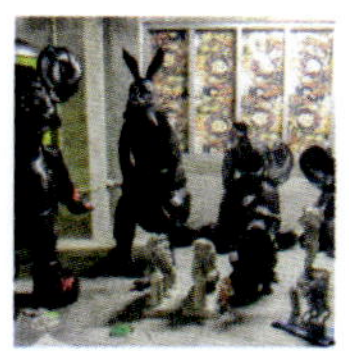
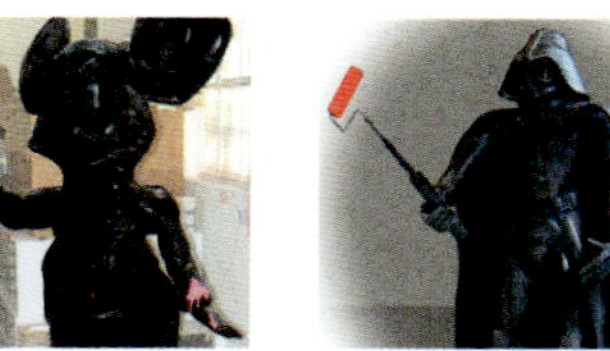
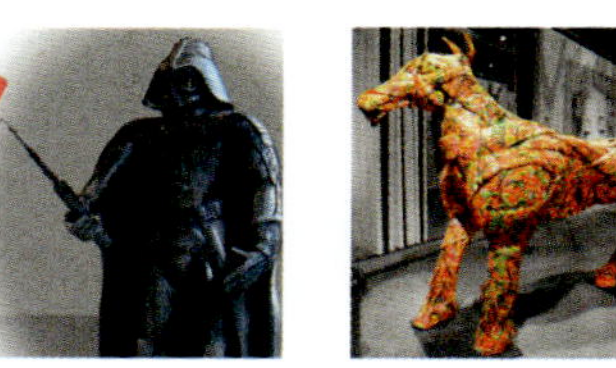
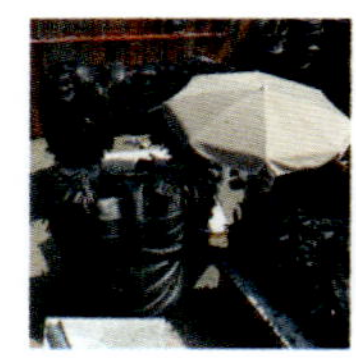
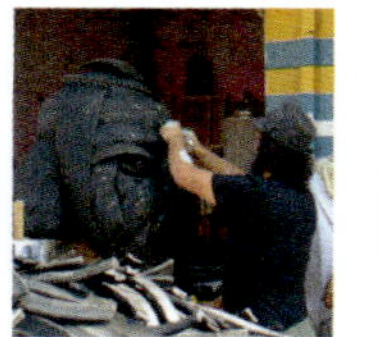
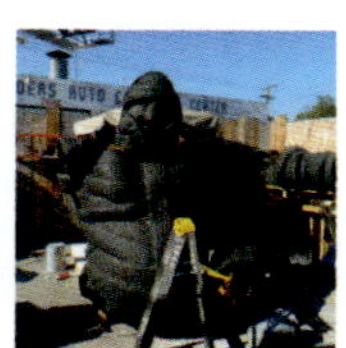
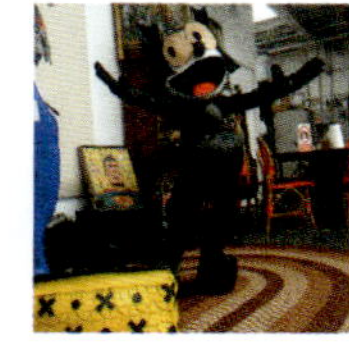
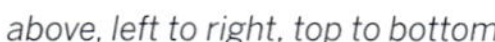

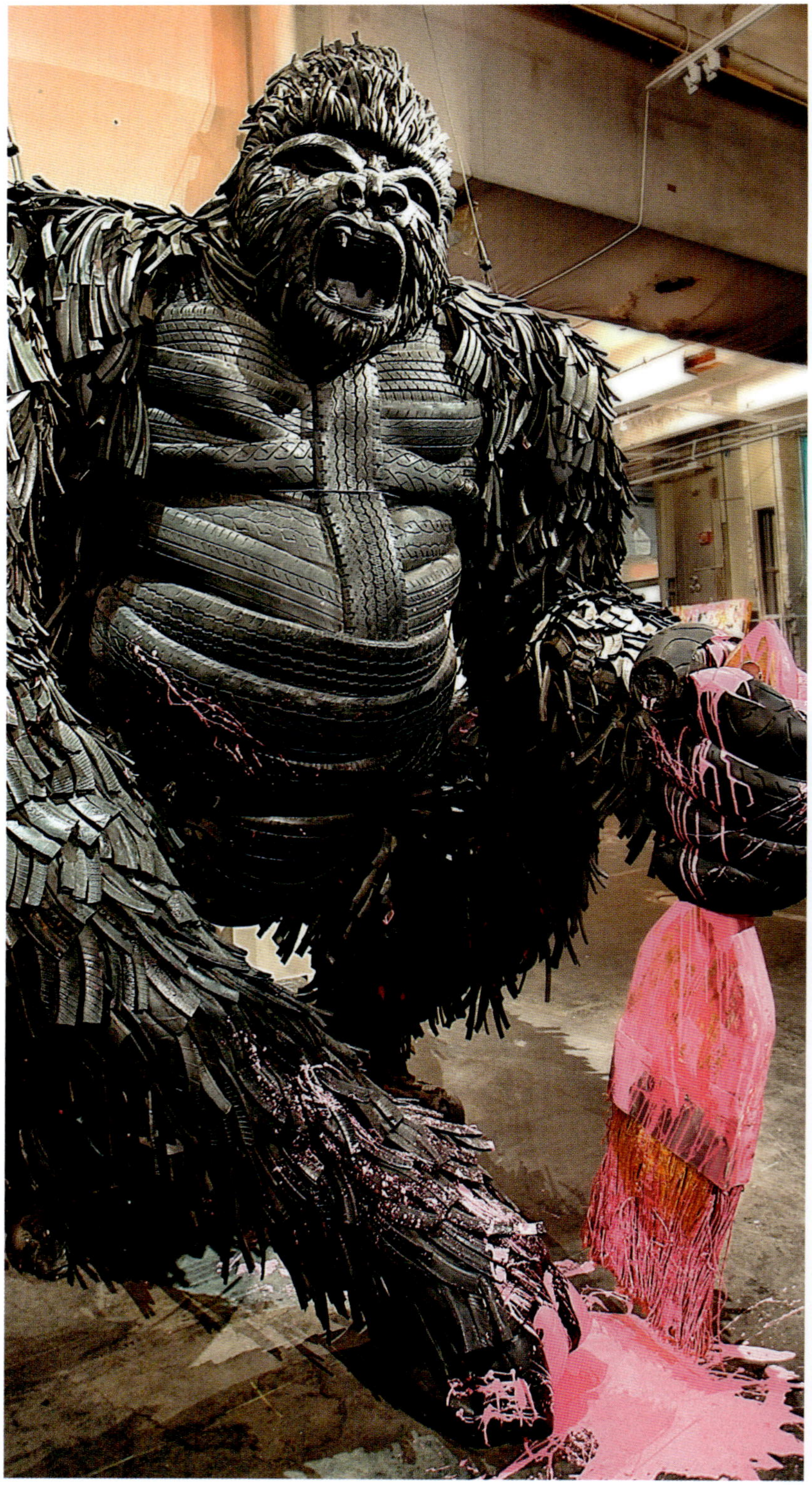

above, left to right, top to bottom

Yoda
58" x 48" x 36"
Tire, wood, and acrylic paint

Michelin Man
72" x 25" x 25"
Tire, wood, and acrylic paint

Elephant
102" x 80" x 70"
Tire, wood, and acrylic paint

Horse
96" x 120" x 48"
Tire, wood, and acrylic paint

King Kong
15 feet tall
Tire, wood, and acrylic paint

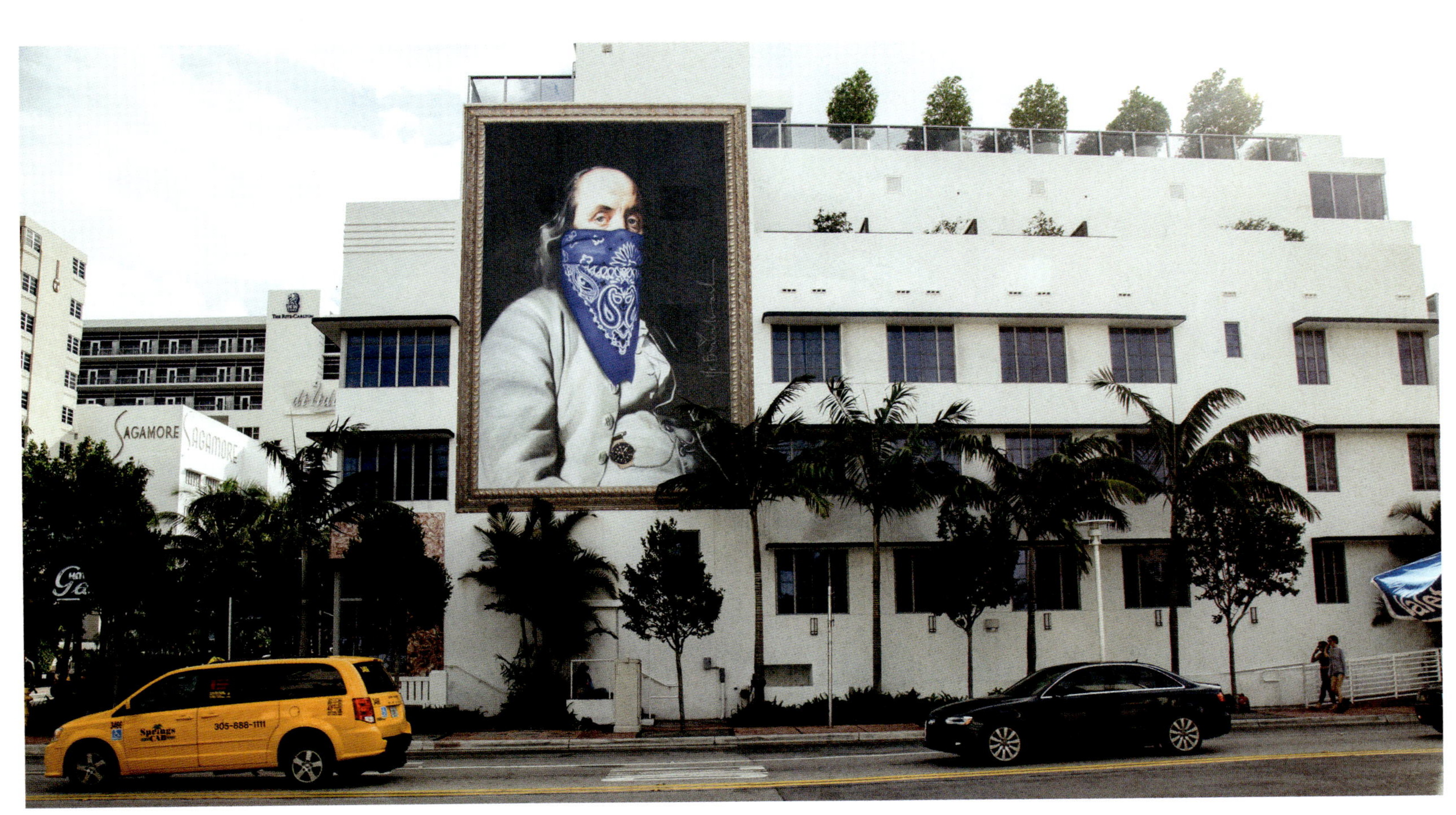

Art Basel Miami Beach

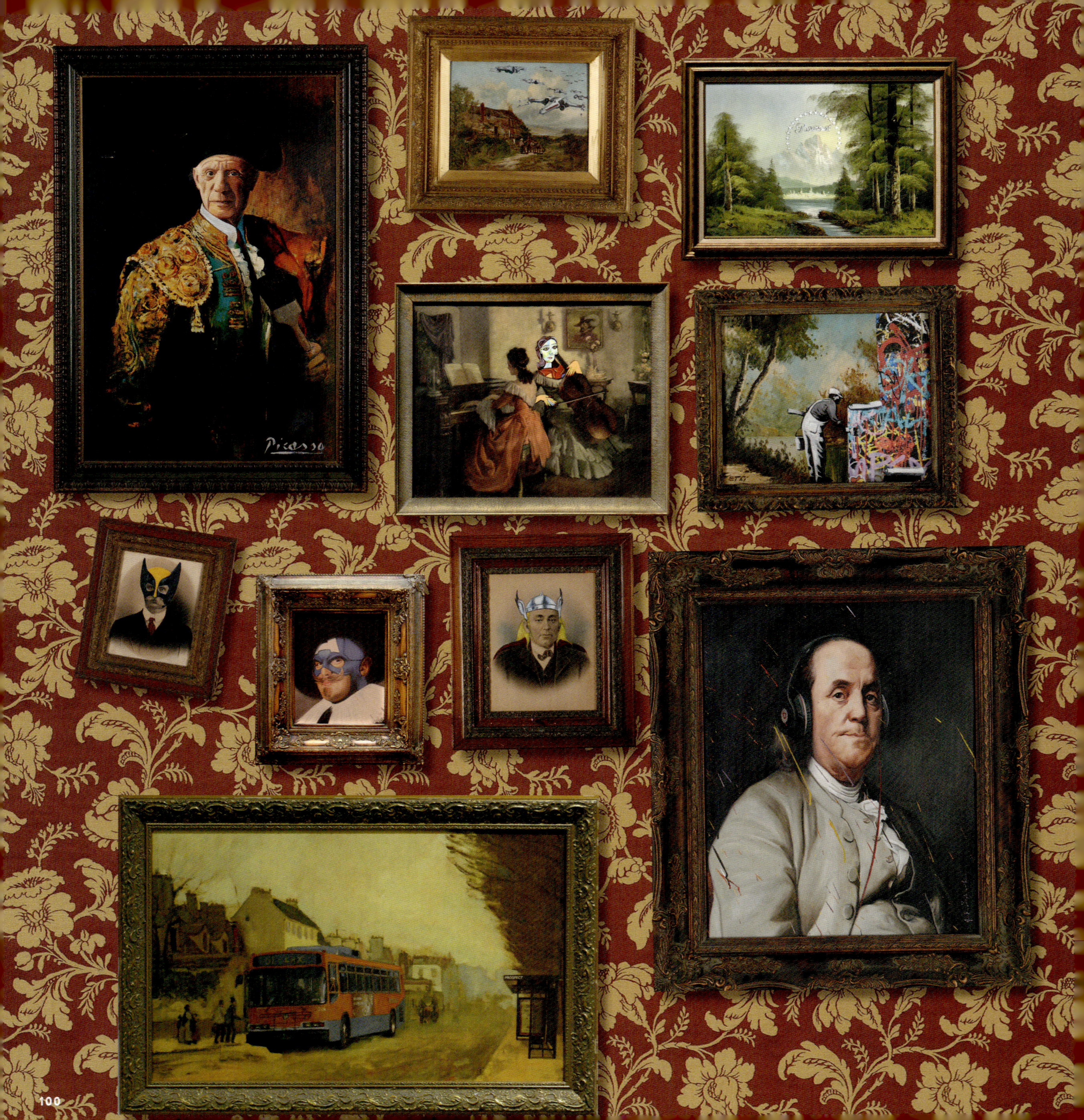

Picasso

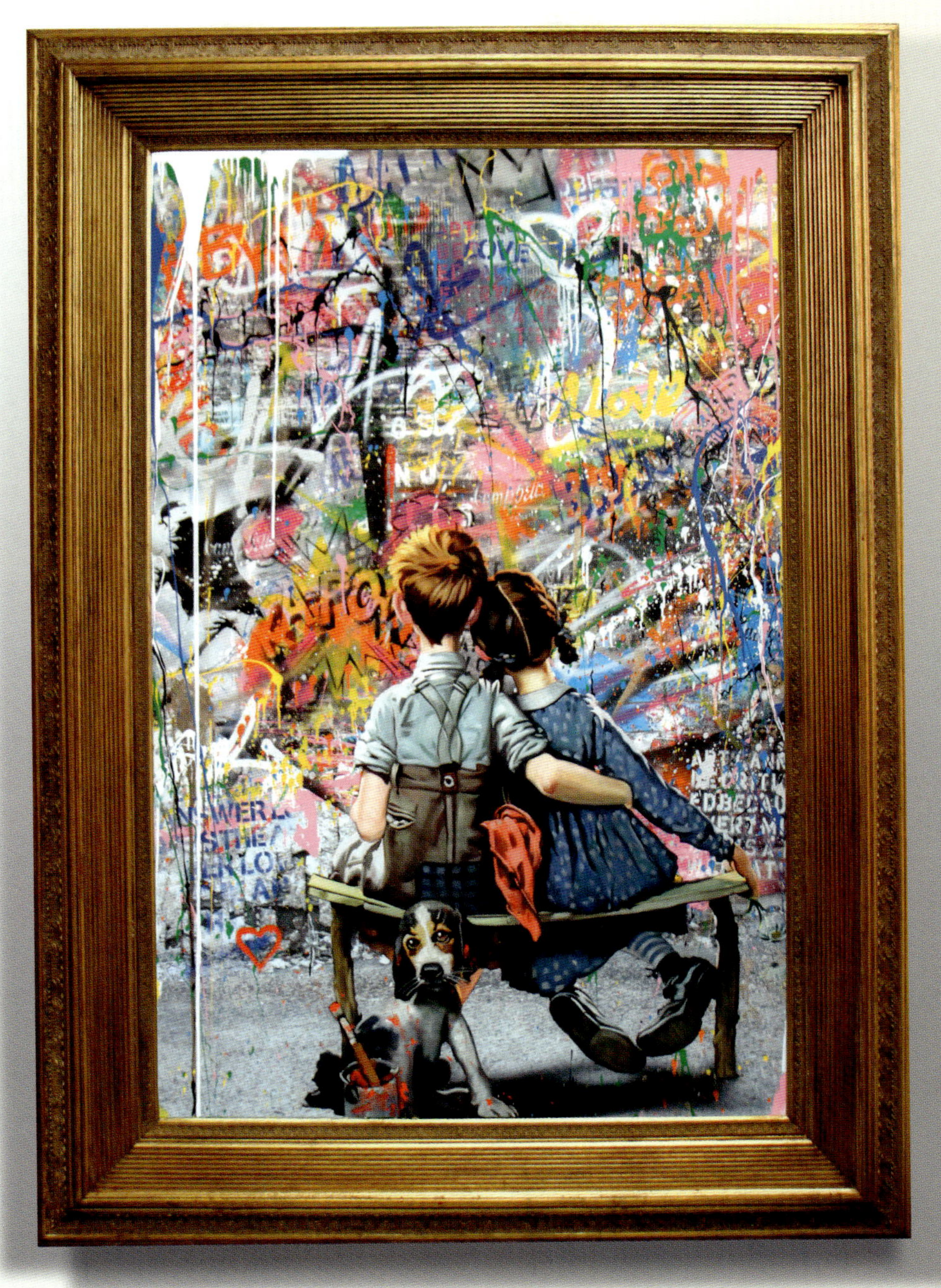

Untitled
90" x 66"
Oil paint on canvas

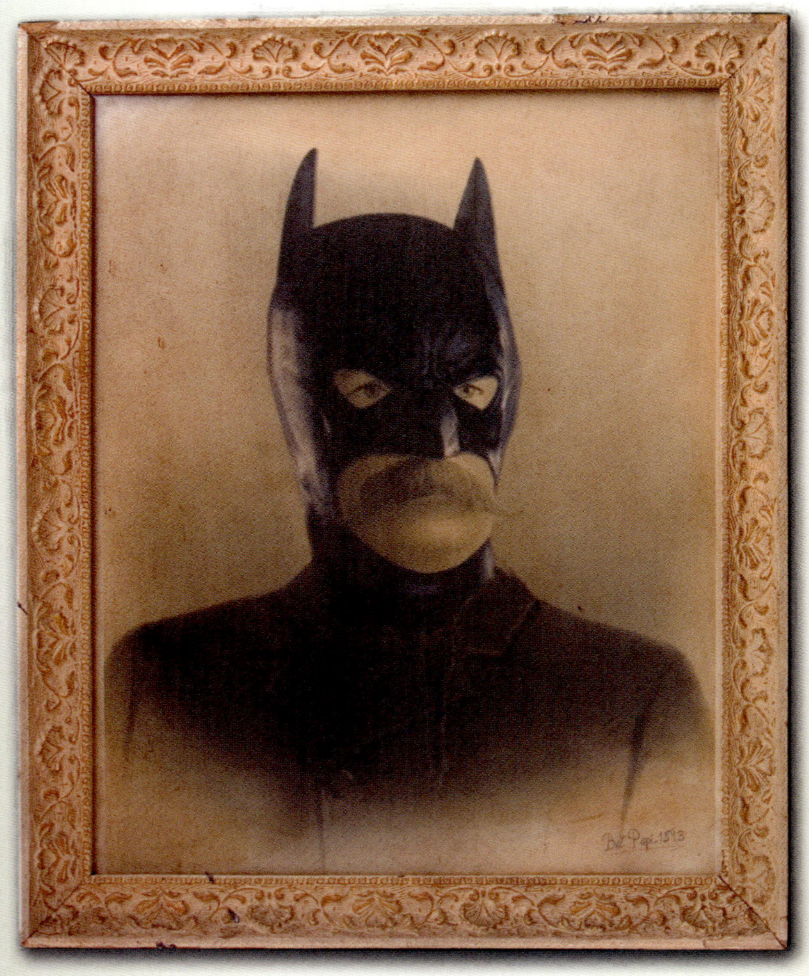

Bat Papi
25" x 21"
Oil paint on canvas

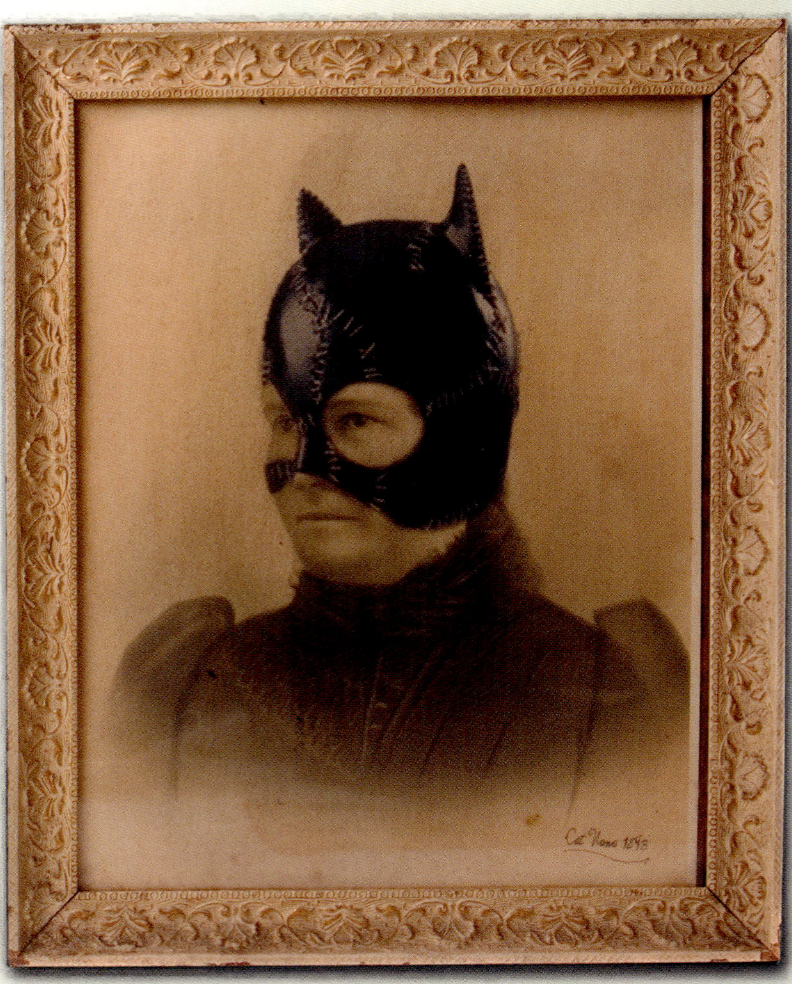

Cat Nana
25" x 21"
Oil paint on canvas

"IT SAYS BAT PAPI, 1893. IT'S BEFORE BATMAN.
IT'S BAT PAPI, THE GRANDFATHER OF BATMAN.
THAT'S WHERE IT STARTED."

MR. BRAINWASH, EXIT THROUGH THE GIFT SHOP

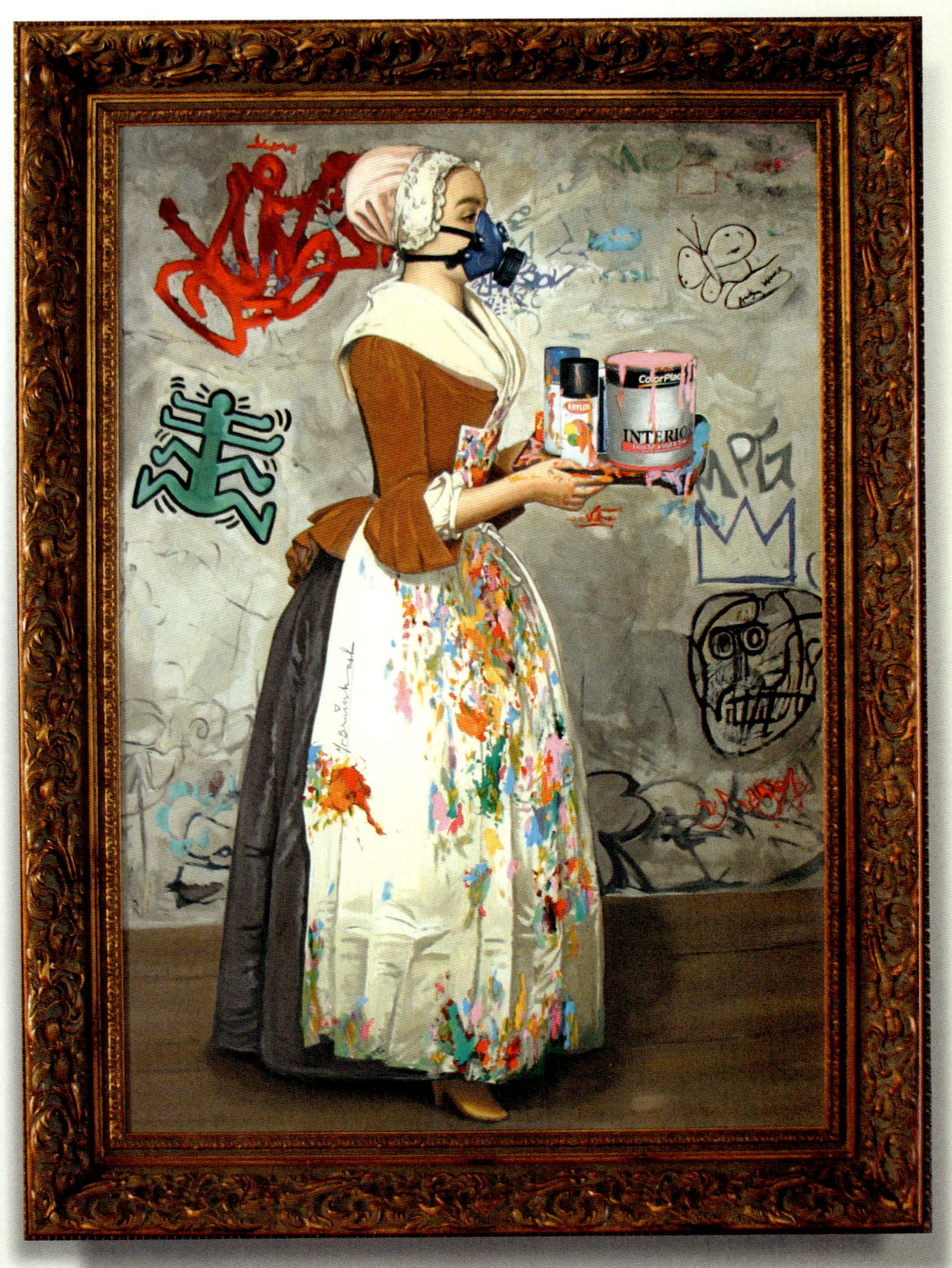

Chocolate Vandal
52" x 40"
Acrylic paint on canvas

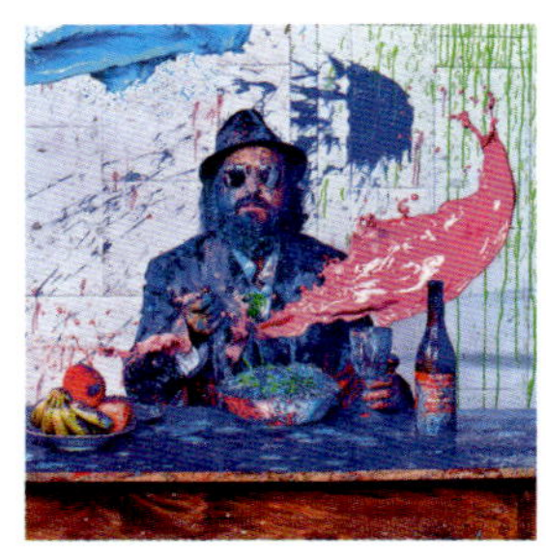
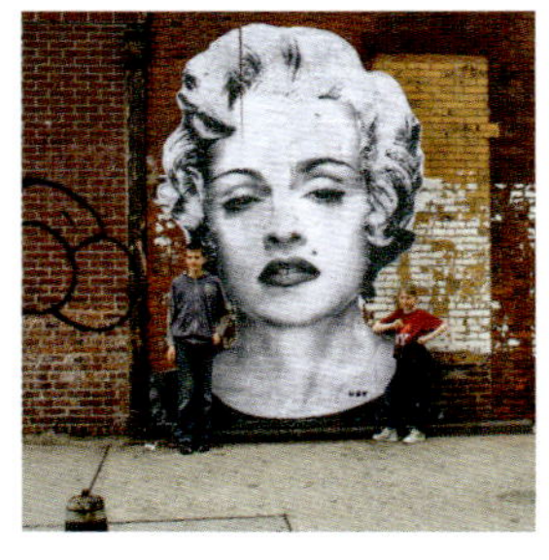
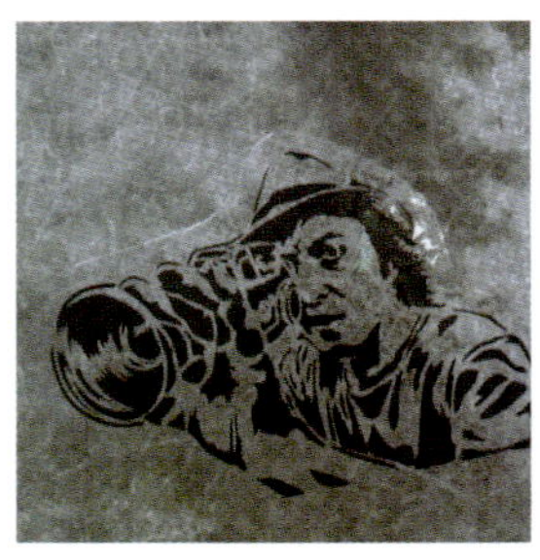

A Y THE ART
WITH YOU
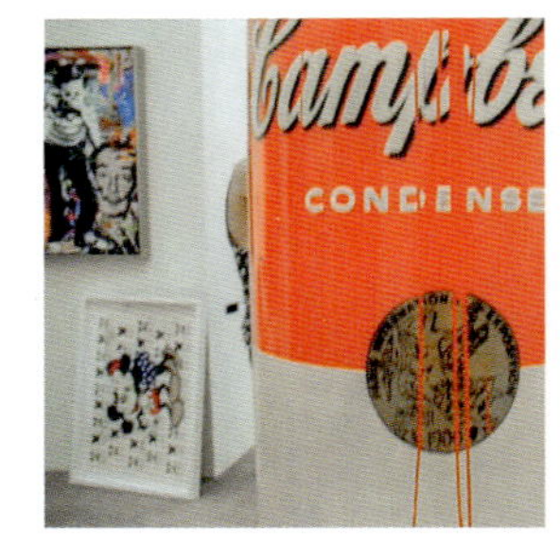
Campbell
CONDENSE
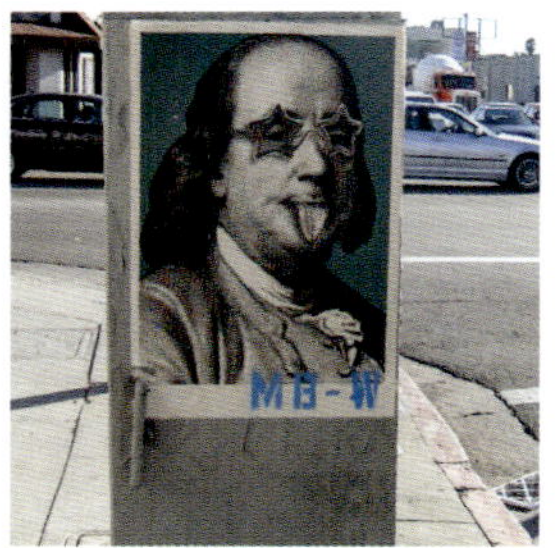
MB-W
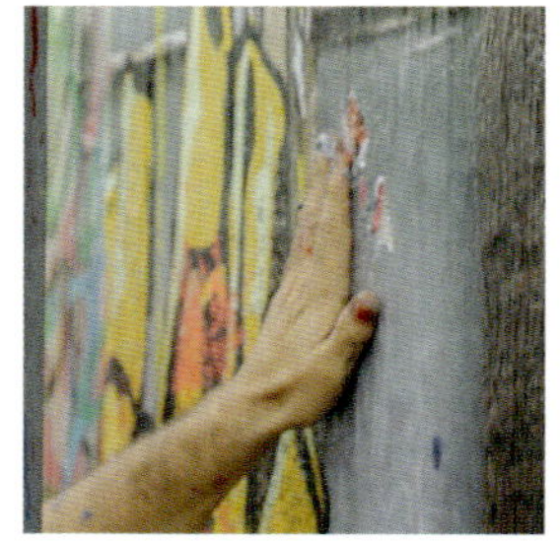
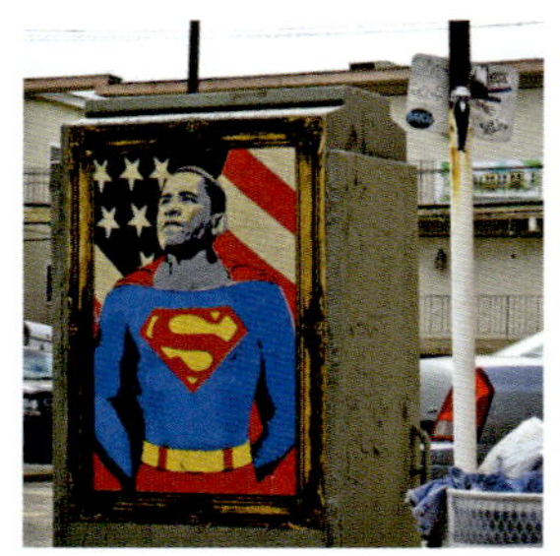
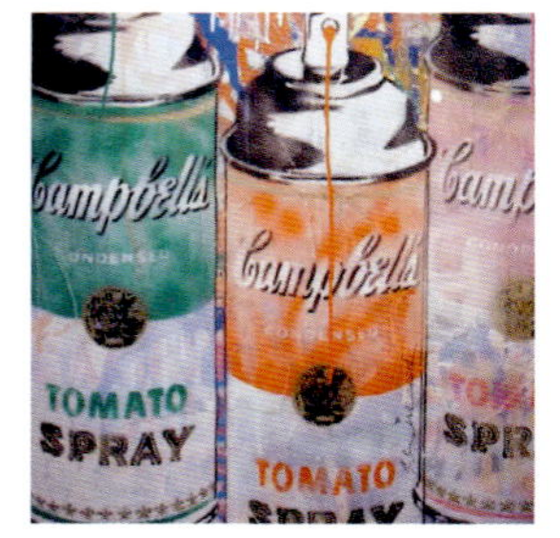
Campbells
Campbell
Cam
TOMATO
SPRAY
TOMATO
SPR
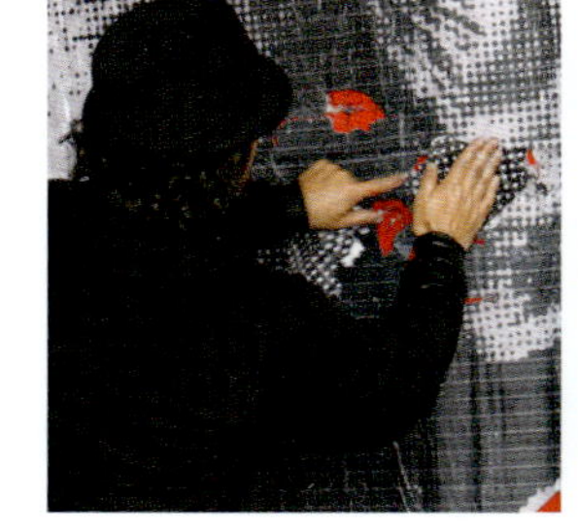
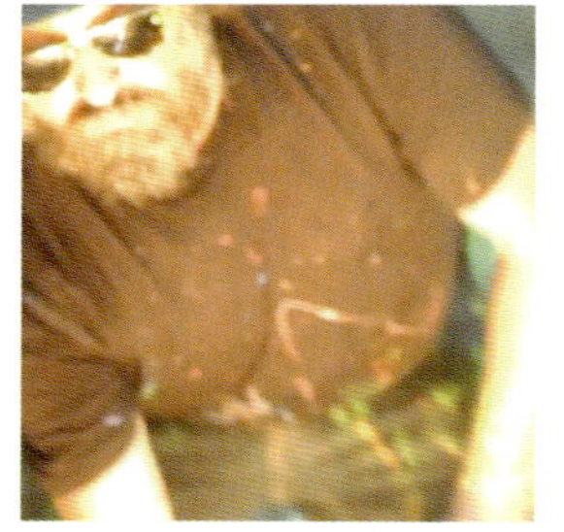
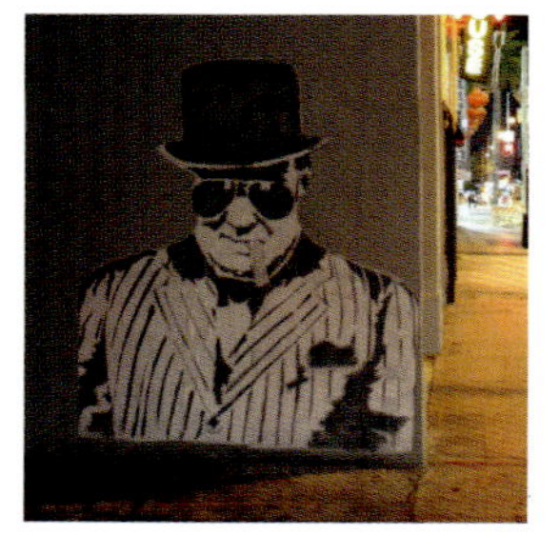
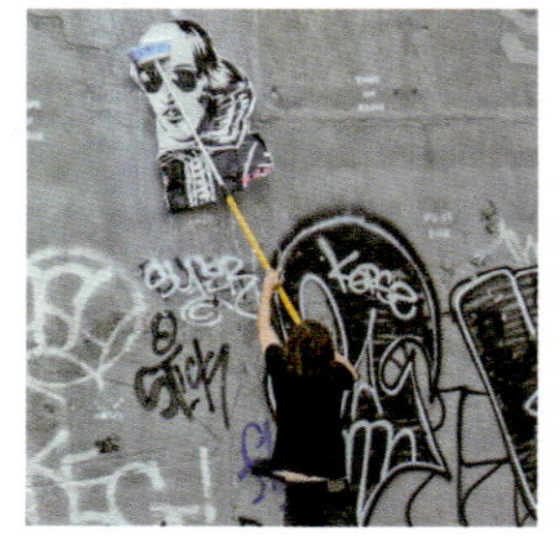
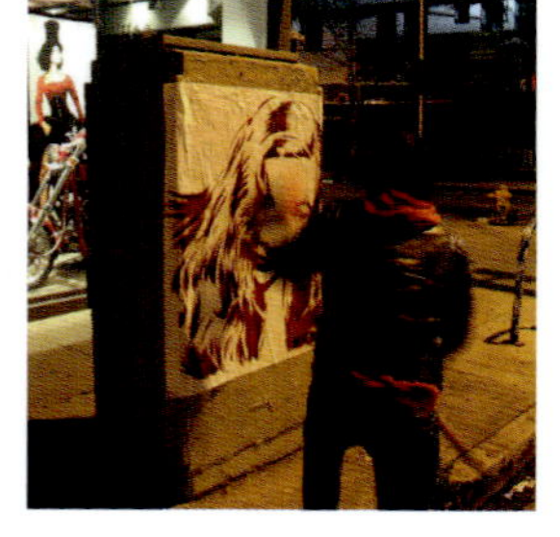
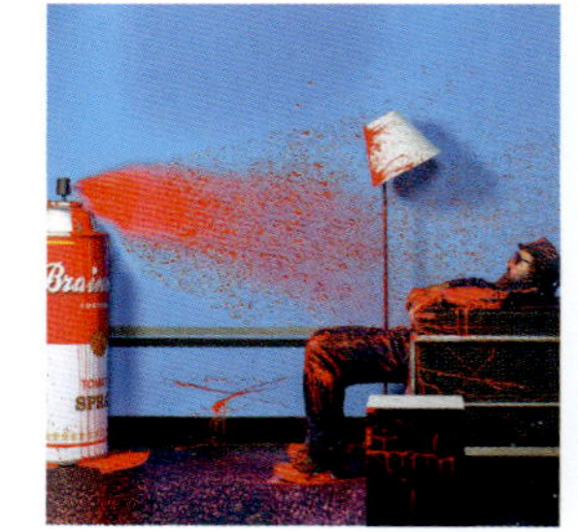
Bra
SPR
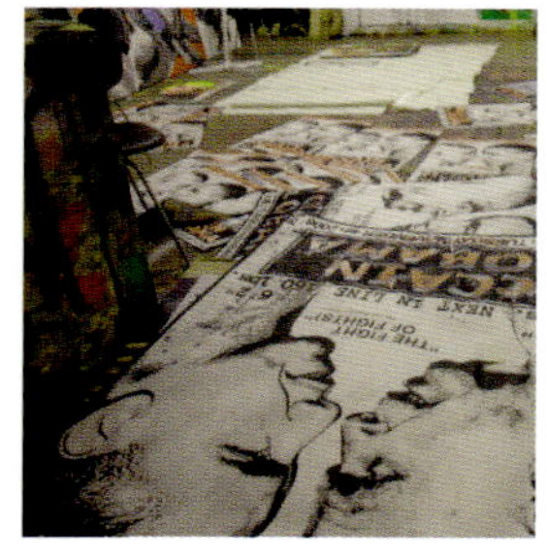
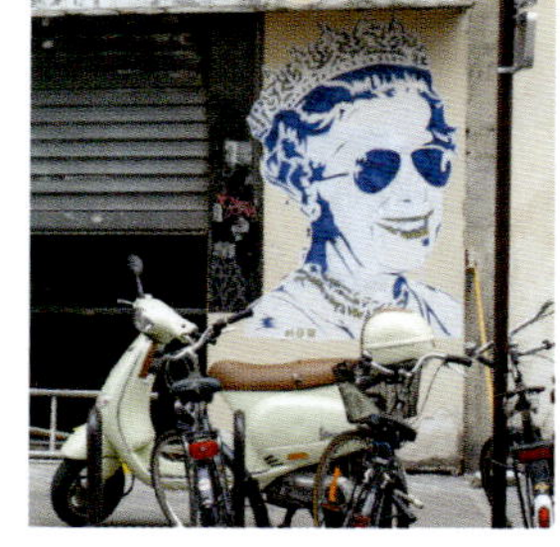
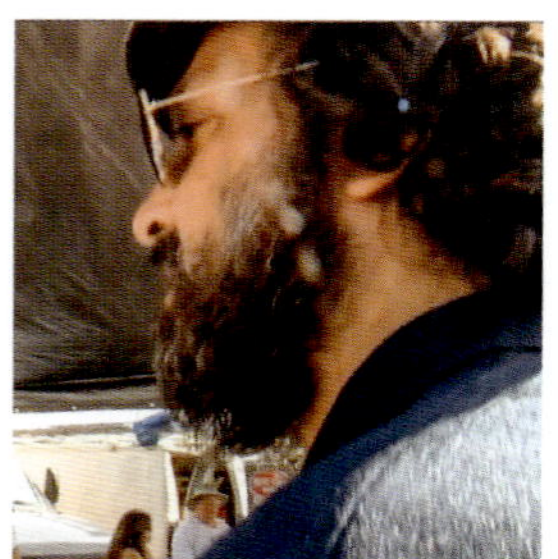
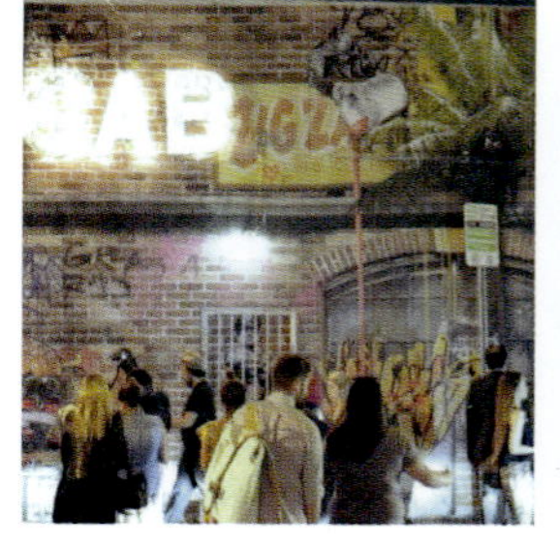
AB
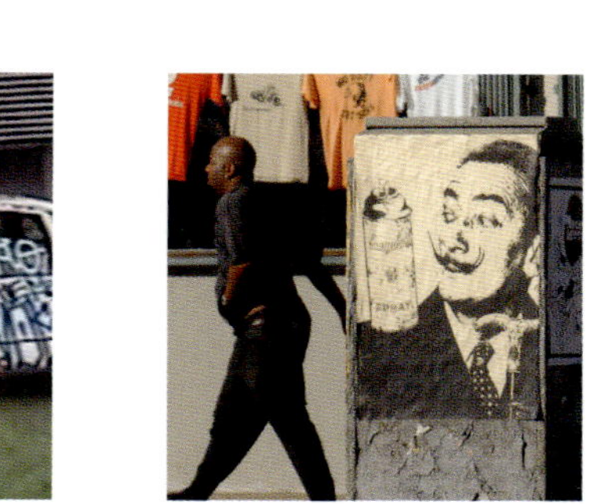
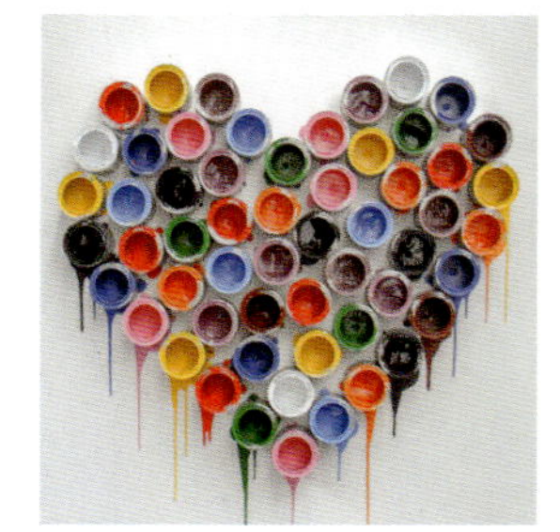
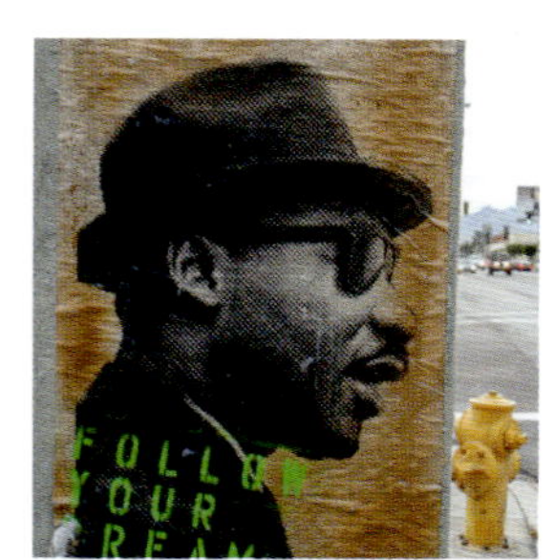
FOLLOW
YOUR
REAM
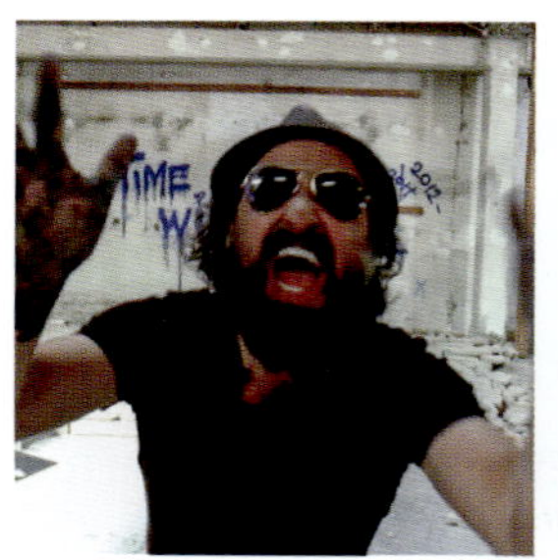

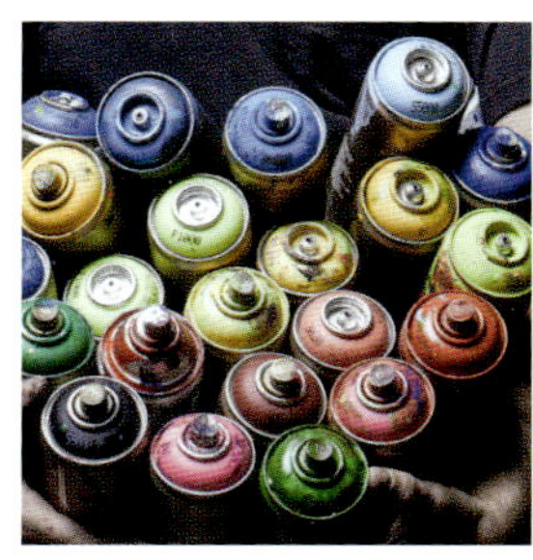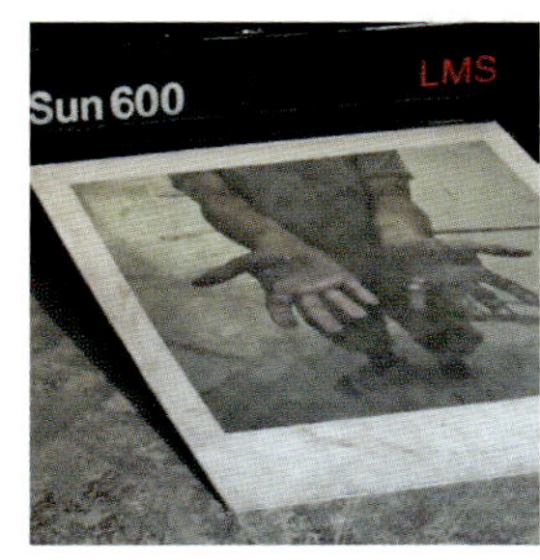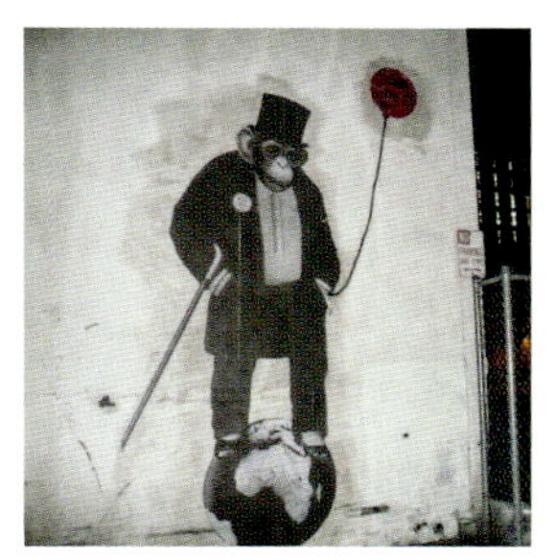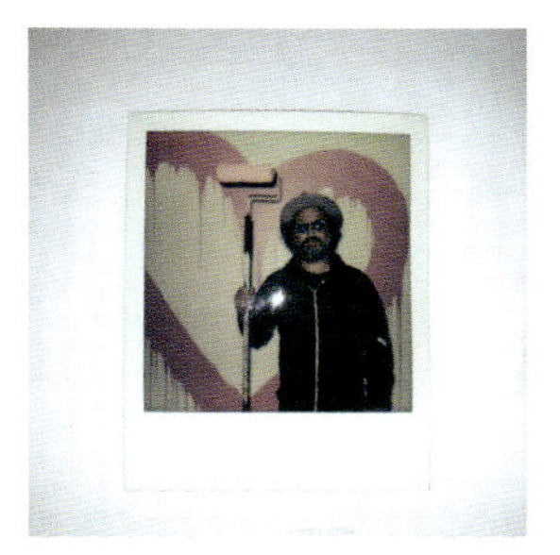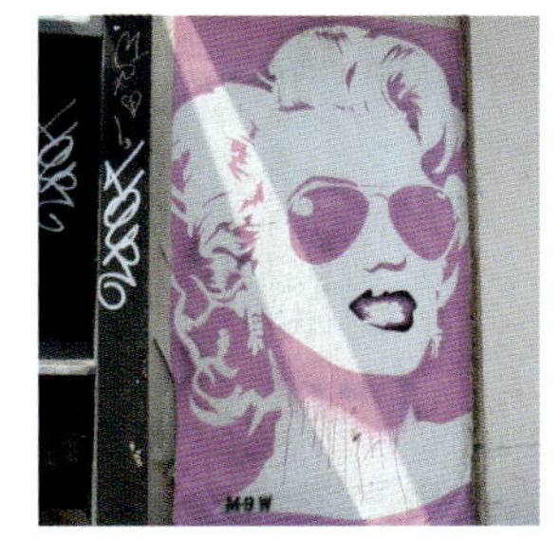
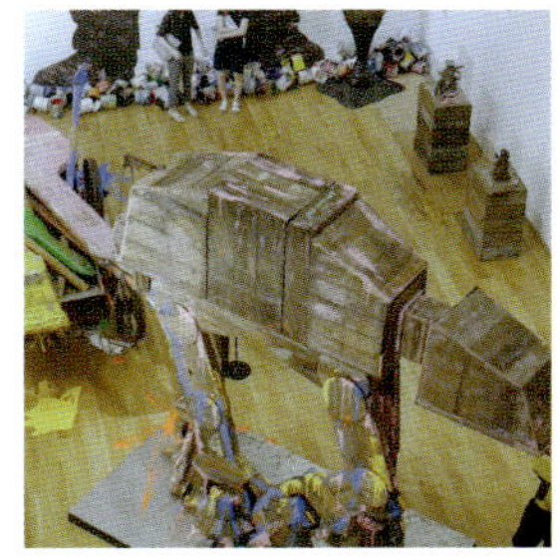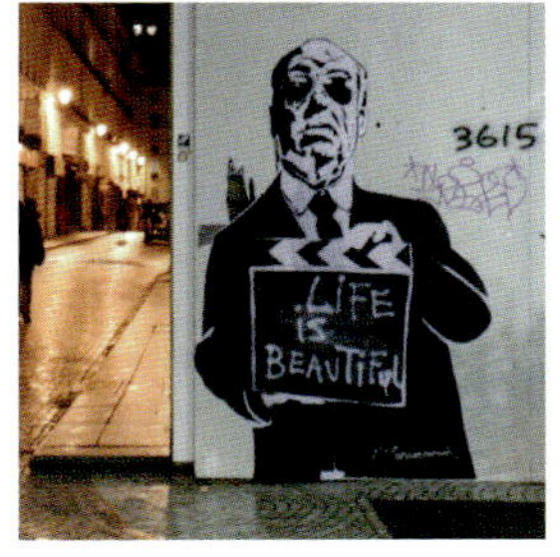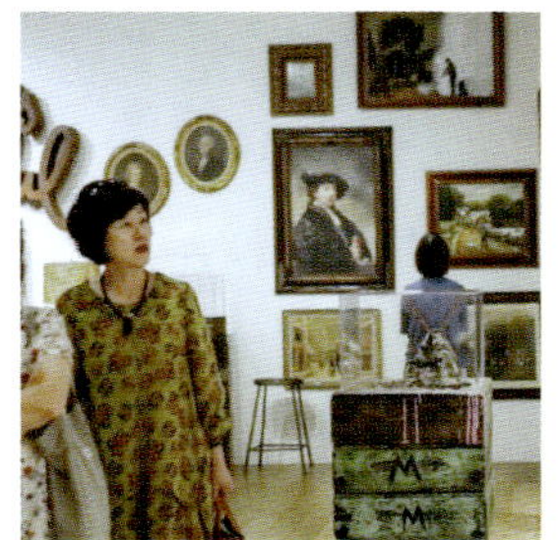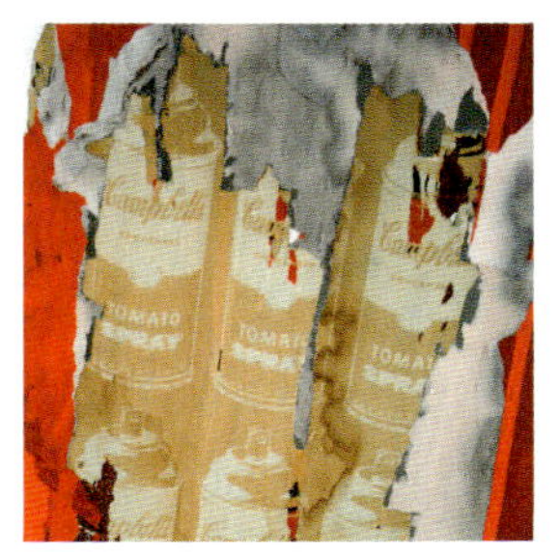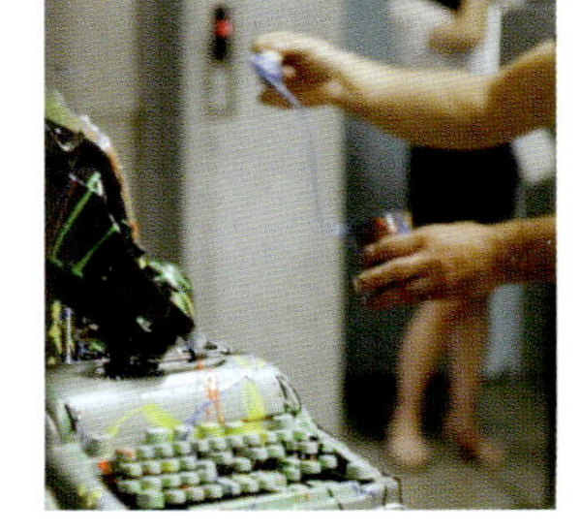
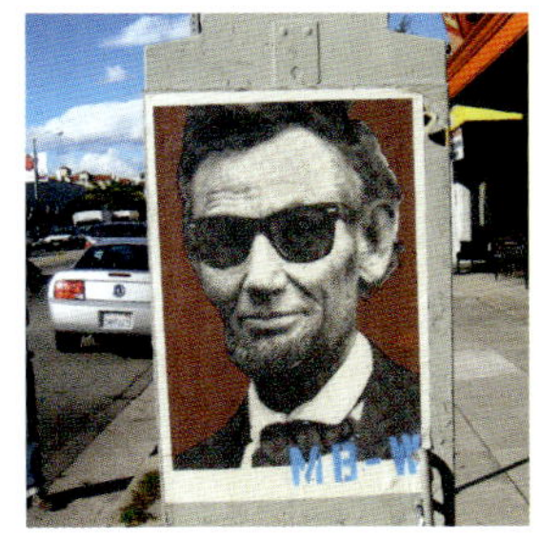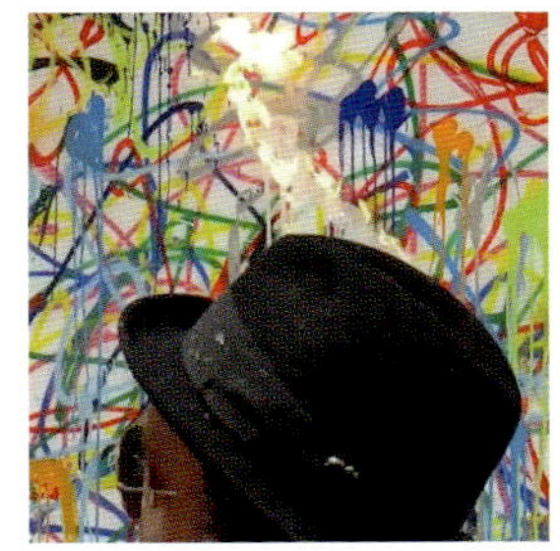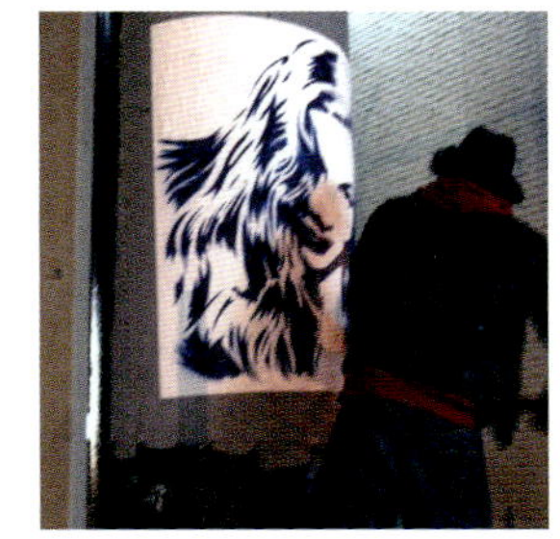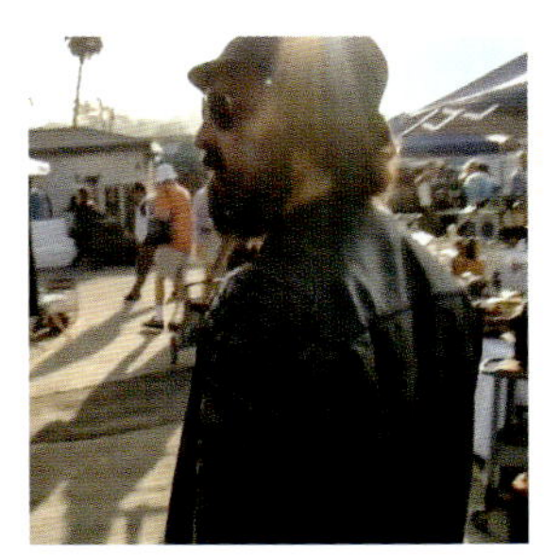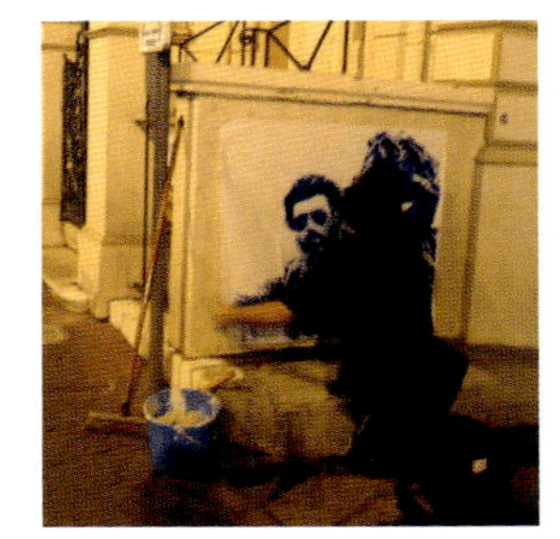
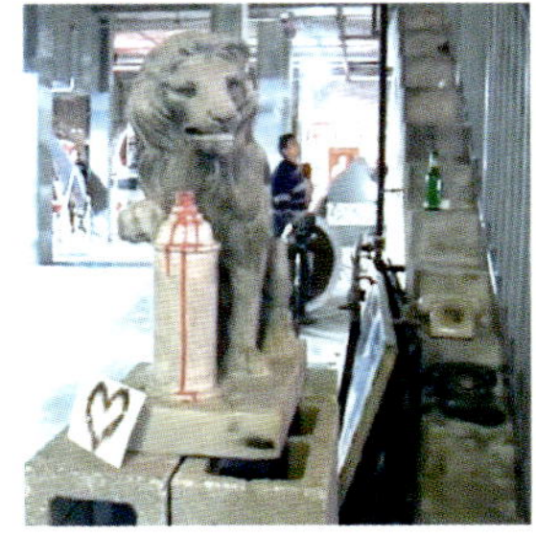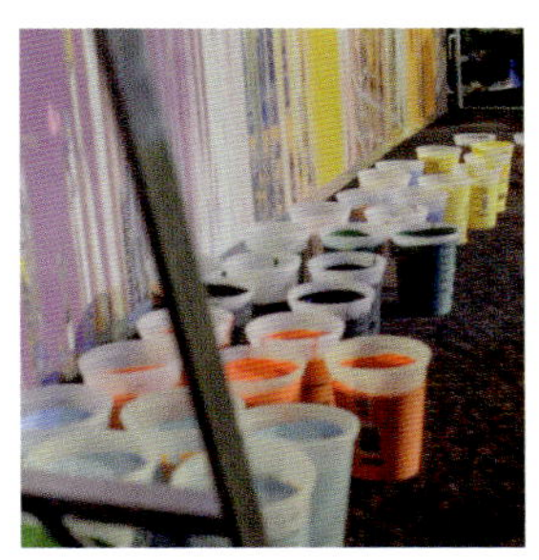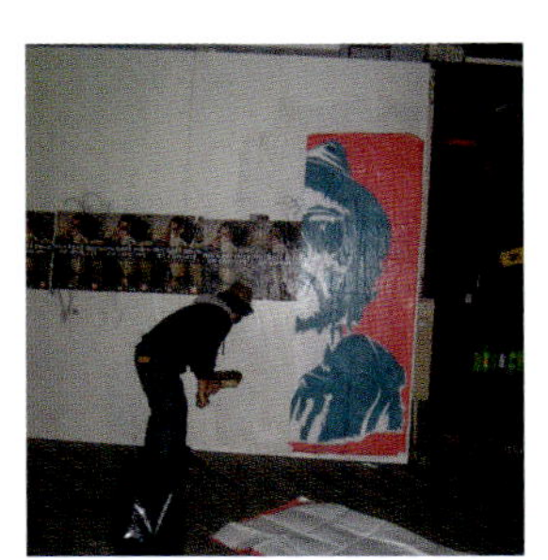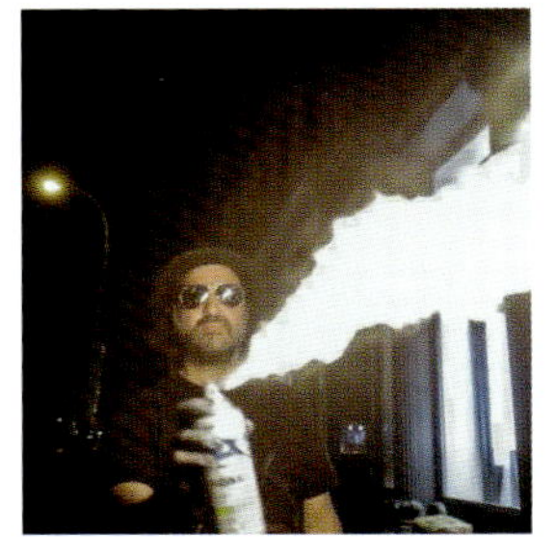
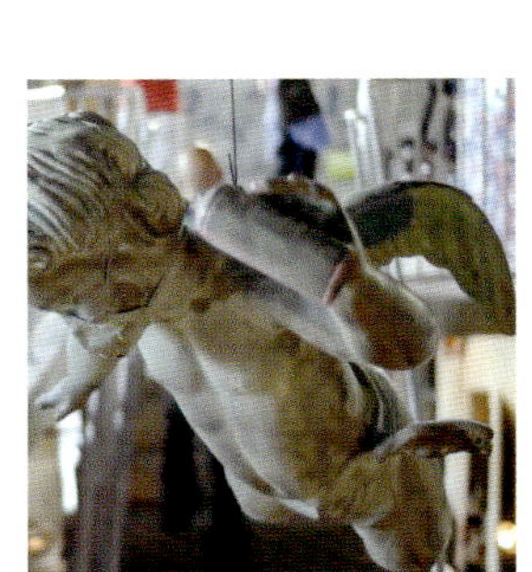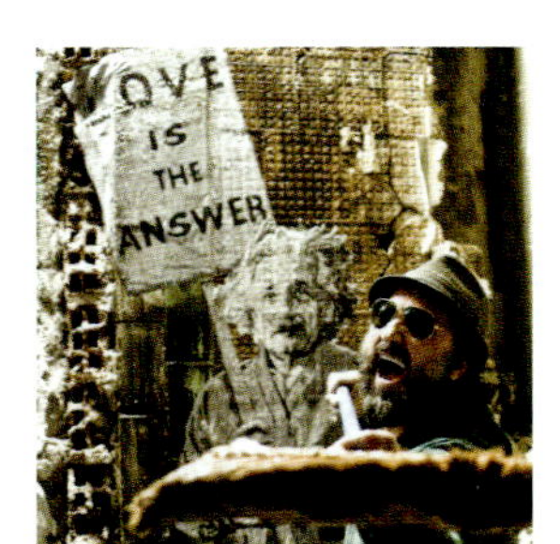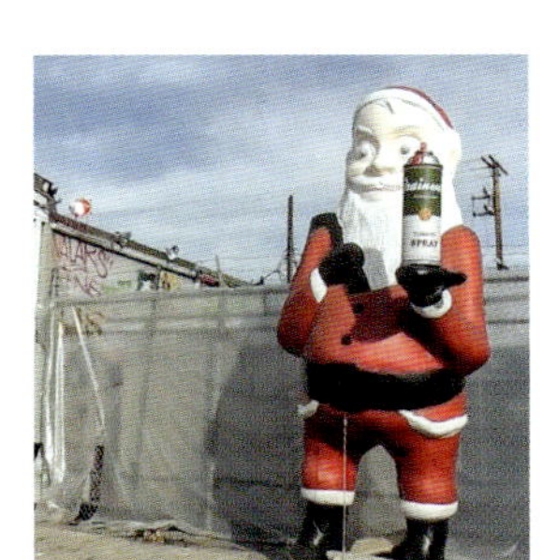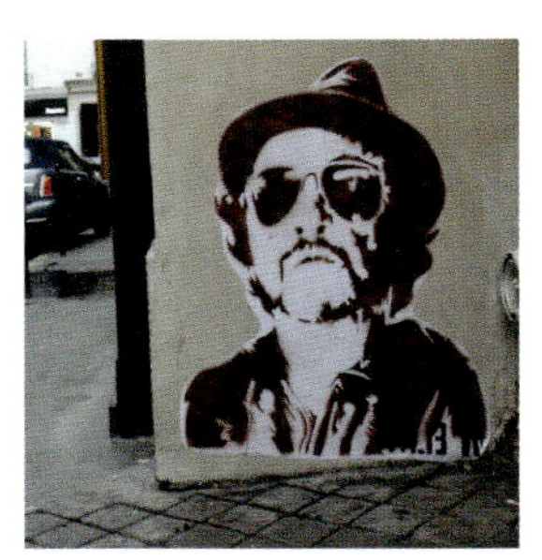

THE WHITE HOUSE

March 14, 2016

Mr. Brainwash
Beverly Hills, California

Dear Mr. Brainwash:

I want to thank you for all your help with the successful celebration of the first anniversary of Let Girls Learn on International Women's Day.

Since launching the Let Girls Learn initiative, I have been inspired by the incredible momentum around increasing access to education for girls around the world. The beautiful mural at Union Market stands as a testament to all of those efforts and a visual reminder to everyone that this work is so important.

Again, thank you, and I wish you all the best.

Sincerely,

Michelle Obama

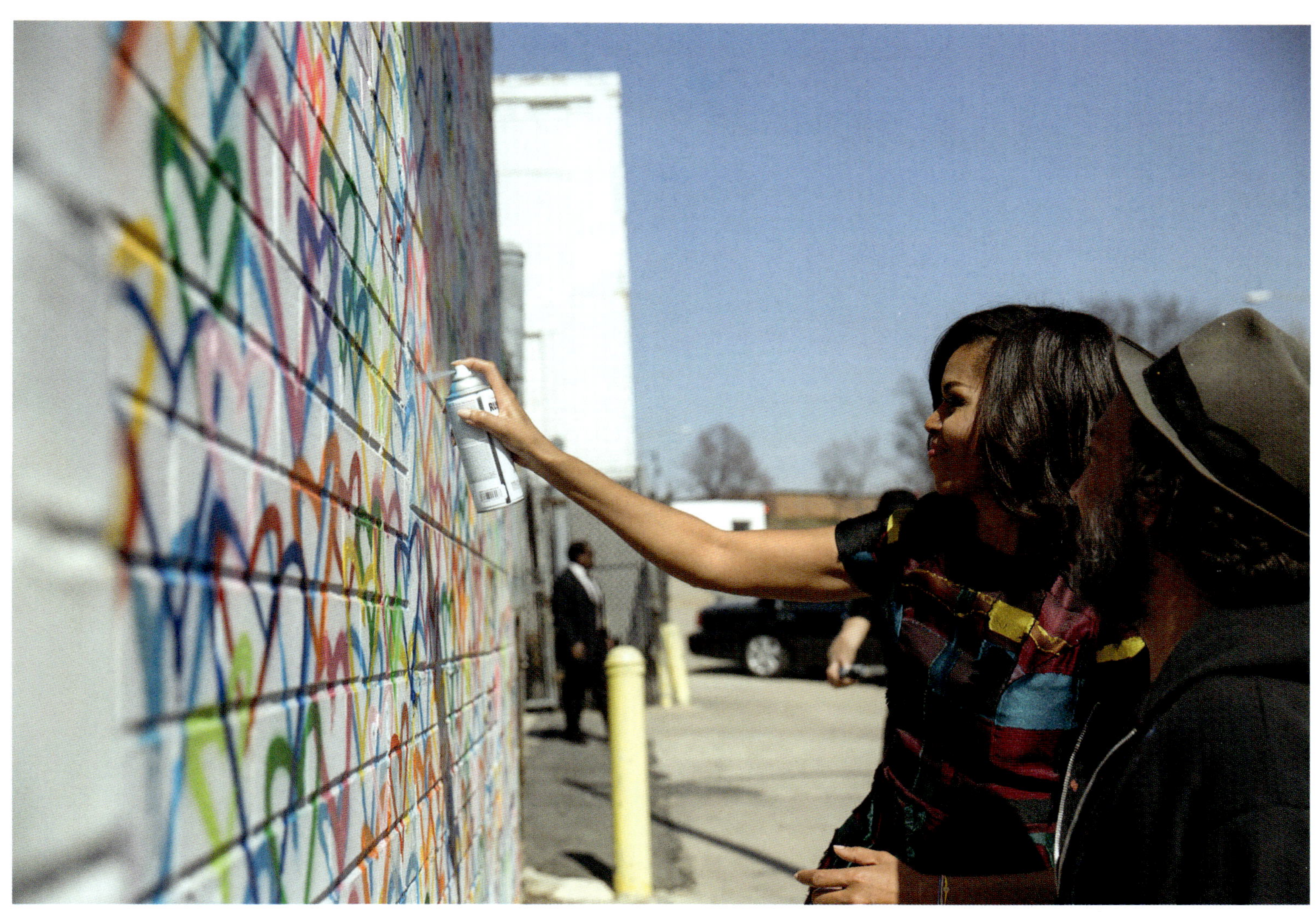

Mr. Brainwash unveiled a series of murals at Union Market in Washington, DC with First Lady Michelle Obama to celebrate International Women's Day with Let Girls Learn, the Obama administration's initiative to help adolescent girls worldwide attend and complete school. The artist created other images, artworks that featured messages and iconic imagery on Union Market's exterior.

Michelle Obama was on-site in the Union Market district to celebrate the first anniversary of Let Girls Learn and asked Mr. Brainwash to teach her how to spray paint. Together they added a few more hearts and signed the inspiring work of art. The mural attracted national and international attention, making it onto the first page of the White House website and newspapers.

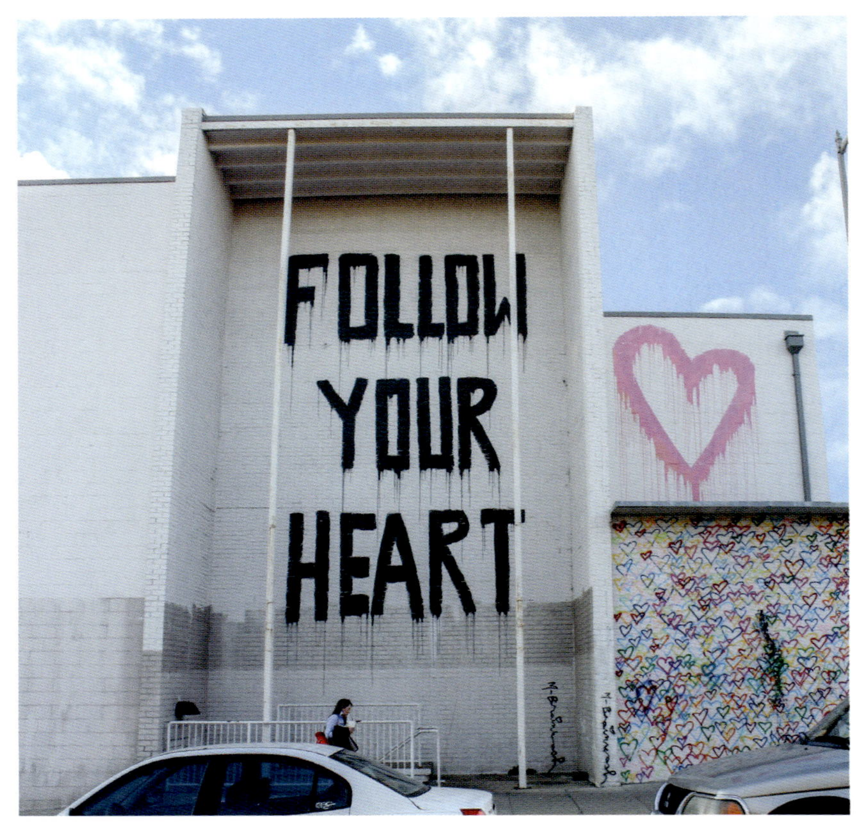

FOLLOW
YOUR
HEART

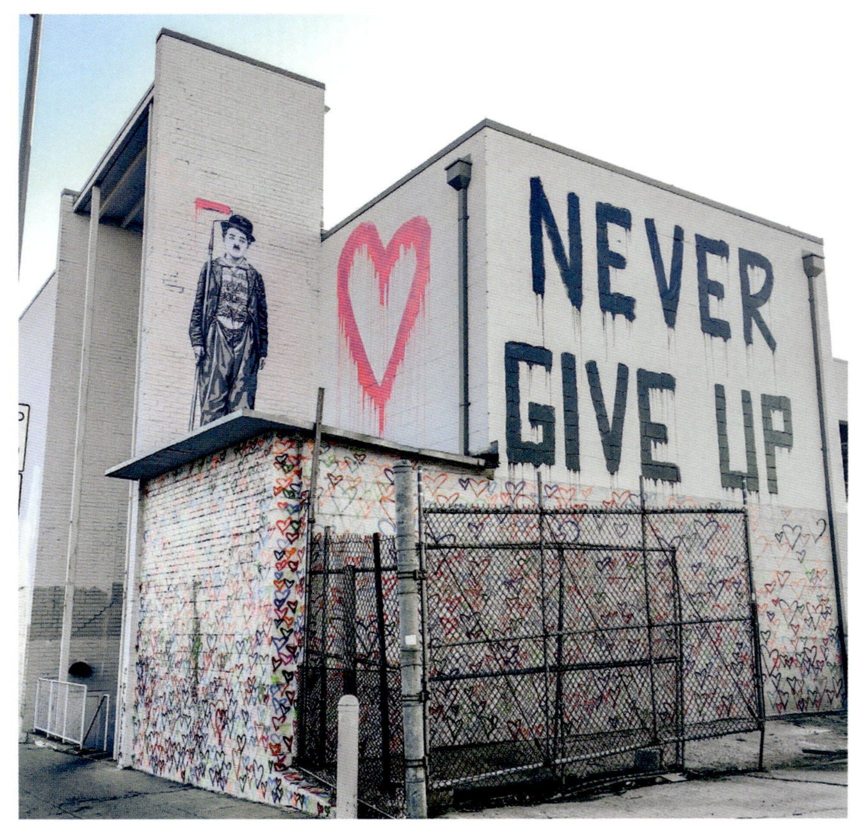

NEVER
GIVE UP

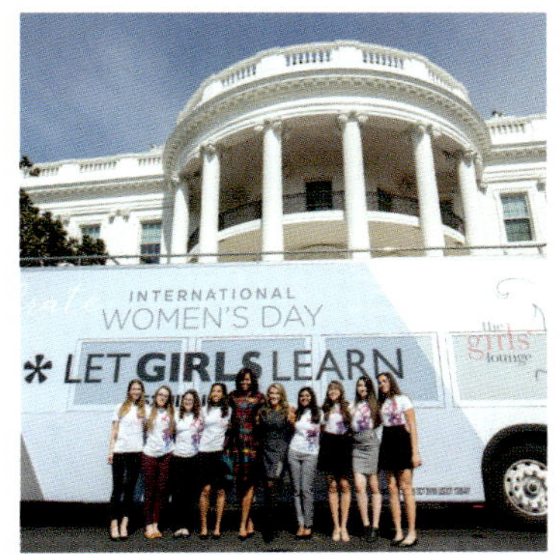
INTERNATIONAL WOMEN'S DAY
* LET GIRLS LEARN

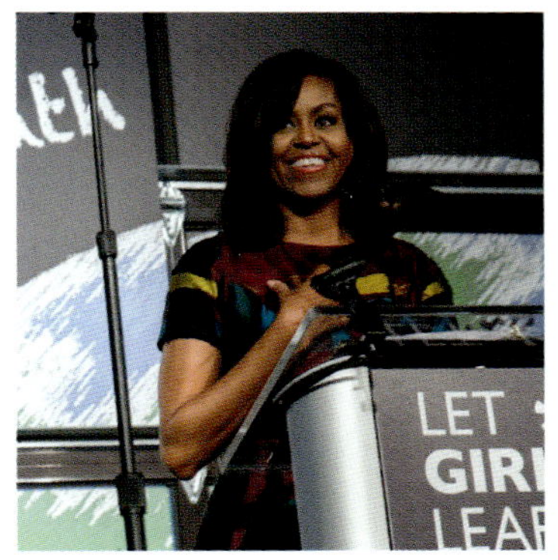

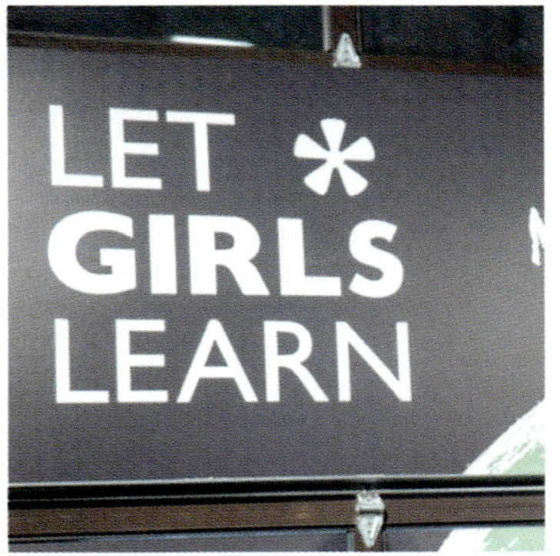
LET * GIRLS LEARN

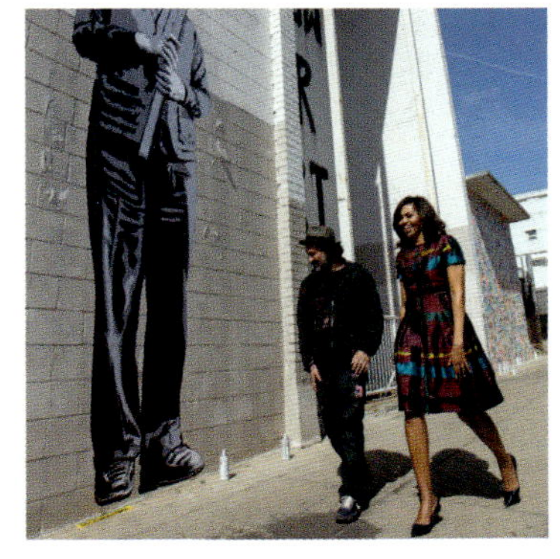

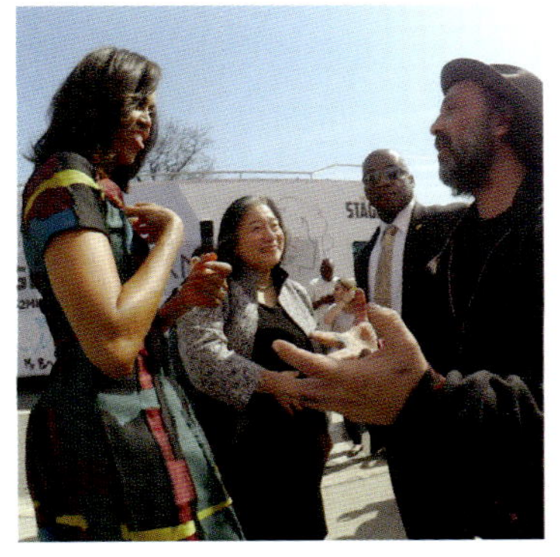

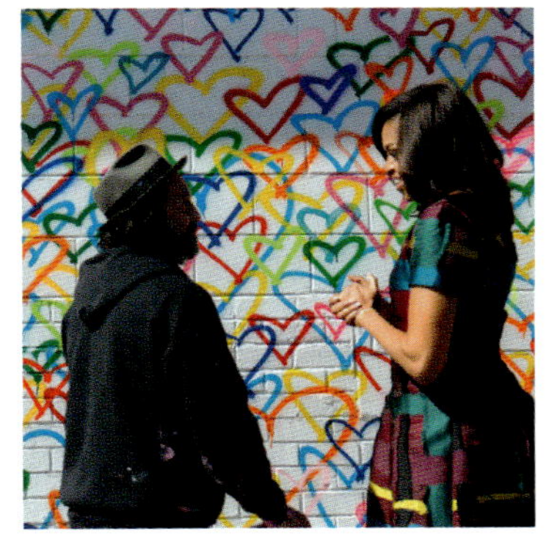

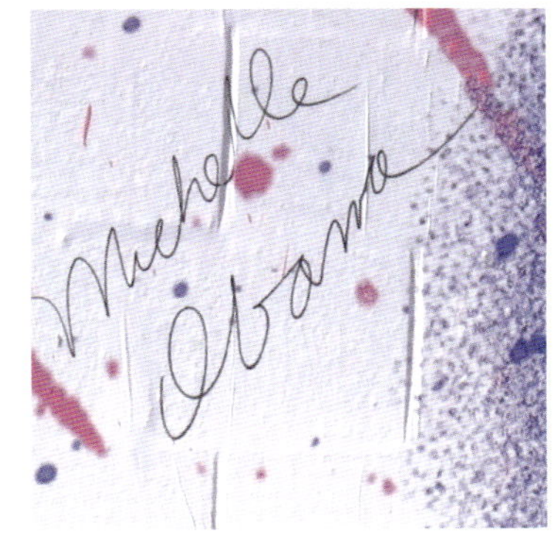
Michelle Obama

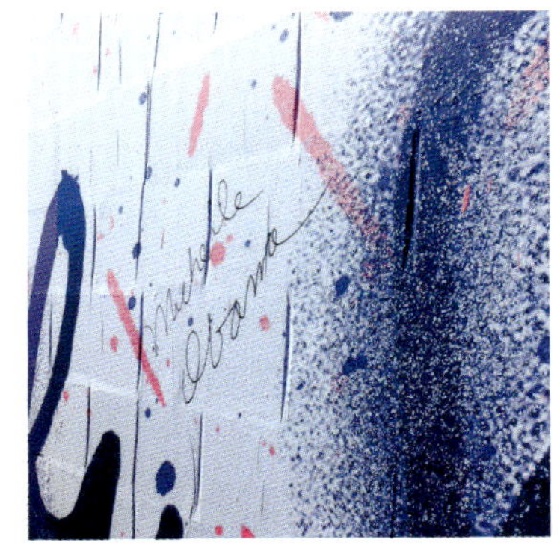
Michelle Obama

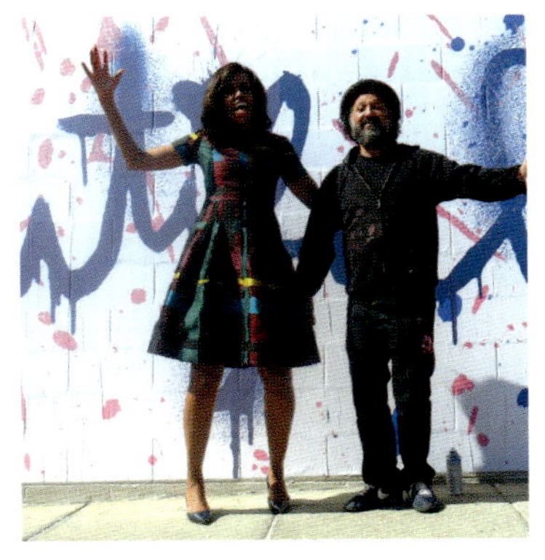

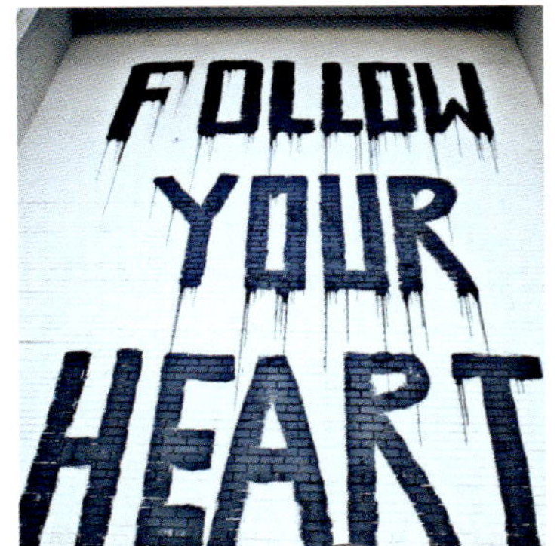
FOLLOW YOUR HEART

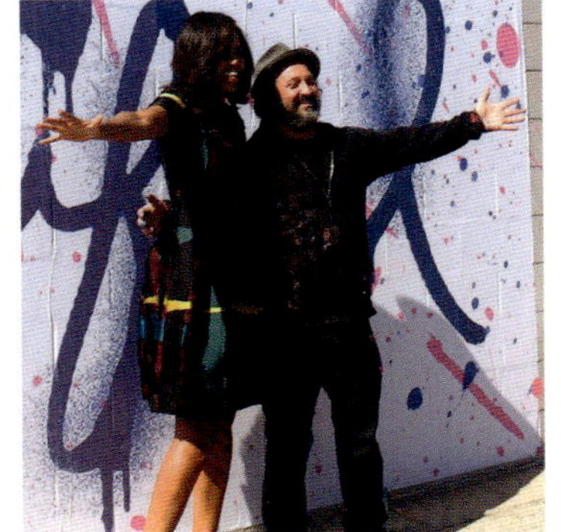

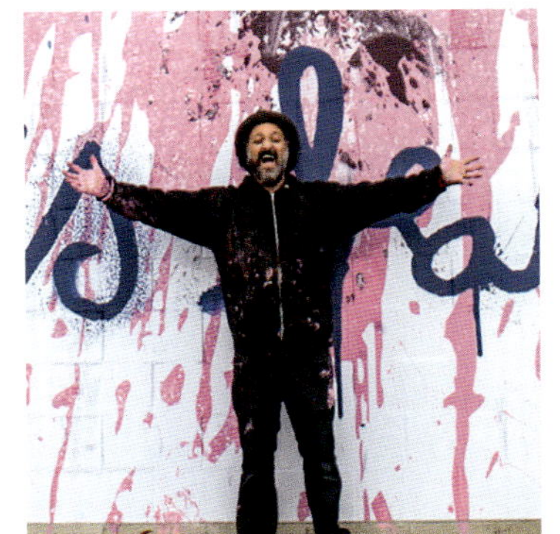

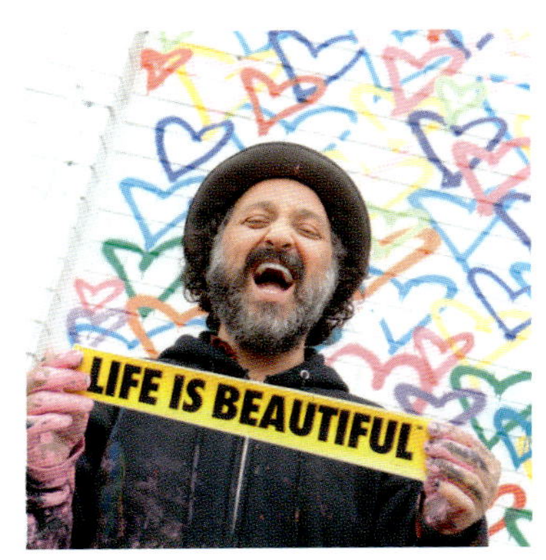
LIFE IS BEAUTIFUL

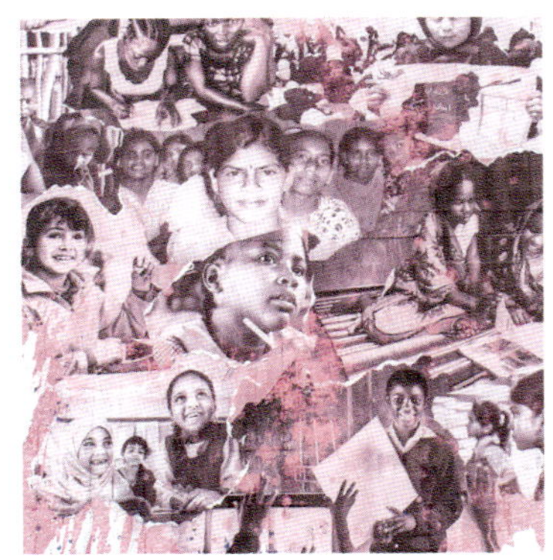

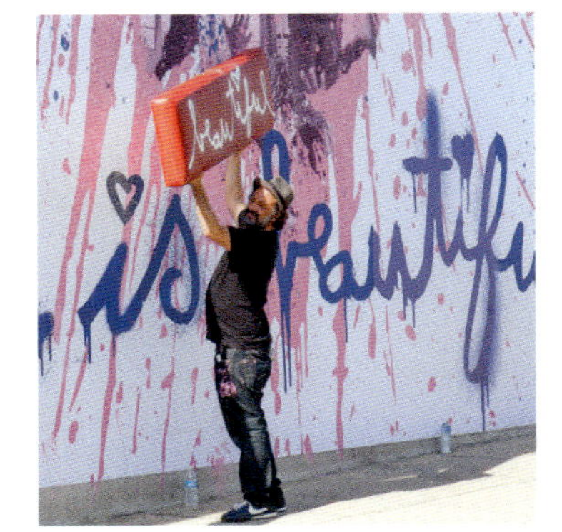

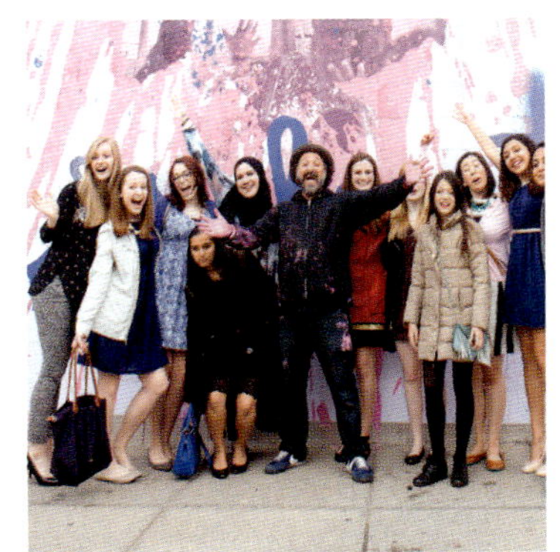

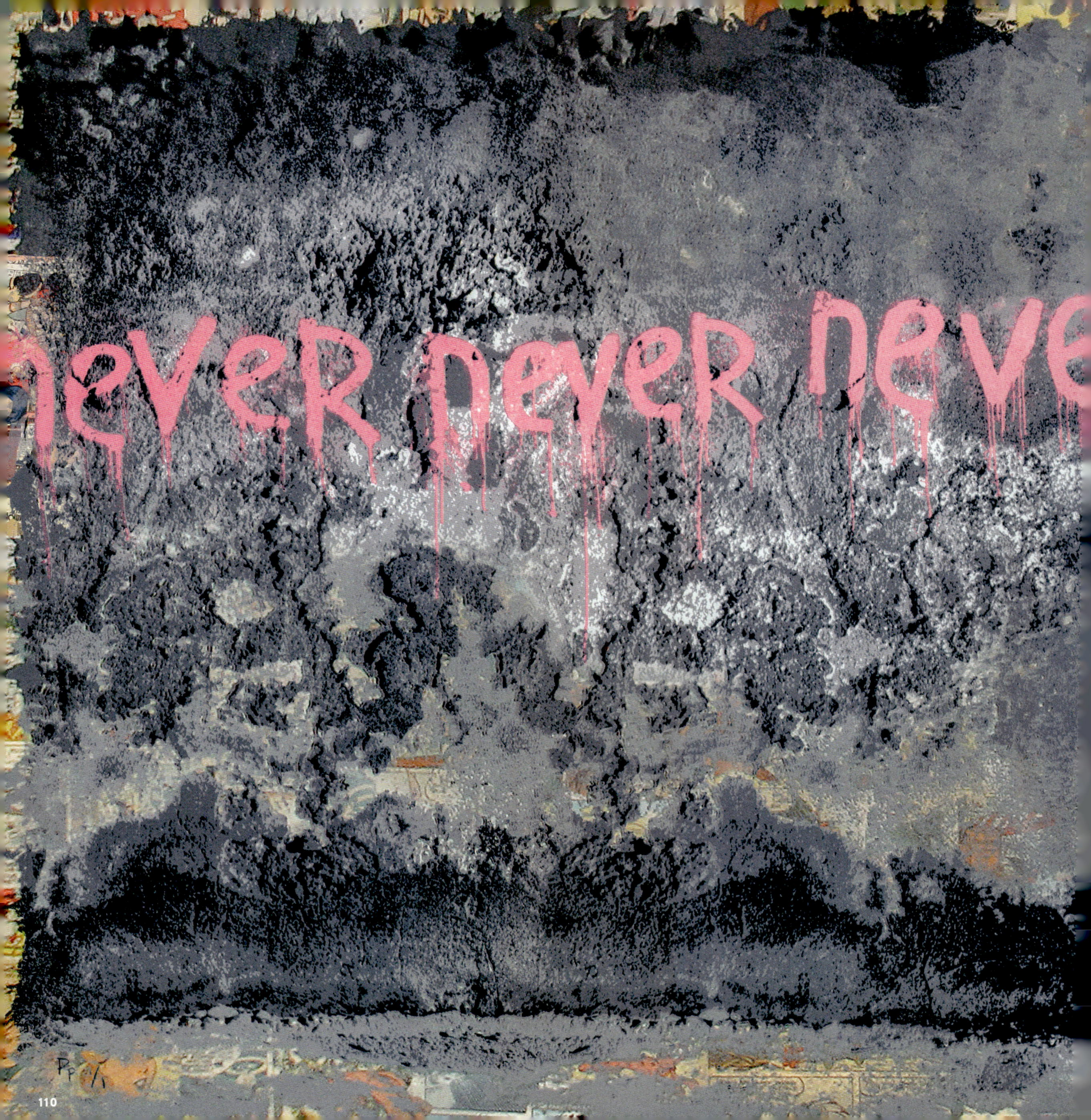
never never never neve

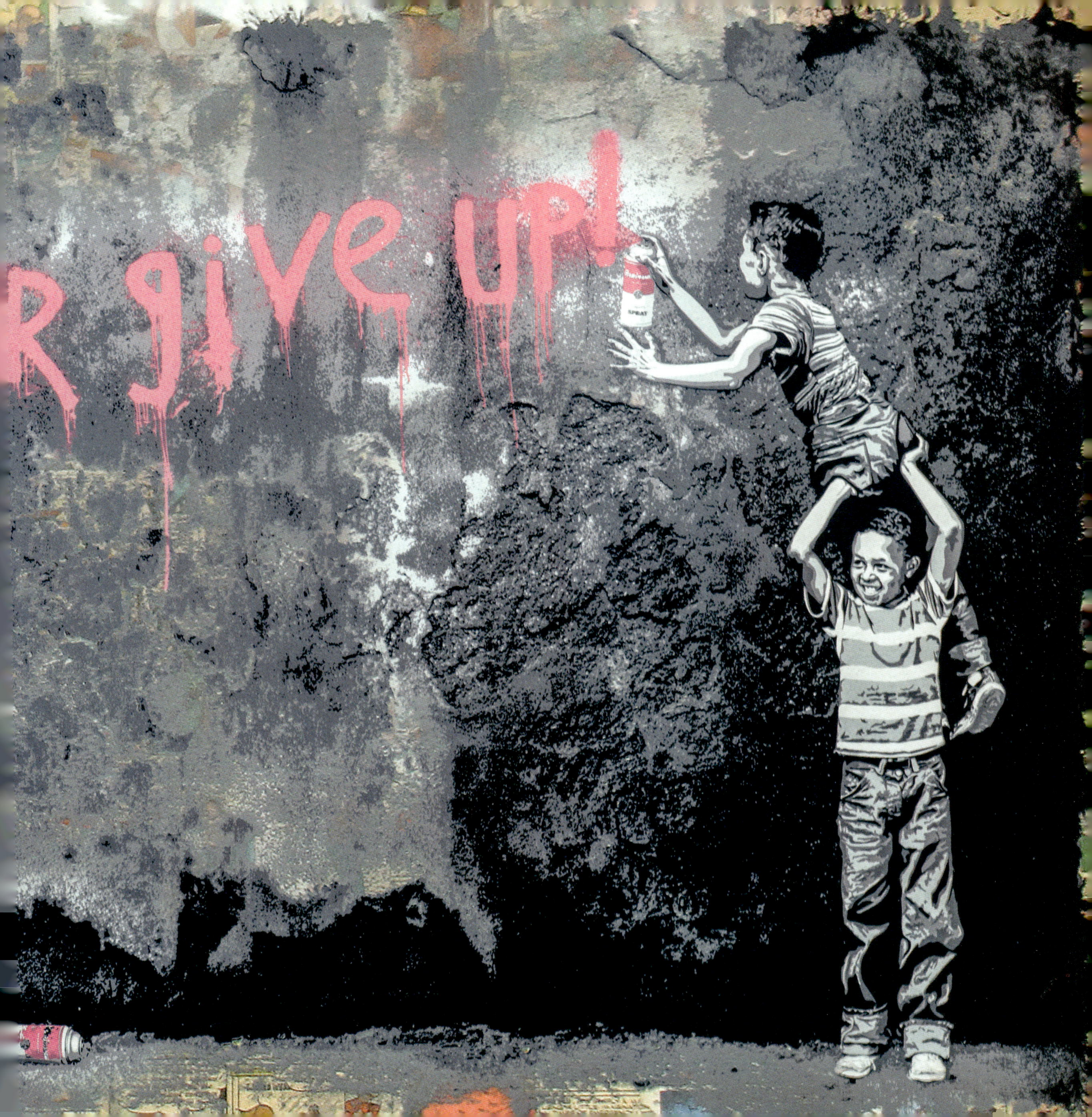
R give up!

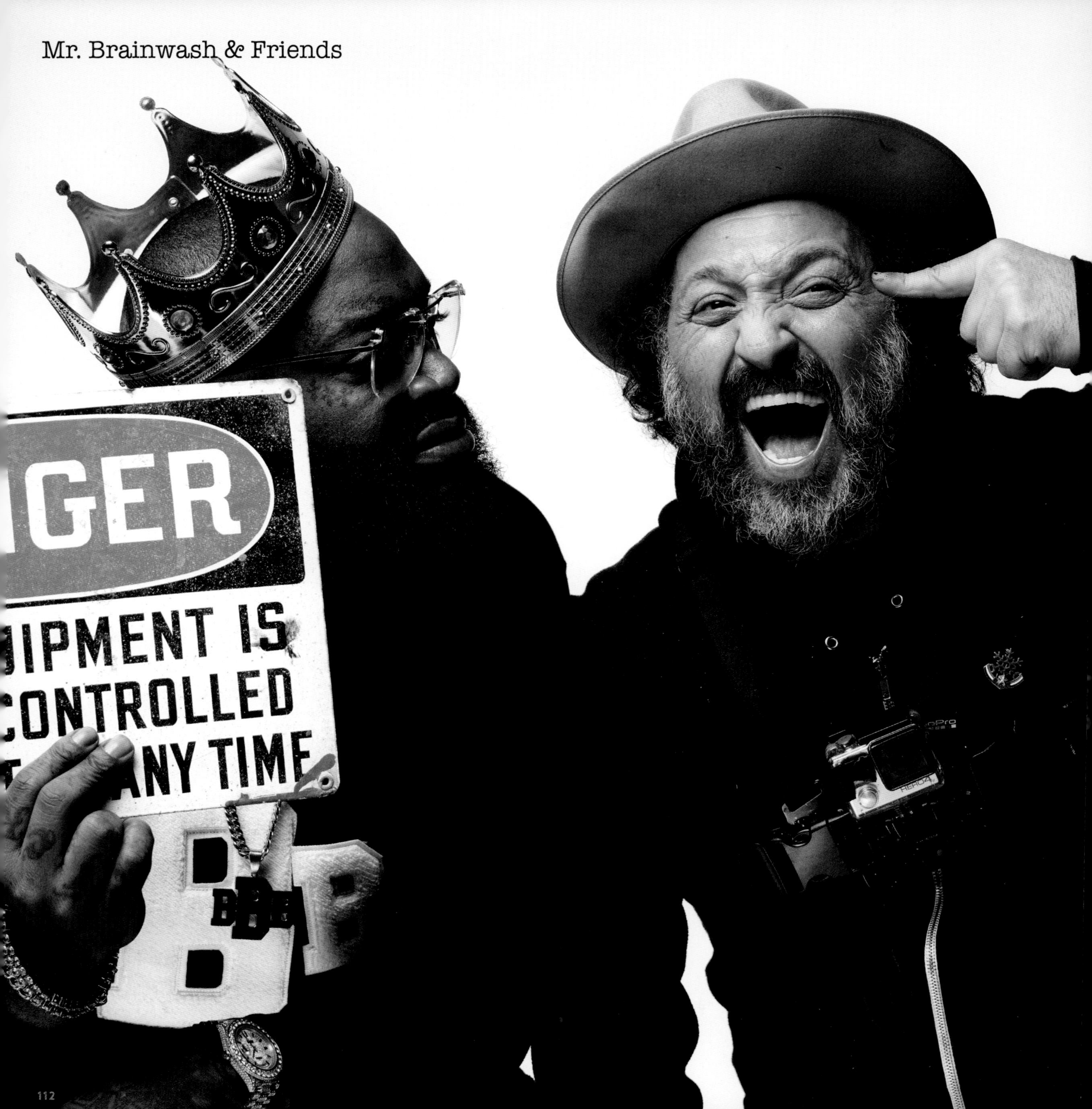
GER
JIPMENT IS
CONTROLLED
ANY TIME

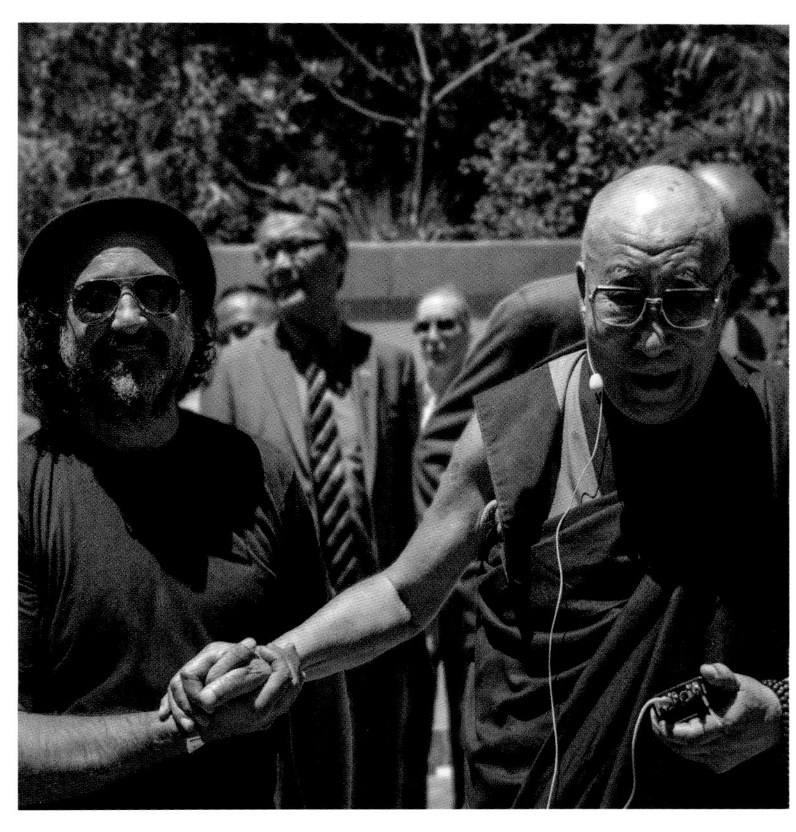
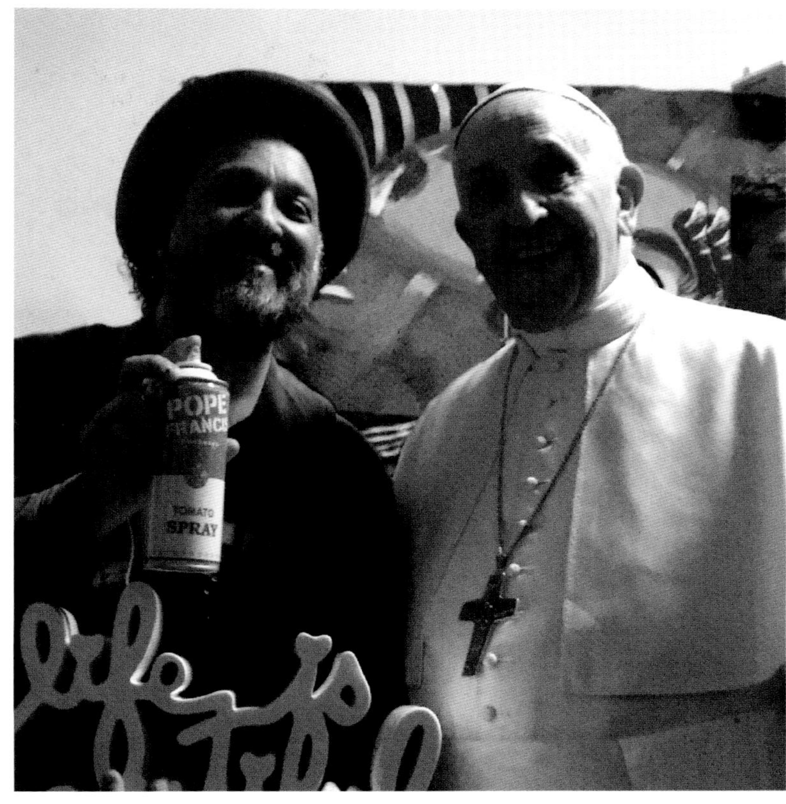
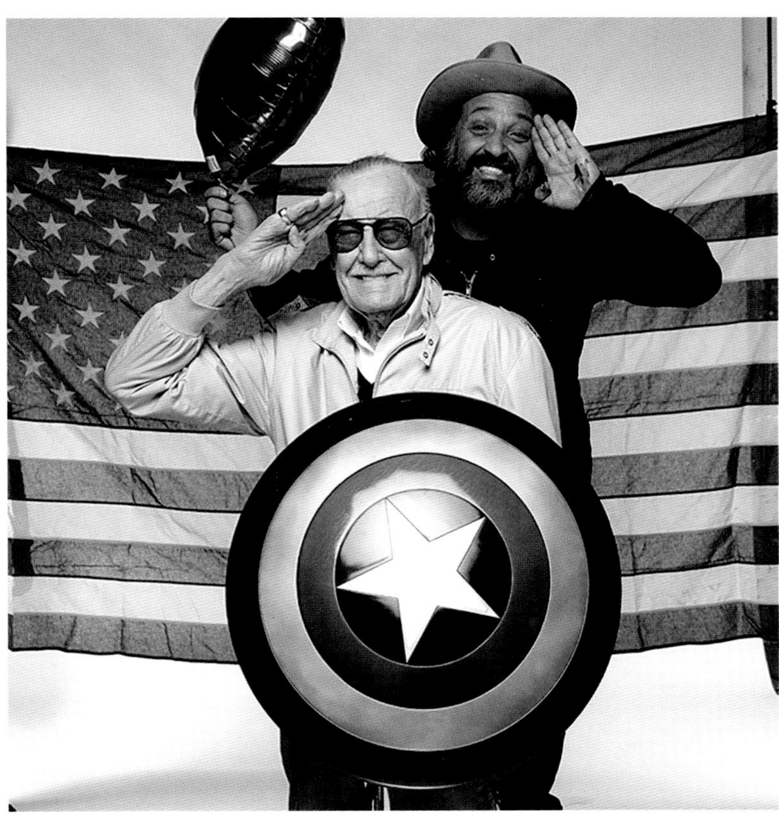
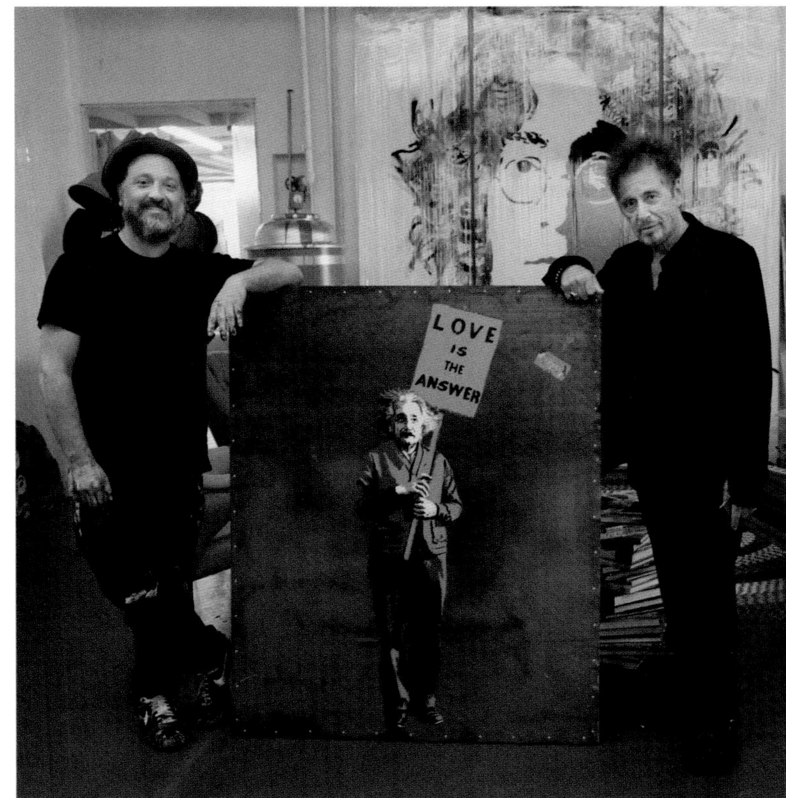

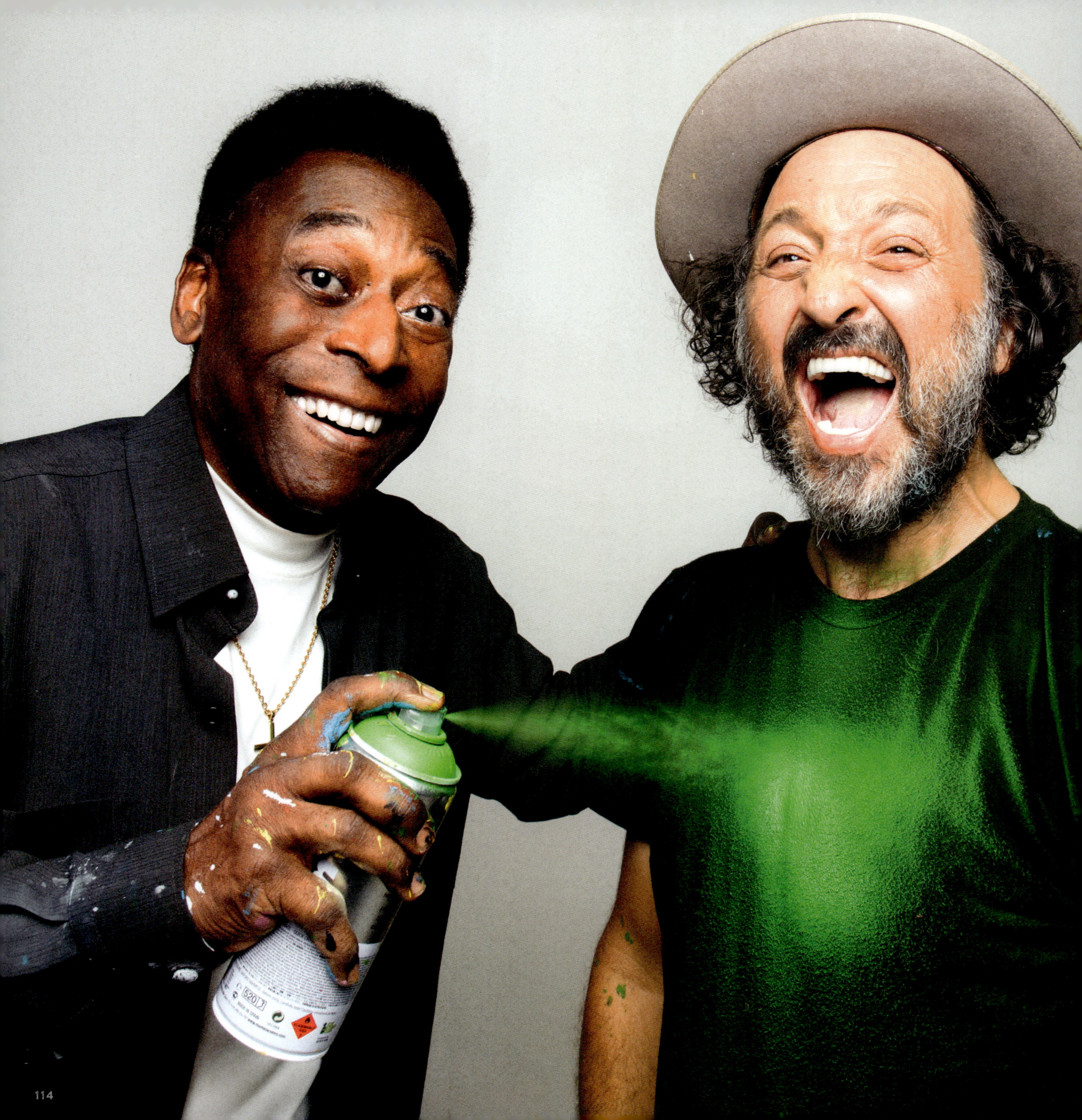

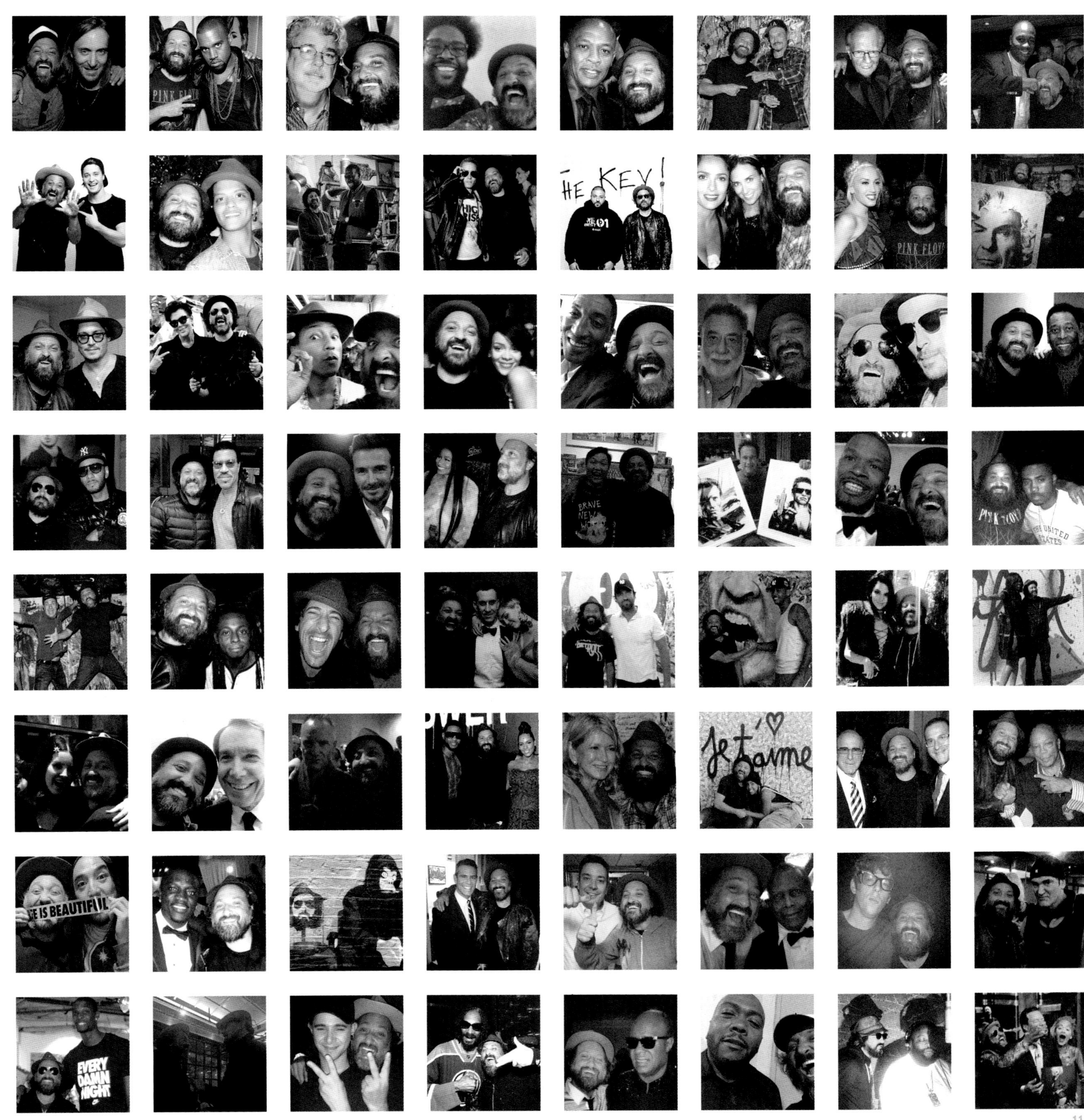

Mr. Brainwash is a force of nature,
he's a phenomenon.
And I don't mean that in a good way.

— BANKSY

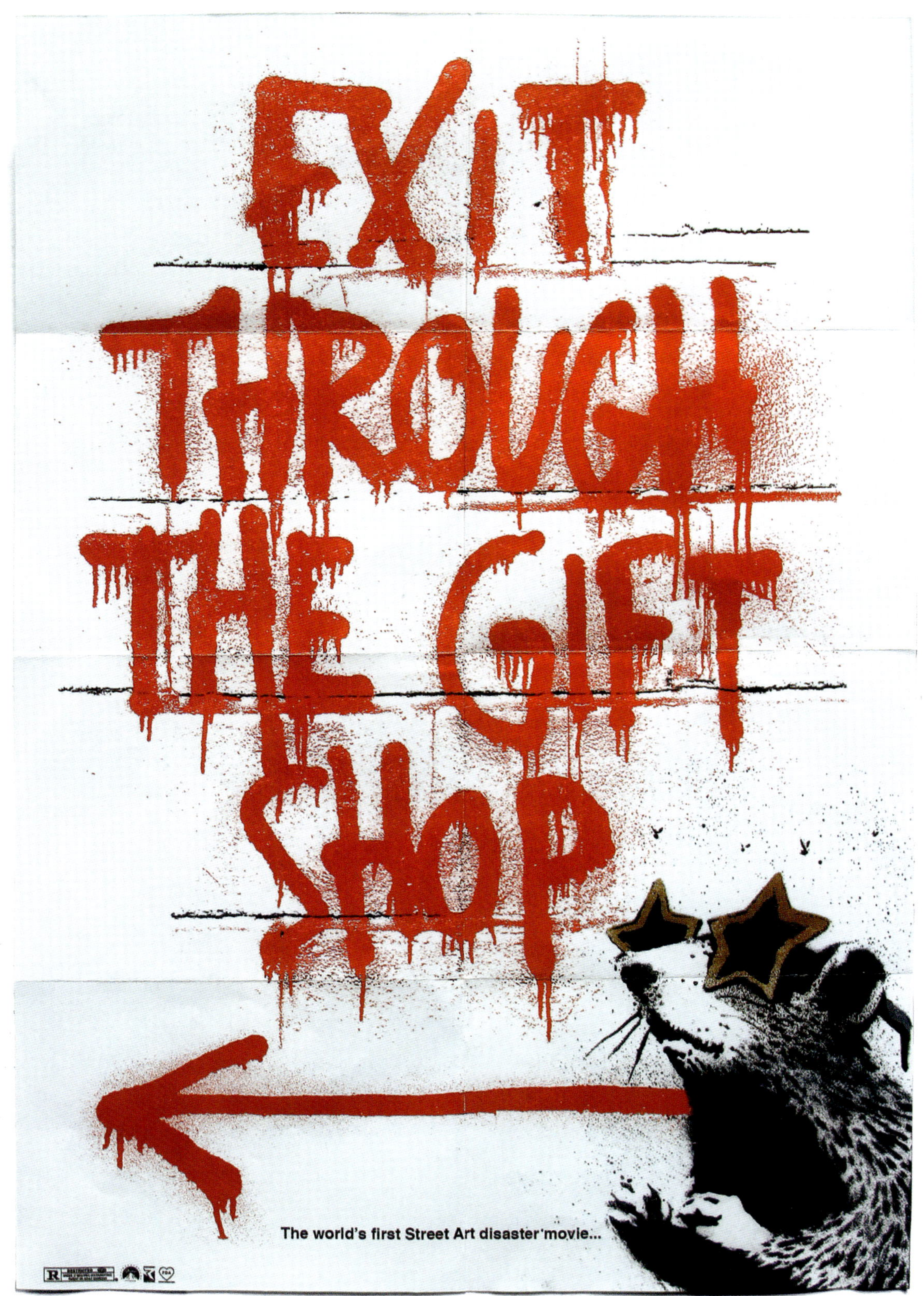

EXIT
THROUGH
THE GIFT
SHOP
The world's first Street Art disaster movie...

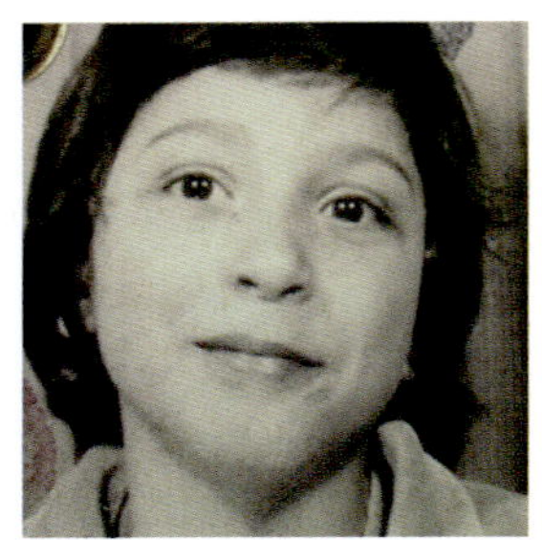 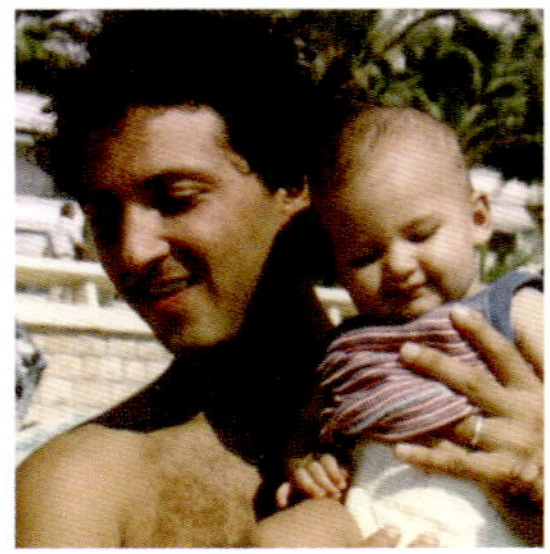 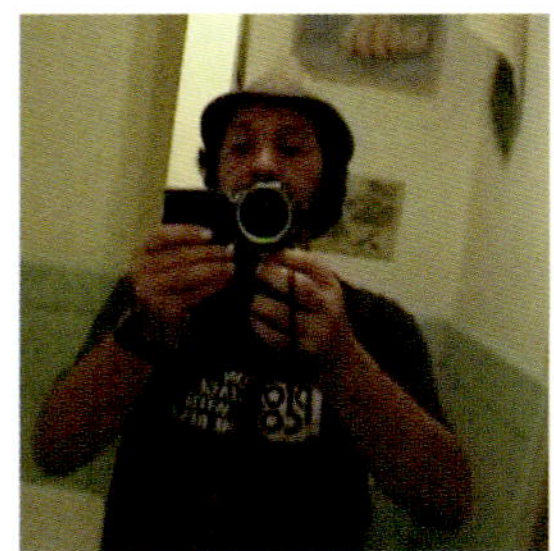 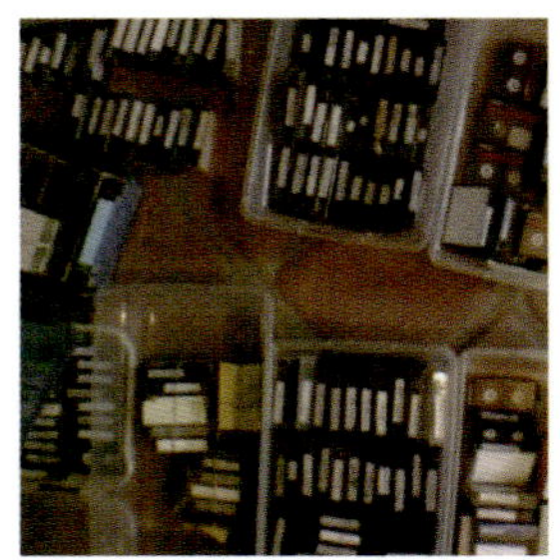 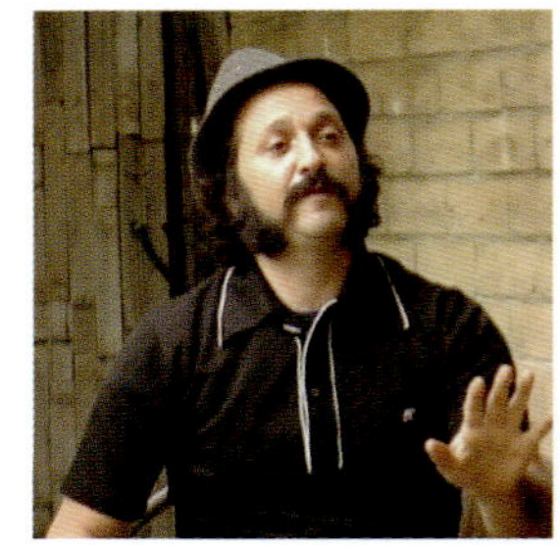

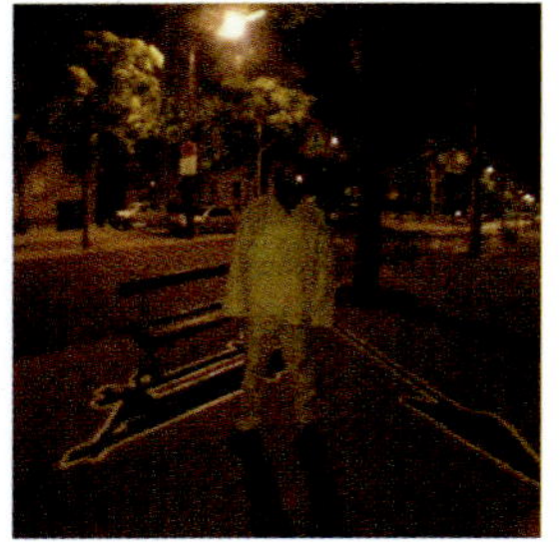 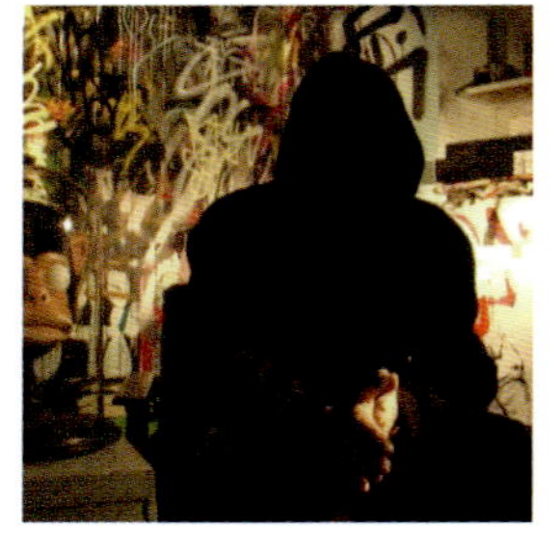 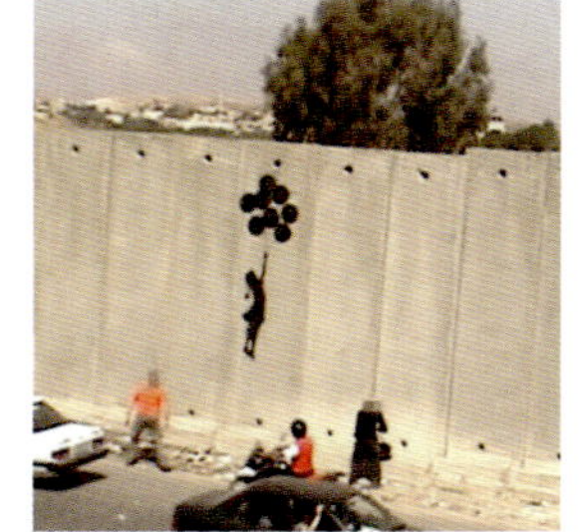 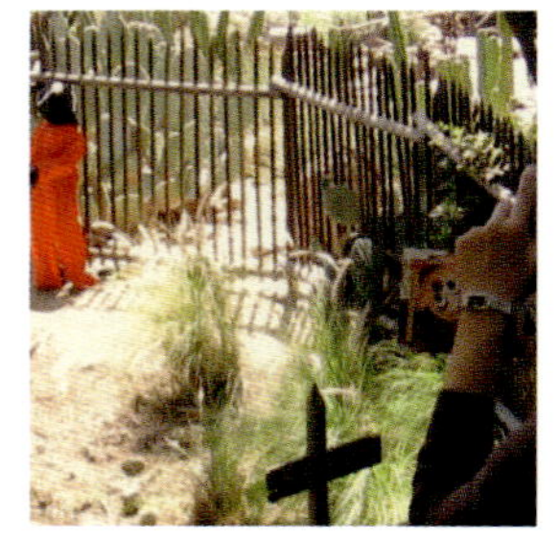 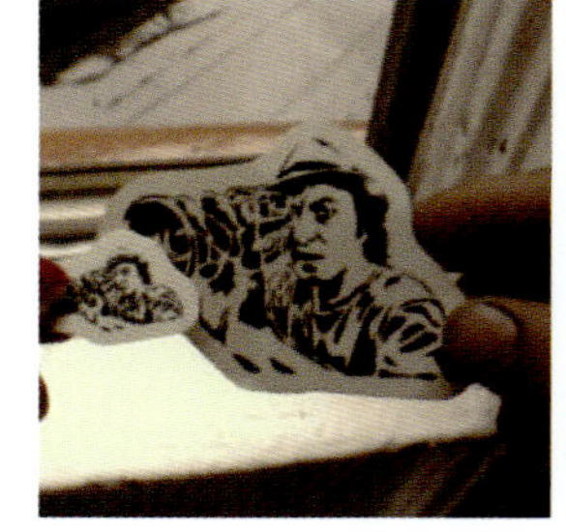

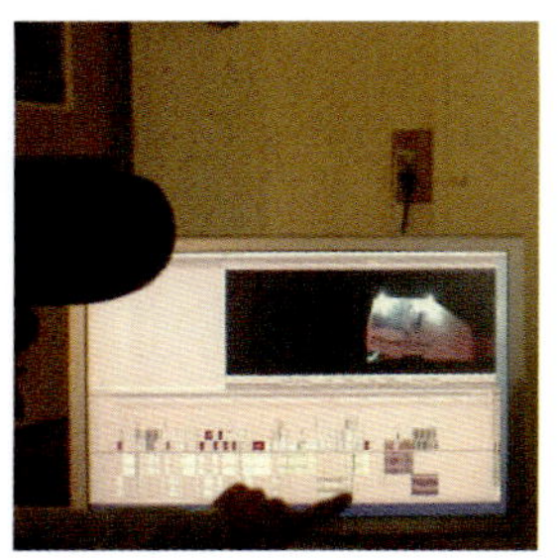
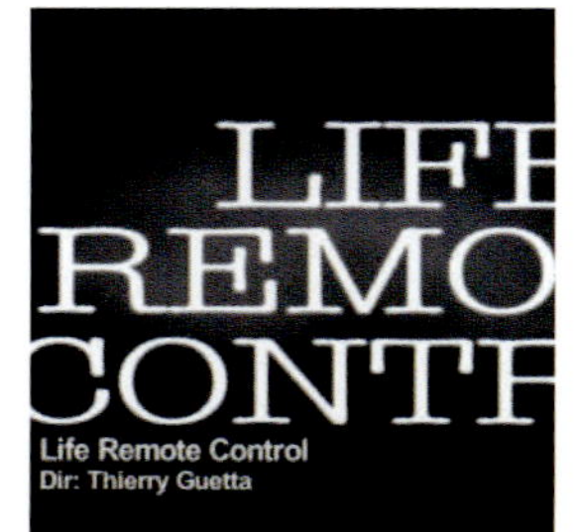

LIFE
REMO
CONTR
Life Remote Control
Dir: Thierry Guetta

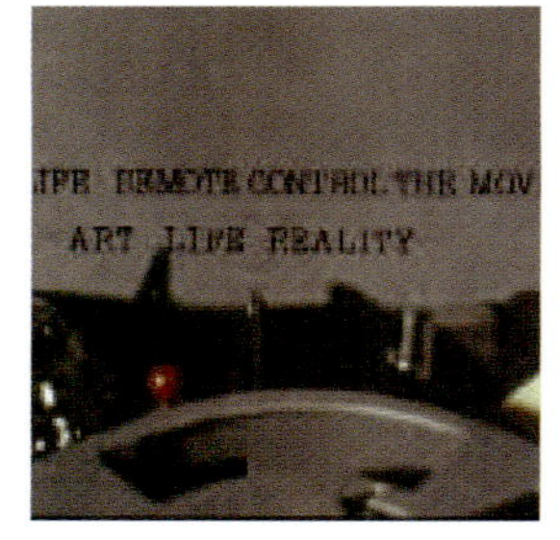

LIFE REMOTE CONTROL THE MOV
ART LIFE REALITY

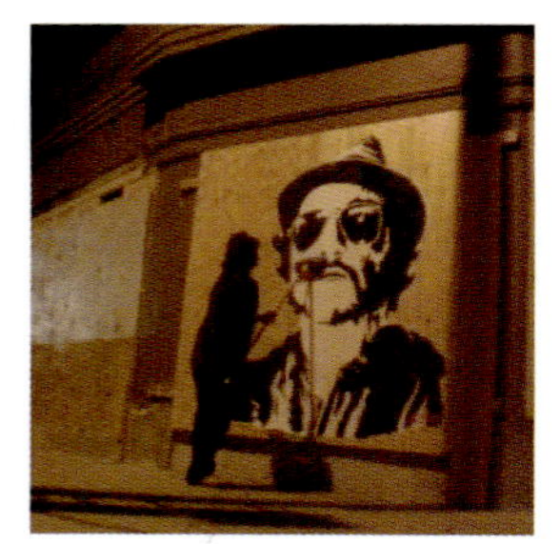 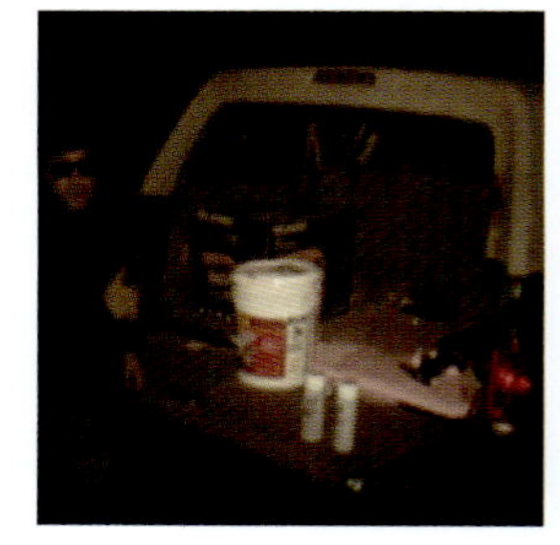

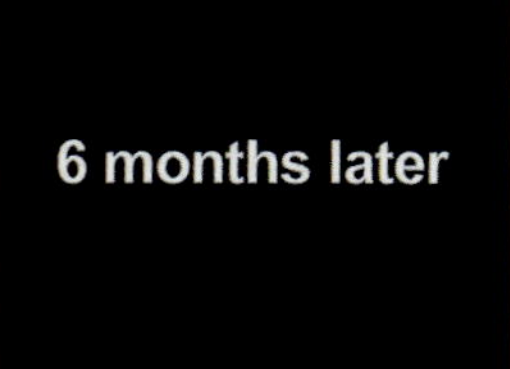

6 months later

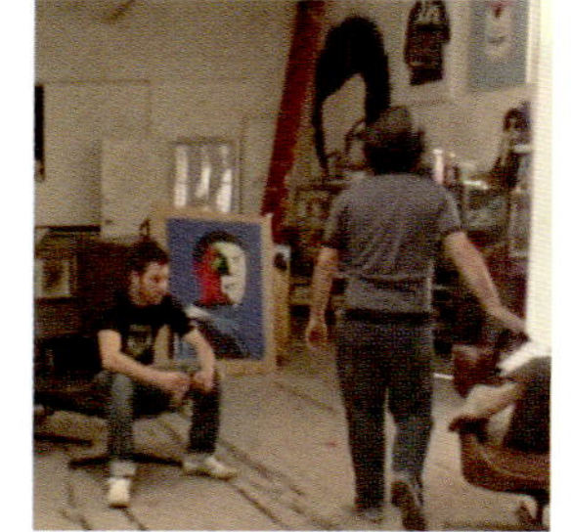 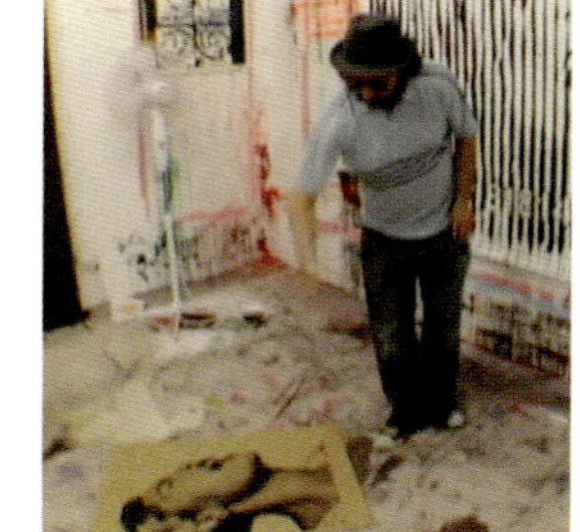 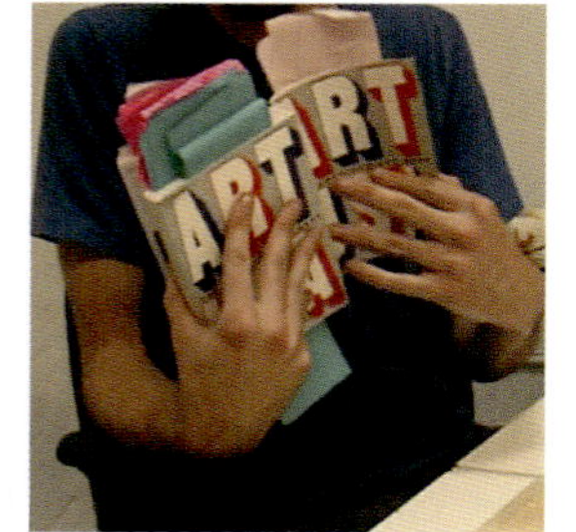 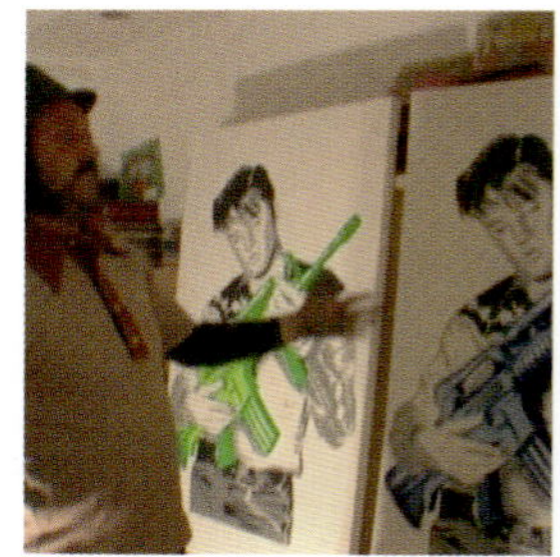

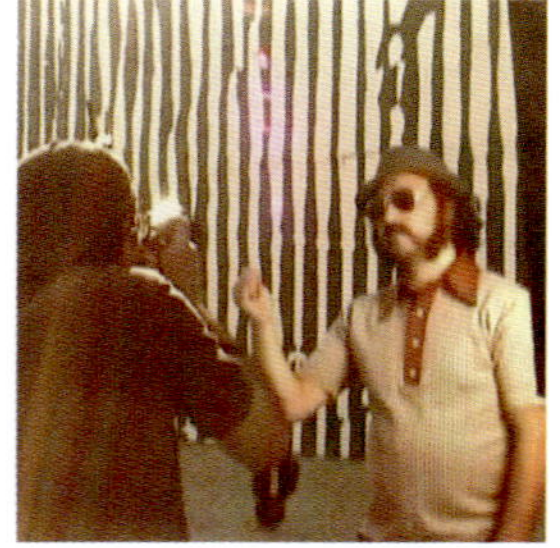 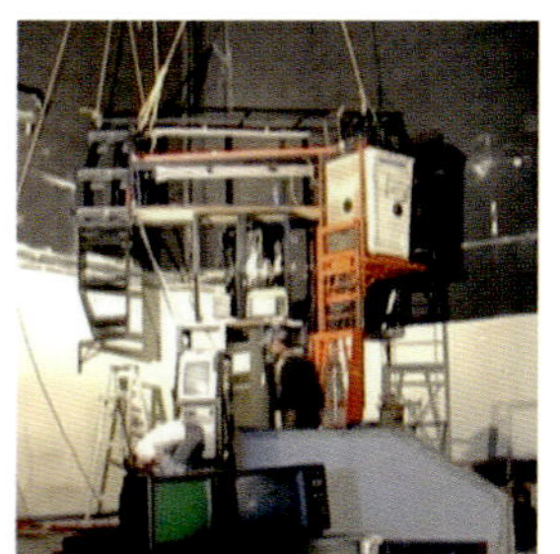 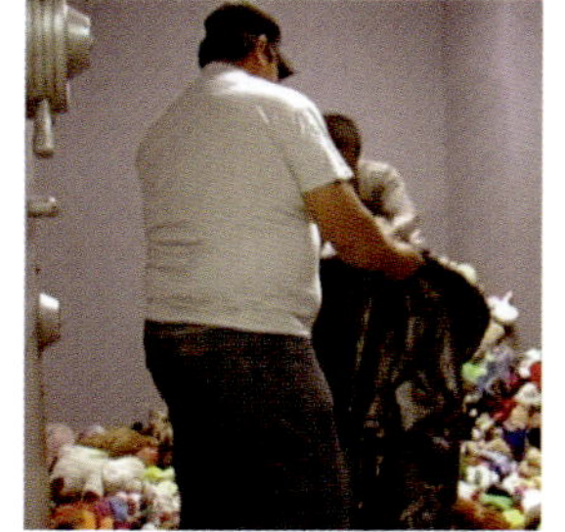 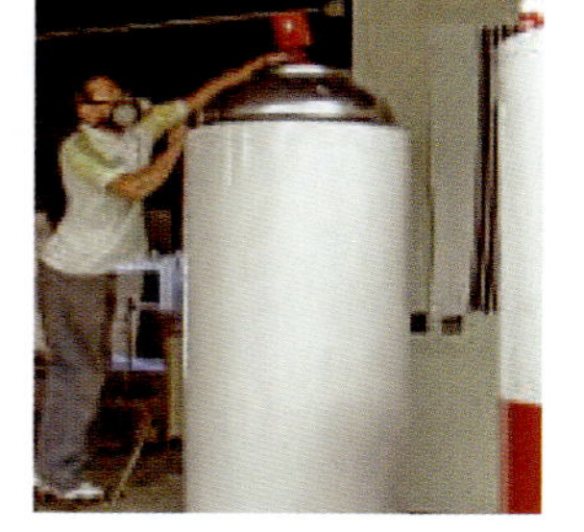 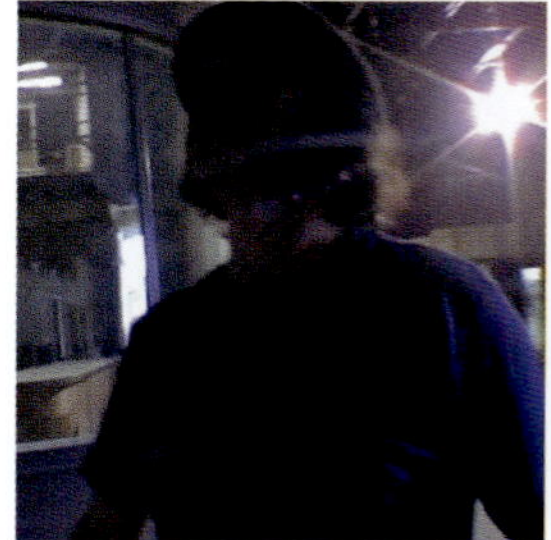

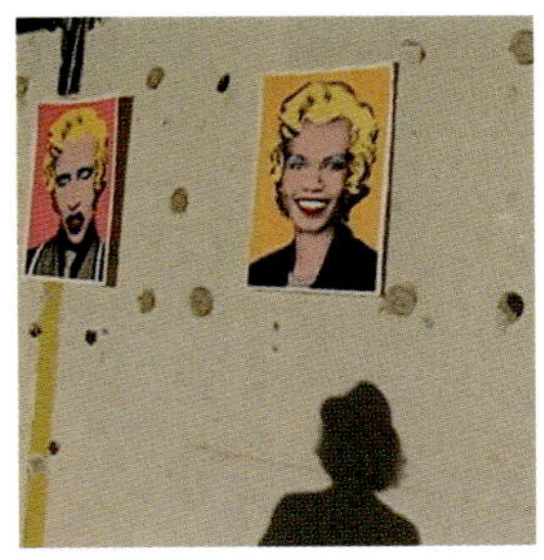
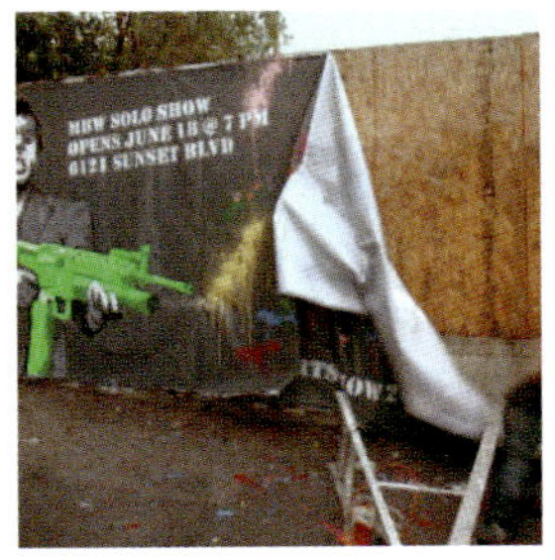

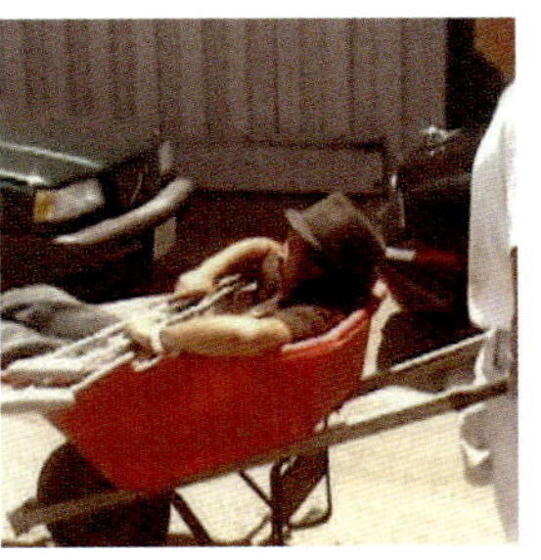
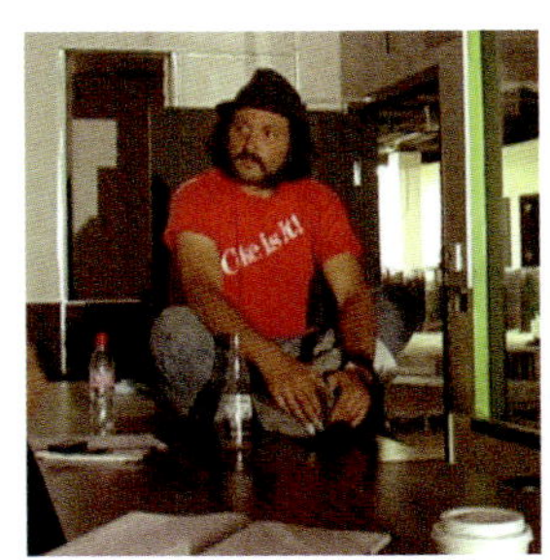

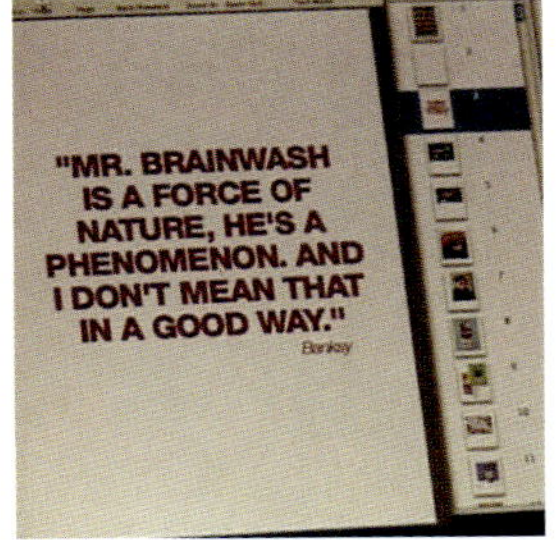

Former CBS Studio
Opens Wednesday
6121 W Sunset Blvd
www.artshow2008.c

Mr. Brainwash is an
infuriating, almost i
MBW is definitely a
started documentin

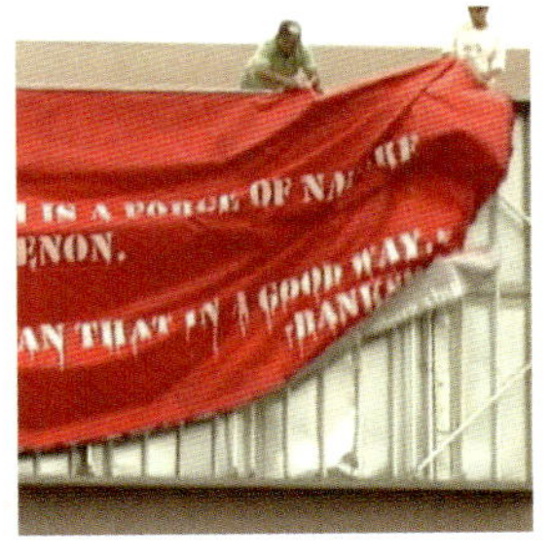

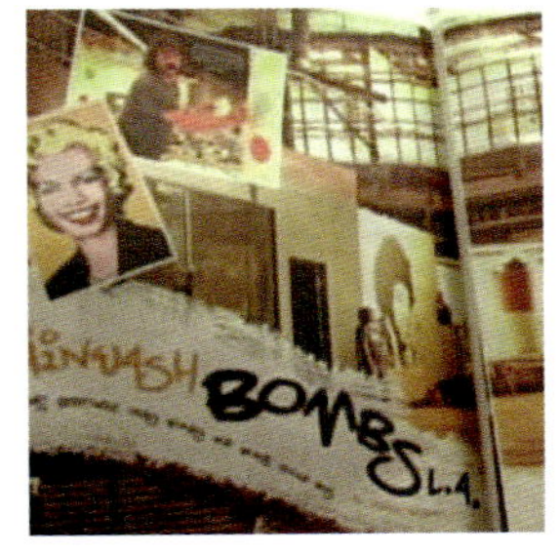

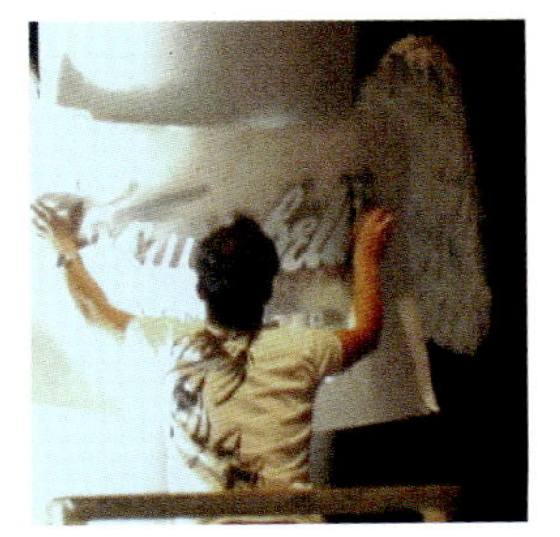
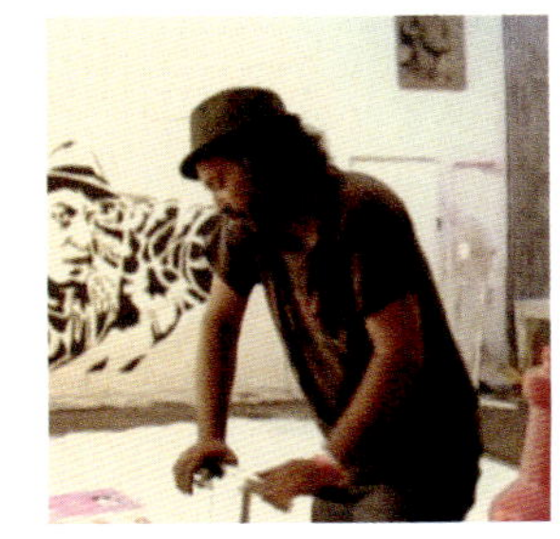
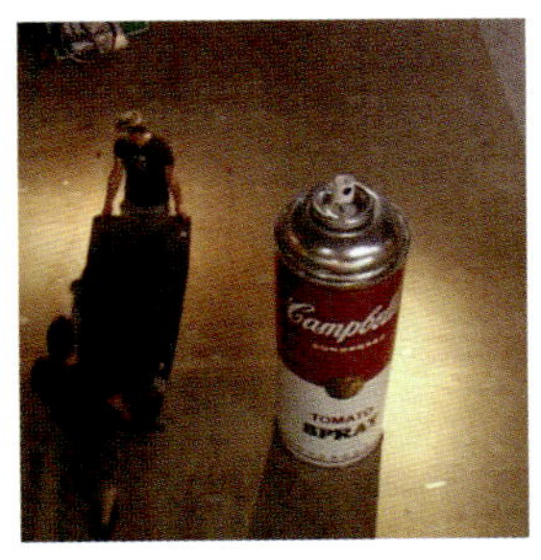

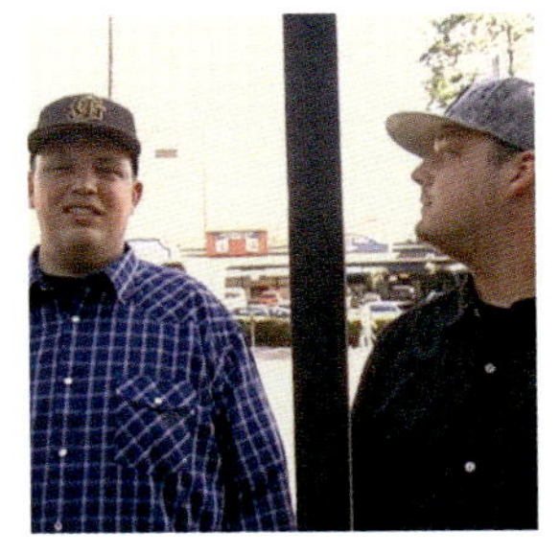
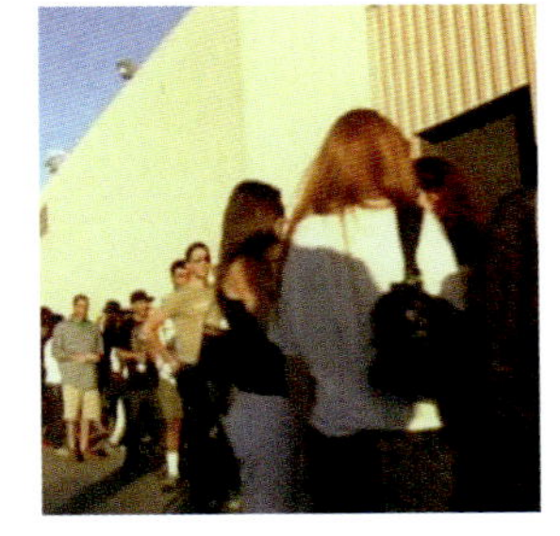
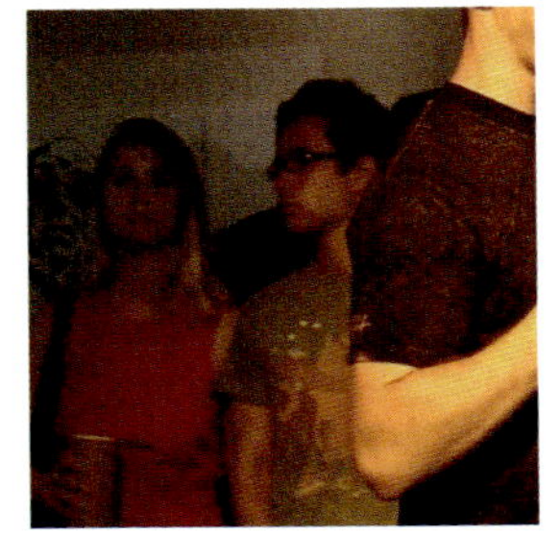
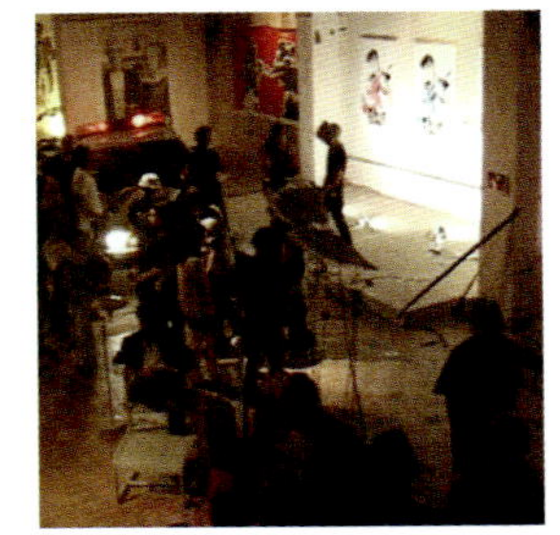
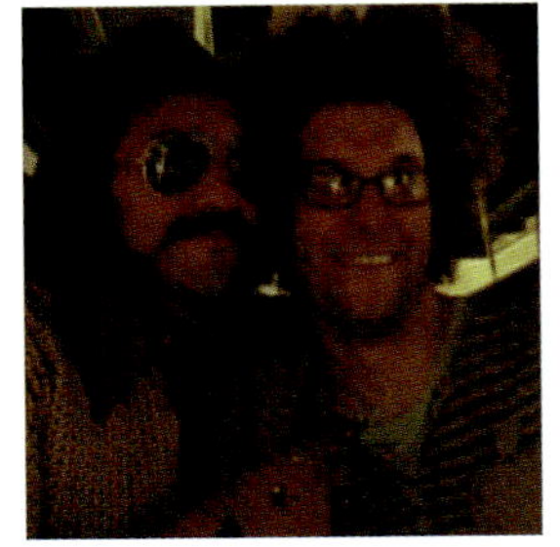
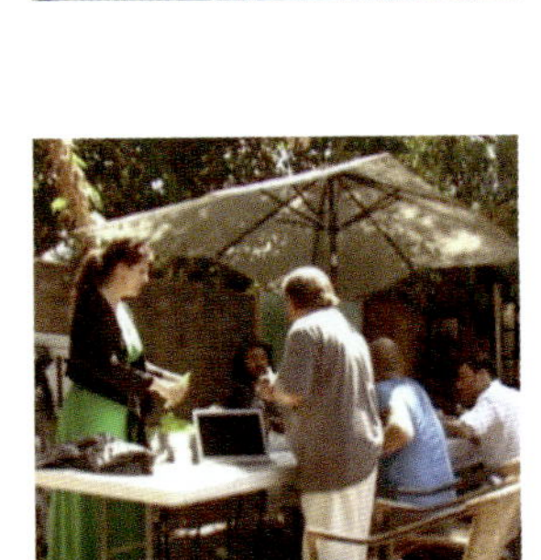
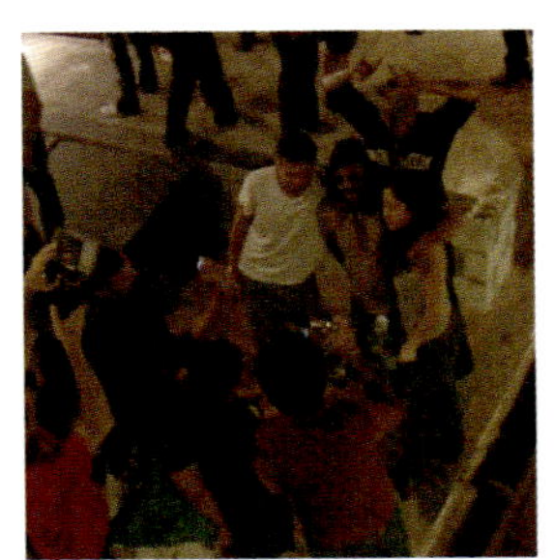
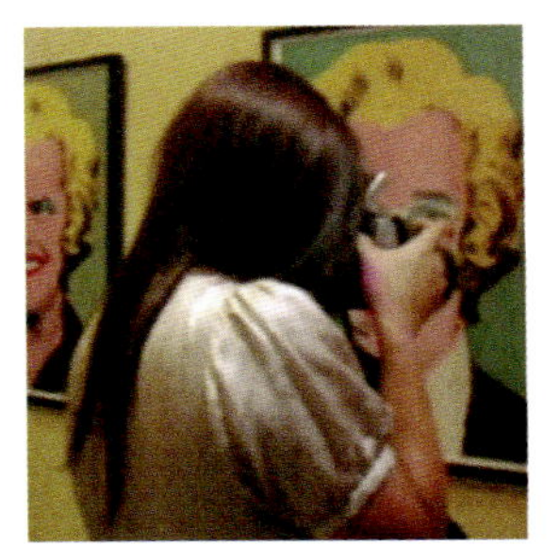
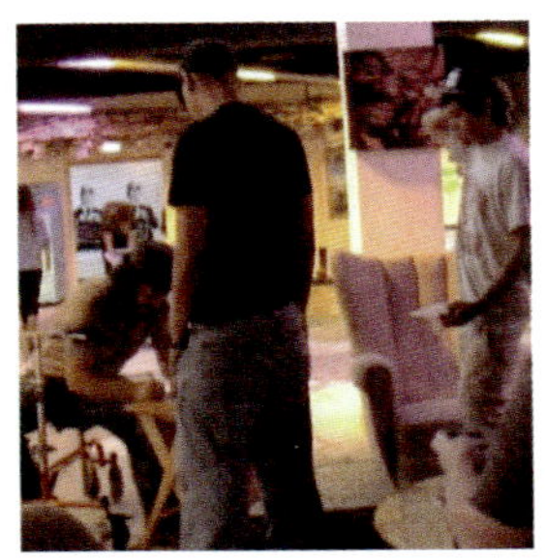
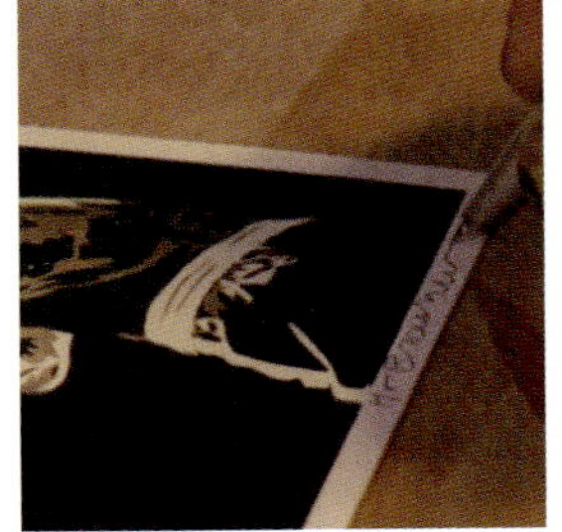
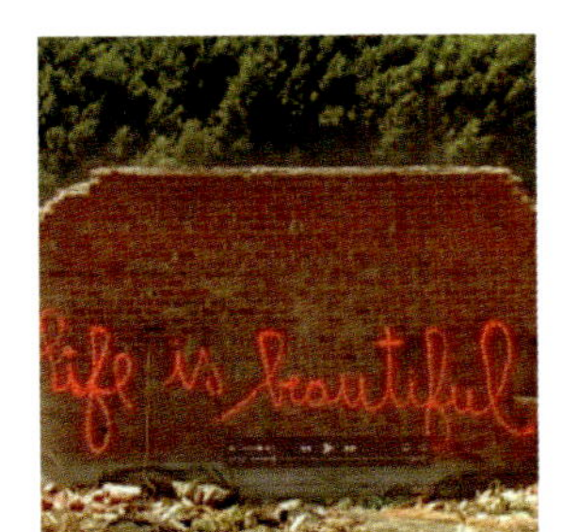

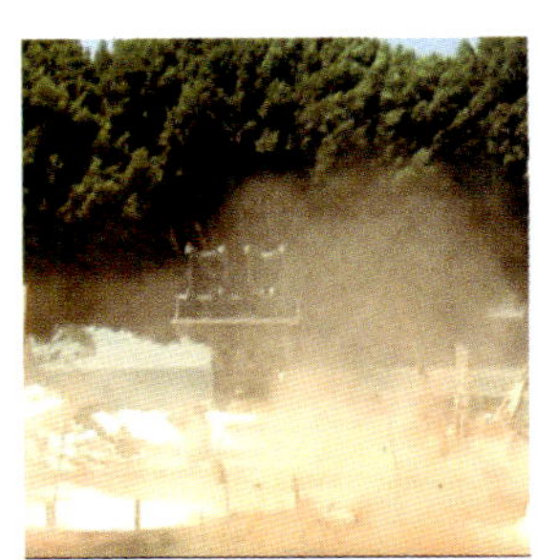

LIFE IS BEAUTIFUL: ICONS
New York City, 2010

In 2010, Mr. Brainwash invaded the Meatpacking District with *Life Is Beautiful: Icons*, his first New York solo show. This show was bigger than ever, covering a 15,000-square-foot, multistorey warehouse. Mr. Brainwash's evocative portraits of music legends, constructed from bits of broken records, were displayed downstairs. The exhibit also featured a 10-foot-tall boom box and a life-size NYC taxicab in Matchbox toy car packaging. *Icons* was so popular that it was extended for three months, reopened as *Life Is Beautiful: Icons Remixed*, with new installations, and extended for an additional three months.

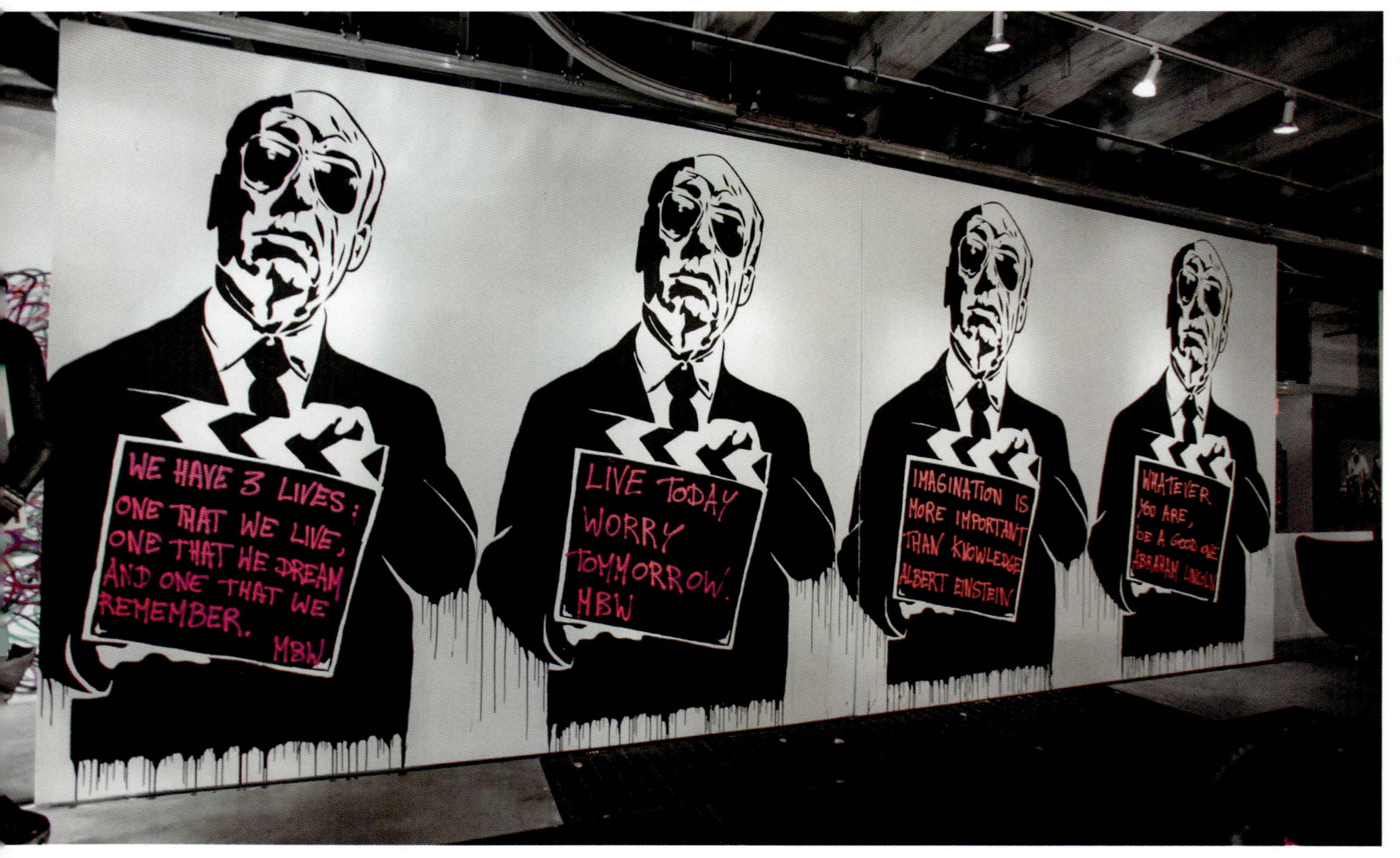

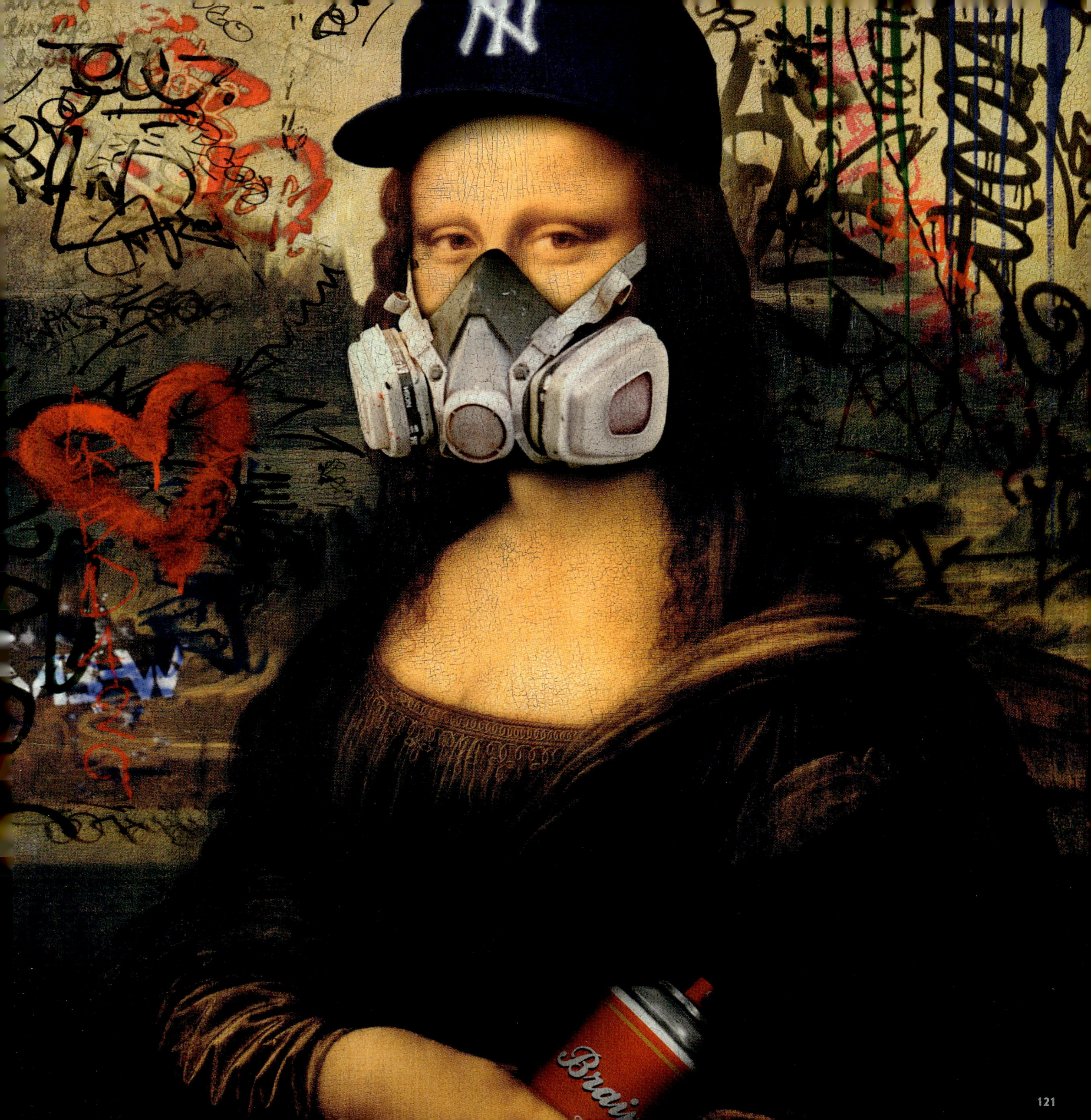
Brai

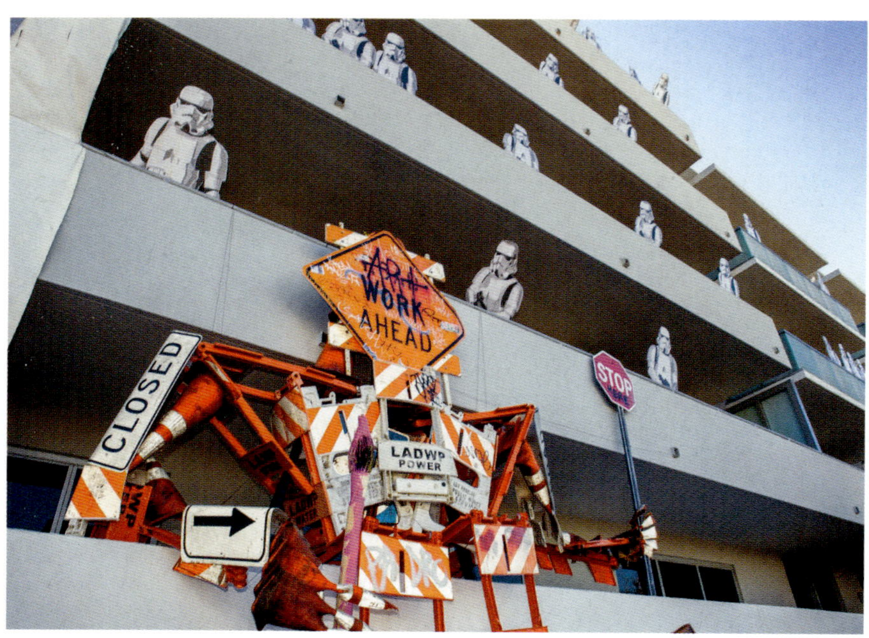

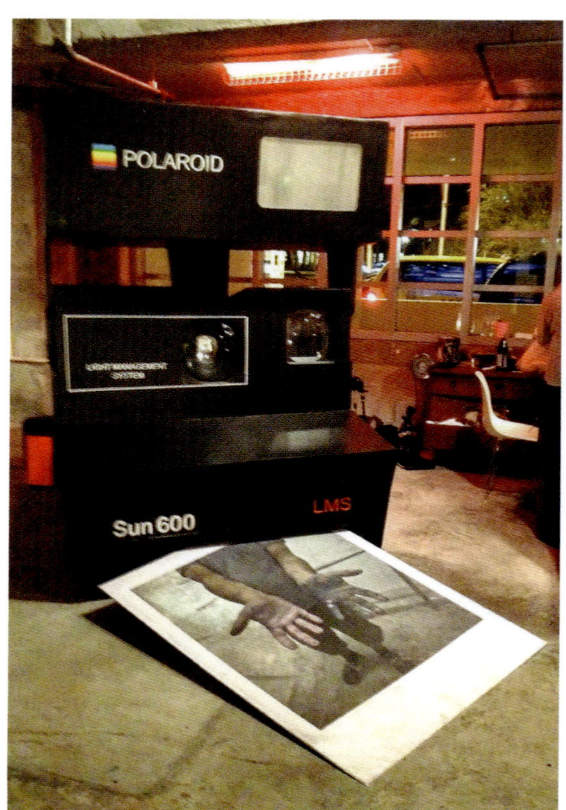

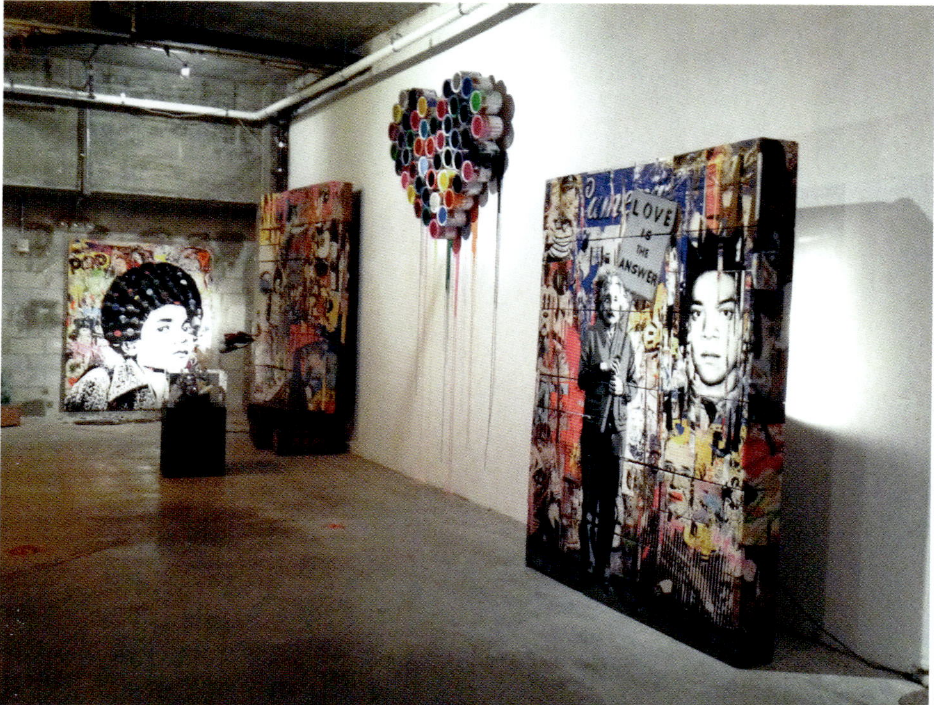

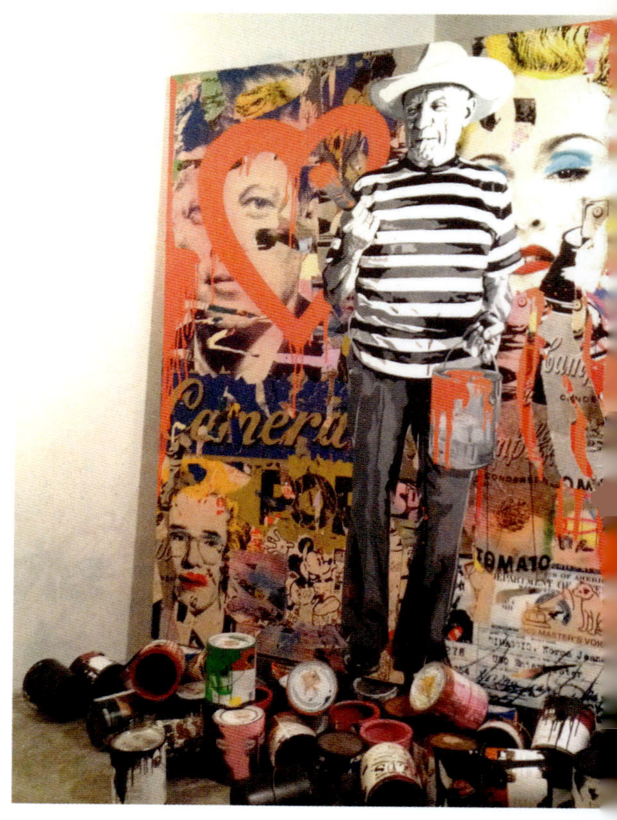

LIFE IS BEAUTIFUL: UNDER CONSTRUCTION
Art Basel Miami Beach, 2010

Mr. Brainwash's Art Basel debut came unannounced to Art Basel Miami Beach and caused a stir with *Life Is Beautiful: Under Construction*. The pop-up show consisted of stormtroopers looking out from various floors of the building, and housed works from Mr. Brainwash in all kinds of mediums.

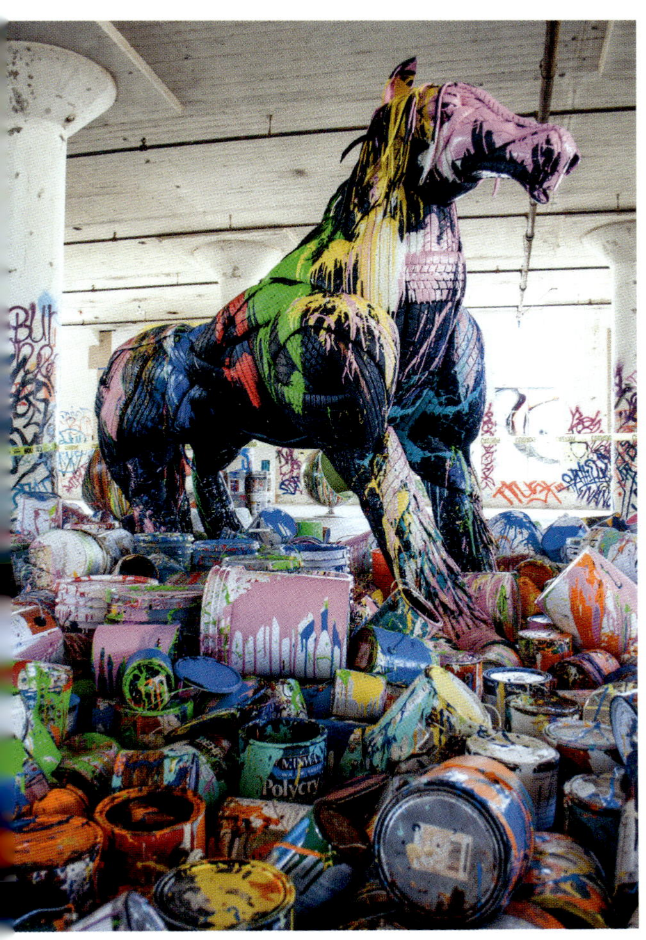

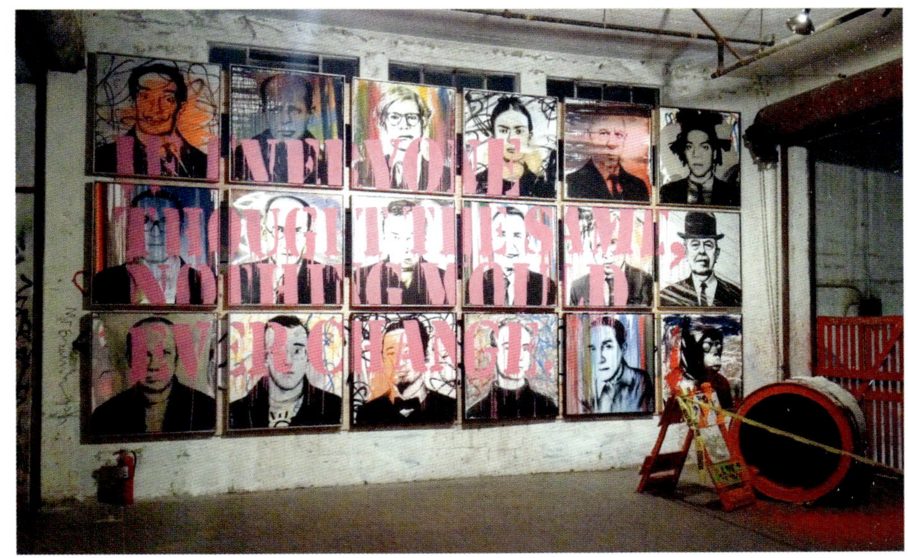

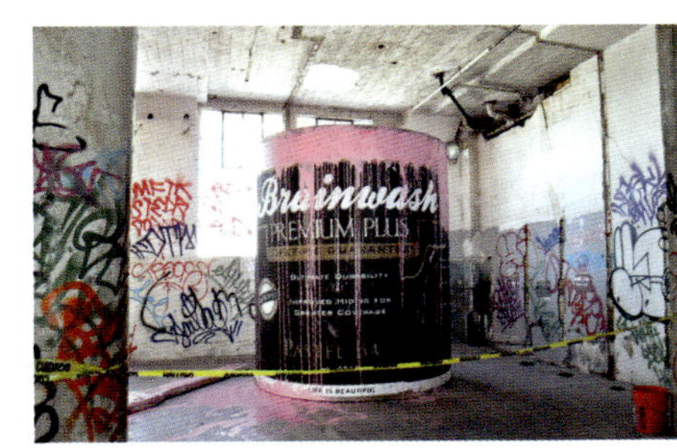

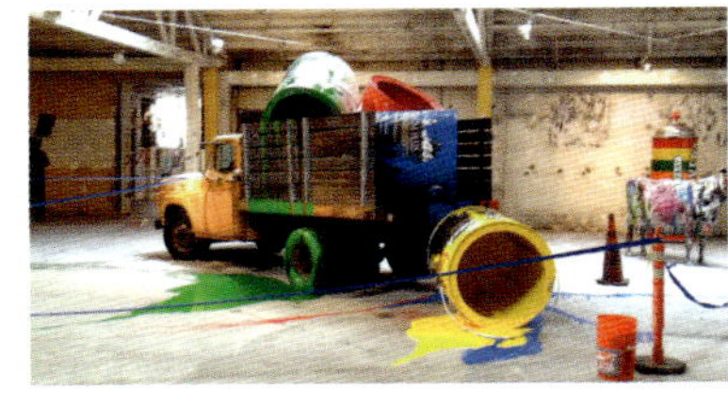

LIFE IS BEAUTIFUL:
ART SHOW 2011

Mr. Brainwash returned to the home of his first solo show, Los Angeles, with *Life Is Beautiful: Art Show 2011*. This show was his biggest yet, taking over an 80,000-square-foot building in the center of the city. Each day, thousands of people gathered to see this thrilling monster of a show, which embraced Los Angeles, the epicenter of pop culture.

Mr. Brainwash also gave artists the opportunity to be a part of the show. He donated over 20,000 square feet of space to showcase works from around the globe. Artists were invited to mail in their art or install the artworks themselves.

The first 300 people to arrive received a special edition print that was numbered, hand-finished, thumb-printed and signed by Mr. Brainwash himself.

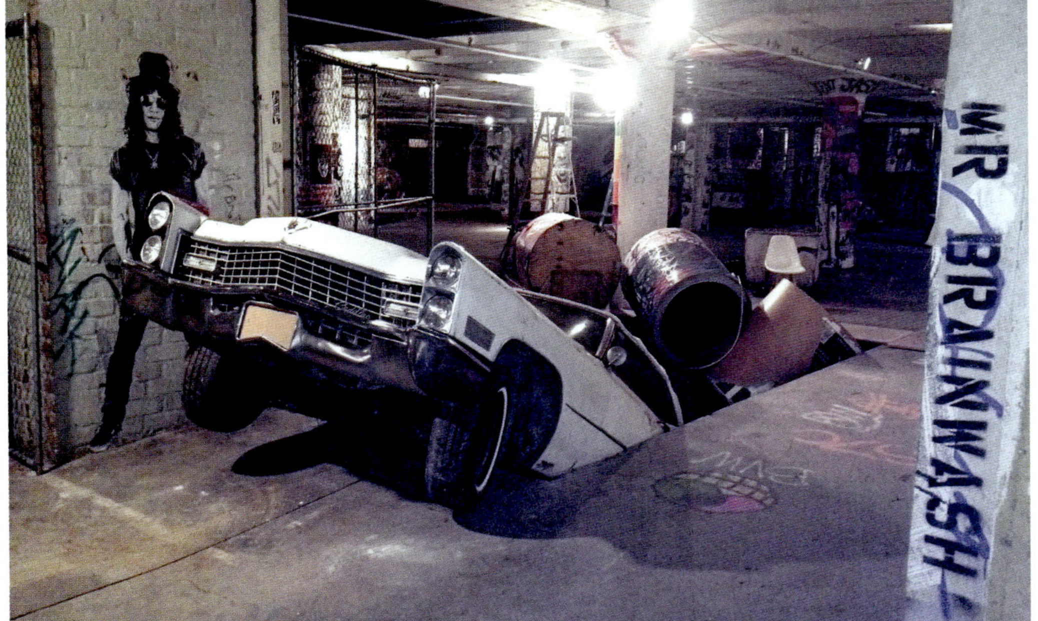

LIFE IS BEAUTIFUL
London 2012 Olympic Games

When the Summer Olympics arrived and the whole world had its eyes on London,
Mr. Brainwash made his UK debut. Already a well-known name because of his collaborations
with Banksy, he invaded the Old Sorting Office, a colossal space only steps from the British
Museum. The first thing visitors saw was a 6-storey-tall Queen Elizabeth II, in her
coronation attire, holding a Union Jack spray can, painted on the side of the building. The
show saw large crowds each day and became Mr. Brainwash's most attended show to date.

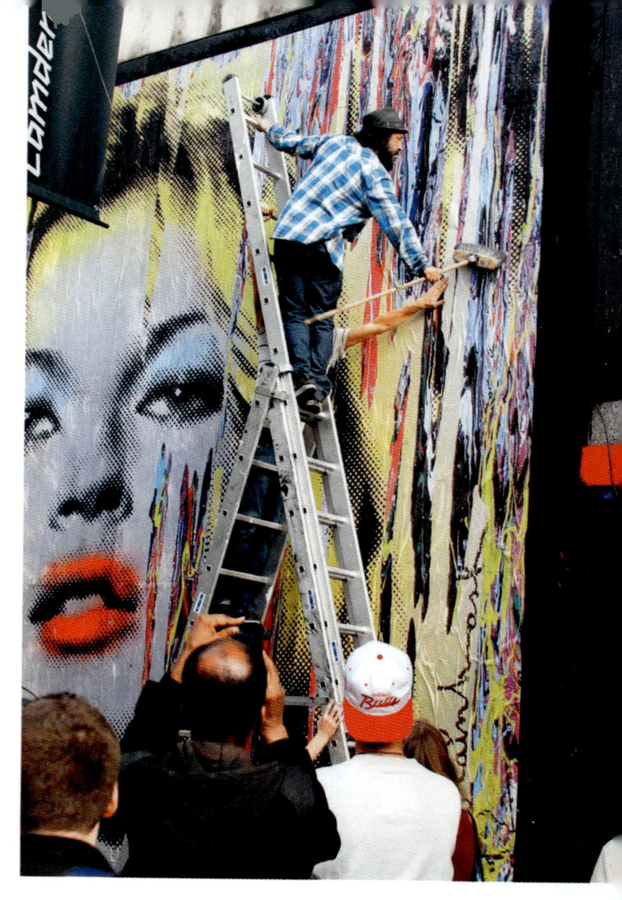

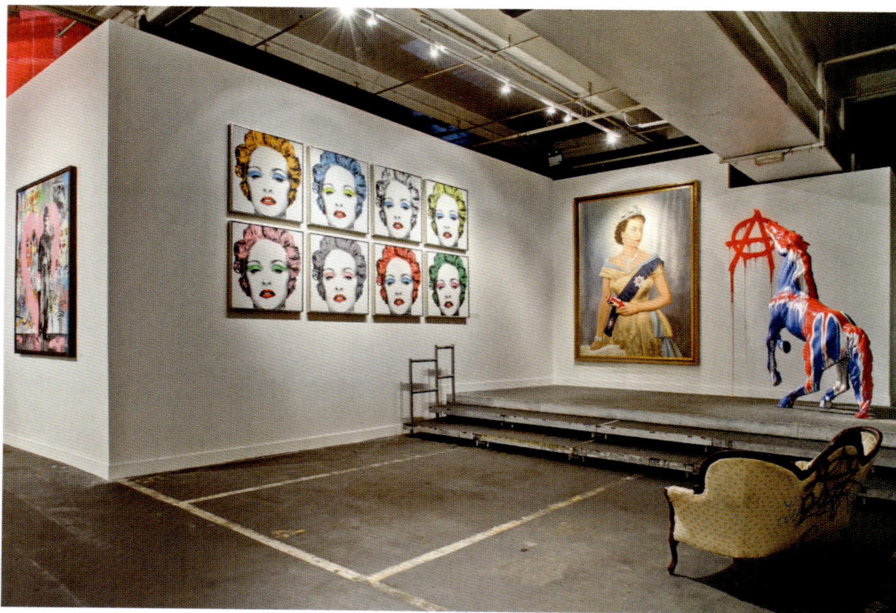

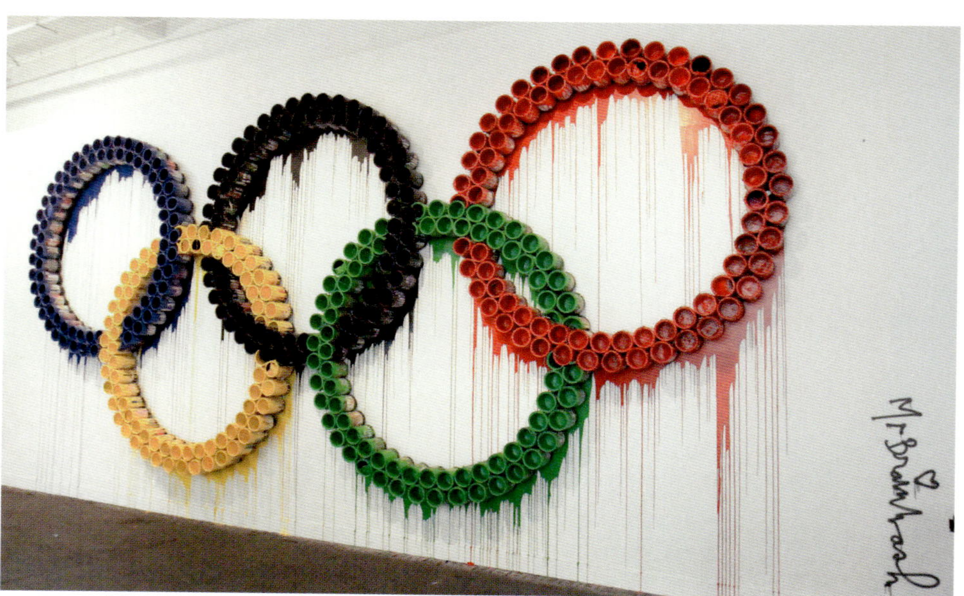

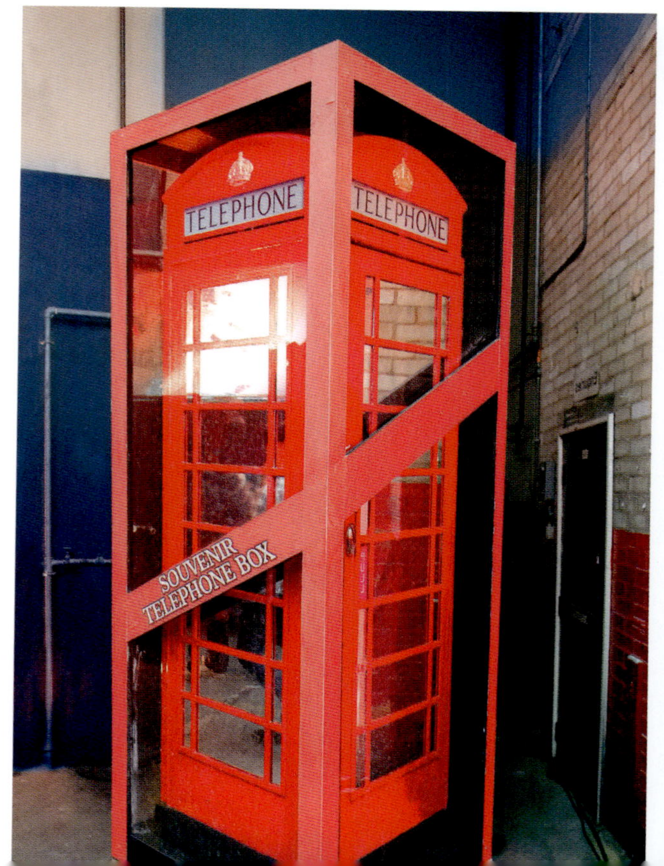

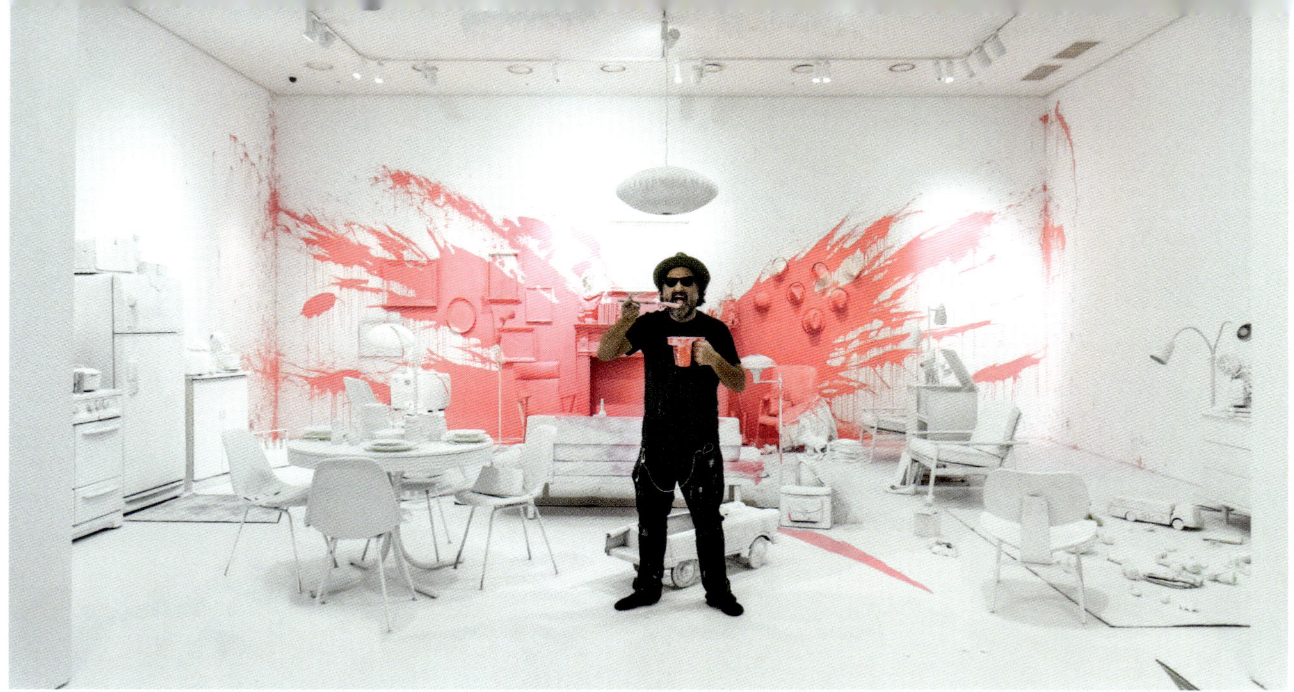

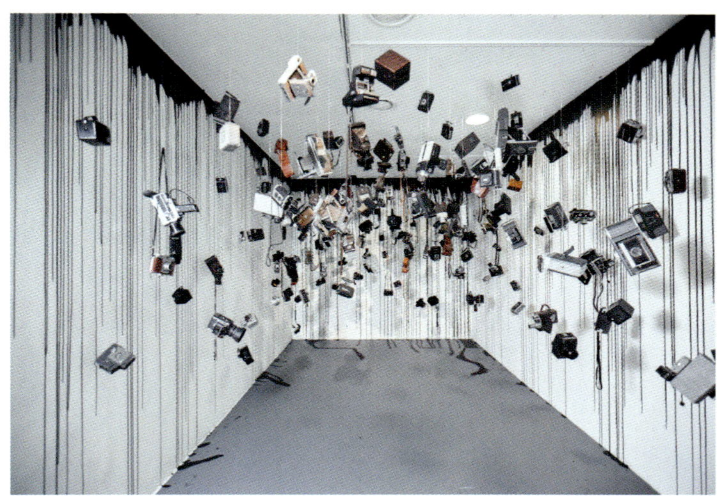

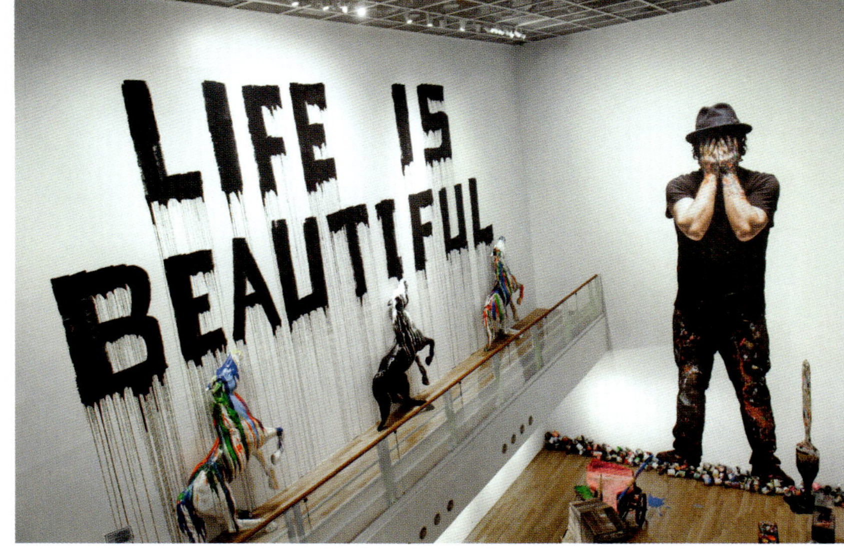

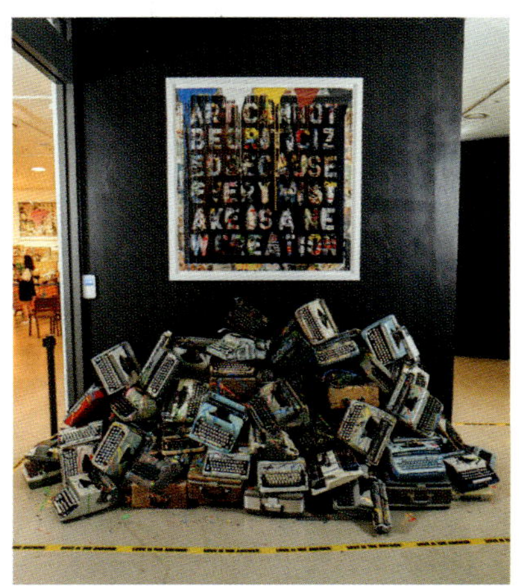

LIFE IS BEAUTIFUL

Seoul, South Korea, 2016

June 2016 marked the debut of Mr. Brainwash's spectacular solo shows in Asia. He opened his first exhibition in South Korea at the ARA Modern Art Museum in Insadong in Seoul. Large mixed media murals were on display showcasing Mr. Brainwash's iconic artwork and larger-than-life scope. Highlights included a massive 15-foot-tall wooden AT-AT from the Star Wars movie franchise, a room full of vintage cameras hanging from the ceiling, and a white room splashed with pink paint.

Mr. Brainwash collaborated with musicians from YG Entertainment, the label-home of K-pop artists Big Bang and 2NE1 to name a couple, to create one-of-a-kind artworks.

1600 Pennsylvania Avenue

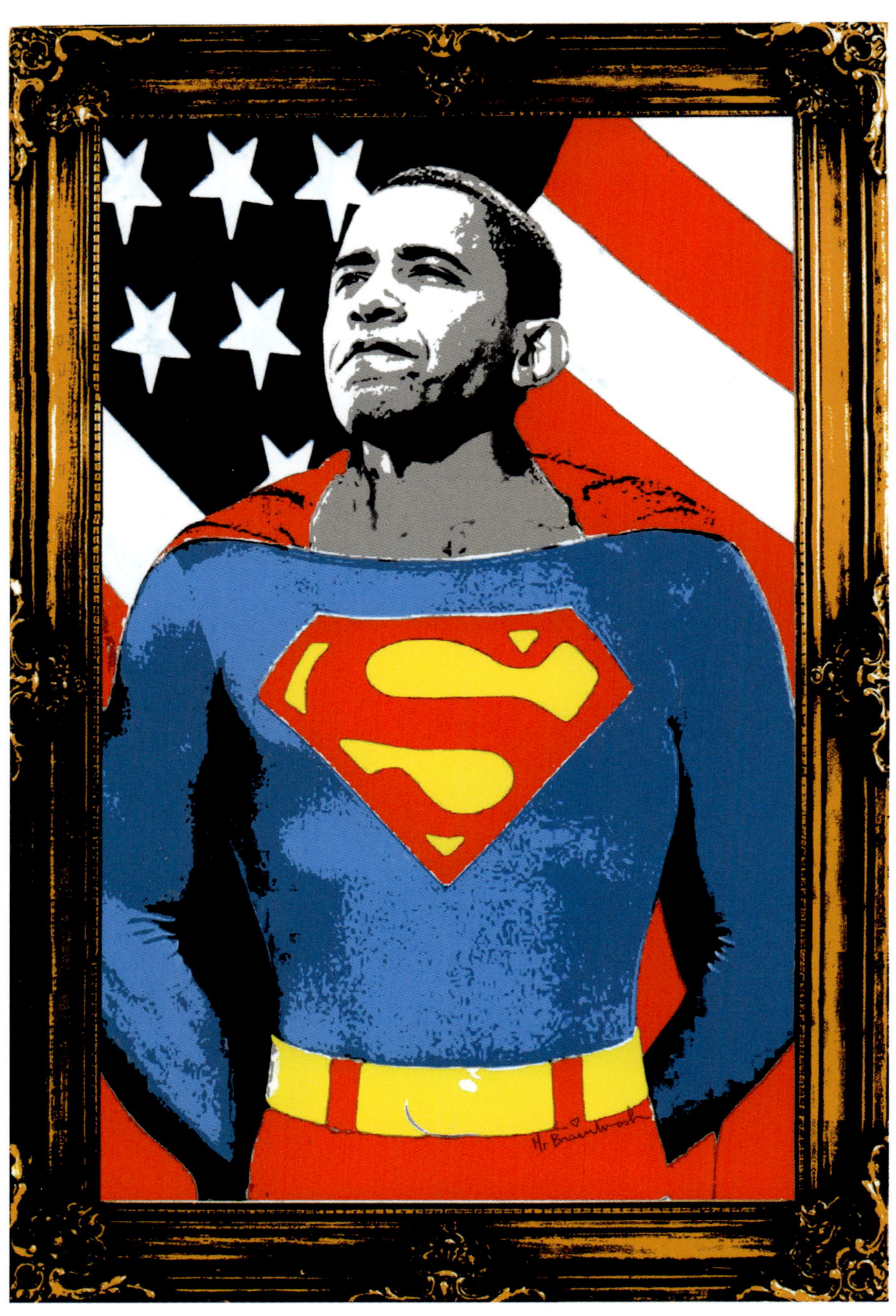

Obama Superman
42" x 29"
Silkscreen edition print

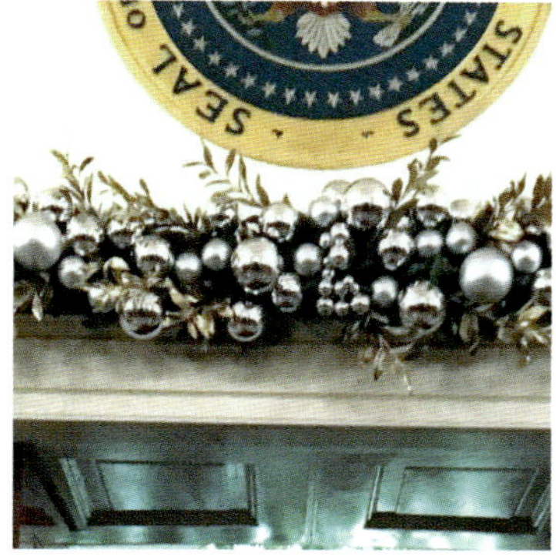

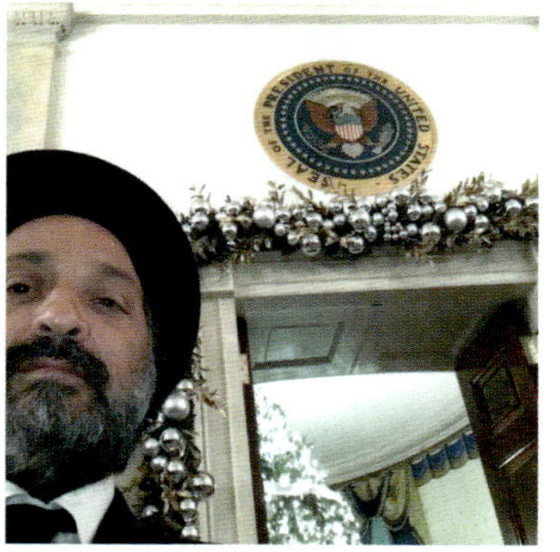

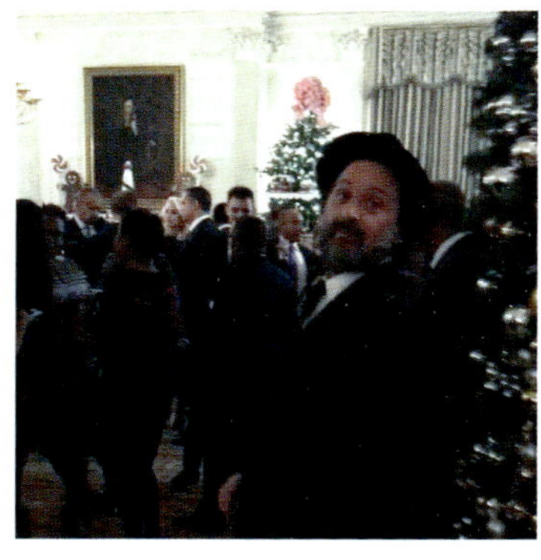

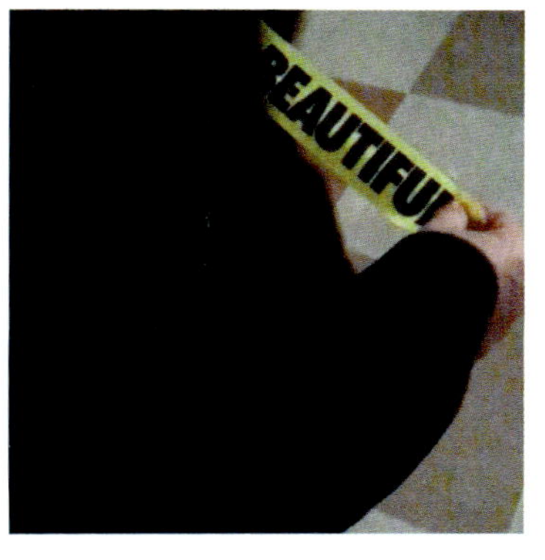

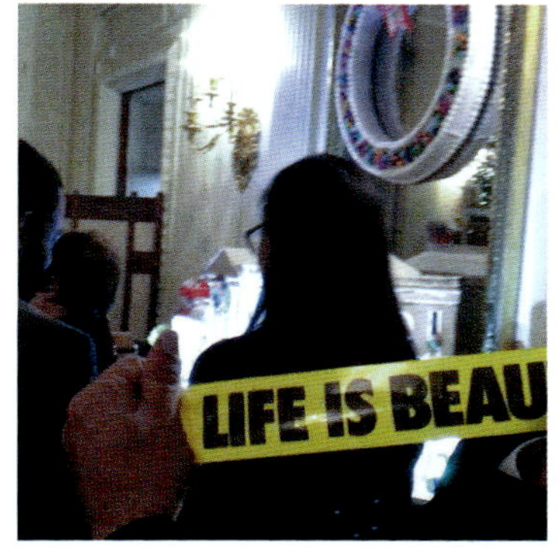

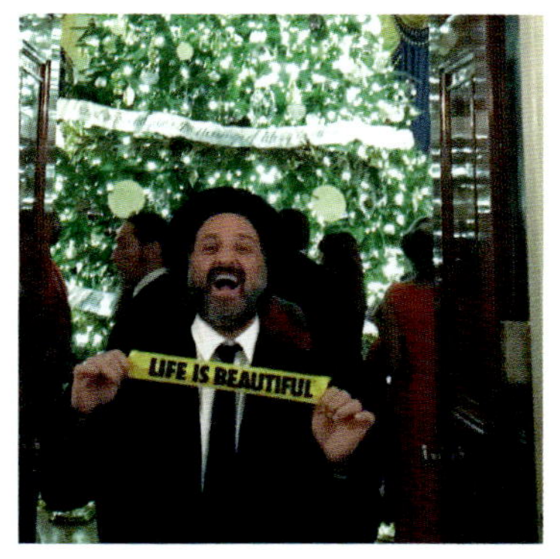

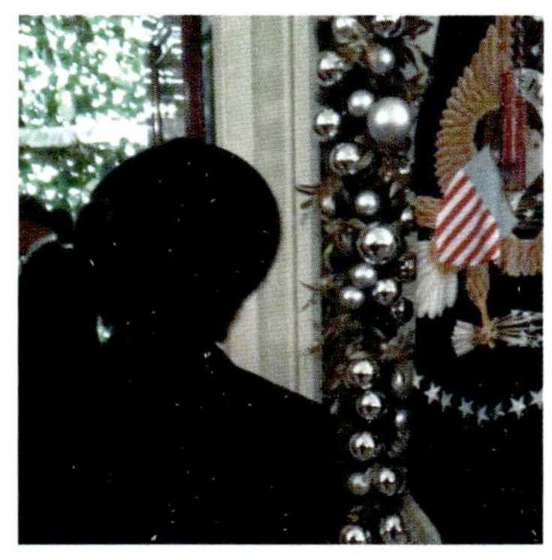

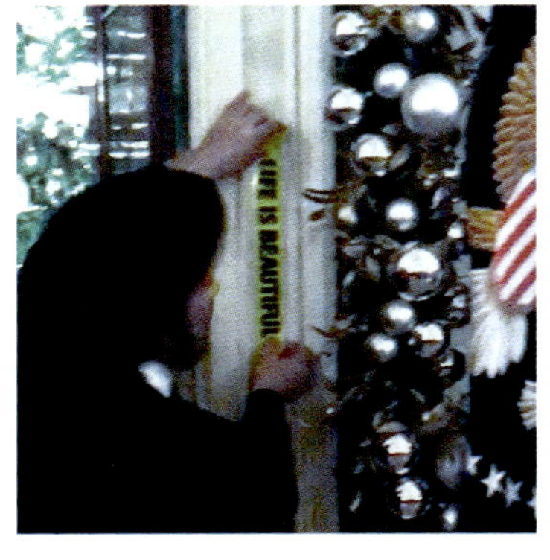

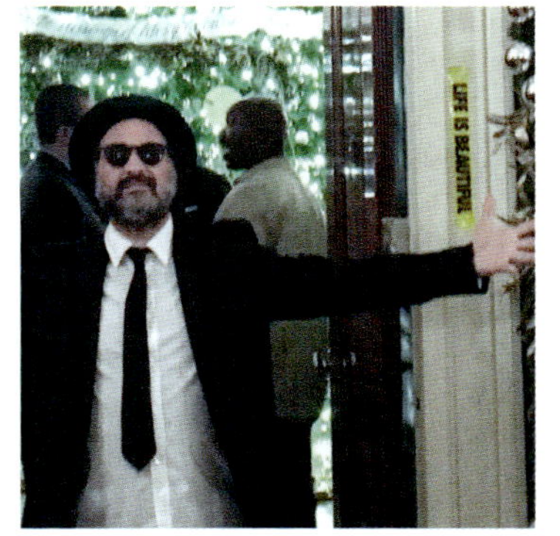

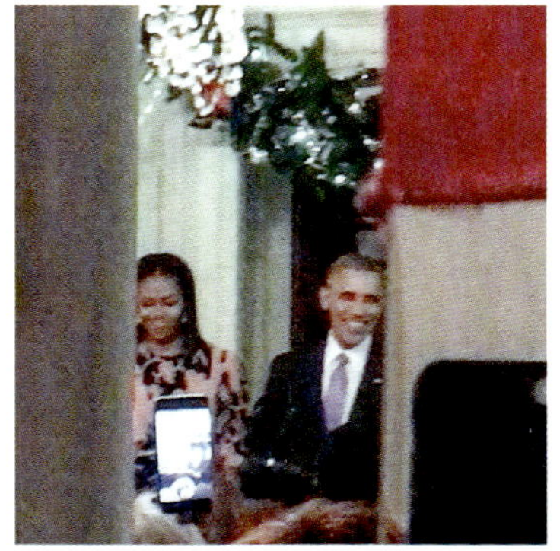

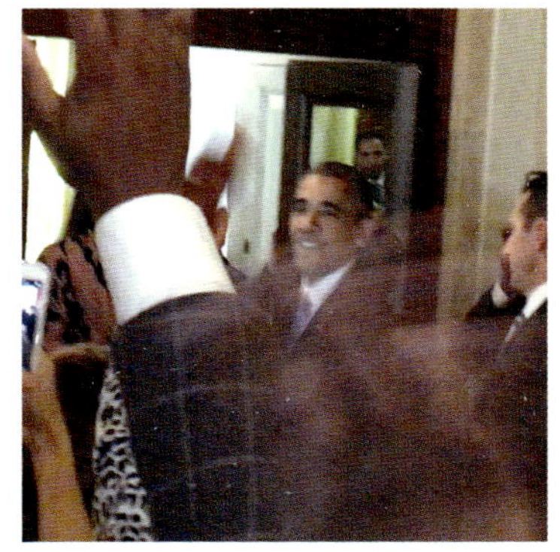

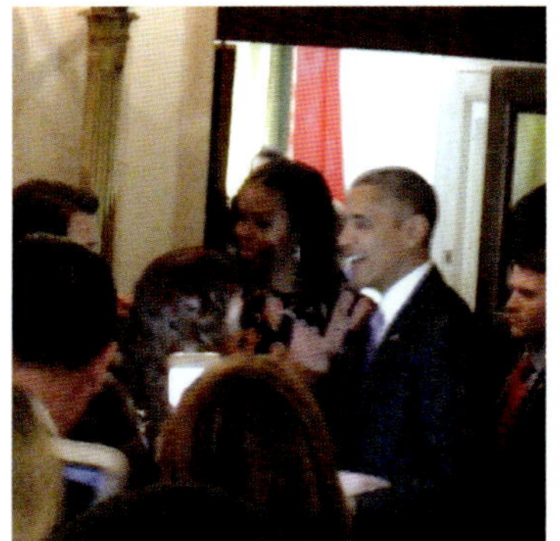

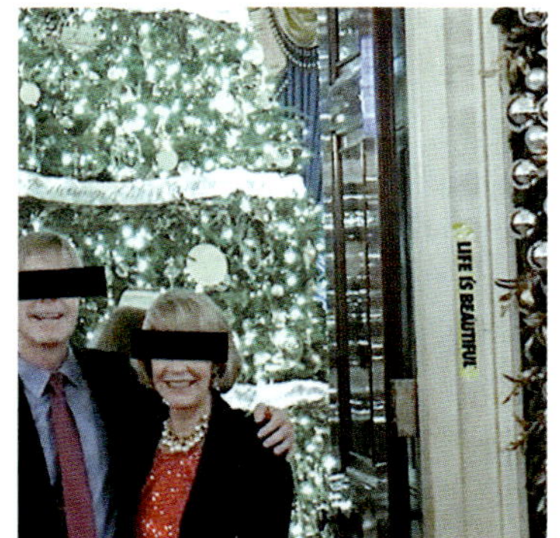

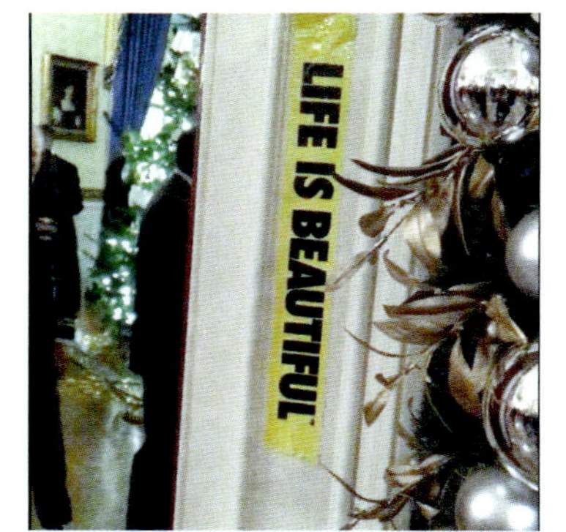

In December 2016 Mr. Brainwash was invited to the annual White House holiday party. During the event he stuck a *Life Is Beautiful* sticker onto the dining room doorframe, where it photobombed unsuspecting guests all night long. For one night only, 1600 Pennsylvania Avenue was brainwashed.

LIFE IS LIKE A GAME
OF CHESS.

I DON'T KNOW HOW
TO PLAY CHESS.

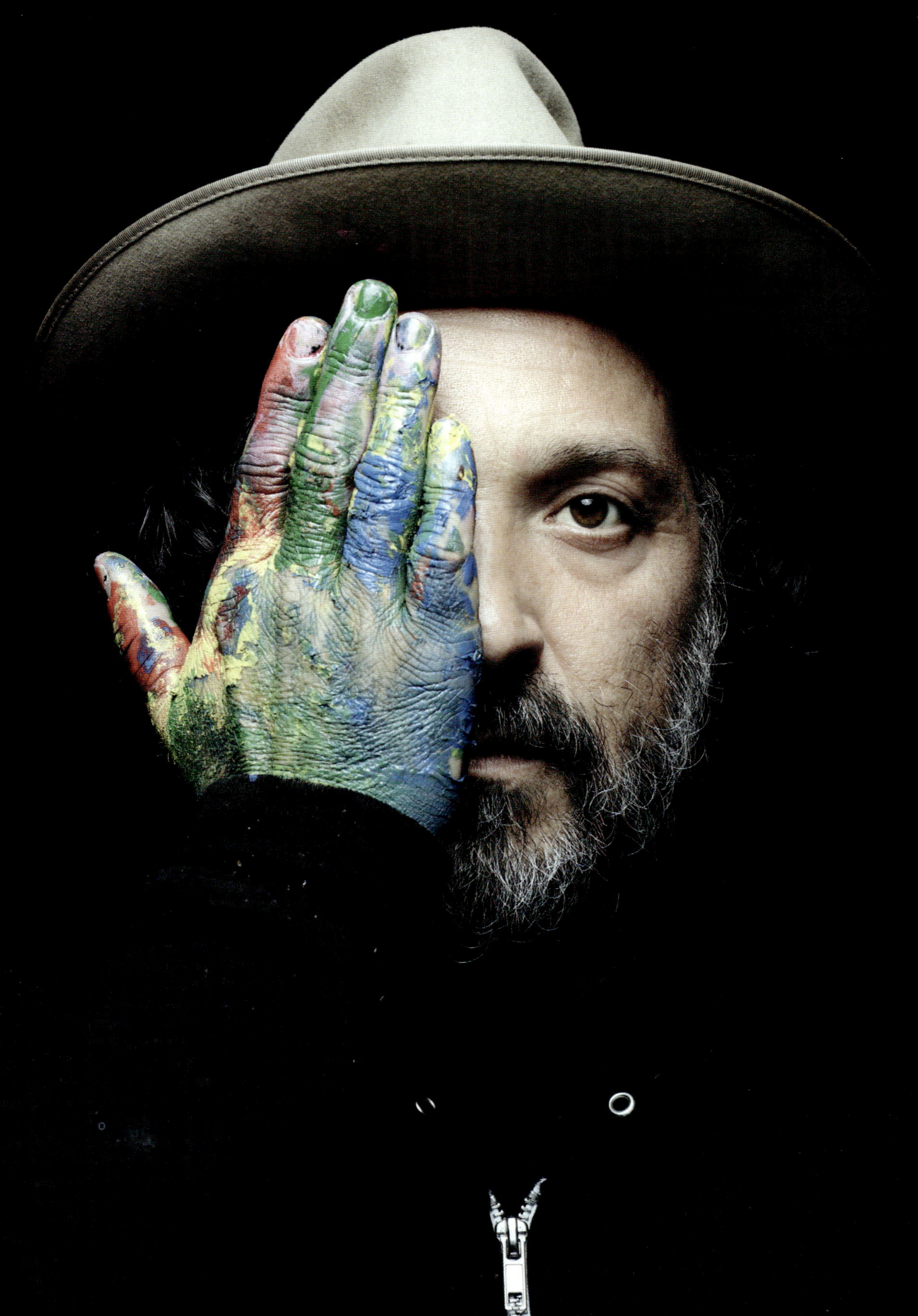

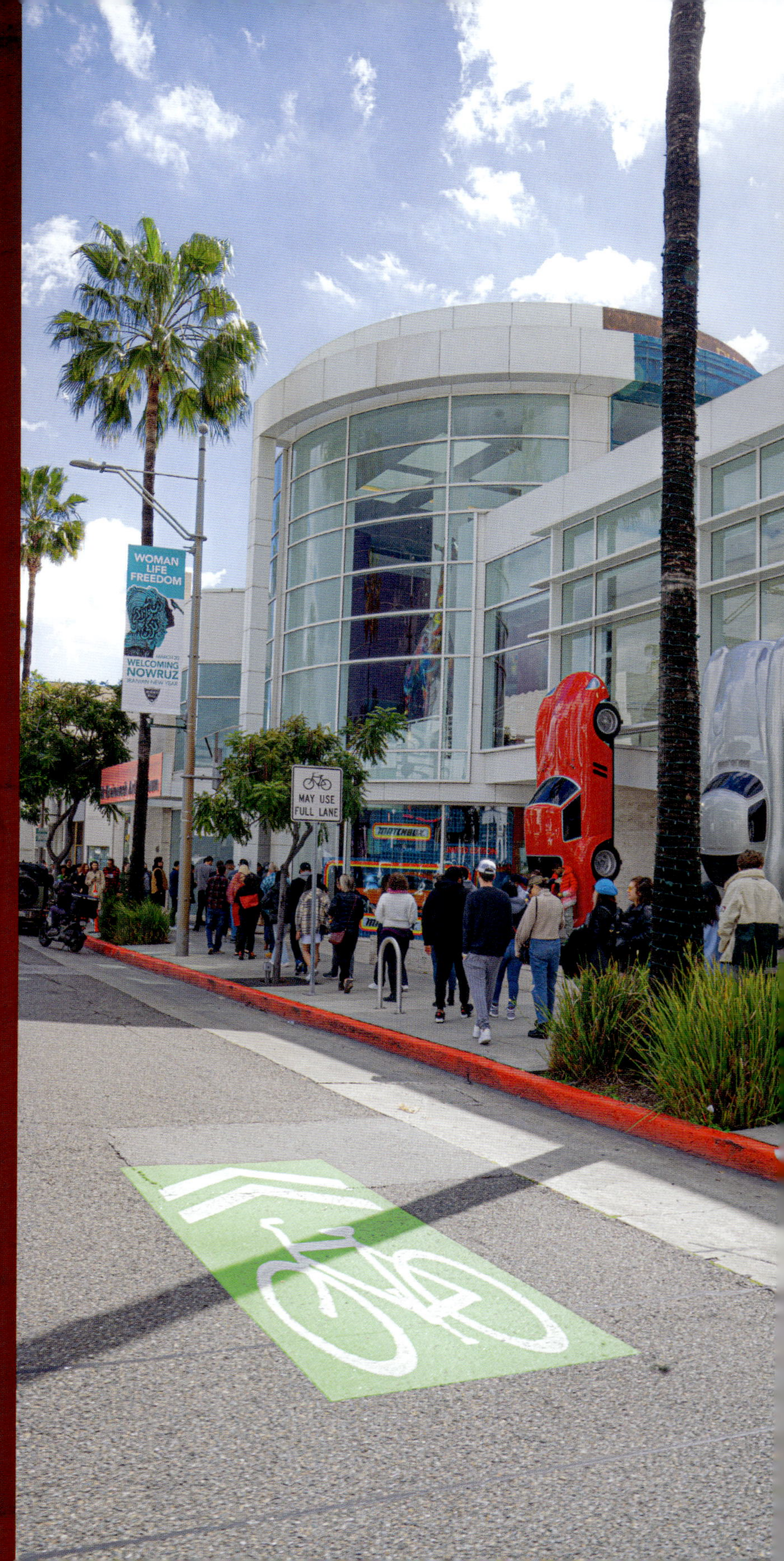

2022
MR. BRAINWASH ART MUSEUM
465 N Beverly Drive, Beverly Hills, 90210

Founded by Mr. Brainwash and opening in December 2022, the Mr. Brainwash Art Museum is an immersive museum located in Beverly Hills showcasing a new world of art. Upon entering the museum, visitors are greeted by a clash of color and a sense of wonder. The space itself is a reflection of Mr. Brainwash's unconventional approach to art and provides an insightful journey through his artistic evolution.

The museum features a wide range of artwork, pop culture references, and reinterpretations of iconic images. Visitors can expect to see a stunning mix of vibrant murals, sculptures, large installations, and even interactive pieces inviting them to become a part of the work. This mix of media and themes within the museum reflects Mr. Brainwash's playful and creative approach to creating art.

One of the museum's standout features is its ability to surprise and challenge conventional notions of art. It's a space where visitors are encouraged to question the boundaries of artistic expression and to engage with art in unexpected ways. Mr. Brainwash's work often carries a message, and visitors may find themselves pondering the deeper meaning behind the awe-inspiring pieces.

Overall, the Mr. Brainwash Art Museum offers a dynamic experience that appeals to art enthusiasts, fans of street art, those curious about the thought-provoking world of Mr. Brainwash's art, and even those just passing by. It's a testament to the ever-evolving nature of contemporary art and the ability of artists like Mr. Brainwash to display the boundaries of creativity.

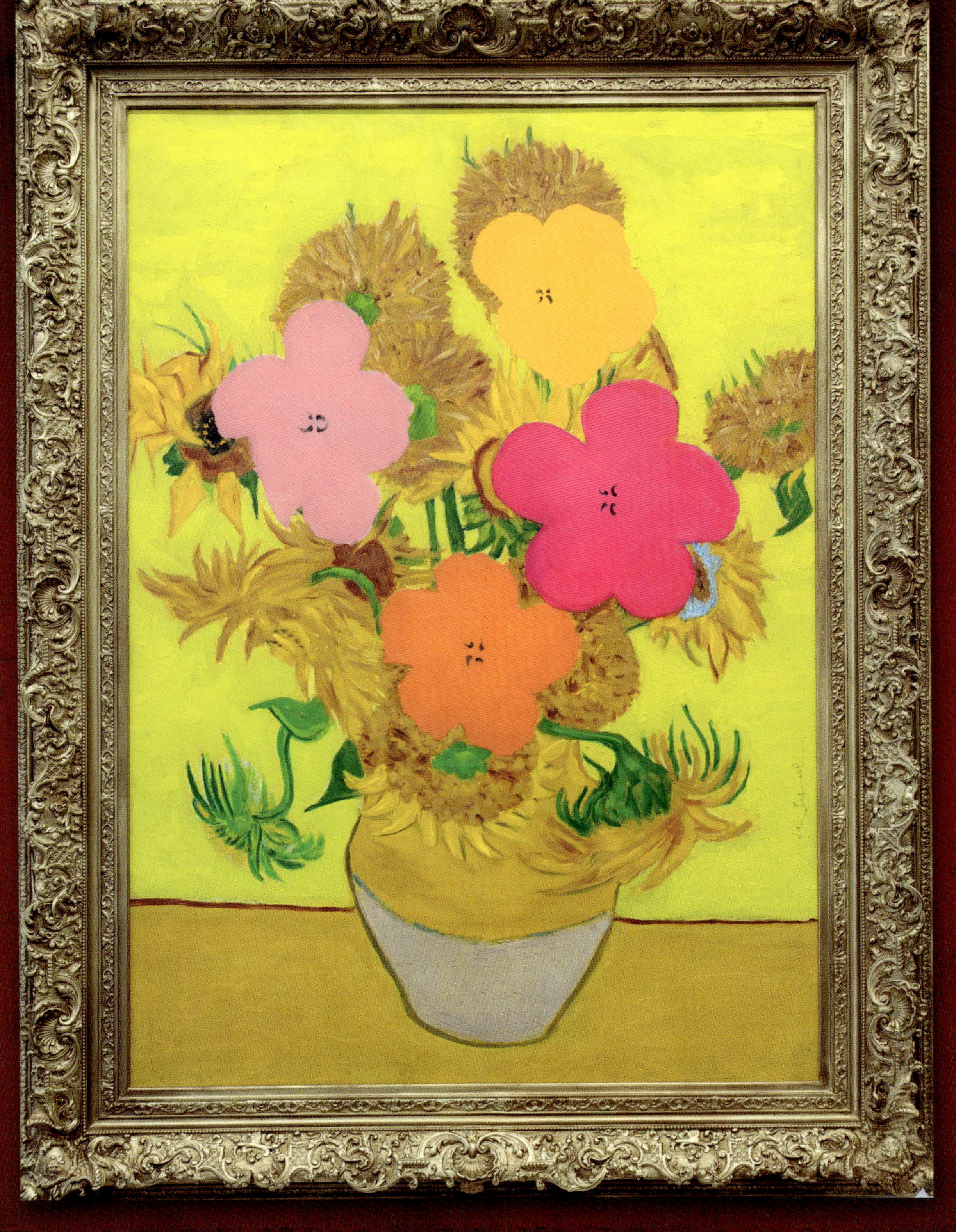

MASTER BRAINWASH

An intimate gallery of experimentation and expression that explodes all expectations—here the great artists and archetypes of art history have been thoroughly brainwashed in anticipation of your thoughtful interpretation. We hope you enjoy these energetic engagements with the imagination, in which past blends with present in provocative new ways...

"Art Is Fun."
Mr. Brainwash

LISA LISA LISA

Discover the imaginary lives of Mona Lisa... She has been a solitary portrait hanging alone at the Louvre for over 200 years, Mr. Brainwash decided to help this most famous of Italian noblewomen explore and express her various personalities and passions, to engage in a renaissance of possibilities!

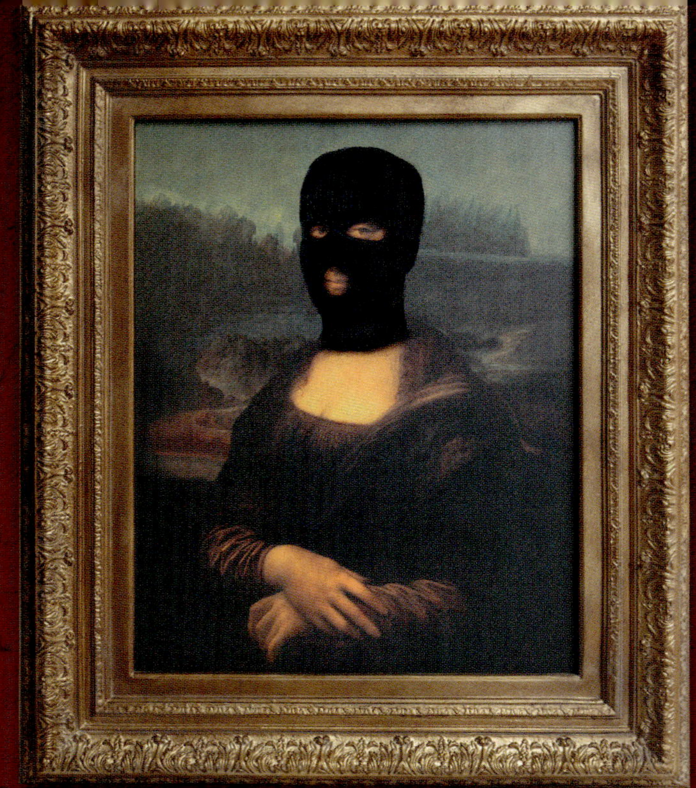

MONA LISA

Considered an archetypal masterpiece of the Italian Renaissance, this half-length portrait painting by Italian artist Leonardo da Vinci has been housed at the Louvre in Paris since 1797. The artwork's global fame stems from its theft in 1911 by Vincenzo Peruggia, who believed the painting should belong to Italy—a sensational act that generated unprecedented publicity for art theft!

"Smile"

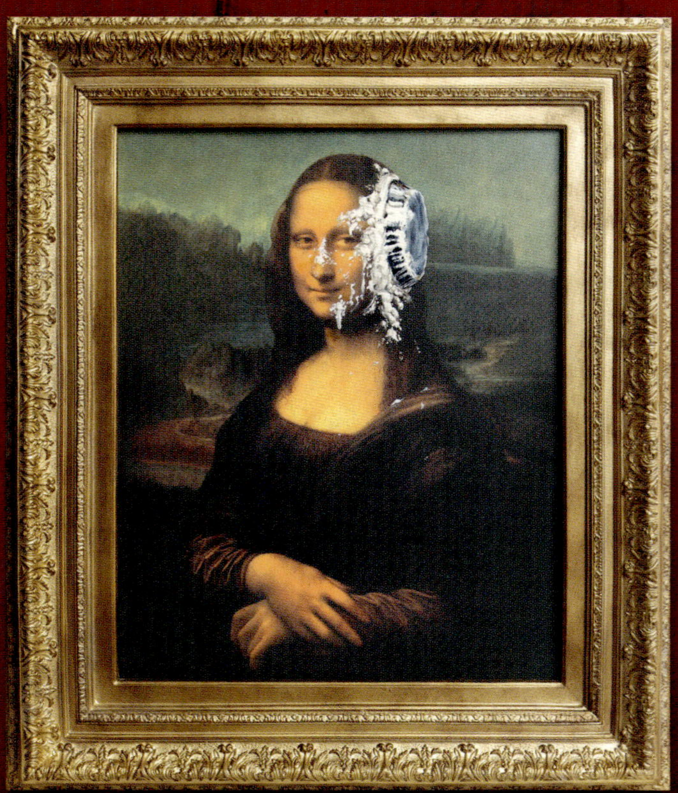

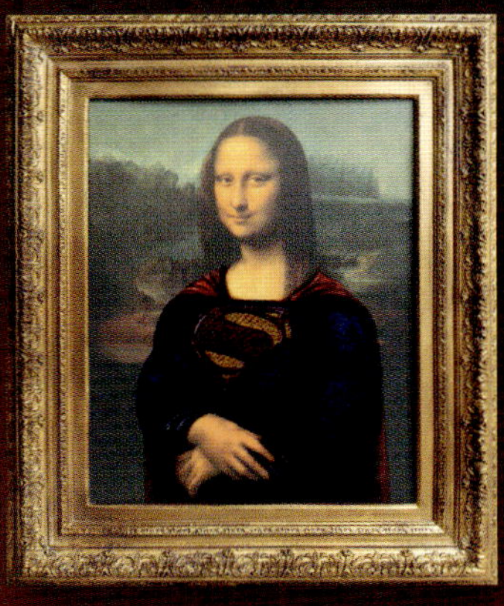
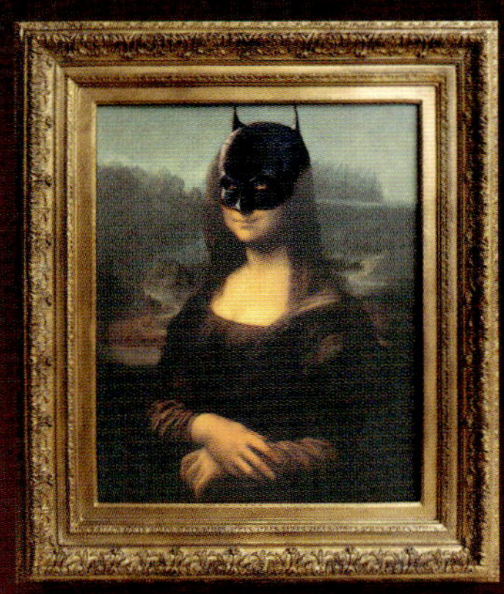
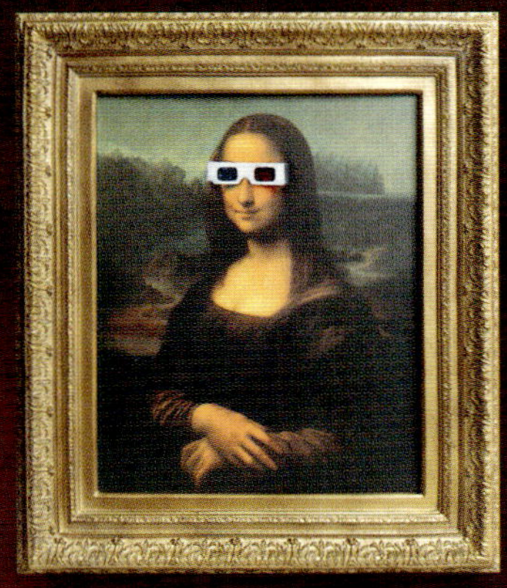
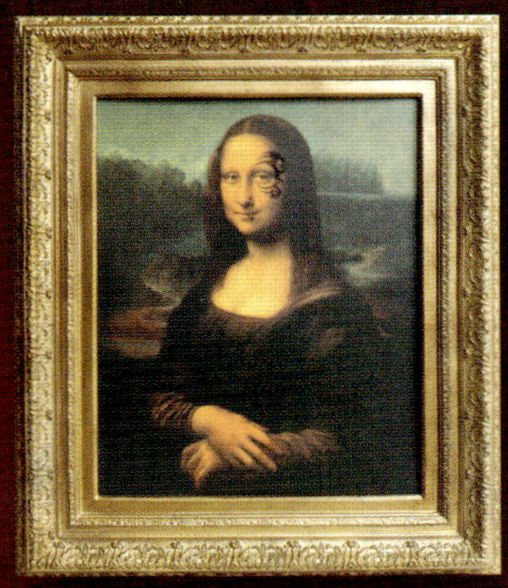
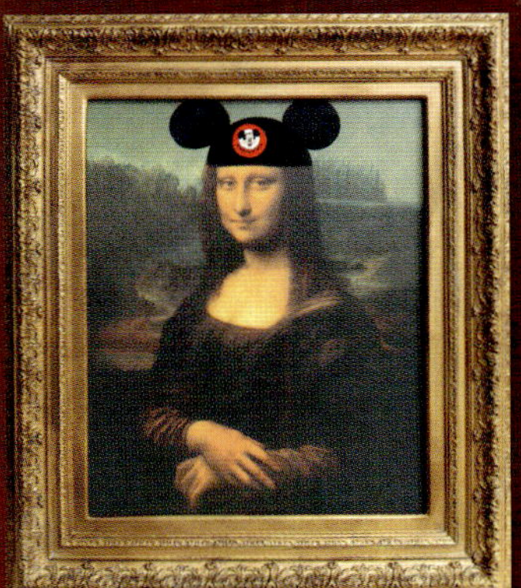
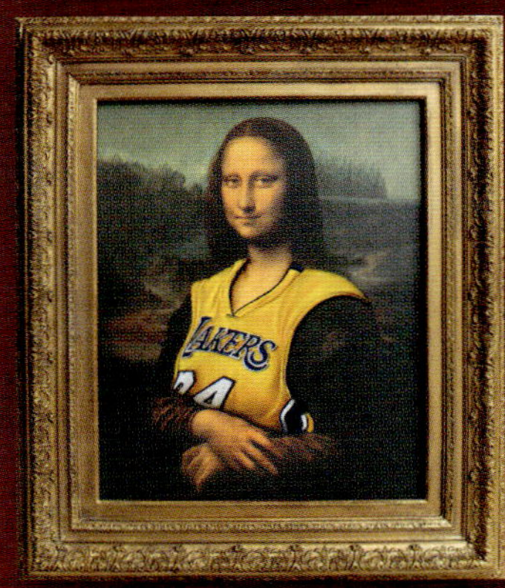
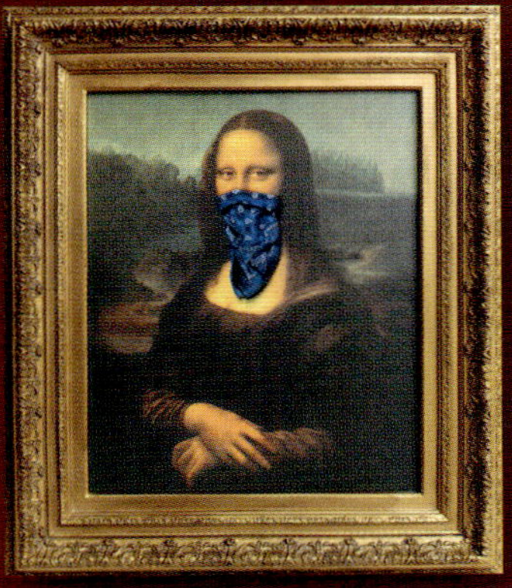
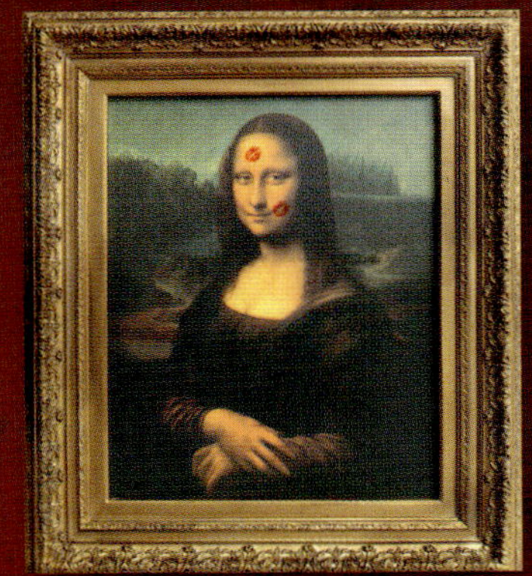
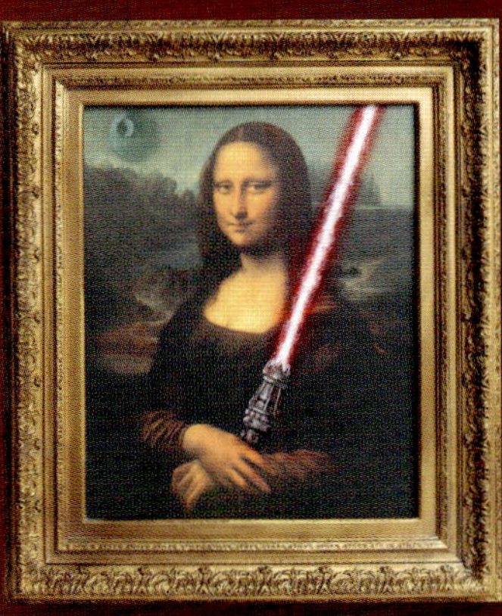
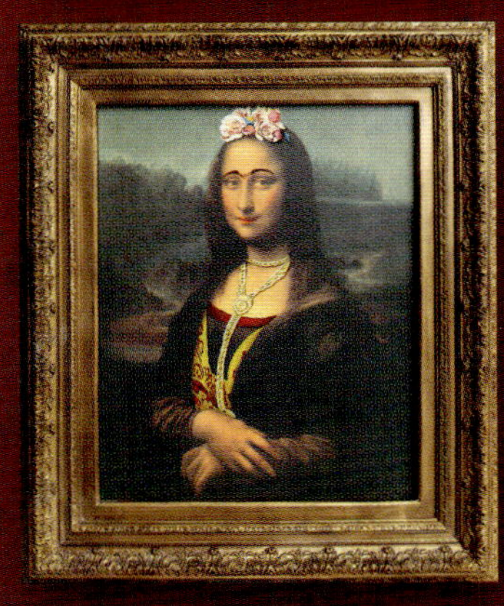
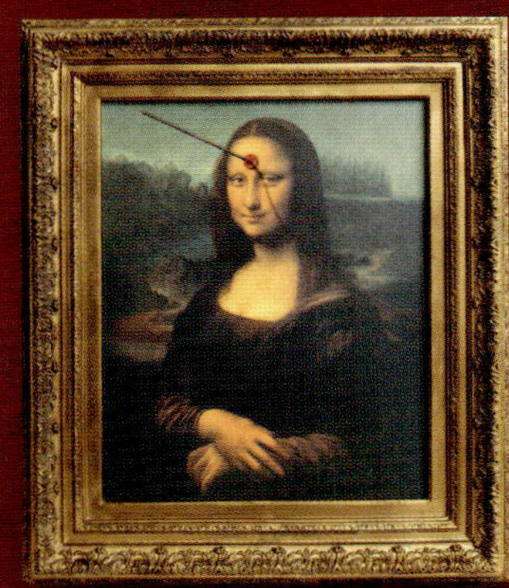
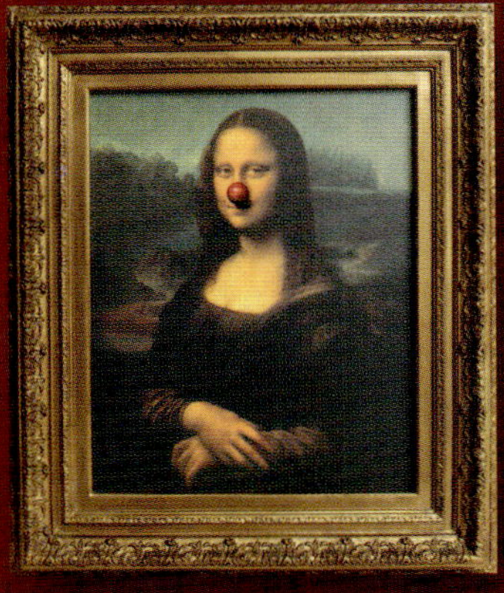
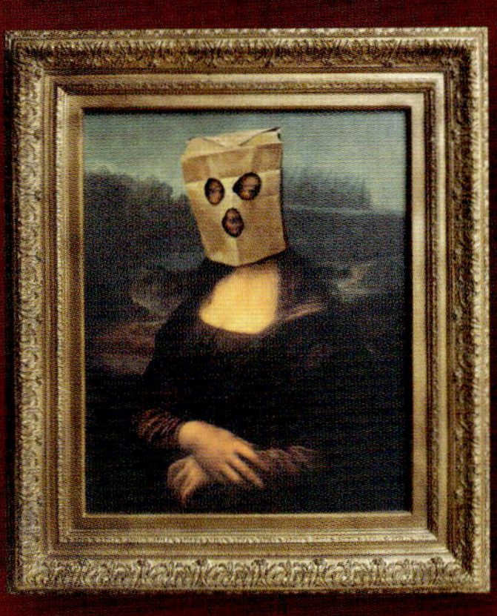
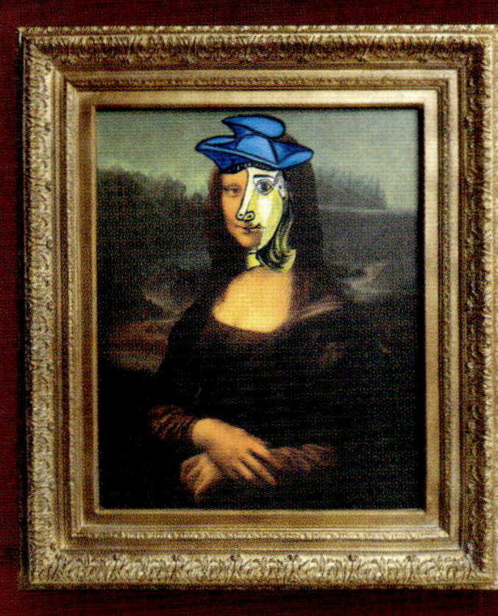
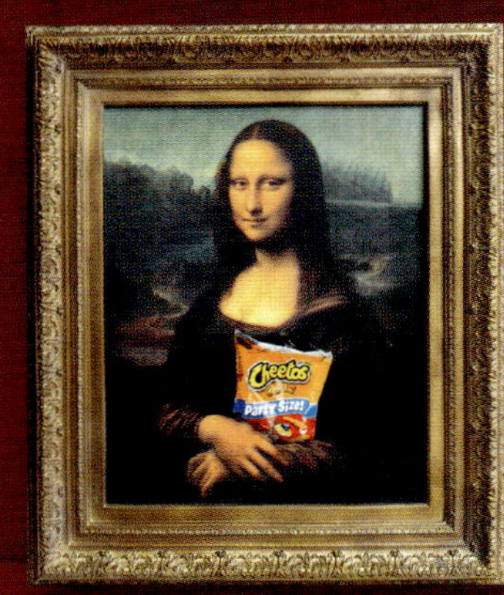
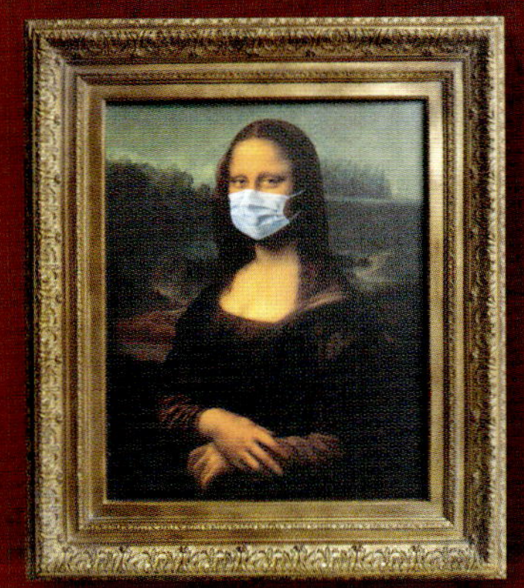

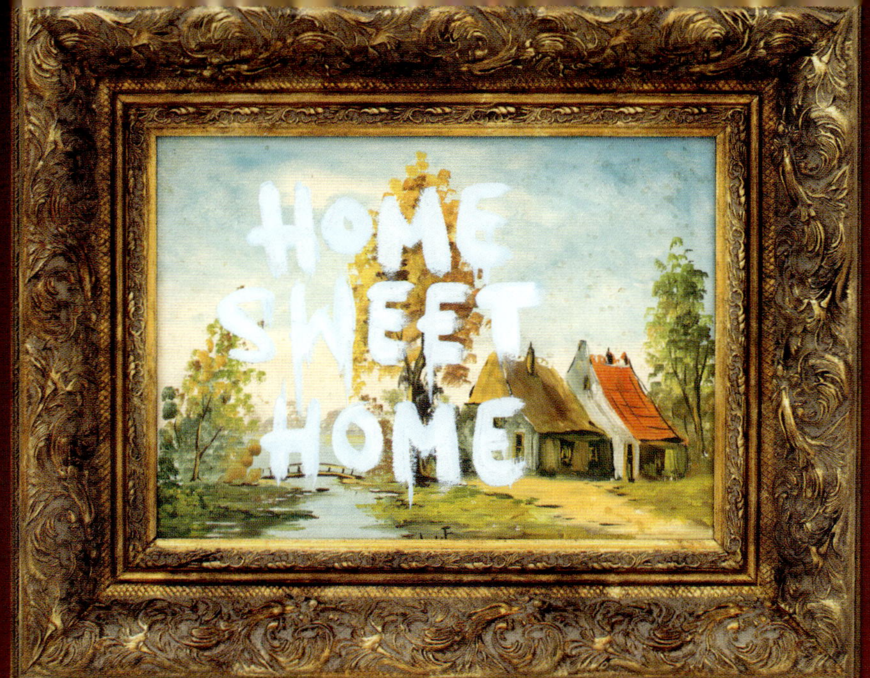
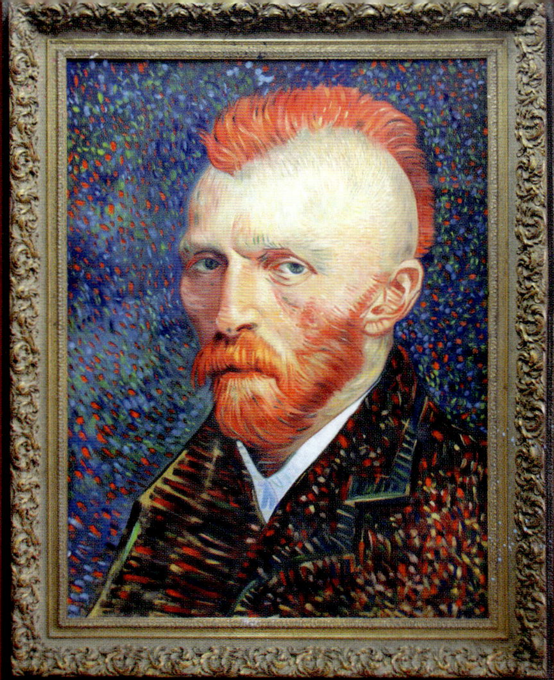

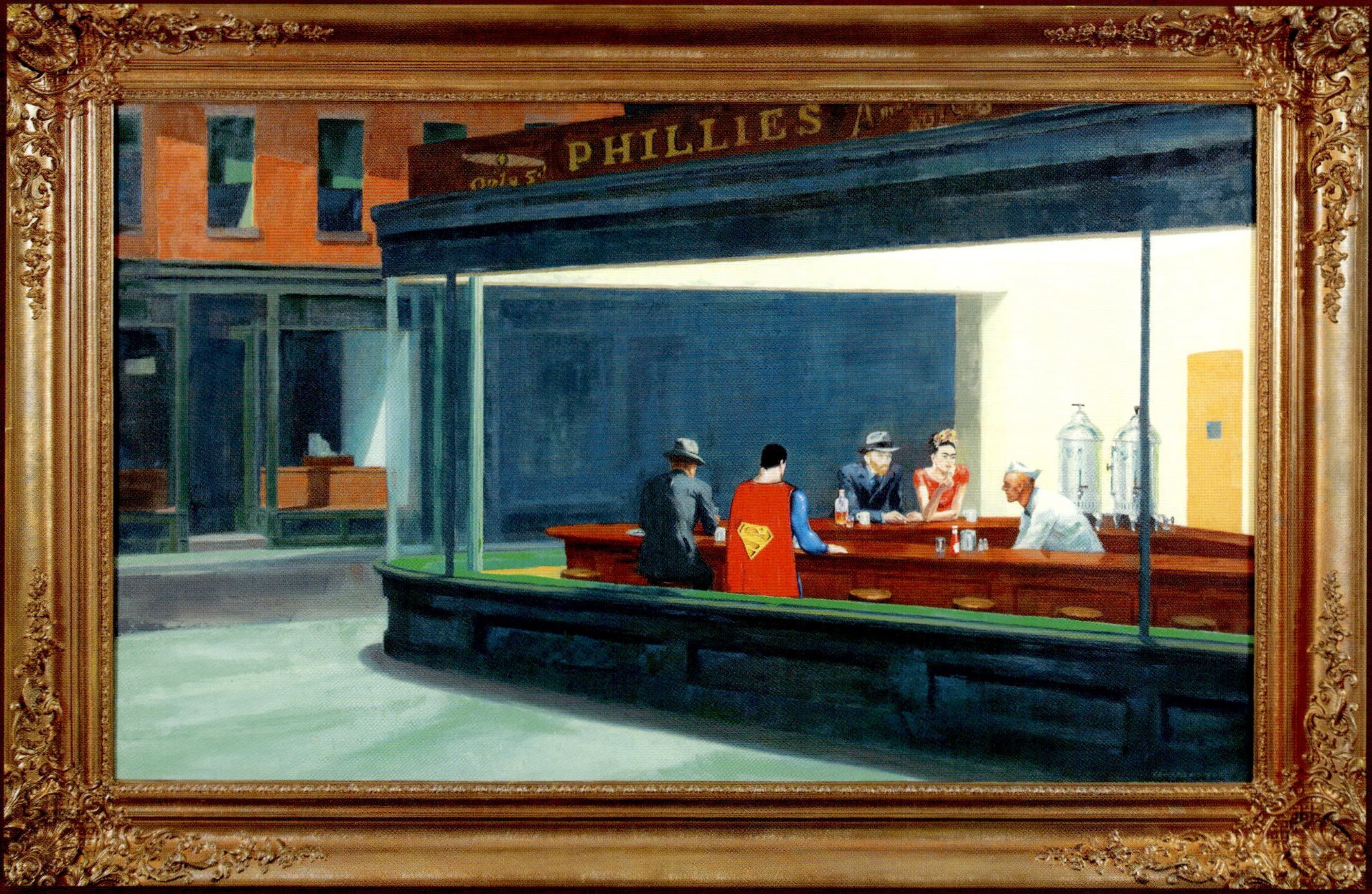

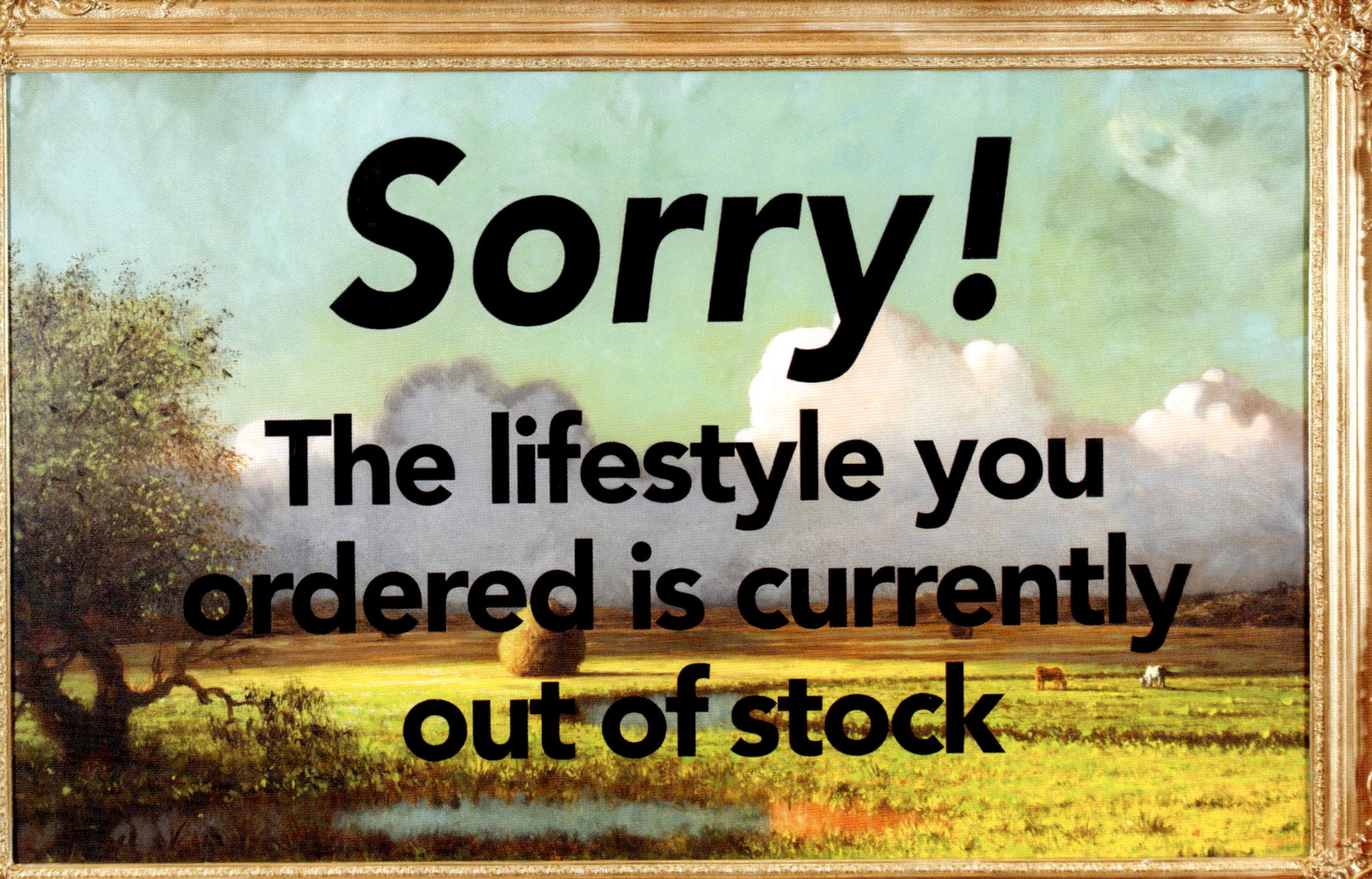

Sorry!
The lifestyle you ordered is currently out of stock

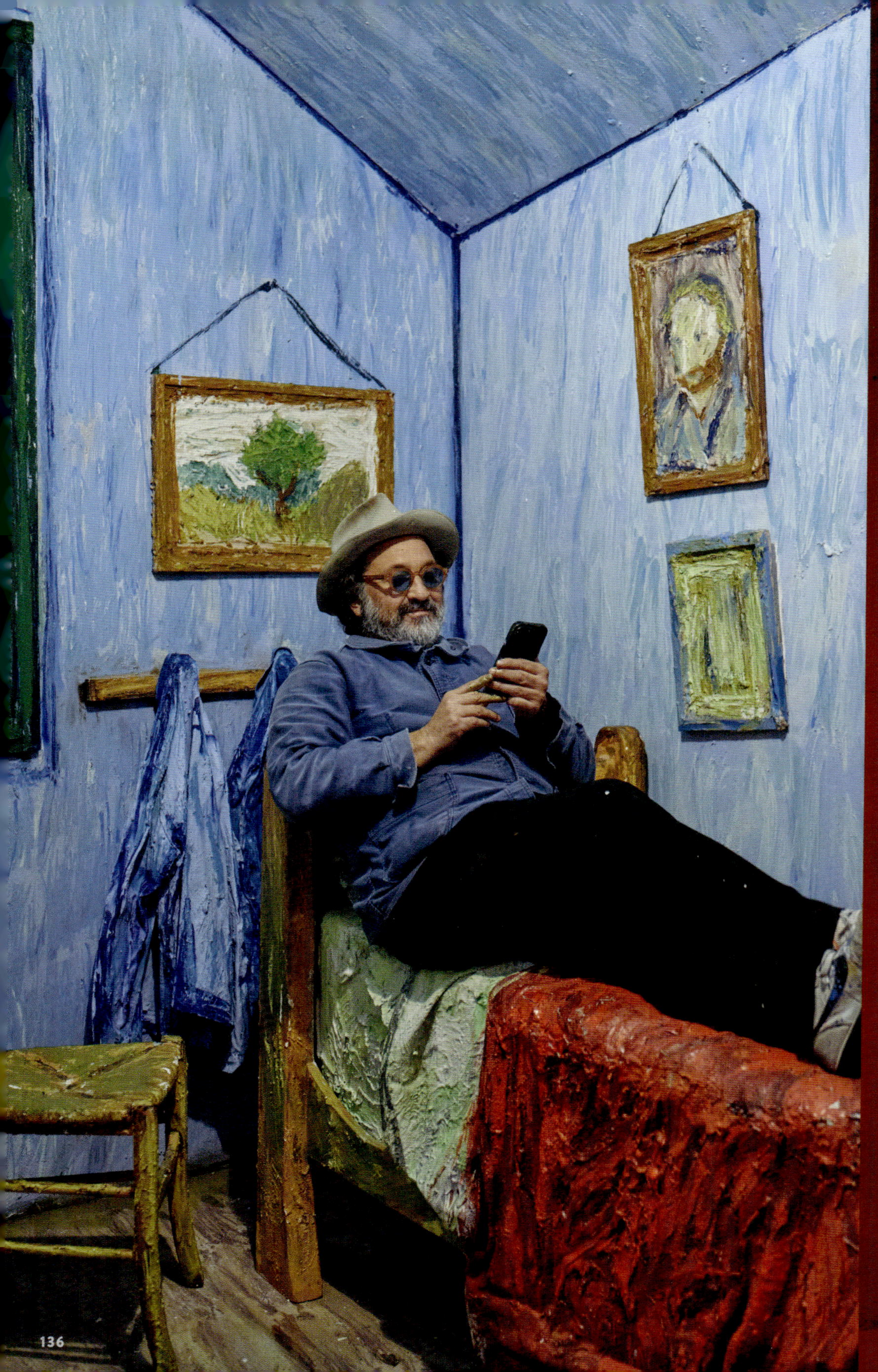

ENTER THE PAINTING

Live in the past moment, right now! Break free from the rules of perspective and find your way into a new frame of mind. Put yourself in the picture, and become part of the most iconic bedroom still-life ever.

VINCENT VAN GOGH

Though he is now one of the most famous and influential figures in Western art history, van Gogh was unsuccessful and unrecognized during his lifetime. Nevertheless, he created around 860 oil paintings, among them the famous "Bedroom in Arles" (1888), which depicts van Gogh's bedroom at 2, Place Lamartine in Arles, France, now known as the Yellow House.

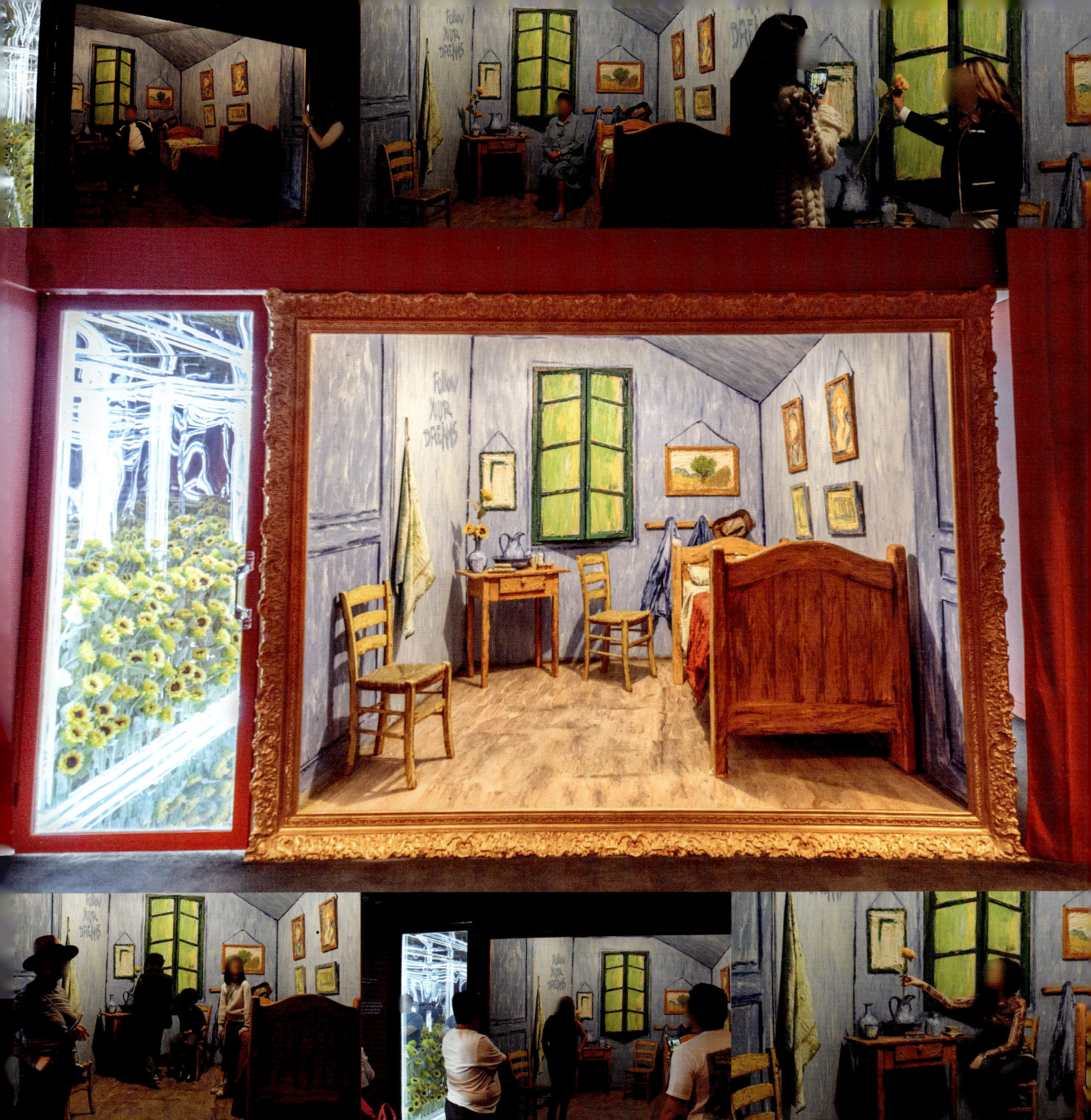
Follow
Your
Dreams

1973 PORSCHE 911 CARRERA RS MATCHBOX
Petersen Museum, Los Angeles

The Petersen Automotive Museum, founded on June 11, 1994, by magazine publisher Robert E. Petersen and his wife Margie, is a $40-million institution in Los Angeles, owned and operated by the Petersen Automotive Museum Foundation. Initially housed within the Natural History Museum of Los Angeles County, it later found its permanent home in a historic department store designed by Welton Becket, which had been opened in 1962 as a U.S. branch of Seibu Department Stores and was later an Orbach's department store from 1965 to 1986. Selected by Petersen for its predominantly windowless design, the building offered an ideal space for display, protecting artifacts from harmful exposure to direct sunlight.

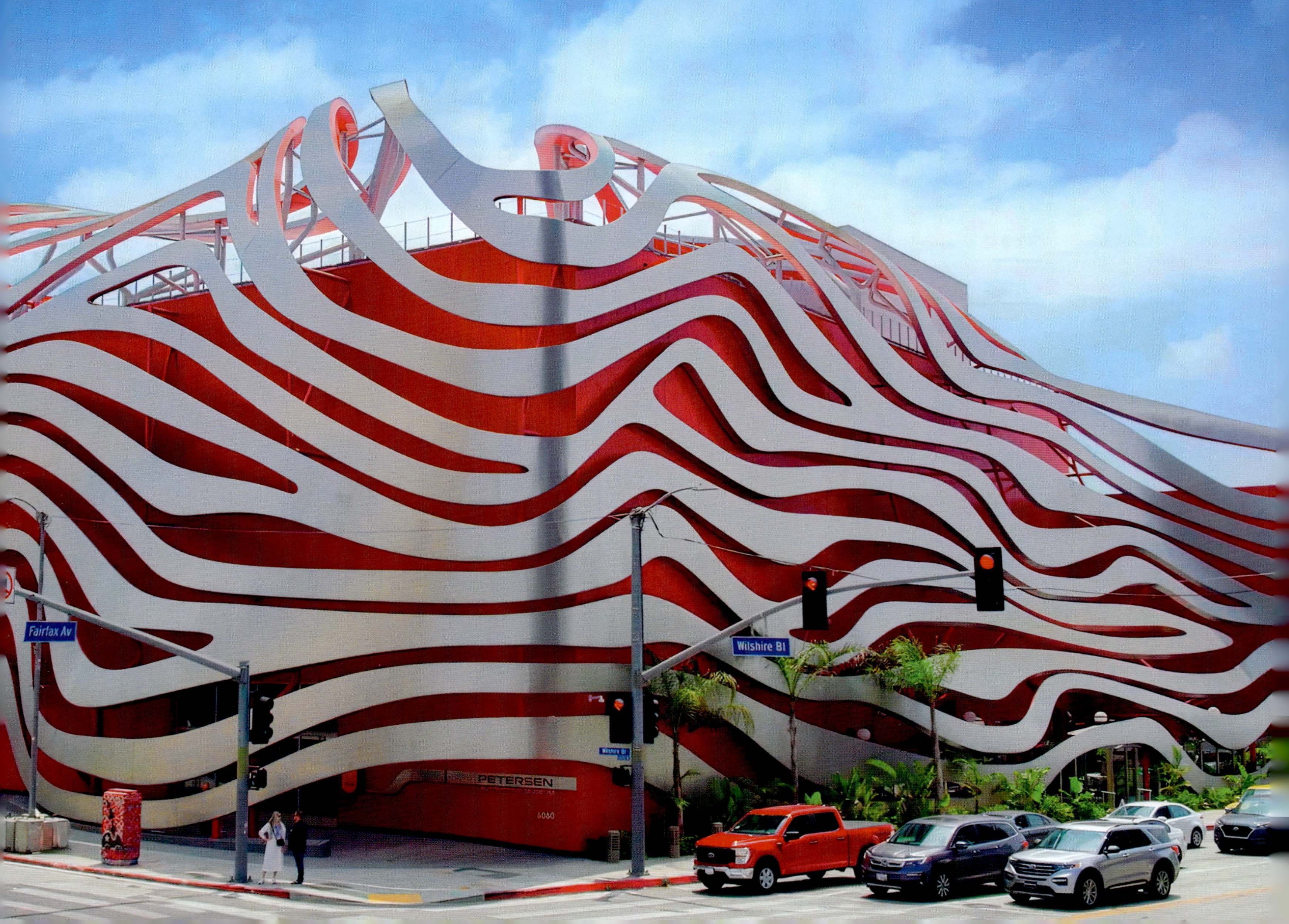

Among its diverse exhibits, the museum showcases championship-winning race cars, art cars, notable motorcycles, vehicles from Hollywood films, and other memorable automotive pieces. Displays include concept cars from the 1950s and 1960s, the Batmobile from the *Batman* comics, Steve McQueen's former Jaguar XKSS, the 1964 Aston Martin DB5 driven by James Bond in *Goldfinger*, and the Ferrari driven by Magnum P.I. in the 1980s TV series.

Embracing the nostalgia of classic automobiles, Mr. Brainwash emphasizes their significance, stating that "A car is a sculpture that can drive... it's going to drive you back to your memory."

Reflecting this sentiment is the full-sized Matchbox Porsche 911 Carrera RS, unveiled in 2023 at the *We Are Porsche* exhibition held at the Petersen Museum. Inspired by an earlier work by Mr. Brainwash, this unique piece embodies the enduring appeal of the Porsche brand, symbolizing the inner child in every enthusiast.

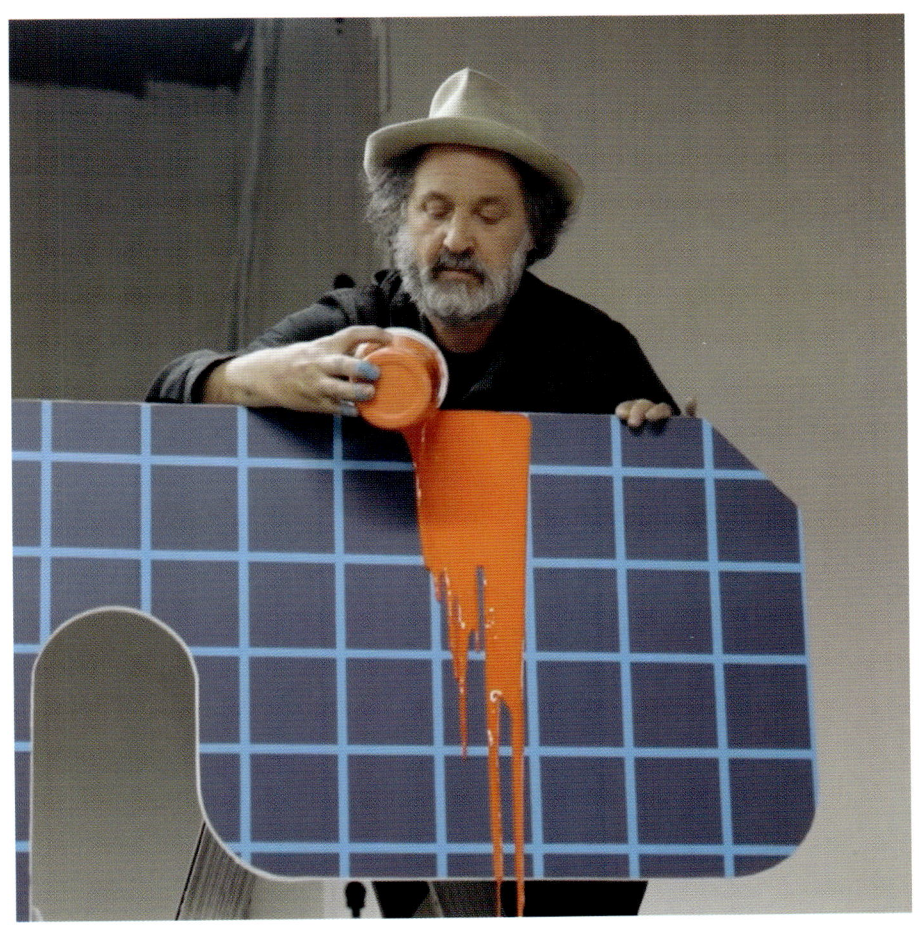

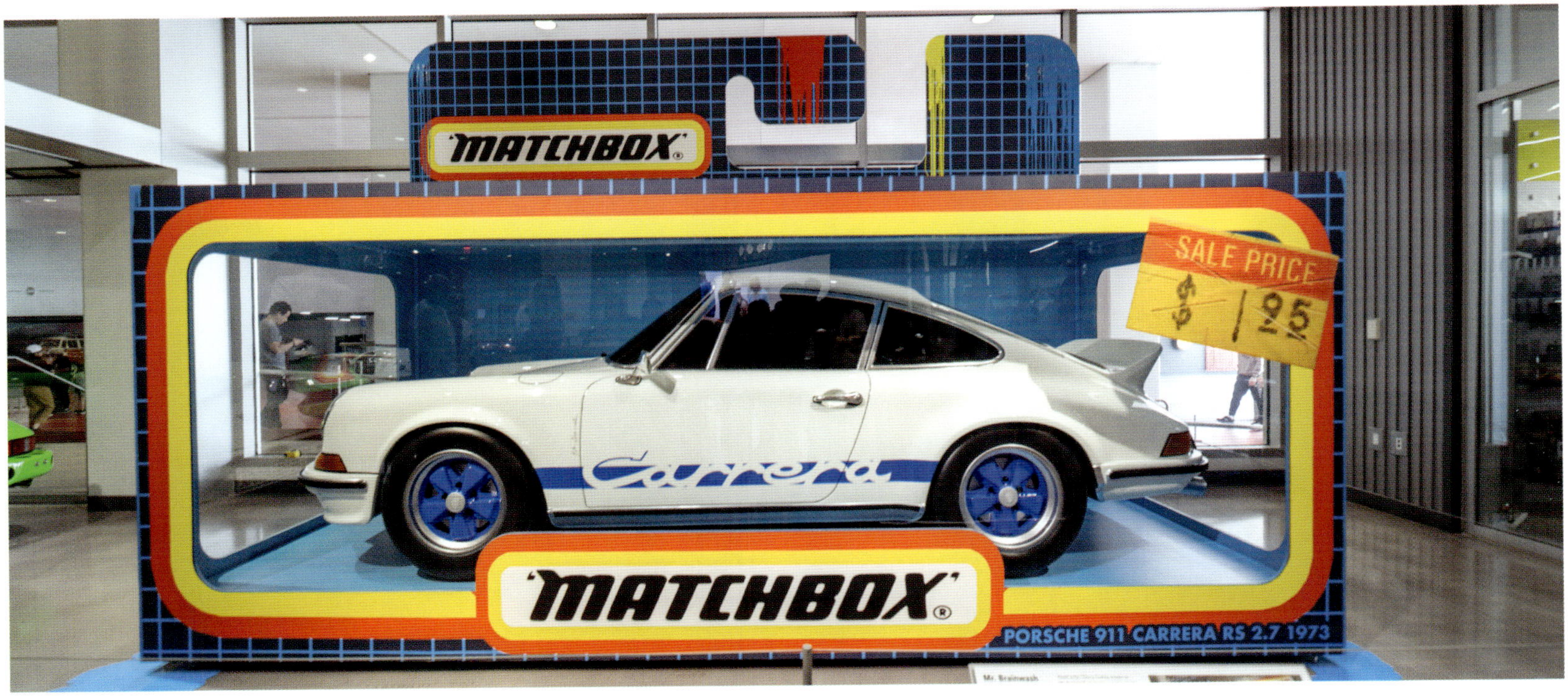

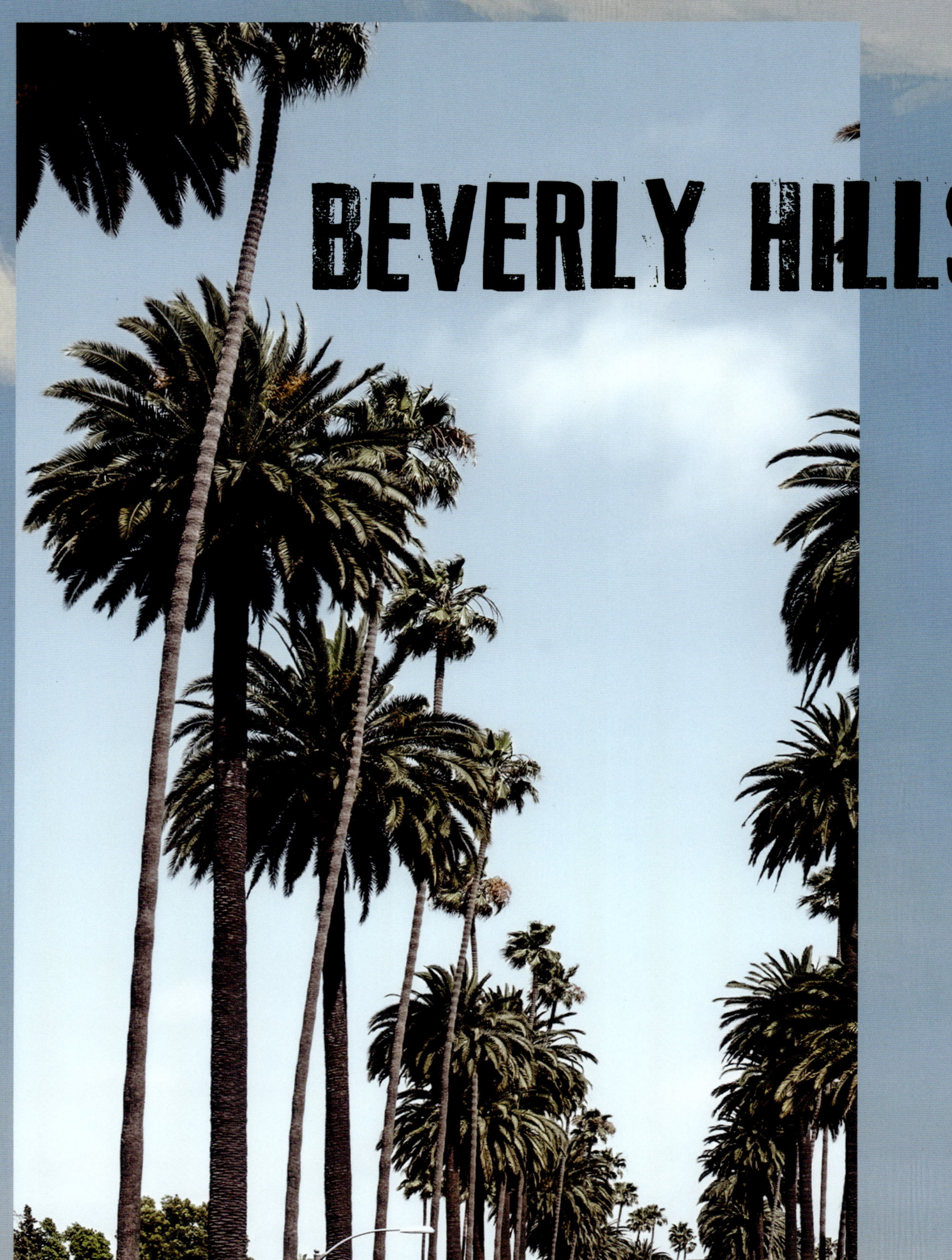

BEVERLY HILLS

2023
IMAGIRO
Rodeo Drive, Beverly Hills, 90210

Origami is an art form that has nearly defined beauty for centuries on end. The elegant matter of creating something magical with material as simple as paper is so unique that it brings together all ages and cultures. When Mr. Brainwash was a child, he turned to origami as a special way to express himself. He wanted to reignite that same feeling he had for origami the first time he ever tried this art form. He discovered that there is no better way to capture that fleeting feeling than to make origami timeless.

Mr. Brainwash then began working on "IMAGIRO", a form of origami made of metal that endows memories and creations with a stable place in the world. Since origami is commonly made out of paper, its fragility plays a huge factor as it can be destroyed at any moment. Mr. Brainwash found a way to make a delicate form of art last forever and the 12 unique sculptures of "IMAGIRO" on Rodeo Drive show that even the delicate nature of origami can be captured in time.

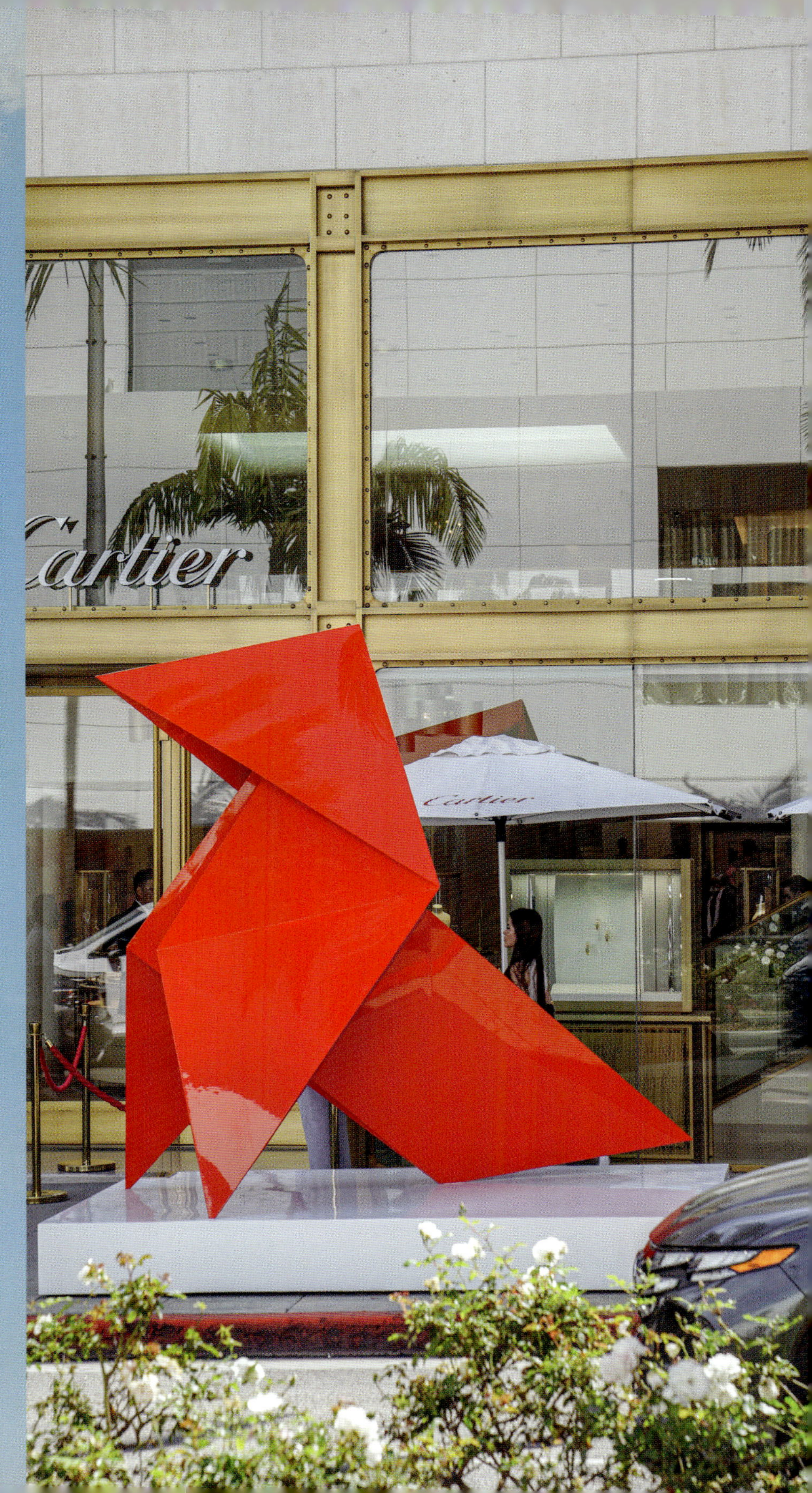

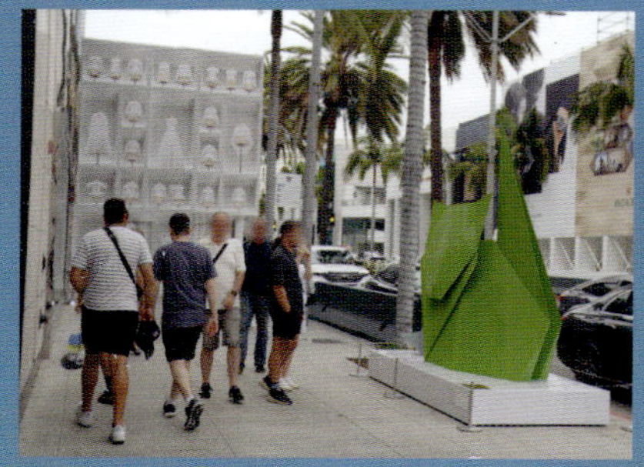
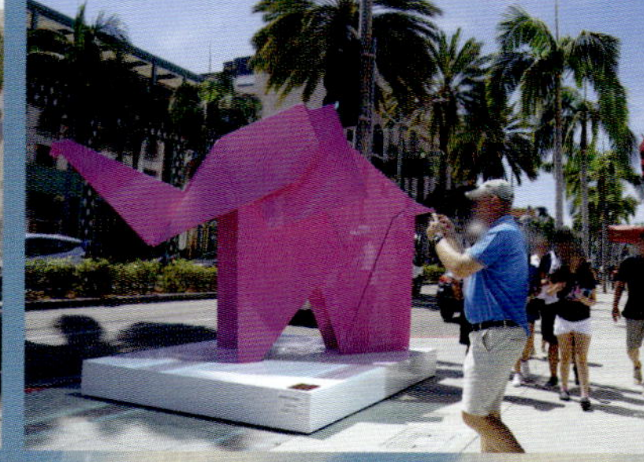
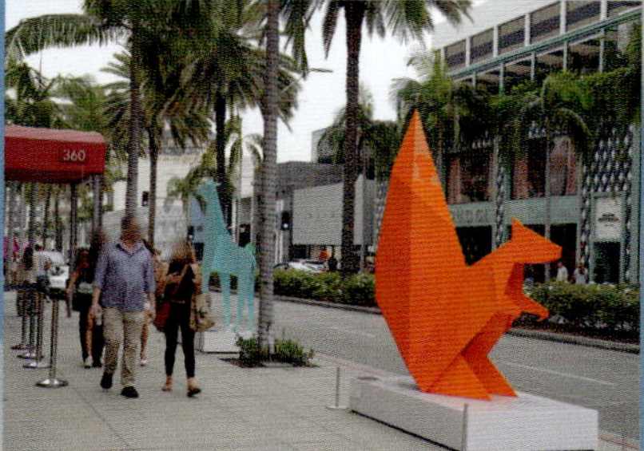
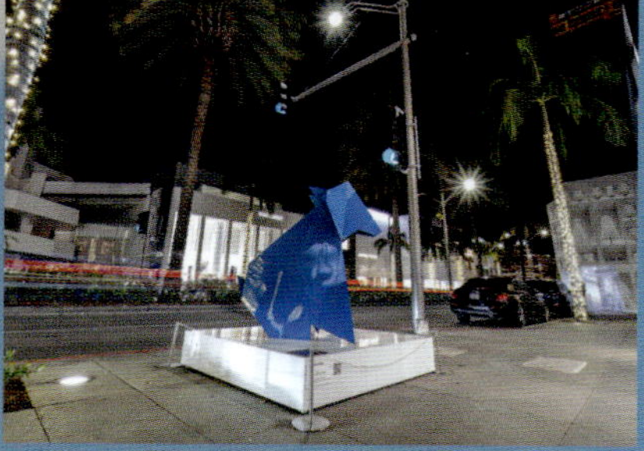
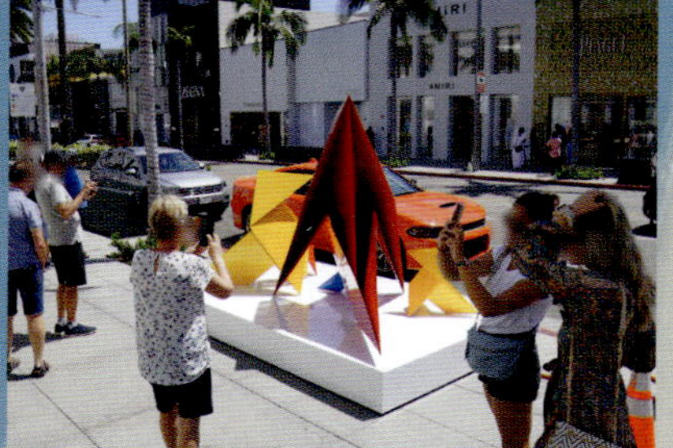
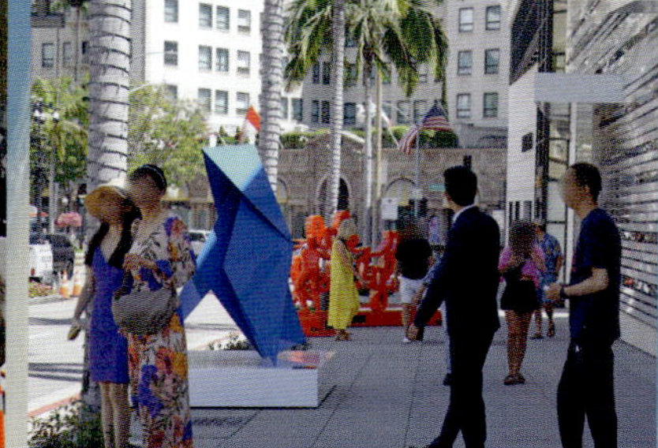
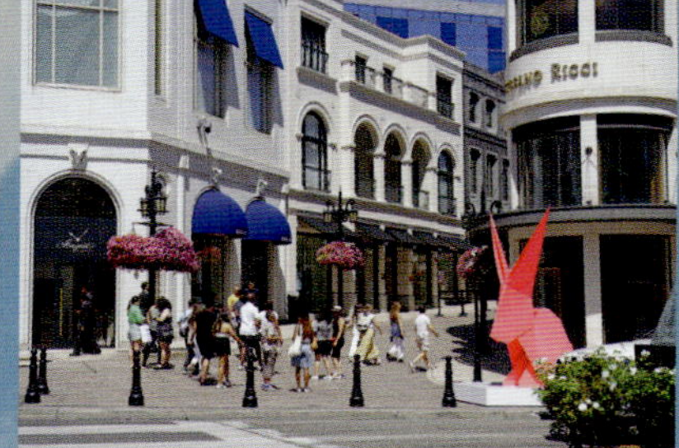
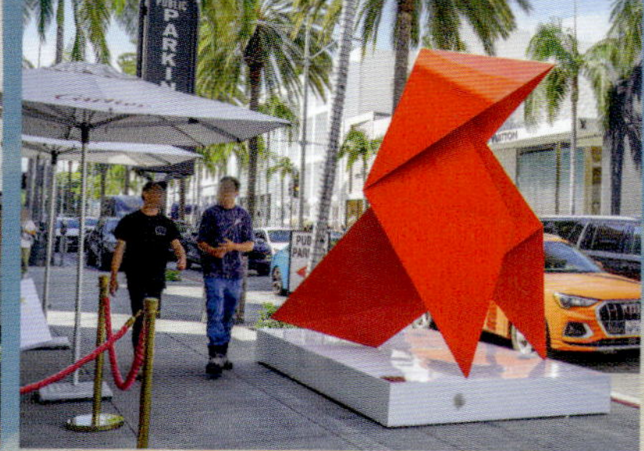
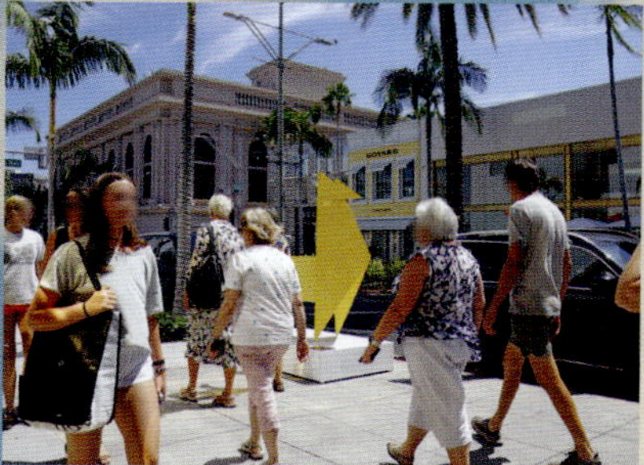
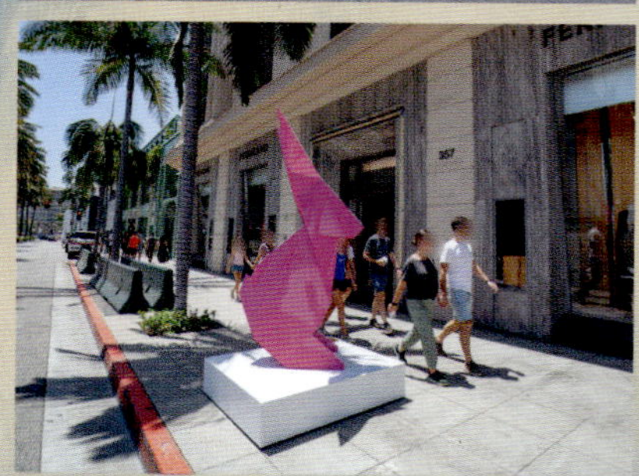

IMAGIRO ♥

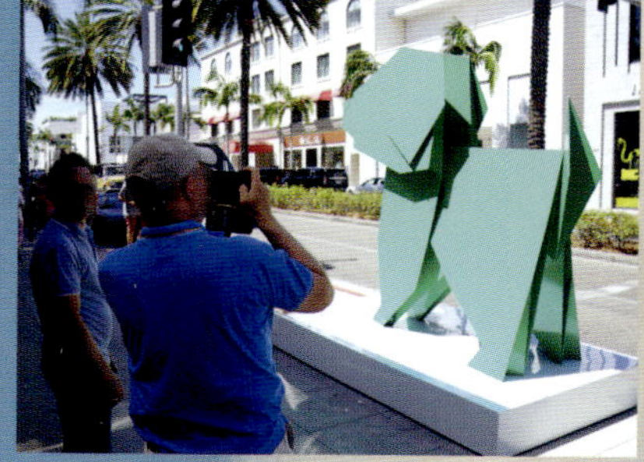
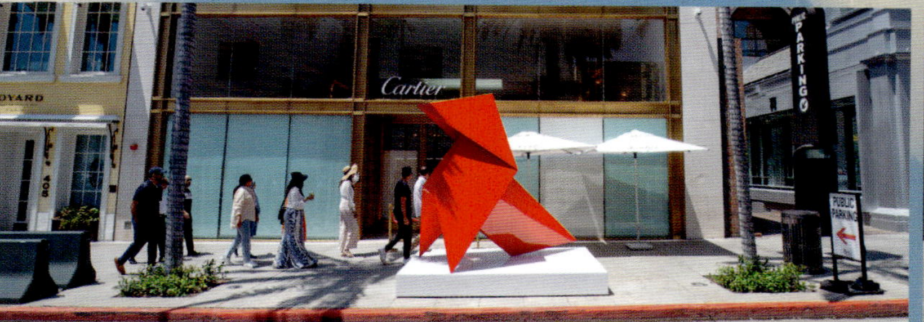
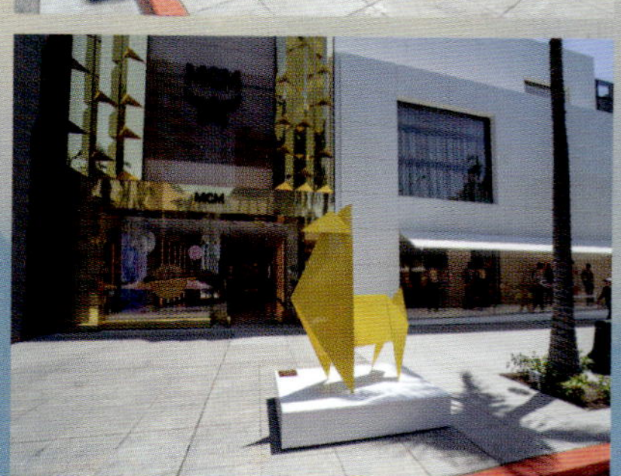
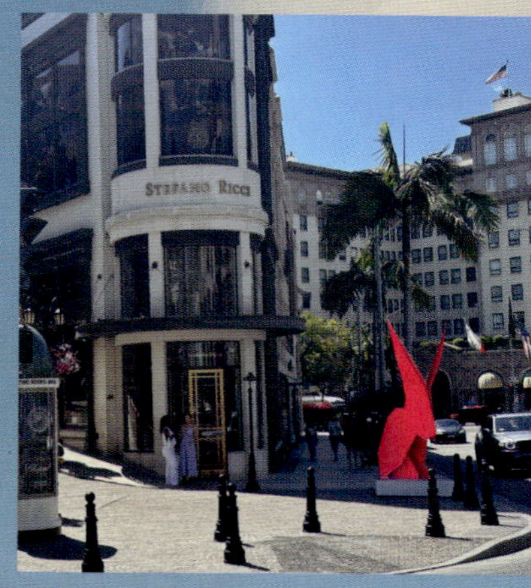
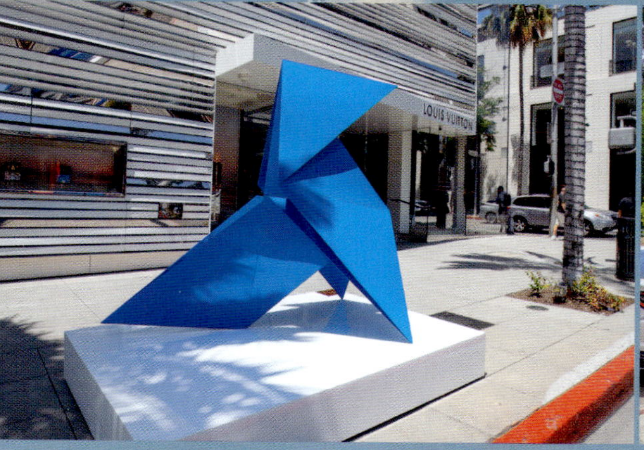
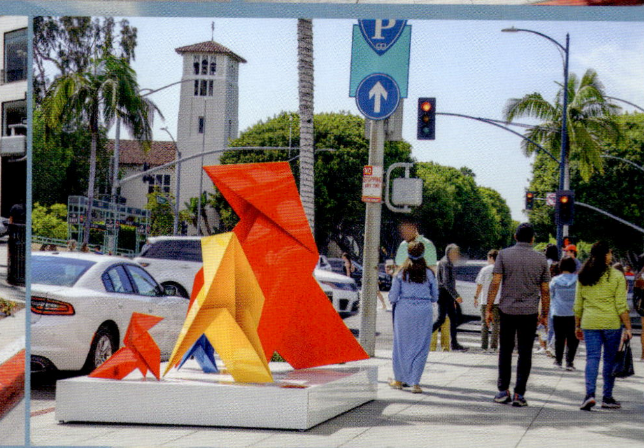

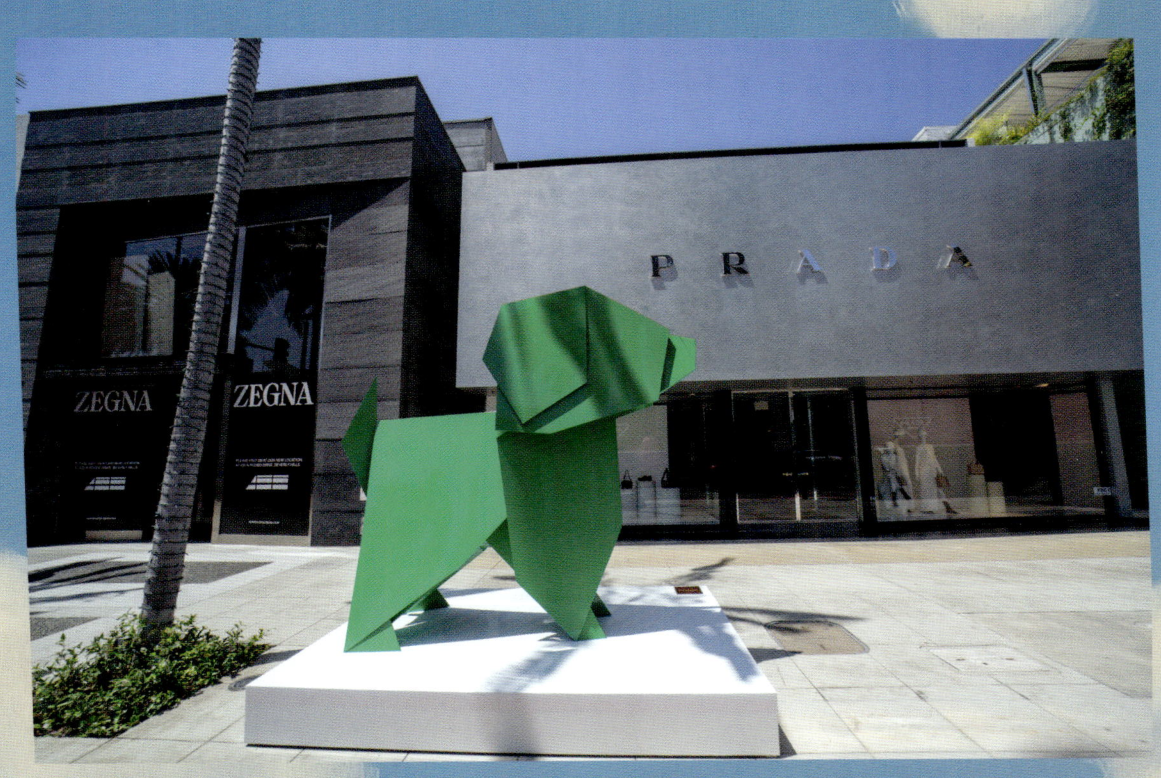

PRADA
ZEGNA
ZEGNA

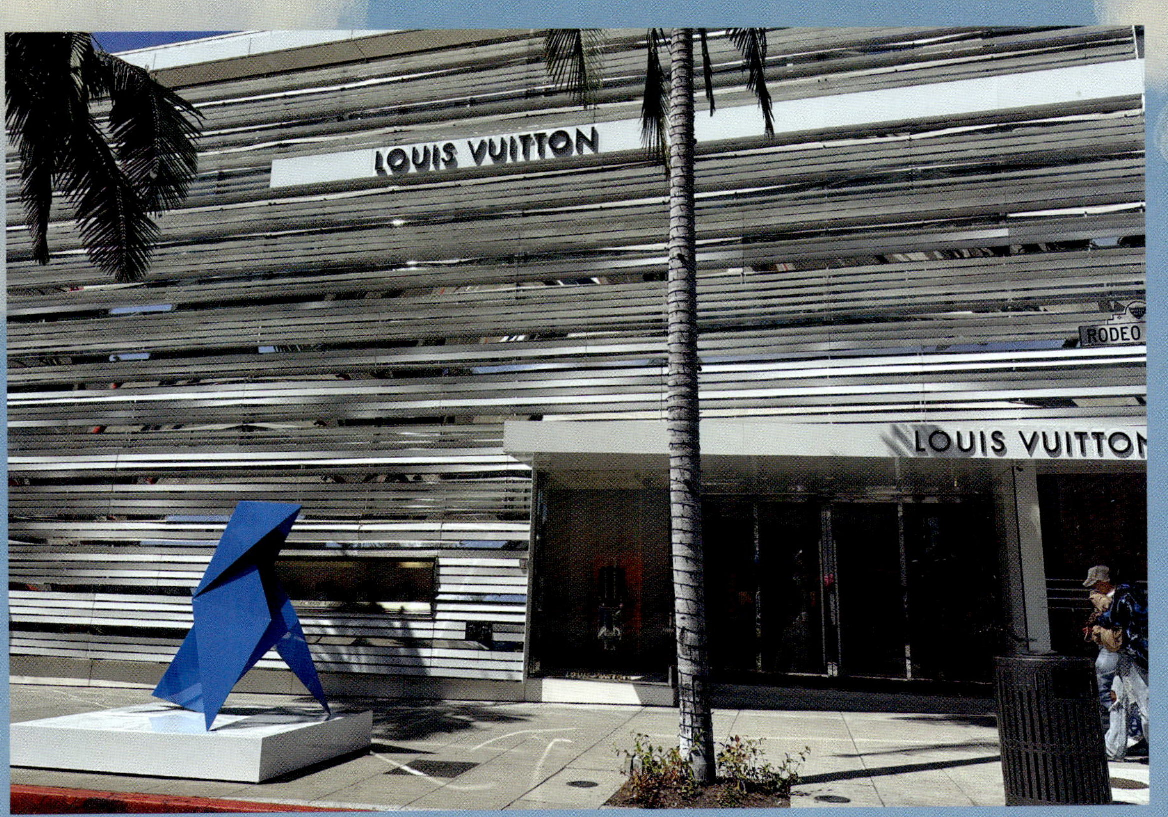

LOUIS VUITTON
LOUIS VUITTON
RODEO

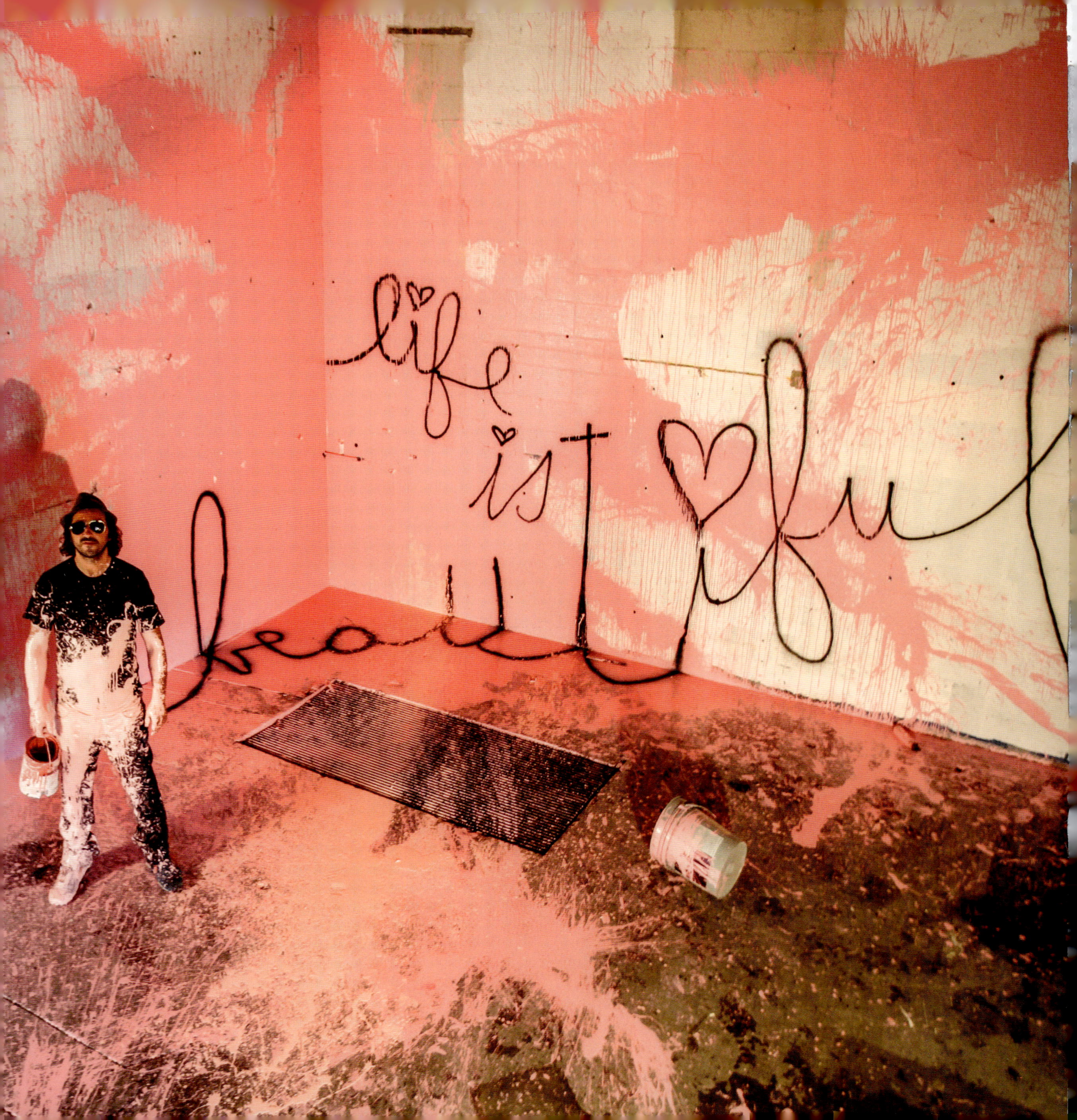
life
ist
beautiful